Caryl Emerson (a literary specialist) and Robert William Oldani (a music historian) take a new and comprehensive look at the most famous Russian opera, Modest Musorgsky's *Boris Godunov*. The result is both a historical study of a famous work and an interpretive piece of scholarship. The topics discussed include: the "Boris Tale" in history; Karamzin's history and Pushkin's drama as literary sources; Musorgsky's innovations as a librettist and as a theorist of the sung Russian word; the strange story of the opera's composition and revision; its first productions at home and abroad; and an in-depth musical analysis. In the process, several often-met errors in Musorgsky scholarship are clarified and corrected. A final chapter speculates on the opera's themes of political murder, guilt, and legitimacy – so important to Russian literary and national identity in the nineteenth and twentieth centuries – and the new role the "Boris plot" and its composer might come to play in more recent open phases of Russian cultural life. The volume contains a selection of classic texts in criticism, numerous production photographs, a bibliography and discography.

The book will be of interest to scholars and students of opera, music history, and Russian literature and culture as well as to opera enthusiasts.

Modest Musorgsky and *Boris Godunov*

First page of the composer's holograph full score of *Boris Godunov*

MODEST MUSORGSKY AND *BORIS GODUNOV*

MYTHS, REALITIES, RECONSIDERATIONS

CARYL EMERSON
PRINCETON UNIVERSITY

and

ROBERT WILLIAM OLDANI
ARIZONA STATE UNIVERSITY

CAMBRIDGE
UNIVERSITY PRESS

Published by the Press Syndicate of the University of Cambridge
The Pitt Building, Trumpington Street, Cambridge CB2 1RP
40 West 20th Street, New York, NY 10011-4211, USA
10 Stamford Road, Oakleigh, Melbourne 3166, Australia

First published 1994

Transferred to digital printing 1999

Printed in the United Kingdom by Biddles Short Run Books

A catalogue record for this book is available from the British Library

Library of Congress cataloguing in publication data
Emerson, Caryl.
Modest Musorgsky and Boris Godunov: Myths, Realities,
Reconsiderations/by Caryl Emerson and Robert William Oldani.
p.   cm.
Includes discography, bibliographical references, and index.
ISBN 0 521 36193 1
1. Mussorgsky, Modest Petrovich, 1839–1881. Boris Godunov.
I. Oldani, Robert William.
ML410.M97E43 1993
782.1'092 – dc20 93-18164 CIP

ISBN 0 521 361931 hardback

CONTENTS

ILLUSTRATIONS

TABLES

PREFACE AND ACKNOWLEDGMENTS

Musorgsky's *Boris Godunov* is the greatest Russian opera – and surely one of the most controversial. With its troubled textual history, its multiple versions (some by very gifted hands), the problematic personality of its author and its half-century of subjugation to Soviet ideology, *Boris* and its creator have generated an array of legends unusual even for Russia, a culture traditionally possessed by its art. One of the goals of the present volume is to challenge some of these entrenched perspectives, which in our view misrepresent Musorgsky's musical creativity, his relations with other composers (both Russian and West European), and his dealings with St. Petersburg's musical establishment. To our deep satisfaction, Russian scholars currently examining Musorgsky's life and manuscripts for the first Academy Edition of his works – projected to begin in the early 1990s with the 1869 version of *Boris* – appear to be engaged in a similar rethinking.

Part I of the book provides basic literacy for examining the opera: its historical material, its most immediate literary sources, the operatic plot, the work's genesis, and an account of the famous premieres, both East and West. Part II attempts to reflect the rhythms of *Boris*'s reception and performance from the composer's day to the present by stitching together in separate narratives both relevant censorship decrees and classic documents of criticism. Part III is interpretation: the poetics and dynamics of the libretto, an analysis of the opera's musical structure, and a speculation on the potential of the "Boris Tale" in Russia's post-Communist future. The book concludes with a discography and select bibliography. Many of the illustrations in this volume are reproduced from copies of early and rare photographs, whose quality is less than optimally clear. Cambridge University Press has made every effort to present them with a clarity that approaches that of the originals.

Although our work is collaborative in that we each have examined every sentence, primary responsibility for the various chapters rests with one or the other of us according to our professional interests and experience. Thus,

Caryl Emerson is largely responsible for Chapters 1, 2, 8, and 10; Robert William Oldani for Chapters 3, 4, 5, 6, and 9. Both authors answer for the selection, translation, and headnotes in Chapter 7. Ellipses in our source texts in chapters 6 and 7 are presented as they occur in the text. Ellipses that we have introduced are enclosed within square brackets.

Use by scholars of many different systems of transliteration from the Cyrillic alphabet has produced many variant spellings in the literature concerning *Boris Godunov* published outside Russia. One finds, among others, Modeste and Modest, Petrovitch and Petrovich, Moussorgsky, Mussorgski, and Musorgsky, and Godounoff, Godounov, and Godunov. In the interest of consistency, we have chosen to standardize spellings (following *The New Grove Dictionary*) in quotations incorporated in the text and in the textual part of endnotes. In bibliographic citations we have reproduced transliterated names and words exactly as they appear in the source. In our own transliterations, we have attempted to approximate English spelling in the text but have adhered to the conventions of Cambridge University Press in both endnotes and bibliography. Thus, for example, the forms Tchaikovsky, Bessel, and Alexander appear in the text, whereas Chaykovsky, Bessel', and Aleksandr appear in the documentation.

Unless otherwise indicated, we give pre-revolutionary dates according to the Julian calendar (Old Style), which remained in use in Russia until January of 1918. The Julian calendar lagged twelve days behind the Gregorian (New Style) in the nineteenth century and thirteen days behind in the twentieth. We cite documents prepared in the West, where the Gregorian calendar was in force, according to the conventional dual system in which the Julian date is given first, the Gregorian second, thus 4/16 September 1885.

We wish to thank our colleagues and friends – foremost among them Roland John Wiley and Richard Taruskin – who have aided our work at various stages of its gestation. Without their help our lot would have been much more difficult, and we can think of no happier way to acknowledge our debt than to paraphrase Musorgsky's own dedication of his opera: to all those who, with good advice and sympathetic concern, enabled us to realize the present work, we offer our heartfelt thanks. We thank as well the editors and publishers of the following publications for permission to draw upon and freely incorporate, at various places throughout the book, material that originally appeared in their publications: *19th-Century Music*, *Liberal Arts Review* and its successor *Liberal and Fine Arts Review*, *The Opera Quarterly*, The English National Opera's opera guide series, UMI Research Press's series in Russian music, Gordon and Breach's series in musicology, and Indiana University Press. We acknowledge and deeply appreciate the work of Jeffrey

Nevin, who prepared the music examples using computer software. Caryl Emerson would like to thank her long-standing Moscow friend and passionate advocate for Russian music, Mikhail Feldshtein, who has been on "Boris Watch" for materials, performances, and new publications for longer than either of them can remember. Robert Oldani acknowledges with pleasure the support of the Graduate College, the College of Fine Arts, the School of Music, and the department of Humanities at Arizona State University; each of these units, either by financial or release-time support, has contributed to the successful completion of this book.

The sources of our illustrations are as follows: Frontispiece and no. 4 from Modest Petrovich Musorgsky, *Boris Godunov* (holograph full score), St. Petersburg, Central Music Library of the Kirov Theater MS 3695; nos. 1, 2 from A. Orlova, *Trudy i dni M. P Musorgskogo: Letopis' zhizhni i tvorchestva* (Moscow: Gos. Muz. Izd., 1963); nos. 3, 9, 16 from R. Shirinyan, *M. P Musorgsky Al'bom* (Moscow: "Muzyka," 1987); nos. 5, 6, 7 from A. I. Sharleman', *"Boris Godunov": Risunki dekoratsy k tragedii A. S. Pushkina* (St. Petersburg: Izd. M. A. Shishkova, 1870); nos. 8, 10, 12–15 from R. Sarkisyan, *F. I. Shalyapin Al'bom* (Moscow: "Muzyka," 1986); and no. 11 from A. Gozenpud, *Russky operny teatr XIX veka, 1873–1889* (Leningrad: "Muzyka," 1973).

PART I

BACKGROUND

I

TSAR BORIS IN HISTORY

The rise and fall of Boris Godunov is one of Russia's most popular plots – and to a certain extent, Western Europe's as well. Over the past three hundred years, this story has inspired dozens of dramas, musical settings, poetic sketches, and historical novels. The Boris Tale received its most distinguished treatment, however, in the Russian nineteenth century. In the fifty years between 1824 and 1874, it was cast in three different genres by three of the nation's greatest masters: as history in the sentimentalist mode by Russia's first popular historian, Nikolay Karamzin; as drama by Russia's greatest poet, Alexander Pushkin; and as opera by Russia's greatest nationalist composer, Modest Musorgsky.

Historian, dramatist, and musician each linked his version of the tale with a larger ambition: the crafting of a specifically Russian or national genre within their respective fields. Since the time of Peter the Great, high culture in Russia had been marked by massive borrowings and imitations from Western Europe, which included authoritative models in such fields as German historiography, French tragedy, and Italian opera. To be sure, our three artists were not the first to seek independence from imported models (in opera, Glinka's *Life for the Tsar* and *Ruslan and Lyudmiia* preceded Musorgsky by two decades); nor were their creative products exempt from the beneficial influence of Western masterpieces that continued to flood the capitals (the influence of Verdi on Musorgsky is a good case in point).[1] But by the 1820s in literature and the 1860s in opera, a culturally specific Russian "language" and style had matured. Thus each of these retellings of the Boris Tale stimulated major controversy. Authors, advocates, and detractors alike deployed these new genre-models polemically, as propaganda for "Russian-ness" and as ammunition against dominant borrowed European models. In each case, then, the familiar story of Boris Godunov became the vehicle for purposely national forms of art.

Musorgsky's contribution to the cultural evolution of this story is the topic of Chapters 2 and 8. In this opening chapter we attempt something both simpler and, paradoxically, more problematic. By the twentieth century, Musorgsky's version of the tale had eclipsed all others; indeed, for most audiences in the West, Boris Godunov is a story that has always been sung. So popular, in fact, did Boris Godunov become in art – and specifically in operatic art – that only much later and with considerable difficulty was his image reconstituted on the basis of historical evidence. This evidence often contradicted the biography that had been canonized in literature and music. But these later "adjustments" to the story, for all their factual documentation, did not liberate Godunov – as they did not Richard III – from his traditional "aestheticized" plot. Who was the historical Boris? We present below the basic outlines of his story and his reign as Soviet and Western historians now tend to reconstruct them.[2]

In 1580, Tsar Ivan IV, the Terrible, celebrated a double wedding. He took for himself as his seventh wife Maria Nagaya, and he married his younger son, Feodor, to Irina Godunova. Irina was not of noble rank. She and her brother Boris, orphaned as young children, came from an old Russian boyar (or serving) family and had been raised at the Muscovite court as wards of the Tsar. In this way they became intimates of the royal family at a time when princely lineage was viewed as potentially seditious and even as a liability. It was safer to be low-born; during the most internally disruptive years of Ivan's long reign (1533–84), the old families were systematically decimated.

The Tsarevich Feodor was gentle and devout, but physically backward and feebleminded. By marrying him into the Godunov clan, which had a record of loyal service to the crown, Tsar Ivan was assured that his younger son would have the guidance and protection of a strong, able family. Feodor was clearly not fit to rule. For matters of state and succession – where intellectual and physical vigor was primary – Ivan IV relied on his elder son and heir, the Tsarevich Ivan. The young man had been trained in statecraft and gave promise of being a strong leader.

During the next year and a half, two events occurred in the royal family that history would later deem fateful. One day, enraged over what he took to be an insubordinate comment, Ivan the Terrible savagely struck his son Ivan and his son's pregnant wife; the wife suffered a miscarriage and Tsarevich Ivan died. Some months later, Tsaritsa Maria gave birth to a son, Dmitry. As the offspring of a union not blessed by the Russian Orthodox Church (canonical Church law permitted only three marriages), the infant Dmitry's claim to succession was tenuous. When Tsar Ivan died in 1584, therefore, the dynasty became suddenly and dangerously insecure. Of the two claimants to the throne, one was the feebleminded and still childless Feodor, the other was his two-year-old, quasi-legitimate half-brother.

4

Feodor was duly crowned, although no one expected him to rule. The new Tsar exiled the toddler Dmitry together with his mother and her brothers – in effect the whole ambitious Nagoy clan – to the appanage city of Uglich north of Moscow, where they maintained a minor court and retinue. Feodor then turned over the practical side of his reign to his wife's gifted brother. For fourteen years, Boris Godunov (addressed in official documents as "the great sovereign's Brother-in-Law, Ruler of the Russian Lands") openly presided over the country, with great energy and success. He made peace with Lithuania, stabilized Russia's northern front that had so drained the resources of Ivan IV, and kept in check the ruinous Tartar raids from the south. Through a mix of skill and guile, he manipulated the reluctant hierarchy of the Eastern Orthodox Church into granting Russia its own patriarch. Moscow's diplomatic ties with Europe (and especially with England) were strengthened, and organized state support was at last offered to the fur traders and Cossacks who had begun to colonize Siberia. To be sure, along with these successes there were also setbacks. The chronic demand for a reliable labor force and a stable tax base in the countryside led the government gradually to restrict the right of peasant movement from landlord to landlord, and also to extend and protect the landlord's right of forceable return. Thus the administrative machinery of serfdom was first laid down during Godunov's term of governance – measures that won Boris much support among the urban classes and rural gentry, although they were deeply unpopular with the peasants. There was in addition the constant threat of treason from the old princely families. An untitled boyar as the power behind the throne was a standing rebuke and a reminder of the princes' disenfranchised state. The Mstislavsky and Shuisky clans in particular found common cause with Russian merchants and churchmen, who railed against restrictions on monastic properties and against privileges that Boris – following Ivan IV's precedent – continued to grant to cunning and infidel foreign traders, primarily the English. Plots proliferated. In 1586, those two clans spearheaded a drive to divorce the Tsaritsa Irina from Tsar Feodor on grounds of barrenness, and thus to rid themselves of the Brother-in-Law as well. Feodor was mortified at the insult (Irina was not infertile; she had suffered several miscarriages) and instructed Boris to take proper measures. Several princes were forcibly tonsured and exiled. Each of these challenges to Boris's authority, in fact, served further to consolidate his power.

Half-way through Feodor's reign, in 1591, the Tsar's nine-year-old half-brother Dmitry was found one May day in the Uglich palace courtyard with his throat slit. The boy was an epileptic; he had been playing knife-toss with friends when a fit came upon him. The Nagoy clan, long chafing at their exile and now desperate over the loss of the "heir," clamored that the death was in fact a murder. The town was roused to vengeance, and in the resulting drunken turmoil half a dozen Muscovite officials were killed. When news of these events reached Moscow, Boris appointed an official commission to investigate, headed by one of his craftiest opponents at court, Prince Vasily Shuisky. The commission's report concluded that Dmitry's death had indeed been self-inflicted during an attack of the "falling illness," and was thus an act of God.

A year later (1592) Irina Godunova bore Tsar Feodor a daughter, but the child died in infancy. When Feodor himself died in 1598, therefore, the Rurikovid dynasty – which had ruled Russia since the ninth century – came to an end. On his deathbed Feodor passed the crown to his wife. But the widowed Irina, prostrate with grief and guilt for not having produced an heir, entered a convent. Moscow was aflame with rumor and warring factions. After a nervous interregnum, which involved much delicate maneuvering, manipulation of easily aroused crowds, and strategic shows of reluctance from the Brother-in-Law, a *zemsky sobor* or "Assembly of the Land" elected Boris Tsar. Understandably apprehensive (an elected tsar was unprecedented in Russian history), Boris required that elaborate loyalty oaths be taken to himself and his family, and set in place an efficient security apparatus.

The first three years of Tsar Boris's reign were relatively prosperous and peaceful. Although constantly the target of plots, attempted poisonings and witchcraft against his person (a charge taken very seriously in the sixteenth century), Boris never responded with a reign of terror. In fact, the demotion and terms of exile suffered by his enemies were, for the times, remarkably benign. As a sixteenth-century Muscovite, the Tsar believed deeply in sorcery and miracles. But he was also keenly – and for Russia, uncommonly – interested in Western medicine, book-printing, and education; he even dreamed of founding a Russian university on the European model. As a preliminary step, he sent young men of noble birth abroad to study (none, however, returned). Contemporaries praised Tsar Boris for his hard work, statesmanship, royal demeanor, and generosity. Russia seemed to have regained the mandate of God that Ivan the Terrible had so sorely tested.

In 1601, this initial good fortune began to turn. A series of natural disasters, which included massive spring floods and a killing frost in August, ruined the harvests throughout Russia. In the Muscovy of those times, crop failure was hardly rare. But in a normal cycle, bad years alternated with good ones, permitting the poor peasant to sustain losses and not be ruined. In the early seventeenth century, all of Europe experienced a general cooling of the climate for several consecutive years. This spelled disaster for a northern country as vast and underdeveloped as Russia, with her already marginal growing season, subsistence agriculture, primitive sowing, harvesting and storage techniques, and rudimentary network of food distribution. By 1603, Russian villages had literally nothing to sow. What is more, the great famine of 1601–03 was the first major famine to occur in conjunction with enserfment – that is, after the Decree of 1597 annulling the traditional right of any debt-free peasant to leave his master on St. George's Day. Starvation was coupled with immobility. In some contemporary accounts it is written that one-third of the population of Muscovy perished from starvation or disease; in any event, the suffering was pervasive and immense.

This socioeconomic crisis coincided precisely with Boris's tenure on the throne. He reacted generously, opening state coffers of grain to the needy and severely punishing hoarders. But these measures only encouraged a disastrous emigration of starving peasants to the cities and furthered civil collapse. At a loss to explain events and always prone to apocalyptic scenarios, many Russians held their "Father Tsar" personally responsible; for inscrutable but momentous reasons, he had lost the mandate to rule. Boris, by now plagued with various chronic illnesses and desperate to make sense out of events, increased surveillance against many princely and boyar families (especially the Romanovs), accusing them of witchcraft and treason. Many were banished to Siberia or forced into monasteries. As peasant unrest continued to rise, the Tsar reinforced his internal police with a network of informers. Brutal tortures, rare since Ivan the Terrible's reign, again began to become the norm.

In the midst of this domestic crisis, sometime in the early spring of 1602, a young man turned up in Poland claiming to be the Tsarevich Dmitry. According to the story he circulated, he had been miraculously saved from the attempt on his life in Uglich in 1591. This Pretender, promptly identified by the Muscovite authorities as the runaway monk Grigory Otrepiev, apparently had been at one time in the service of the Romanovs; quite possibly he had been groomed by them for this risky but tantalizing mission. The young man was not without talent. A veteran of several monasteries, where his skill at transcribing books and composing sacred canons had attracted some attention, Grigory even served as deacon for a year at the prestigious Monastery of the Miracle. It was there he first expressed, to a horrified fellow monk, his ambition to become "Tsar in Moscow."

Once across the border, the would-be Pretender had some difficulty finding a patron. But historical and political circumstances came to his aid. The southern reaches of Muscovy were on the brink of civil war; the countryside was demoralized, the Don Cossacks in open revolt. Poland, a rival country always ready to exploit Russian weakness and experienced in using pretenders to unseat neighboring regimes, produced enough ambitious parties willing to make of this Pretender a pretext for war. In support of this massive fiction, both territorial and religious ambitions came into play. Ever since the time of the Teutonic Knights, the Catholic Church had entertained the possibility of "winning the East back into the Roman fold," and Poland-Lithuania was now a robust, expansionist state. Neither the Polish King Sigismund III nor the Pope was bold or foolhardy enough to back the Pretender's claims too openly with large, well-funded troops. Both did give their unofficial encouragement, however, and the False Dmitry was formally converted to the Catholic faith. He then affianced himself to Marina Mniszech, beautiful daughter of a wealthy Polish magnate, by promising to his ambitious bride the Muscovite crown and to her father large tracts of Russian territory, including the rich Western Russian cities of Novgorod, Pskov, and Smolensk. On both sides of the border, the Pretender found himself riding a wave of anti-Godunov sentiment.

In 1604, the False Dmitry crossed over into Muscovy with a motley invasion crew of 2,000 mercenaries and Polish adventurers. So small a force would have presented little danger were it not for the Don Cossack army, which spontaneously joined the effort, and the numerous bands of desperately impoverished peasants eager for some change of luck. The whole southern frontier soon rose in inchoate revolt. The ideological standard of this alliance, it must be said, defied any logical description: the purported son of Ivan the Terrible, returning to the Orthodox throne of his fathers by challenging the godless "usurper" Tsar Boris, was marching under the banner of infidel Poles and Jesuits. But in the confusion this indiscrepancy was apparently masked or disregarded – for things went badly for the Pretender from the start.

Late in 1604, the forces of Tsar Boris, vastly superior in arms and men, defeated the invaders and forced them to flee to Putivl. Inexplicably, Boris's commanders did not follow up on their victory. Minimal arms supplies from the Poles and a continual influx of impoverished peasants and rebel Cossacks enabled the False Dmitry to hold out. In January 1605, however, rebel forces were again decisively defeated; again they were not destroyed. Whether for reasons of treason, exhaustion, interrupted supply lines, or simply anger at increasingly brutal punishment for "collaboration," Moscow's armies procrastinated once again. The fortified town of Kromy, headquarters of the rebellious Don Cossacks, survived six months under siege against government troops. Having survived the winter, the False Dmitry was unexpectedly joined by a full-scale peasant uprising in the spring. At this time, key leaders in Boris's own military staff began to defect.

As the Pretender was moving toward Moscow in April 1605, doubtless astonished at his undeserved success, Tsar Boris suddenly died. His son, the sixteen-year-old Feodor Borisovich, ascended the throne, and after a generous distribution of gifts secured an oath of loyalty from Muscovites. But the general amnesty routinely declared upon the death of a tsar allowed many banished persons to return to the capital, and organized rebellion grew. The Pretender's advance troops won over the populace with promises of a "returning true tsarevich" who would regain God's mandate, restore prosperity to Russia, and punish traitors. The Kremlin was stormed; the young Tsar Feodor was mutilated and strangled to death, along with his mother. The Tsarevna Xenia Borisovna, Boris's lovely unmarried daughter, was set aside for the Pretender's pleasure; when Marina Mniszech arrived in Moscow later that year, Xenia was swiftly immured in a convent. This violation and murder of children – Dmitry of Uglich in the beginning, the Godunov adolescents at the end – became the conventional framing events of the Boris Tale.

The False Dmitry entered Moscow in June 1605. The following month his mother Maria Nagaya (long a nun under the name Marfa), "recognized" him as her long-lost son, and three days later he was crowned. Dmitry reigned for less than a year. Although personable and resourceful, the tension between his Russian Orthodox pretensions and Polish Catholic dependence came to a head in May 1606, with the arrival of his bride and her large Polish retinue. Russian boyars and nobles quickly arranged for the Tsar's arrest and death. His ashes, so the story goes, were fired from a cannon in the direction of Poland. For the next five years, Russia was in a state of civil war.

The Boyar Council put forward Vasily Shuisky as the new Tsar. But Tsar Vasily, while a skilled court intriguer, proved incapable of governing amid national crisis. A huge peasant rebellion coalesced again in the south. Led by an energetic Cossack named Bolotnikov who raised his standard in the name of a completely fictional "Tsarevich Peter," the revolt culminated in a two-month siege on the city of Moscow itself in the fall of 1606. A second "False Dmitry" then appeared – whom Marina Mniszech, that remarkably resilient woman, acknowledged as her husband and to whom she even bore a son.

Domestic chaos invited foreign intervention. By 1609–10, both Poland and Sweden had been invited to intervene by various sides in the civil war. These armies began to invade the Russian lands with their own candidates for the Russian throne; finally, King Sigismund III himself indicated a desire to become the Russian Tsar. It was this ultimate Catholic threat, after half a dozen years of unchecked civil violence and devastation, that triggered the creation of a national liberation army in the hinterland in 1612. Under the leadership of a butcher, Kuzma Minin, and Prince Pozharsky (their statue can be seen in Red Square, in front of St. Basil's Cathedral), this liberation army succeeded in uniting the Russian people and at great cost drove the Polish garrison out of the Kremlin.

Thus did this terrible period in Russian history, the so-called *Smuta* or "Time of Troubles," come to an end. In 1613, a *zemsky sobor* was convened to elect a new tsar. It chose the young – and understandably very reluctant – Mikhail Romanov. Sixteen-year-old Mikhail was the son of Filaret Romanov, who had been forcibly tonsured and exiled for treason under Boris Godunov. Filaret in turn was nephew to Anastasiya Romanova, first wife of Ivan the Terrible – and thus a tentative link to the old dynasty was preserved. Many did not expect the new House of Romanov, erected on the ruins of a decade of pretenders, invasion, peasant revolt, and famine, to last out the year. It survived until 1917.

The Time of Troubles is one of Russia's great transitional periods. Boris Godunov came at a moment of break with past patterns of governance and legitimacy; the old was gone, the new was not yet sufficiently instilled. His reign and its immediate aftermath have their equal, perhaps, only in four subsequent historical turning-points: Peter the Great's modernizing measures of the late seventeenth and early eighteenth centuries, Alexander II's Great Reforms and liberation of the serfs in the 1860s, Stalin's brutal industrialization and re-medievalization of the Soviet Union in the 1930s, and Gorbachev's dismantling of the Soviet authoritarian-imperial model in the 1980s. But unlike those later societal cataclysms, all launched in the name of progress and defended as historically inevitable, the lesson of Boris Godunov's watershed was its durable backward-looking quality.

Boris craved traditional legitimacy. In the deeply patriarchal Muscovy of that time, the people perceived the body of the sovereign as mediator between this world and the next, and the hereditary dynasty as the sacred link between Russia's past and her future. Thus Boris had brought his young son forward as co-ruler and co-signer of documents even during Tsar Feodor's reign. Boris's ambitions were not so much personal and "reformist" as they were dynastic. He aimed to survive on the throne until his son could rule as Tsar by right of birth, not election. These hopes were defeated by natural accident and preternaturally bad timing – which, in the belief systems of the time, could be read only as divine retribution or fate. This tension between accident and fate is the emotional truth of the opera, and, as we shall see in later chapters, a matter quite separate from the fact-based truth of any particular historical event or personality. Musorgsky had a gift for writing from within a given belief system, for penetrating the spirit of a historical era and dramatizing an event as it must have appeared to its participants. In watershed times when whole worldviews erode, this required special genius.

One cost of this gift was a bleakly unsentimental attitude toward the processes of history. Musorgsky was powerfully attracted to crisis periods in Russian history that sought their legitimacy not forward but backward in time (the spiritual center of his second historical opera, *Khovanshchina*, belongs entirely to the Old Believers, for whom Peter the Great was the Antichrist). Power that is hopelessly wasted or arrested, energy in stasis – for Musorgsky, these were Russia's characteristic recurring traits. In June 1872, the very month he completed the final scene of *Boris* in full score and began sketching out *Khovanshchina*, Musorgsky wrote his friend Vladimir Stasov a revealing letter. All Petersburg was celebrating the Bicentennial Jubilee of Peter the Great's ascension to the throne. But Musorgsky's letter looked back at seventeenth-century Russia in a very different spirit. "The power of the black earth will make itself manifest when you plow to the very bottom," Musorgsky wrote. "Paper, books, they've gone ahead, but [the people] haven't moved . . . Public benefactors are inclined to glorify themselves and to fix their glory in documents, but the people groan, and drink to stifle their groans, and groan all the louder, 'haven't moved!'"[3] Far from being the populist and progressive materialist that Soviet music critics have made of him, Musorgsky was by every indication a profoundly mystical and pessimistic historical thinker. These matters will be discussed in more detail in Chapters 8 and 10.

It is common, when addressing the genesis of the *Boris* libretto out of the Boris Tale, to counterpose two epigrams by the distinguished authors of Musorgsky's two major literary sources. In 1815, Nikolay Karamzin dedicated the first volumes of his *History of the Russian State* to the Emperor Alexander I with the inscription: "The history of a people belongs to the Tsar."[4] In 1825, several months before beginning work on his drama *Boris Godunov*, Alexander Pushkin wrote to his friend, the poet Nikolay Gnedich: "The history of a people belongs to the poet."[5] No one in the 1820s would have suggested that the history of a people belongs to the people. Musorgsky made that move during the 1860s and 70s, decades that experienced an explosion of interest in the newly emancipated peasant and eagerly celebrated the spiritual potential of the Russian folk. He thus profoundly changed the way in which the tale of Boris Godunov was read. In contrast to many of his contemporaries, however, Musorgsky did not glorify the Russian people, or their past, or their future. His "populism" was a curious blend, as well as a creative distortion, of the narratives bequeathed him by Karamzin and Pushkin. We turn now to these earlier versions of the tale.

2

MUSORGSKY'S LITERARY SOURCES, KARAMZIN AND PUSHKIN

In the first quarter of the nineteenth century, two remarkable – and remarkably different – versions of the Boris Tale were written in Russia. The first was by Nikolay Karamzin, Imperial Historiographer to the Russian Court and an accomplished man of letters; it occupied the last several books of his monumental thirteen-volume patriotic history, an instant bestseller upon publication (1818–26). The other, the first serious stage drama written by Russia's greatest poet, Alexander Pushkin, drew heavily on Karamzin's just-published work but was so formally anomalous as drama and so politically ambivalent as history that it lay unpublished for six years.[1] The play was given guarded private readings, met with very mixed reception when it did appear in print, and was not approved for stage performance during the poet's lifetime. Yet the two works, and their two authors, are tightly connected. This chapter examines the work of the historian and the poet who provided Musorgsky with most of the literary material for his libretto – and with a set of contrasting dramatic principles and historical worldviews as well.

I

The appearance, in 1818, of the first eight volumes of Karamzin's *History of the Russian State* was a pathbreaking cultural event.[2] In part this impact was due to the skills of Karamzin himself as researcher, poet, and storyteller of the Sentimental school. (Two decades earlier, before turning to history, Karamzin had championed linguistic and stylistic reforms aimed at making the literary Russian language less "ecclesiastical" – less like Latin and Slavonic – and more like French in its syntax and expressive potential.) The success of the *History* was equally due, however, to the political and cultural climate of post-Napoleonic Russia. The sacrifices exacted by the French invasion and the burning of Moscow had stimulated interest in heroic stories from the national past, which in turn fed Russia's emerging sense of herself as a world power. This new hunger for historical identity was reinforced by a more general change in the status of history as a profession. During the liberal early years of Alexander I's reign (1801–25), historical societies had been established, journals founded, and archival materials published and codified. When Karamzin was appointed court historian in 1803, more documentation was available to him than to any previous Russian historian.

However, this new quantity and visibility of state decrees, records, chronicles, and geographies did not yet constitute a history. In fact, the very profusion of materials emphasized their incoherence. What was needed was a satisfying, readable narrative for the general public – and happily, the release of historical materials in Russia coincided with a general revival of interest throughout Europe in historical genres. Romantic writers had begun to "make them literary": it was an age of memoirs, fictional diaries, historical novels, the personal letter designed for public reading. The aesthetics of Romanticism tended to disregard rigid boundaries between genres; poetry partook of music, history of poetry, and the conventions for reading texts were themselves in dispute. In this spirit, Karamzin intended his *History* not only to educate and uplift his fellow Russians – a virtue expected of all eighteenth-century art – but also to change the very way history was written. So successful was he that his work quickly became required reading in Russian schools as well as a major source for nineteenth-century novelists, poets, playwrights, and librettists wishing to reconstruct pre-Petrine Russia in their historical fictions.

As we shall see, the image of Russia and of Tsar Boris that dominates the final volumes of the *History* left a deep trace on the revised version of Musorgsky's opera, a debt that the composer freely acknowledged. Until recently, however, Soviet-trained scholars have underplayed this influence, largely because the politics of the monarchist Karamzin was deemed reactionary and thus his influence on the "progressive" Musorgsky an ideological embarrassment.[3] (Soviet critics have routinely taken pains to demonstrate not only Musorgsky's progressiveness, but also his victimization by Imperial Russian institutions and society.) Only in the late 1980s did such canonized political formulas decisively break down. Now Karamzin's monarchism – with all its sentimentalism of style and its celebration of state and autocrat – can again be read in the Russian homeland for what it is: a sophisticated, skeptical, somewhat fatalistic revisioning of Enlightenment historiography.[4] Critical to Karamzin's historical experiment was his treatment of Boris Godunov.

To understand the Boris Tale in its first quasi-literary expression, a few words are in order about Karamzin's *History*. Before Karamzin, history in

Russia was practiced in two modes. Neither much attended to the literary appeal of its product. The first "monarchical" school produced patriotic tracts that glorified the state or dynasty; the second school, largely emigré German philologists, analyzed isolated historical documents. These two options might be seen as embodying the ancient debate between history as utility (rhetorical art) and history as truth (objective science) – and Karamzin found both extremes wanting. Reared amid eighteenth-century debates over the effectiveness of fiction versus history as means of moral instruction, he hoped to fuse the two modes in a new type of history that would be both partisan and true, and that would provide an irresistibly good story as well. The *History* achieved this dual aim through a dual structure.

On one "archival" level, Karamzin appended to each volume, in a section entitled *Primechaniya* or *Notes*, a vast number of annotated documents, selectively correlated to his historical narrative. At the same time, the historian anachronistically supplied psychological and moral motivation to the story-line level of the *History*, and especially to its later volumes, where the rise and fall of whole epochs are traced in terms of the personal virtues and vices of Russia's rulers. Such an individualized, ethical inner perspective could not of course be found in most of the early and medieval chronicles that were the historian's major primary source. As he approached the time of Godunov's reign, Karamzin increasingly laced his chronicle sources with an emotional, didactic narrator who judged persons and events not with a medieval but with a nineteenth-century vocabulary.[5] Thus were the political lessons of history made more inescapable to contemporary readers, and the lives of the Muscovite tsars made more compelling to an audience raised on Romantic texts. By volume IX (on Ivan the Terrible, and highly critical of his reign), moral choice and personal conscience are already firmly in place as part of a character's image. By the beginning of Boris's story (volumes IX through XI), medieval tsar has been transformed into modern Romantic hero.[6] This hero is no longer solely the product of fate or of dislocated events in his own time, but is an agent forced to negotiate eternal crises of good and evil.

In its time, Karamzin's didactic narrative was read as very fine literature. But it is not, and was not intended to be, a fiction; the historical documents in the *Notes* do contain the story Karamzin tells, as well as many others stories not told. The main narrative was designed to be "rhetorically useful" and the *Notes*, of great discrimination and length, were "scientific." What precisely was the utility that Karamzin aimed to serve?

The historian died in 1826, working on the thirteenth volume (civil war during 1610). According to his biographer Yury Lotman, Karamzin, even before his final illness, had intended to conclude his labors on the Time of Troubles.[7] Part of the Hegelian movement of the *History*, after all, was its assumption that increasingly terrible national trials were met by increasingly triumphant reconstitutions of the state; thus the desperate crises of the Time of Troubles prefigured perfectly the glorious founding of the Romanov dynasty, to whose reigning tsar the *History* was dedicated. Thus we might read Karamzin's image of Tsar Boris as an emblematic culmination, a master trope for tragic biography at the national level. Central to this image are two assumptions: first, that Boris, although legally elected to the throne, is nevertheless illegitimate; and second, that for all his many talents Tsar Boris is fatally guilty of a dynastic crime – the murder of the Tsarevich Dmitry – that he could have chosen not to commit, and this crime brought down the Russian state.

As we saw in Chapter 1, both these assumptions are profoundly suspect today. But Karamzin's sources spoke otherwise. Powerful political and religious forces conspired early in the seventeenth century to "confirm" Boris's guilt and to register it in writing. The Orthodox Church – despite its achievement of a Patriarchate under Boris as Brother-in-Law – had little use for Godunov after his death. Official distrust began in 1606, when Tsar Vasily Shuisky, in an effort to fasten Dmitry of Uglich in his grave and prevent further pretenders to his name, ordered the canonization of the "martyred Tsarevich." From 1606 on, in the eyes of the Church, Boris Godunov was both *tsareubytsa*, tsarecide, and *svyatoubytsa*, murderer of a saint. Civilian authorities were equally ungenerous to Boris's memory. The Romanov clan, which had suffered such persecution under Tsar Boris, lost no time in censuring their predecessor once they themselves occupied the throne. Up through the nineteenth century, then, almost all surviving state documents and chronicles (compiled by government clerks or by monks in monasteries, not unlike Pushkin's and Musorgsky's Pimen) condemned the Godunovs in the harshest possible terms.

There were, however, reasons quite beyond the stories told in the historical sources that made a guilty and illegitimate Boris attractive to Karamzin. These reasons have more to do with Karamzin's own era than with any events of the sixteenth century. To put them in context we might go back to 1802, sixteen years before the first volumes of the *History* appeared, to an essay that Karamzin wrote entitled "Reminiscences on the Road to Troitsa" (the Troitsa-Sergeevo Monastery near Moscow, where the Godunov family is buried).[8] In this essay Karamzin reprimands the seventeenth-century chroniclers for their cruel judgment of the Godunovs. Boris's services to Russia as Brother-in-Law and as Tsar were so great, he writes, that later generations would like to doubt evidence that he had cleared his way to the throne by murder. And fortunately, Karamzin notes, this evidence is indeed open to doubt – for the chroniclers, who passed over in silence Boris's positive achievements, readily "incorporated false opinion through senselessness or malicious intent." Karamzin warns against "the timid historian [who] repeats the chronicles without criticism ... [Then] history sometimes becomes the echo of slander."

In this early essay, Karamzin does not deny the possibility that Boris is responsible for Dmitry's death. But he does resist figural interpretation – that is, retroactive reading of a later compromised reputation into earlier and innocent events – and he exercises a healthy suspicion of the sources. He urges that his contemporary readers, who "live in a time when a man can and must use his reason," understand Boris's guilt in a larger context. "The ambition of intelligent men is not always a stranger to evil-doing," Karamzin writes. "God judges secret villainies, but we must praise tsars for everything they do for the glory and welfare of the Fatherland." As friends of the historian were to note, this charitable early image of Boris differs markedly from the canonically negative image that Karamzin later draws in the *History*. What might have provoked the change?

The answer must be sought in contemporary Russian events, against whose backdrop the Boris Tale was (and to this day continues to be) reworked. Alexander I had just ascended the throne, and Karamzin was a fervent admirer of the young and liberal-minded new tsar. It was widely believed that Alexander had assisted in deposing – and perhaps in murdering – his own father, the eccentric and tyrannical Paul I; this alleged tsarecide rescued the country from weak and irresponsible rule and paved the way for a competent claimant to assume power. In 1802, any reference to the death of Dmitry in Uglich would be read as a reference to the recent murder of Paul I in Petersburg. Over the next two decades, however, the subtext changed. A series of cataclysmic events – the dazzling rise of Napoleon, his successful aggression against the old regimes of Europe, his invasion of Russia in 1812, and Tsar Alexander I's own subsequent conversion to a politics of the mystical right – all foregrounded another aspect of the Boris Tale: not Godunov's wisdom and generous deeds, but his illegitimacy and lack of royal blood. Since both Tsar Boris and the Emperor Napoleon had begun their reigns as popular and seductive rulers – "saviors," after a fashion, of their respective peoples – the political point had to be strongly driven home. The lesson for conservative regimes in the post-Napoleonic Age was that the low-born could not achieve political greatness except through regicide and crime.

Karamzin intended his *History* as moral education. The primary vehicle for ethical persuasion was to be the exemplary regal biography – a genre both congenial to Karamzin as an accomplished writer of the Sentimentalist school and congruent with his concept of human progress. As Richard Pipes has remarked, Karamzin always measured progress in moral and cultural, not political or institutional, terms.[9] Since moral growth was perceived as individualized and exceedingly difficult, it is hardly surprising that Karamzin was pessimistic about human nature and wary of popular movements. He preferred "kindly, passive, frugal kings to dynamic reformers," regardless of the wisdom of the reforms. Following Montesquieu, Karamzin advocated for Russia a strong state with undivided monarchical power – albeit one in which the crown obeyed its own laws – and he blamed the collapse of such states on a degeneration of monarchs into tyrants. This logic governed Karamzin's scandalously frank condemnation of Ivan the Terrible in volume IX, and, with the addition of some religious themes, of Boris Godunov in the final volumes as well. The biographies of Russian tsars, especially if flawed, had an important educative function.

To these two sociohistorical justifications for a negative image of Tsar Boris – the bias of state documents and chronicles, and the political lessons of the Age of Napoleon – we must add two more. The first is a fact of literary history. The image of a guilty (and ofttimes a repentant) Boris Godunov fit well into a Gothic and later Sentimental plot very popular at the turn of the century: the tragic hero or hero-villain, tormented by a terrible crime on his conscience, is pursued unto death by the avenging ghost of his innocent victim. It is this dramatic kernel, of course, that Musorgsky eventually extracts out of Karamzin's Boris for the centerpiece of his opera. However, Karamzin – in contrast to the composer two generations later – did not dwell on Boris's inner feelings of guilt; the historian was interested largely in the self-serving criminality of the deed and in God's punishment as meted out to the Russian land. In this approach to his material, we should note, Karamzin was being true to the psychology of his medieval subject. For even in the improbable case that Boris had arranged the death of Tsarevich Dmitry, it is absurd to presume that a successful Russian monarch schooled in sixteenth-century politics would feel "guilt" at eliminating a political rival – as absurd as it would be to ascribe guilt to the workings of Cesare Borgia in Italy a century earlier. In that era, eliminating rivals was dangerous business, but hardly to the soul. No connection can be assumed between the Uglich "murder" and the death of Boris "from an uneasy conscience." That sort of guilt, perhaps proper to eighteenth-century works of literature and to grand opera, is a much later romantic cliché.[10]

Musorgsky, an earnest if idiosyncratic populist, shared with the conservative monarchist Karamzin one additional reason for depicting a guilt-ridden and illegitimate Boris. Both historian and composer drew on a set of quasi-religious folk beliefs, elevated before mid-century into a coherent ideology by Slavophile thinkers, on the nature of the Russian Tsar and his obligations to the Russian people. Early Slavophile thought was deeply apolitical. Its adherents often perceived the Orthodox Tsar as a sort of secular Christ who, in accepting the burden of autocratic rule, took upon himself the guilt of the world, thus rescuing the populace from the compromising and polluting responsibilities of political power. A virtuous tsar could intercede on Russia's behalf with saints and deities; a criminal tsar could not. This tenet of Orthodox faith had immense consequences for the nation's fate. By linking the Time of Troubles directly with Boris's own flawed biography, Karamzin arrived at the refrain of volume XI: "the ruins of Uglich howl to Heaven for vengeance" (XI, 85).

Illegitimate tsars must continue to answer for their nation's sins. And yet they cannot promise a resolution of these sins, or any ultimate salvation. Thus it is no accident that Boris Godunov, Russia's first elected Tsar, was challenged by Dmitry, the first pretender to the Russian throne. By promising a blood link to the ancient dynasty and the restoration of divine blessing, pretenders became a powerful social force during the seventeenth century. And so they remained until well after the French Revolution, in fact, until well into Musorgsky's era. Among the major European nations, in Russia alone could a pretender to the throne still have real political consequences in the nineteenth century.

Another, more specifically Christian prototype also comes into play in the Boris Tale. This is the ancient tradition of the "passion-sufferer" and its companion myth of the Saintly Prince.[11] Early Russian messianism made no distinction between the sacred and secular capacities of its rulers. Thus Dmitry of Uglich was viewed as the last of a long series of martyred princes in an Orthodox pantheon beginning with the first two saints canonized by the Russian Church, Boris and Gleb – two royal brothers, mere teenagers, slain in the eleventh century by an elder brother who wished to secure undisputed title to the Kievan throne. It was this spiritual lineage, as much as the fact of being Ivan IV's son, that would eventually provide the organic link with the past so desired once the ancient dynasty became extinct. The life of Tsarevich Dmitry – which was in no way remarkable, indeed, which was by some accounts rather repellent – mattered less than the spectacle of an innocent child's undeserved and inevitable death.

Hagiographic accounts of St. Dmitry's life were an important source of rhetorical strategies for Karamzin, as they became for Pushkin. One of the most effective scenes in the entire *History*, in fact, is the dramatization of the Uglich "murder," an episode directly influenced by a mid-seventeenth-century version of the Life of St. Dmitry.[12] To be sure, Karamzin had to retrofit the terminology of a post-1606 hagiography into the 1591 death – a death that was, at the time of its occurrence, a very minor event in the annals of Muscovy.[13] Blurring the distinction between his own voice and the voice of a pious chronicler monk, Karamzin sacralized the death, and even interpolated a miracle or two: "The nine-year-old Holy Martyr lay bloody in the arms of the woman who had raised him and who wanted to protect him with her own breast; he *trembled like a dove*, expiring, and died, never hearing the shriek of his desperate mother" (x, 79, emphasis in original). From the later perspective of Pushkin and Musorgsky, then, we might say that Karamzin as historical narrator prefigured the chronicler Pimen.

But figural interpretation and legitimation through a Saint's Life was only one path to the success of the Pretender's challenge. At the time of his appearance in Russia, the False Dmitry drew on a related and incompatible myth. This was the legend of the "returning Tsarevich as true deliverer": the young man of royal birth who emerges from hiding, exile, or disguise to reverse a wicked policy, regain God's mandate, and save his people.[14] Clearly, in one logically motivated sequence of events, both of these myths could not function simultaneously as "true." The Tsarevich Dmitry could not have been murdered at Uglich and then return later as the True Dmitry, the living son of Ivan IV. The two events can be linked solely through resurrection and miracle.

This question of the supernatural can serve as an instructive point of contrast between the historical imaginations of Karamzin and Musorgsky. As a good son of the Enlightenment, Karamzin considers the False Dmitry a fraud and a dreamer; once on the throne, the Pretender becomes an impresario as well, a versatile actor who can play-act any role (Karamzin is much taken by the False Dmitry's theatricality). As a historian, Karamzin knew and exploited the fact that medieval Russian culture connected theater with the demonic.[15] Thus the Pretender became the perfect instrument of the impious Godunov's destruction, and an enabler of the Romanov restoration. Musorgsky, whose mind was much more amenable to wizardry and less wedded to historical ameliorism of any sort, interpreted pretendership more darkly. For him, the demonic was no willing servant of history – although it remained very congenial to theater. Musorgsky's focus is lonely, psychological, and directed almost entirely at Boris himself, at the problems of a gifted medieval psyche forced to make sense out of events at a historical watershed.

We will return to this dilemma when considering the libretto, in Chapter 8.

It remains to sample briefly the flavor of Karamzin's narrative. We draw from those portions of the *History* that most directly shape the image of Boris as a personality, and that subsequently leave their trace on the central events of the opera. Most remarkable in Karamzin's image of Godunov, we note at the outset, is its pre-formed and non-developmental quality. All attributes of his personality are present fully matured from the start, in fact from his first mention in the *History*. Thus the events that befall him illustrate, but cannot fundamentally change, his character.

Boris is first introduced to us in volume IX as richly endowed, "imposing, handsome, sagacious," a young man "in whom both great virtues of statecraft and a criminal ambition had already ripened" (IX, 131–32). After Ivan the Terrible's death and Boris's elevation as Brother-in-Law, Karamzin again has much praise for Boris's gifts – but with increasing intensity he laments Boris's lack of virtue. "Lack of virtue" in this context means ambition inappropriate to rank. "Had he been born to the throne, he would have deserved to be called one of the best monarchs in the world," Karamzin writes. "But born a subject, with an unbridled passion to rule, he could not resist the temptation when evil seemed to his advantage – thus the curse of centuries muffles Boris's positive reputation in history" (X, 7). Every positive achievement (the patriarchate, negotiations with the khans, peace on the northern front) is explained as a step calculated to bring this cunning man closer to absolute power – a desire which, Karamzin assures us, is only natural in a man of such energy and gifts. At all points Boris's pre-formed character is held responsible for its powermongering, and yet Boris is psychologically not free to act otherwise. Thus the murder of the "legal heir" in Uglich was "inevitable" (X, 75–76).

Karamzin describes impartially the complex events of the interregnum after Feodor's death (XI, 3–20). The people's enthusiasm for Boris was high; Boris was unfailingly generous toward them. "It seemed as if Fate smiled on the new monarch . . . in Russia's foreign policy, nothing changed in spirit or in appearance" (XI, 14, 17). The first intimation of future misfortune, and an example of Karamzin's skill at discriminating when necessary among his sources, is the sudden death of the Tsarevna Xenia's Danish bridegroom, Prince Ioann. (This incident is foregrounded in both drama and opera.) "Should we credit the chronicler's story that Boris secretly did not regret the death of Ioann, envying the general love Russians bore toward him and fearing in him a rival for the young Feodor?" Karamzin asks (XI, 32). And he answers: "No, at that time Boris was truly shattered, without hypocrisy, and he felt, perhaps, divine punishment on his conscience, having prepared happiness for his beloved daughter and seeing her a widow in her bridal garments" (XI, 33). But Boris's hypocrisy and criminality – always latent in Karamzin's image – are activated afresh when Russia falls on hard times, two years into the tsar's reign:

The time was drawing near when this wise ruler, then justly glorified in Europe for his intelligent policies, for his love of enlightenment, for his eagerness to be a true father to his fatherland – and finally for his good behavior in social and family life, must taste the bitter fruit of lawlessness and become one of the wondrous victims of divine justice. The precursors were an inner agitation of Boris's heart and various calamitous events, against which he still struggled earnestly with all the firmness of his spirit, only to find himself suddenly weak and, as it were, helpless in the final manifestation of his miraculous fate. (XI, 55)

As Karamzin instructs his readers, Boris's greatness "was purchased at too dear a price" (XI, 56). This expense was initially no fault of his Russian subjects, who appreciated Boris's services. "It should come as no surprise that Russia, in the words of contemporaries, loved its Wearer of the Crown, wishing to forget the murder of Dmitry or at least to doubt it" (XI, 57). The fault was lodged not in externals but in Boris's own conscience:

The Wearer of the Crown knew his own secret, and did not have the peace of mind to believe the people's love; while showing charity to Russia, he soon began to distance himself from Russians ... he appeared rarely, and only in inaccessible finery ... Godunov, appearing not to fear God, feared people more and more, and even before the blows of Fate, before betrayal by fortune and by his own subjects, while he was still peacefully on the throne, sincerely praised, sincerely loved, already he knew no spiritual peace ... This inner agitation of the soul, inescapable for a criminal, was made manifest in the Tsar by unfortunate acts of suspicion which, alarming him, soon alarmed Russia as well. (XI, 57)

Torture and arrest of noble families began, most markedly of the Romanovs. And with this revelation of tyranny in Boris, "the people ceased to love him." "Peoples are always grateful," Karamzin notes. "Leaving it to heaven to judge the secret of Boris's heart, Russians genuinely glorified their Tsar when he seemed to them, under a mask of virtue, to be a father to his people; but having recognized the tyrant in him, they naturally began to hate him, for the present as well as for the past ... and Dmitry's blood showed up all the more vividly on the royal purple of this Destroyer of innocents ..." (XI, 65–66).

There could scarcely be a clearer example of Montesquieu's paradigm, the collapse of a monarch into a tyrant. Karamzin's description of Boris recalls his earlier treatment of Ivan the Terrible – but with one important difference:

Ivan was a hereditary monarch. He could err monstrously, but on the question of legitimacy his heart was at peace. Therefore, unlike Boris, he *developed* into a tyrant; he was not revealed as having been a tyrant from the start.[16] Thus governed by his guilty conscience, the Karamzinian Tsar Boris is a static figure: everything positive he achieves becomes mere cover-up and cunning. His generosity after the famine functioned to "hide the act of divine wrath" (XI, 69). The Tsaritsa Irina's death was a blessing for her and her brother, for she had "shown him the way to the throne, albeit innocently, being blinded by love for him and by the glitter of his apparent virtues" (XI, 73). The rise of general brigandage and of the Pretender Otrepiev was but the final nemesis. The last months of Boris's life are Macbeth-like in their paralysis.

Till the very end, Karamzin presents Tsar Boris as much stronger politically than he was psychologically. Had this energetic Tsar only mounted his horse and led his troops into battle, the historian conjectures, "his great boldness and confidence would have had their effect . . . [but Boris] did not want to confront Dmitry's shade" (XI, 94). For all this prefiguration, however, the Tsar's actual moment of death is recounted matter-of-factly. Boris rose from the table where he was receiving foreigners, and with terrible suddenness "blood poured from his nose, ears, and mouth, and even the doctors whom he so loved could not stop it" (XI, 108). Karamzin discounts the possibility of suicide as cowardly and in any event premature. The Tsar's untimely death, which benefited no one, was rather a punishment to Boris and his country: "Russia, deprived in him of an intelligent and solicitous tsar, became the prey of evil-doing for many years" (XI, 108–09). For was it not Godunov, "more than anyone, who cooperated in the destruction of the throne, by having mounted it as a saint-murderer?" (XI, 109). It was – Karamzin implies – as if the Tsarevich Dmitry's blood, so long contained and denied, had finally flowed forth in expiation.

Thus Karamzin's portrait of Boris and his reign combined in a single image a Saint's Life, a morality play, a psychological study, and a defense of legitimacy that would not be lost on the generation that survived Napoleon. Karamzin's achievement is larger, however, than mere propaganda for legitimatist loyalties. He forged a new genre of historical writing, fitting sacred motifs of sin and retribution together with a more secular language that perceived the causes for events not in heaven but in the human psyche. A gifted, ambitious man is brought low by a single criminal act. This act is "inevitable," but not because God or fate preordained it; at every step of the way Boris has very good inner reasons, both selfish and altruistic, for committing it. Like the ancient tragedians (and like Dostoevsky half a century later), Karamzin, a skilled storyteller, is scrupulous in keeping these reasons in front of his reader. Once the act is committed, however, its consequences cannot be contained. Sentimental and divine determinism combine to condemn Boris. And with his fine sense of Russia's traditional texts, Karamzin at crucial moments adopts the voice of an ancient chronicler and appeals to a deeply engrained religious genre, the Saint's Life, at the center of the Tale.

The Preface to the *History* opens on these words: "In a certain sense history is the sacred book of peoples, its main and indispensable book ... a supplement and explanation of the present and an example for the future" (I, xvii). Karamzin used the Fall of Boris Godunov to stress a moral lesson, to point the way to the enlightened Romanov dynasty, and to draw edifying parallels between Russia's past and her present. A very different mission and evolution of the story was experienced in drama and opera. Boris's guilt became canonical there also. But this guilt, along with the divine vengeance and wholesale devastation that followed in its wake, was not utilized in those later versions the way Karamzin had utilized it – that is, as a cohesive factor imparting sense and shape to chaotic events of national history. On the contrary, Pushkin, and later Musorgsky, achieved their new artistic state-ments by stressing the opposite, the disharmony and incompatibility of part to whole. What Pushkin wanted to say about history was that it did *not* cohere, not in general and not in the minds of those who would later be called its heroes. Pushkin copied Karamzin's image of Boris closely: most of the scenes of Pushkin's drama can be traced to details in the text or notes of the *History*, and many of the same phrases and epithets resonate.[17] But a close copy of particulars within a very different context can signify parody as easily as homage. In Pushkin's play there is none of Karamzin's larger didactic framework, no narrative voice that poses and resolves rhetorical questions. Where Karamzin grants authority to divine providence, Pushkin grants it to rumor and slander. We will now look at the drama that Pushkin, in exile at his family estate during the tense interregnum year 1825, fashioned out of Karamzin's tenth and eleventh volumes.

II

Both Karamzin and Pushkin approached history "poetically," and both experimented with literary genres. Whereas Karamzin, however, sought to mold disparate historical parts into a meaningful sequence, Pushkin (who had curious ideas about fate, but little faith in divine providence) was suspicious of patterning and figural thinking. In particular, Pushkin was impatient with the formulas that had come to govern both romantic and tragic art – borrowed European categories, he argued, that were poorly understood by their Russian imitators. Two brief statements by Pushkin will make his theoretical position clear.

In 1825, the year of his writing *Boris Godunov*, the poet jotted down some thoughts "On classical and romantic poetry."[18] Contrary to common belief, he wrote, the essence of romantic genres has nothing to do with "dreaminess," "superstitions" or "folk legends." (The subtext here could well have been the famous definition by August Wilhelm Schlegel [1808]: the romantic is that which "presents a sentimental theme in a fantastic form.") For Pushkin, "the romantic" deserved a definition in terms of form, not content. And the formal definition he offered was this: romantic genres are ones not known to the ancients or ones in the process of evolving – any form, that is, which encourages innovation and change. To be romantic, therefore, meant to value the unexpected; by definition, a romantic cliché could not exist. That same year Pushkin also expressed himself on tragedy.[19] The stage will never be "realistic," he insisted. And tragedy is in any case the least realistic of all dramatic forms. Those who write for the tragic stage, therefore, should not seek compensation for tragedy's lack of verisimilitude by patching together arbitrary, and inevitably crimping, "unities" of time, space, style. Tragic form should require no fixed rules; rather, "verisimilitude of situations and truth of dialogue – there is the real rule of tragedy." "Interest," Pushkin wrote archly, "is also a unity."

To be sure, Pushkin's brief contributions to these two much-discussed literary traditions are not in themselves original. But they take on some importance when we consider their application to the drama *Boris Godunov* – labeled by Pushkin, in an intriguing conflation, a "romantic tragedy." According to Pushkin's own aesthetic, what are the play's "romantic" and "tragic" components? How do they work to undo Karamzin's Boris Tale, and in what way might they have appealed to Musorgsky?

If Karamzin's telling was a model of cohesion, Pushkin's *Boris* is a model of fragmentation and unexpectedness – spatial, temporal, stylistic. Much of the play's formal inspiration comes from Shakespeare, a debt that Pushkin often and freely acknowledged. Its twenty-three short, unnumbered scenes move from Moscow to Poland and to various borders and battlefields in between. (Pushkin wrote twenty-five scenes in 1825, but voluntarily omitted two of them when the play was published in 1831.) The time of action stretches over seven years. The play mixes not only diction and style (blank verse interrupted by lofty rhythmic passages and then by colloquial, at times inebriated prose, often lasting for entire scenes) but also languages and even typeface. (The sixteenth scene, set in the midst of a battle, is a macaronic jumble of Russian, French, German, French as it sounds to Russians – and is printed in Cyrillic, Latin, and *Frakturschrift*.) Before we speculate on the genre of the play and its historical worldview, however, we provide here a brief overview of its scenes.[20]

PUSHKIN'S *BORIS GODUNOV*: SYNOPSIS OF SCENES

[1] The Kremlin Palace (the year 1598, 20 February)

The Princes Shuisky and Vorotynsky, assigned to keep watch over Moscow, cynically discuss the succession crisis: Boris, crafty and ambitious, will not accept the crown. Shuisky recalls the death of Dmitry in Uglich eight years earlier, and tries to excuse his own complicity in covering up Boris's role in it. But the Ruler is hardly a man to make Uglich an obstacle, Shuisky insists. "He'll step over it; Boris is not that timid!" Both agree that the nobility has lost its mandate to rule.

[2] Red Square

Voices from the crowd lament Boris's "terror at the throne" and the specter of an orphaned, unruled Russia. Shchelkalov, head clerk of the Duma, reports that the council continues to pray for "the Ruler's grief-stricken soul," and that the Patriarch is bringing out the most sacred icons in an effort to persuade Boris to reconsider.

[3] Maiden's Field. Novodevichy Convent [Suppressed by the censor from the 1831 text]

Voices from the edge of the crowd, this time openly cynical. One mother hushes her infant and then, when a loud supplication is called for, throws it on the ground to add its wailing to the din; others ask for onions or wet their eyes with spit to simulate weeping. Finally the news reaches the outskirts of the crowd: Boris has consented.

[4] The Kremlin Palace

Boris addresses the boyars and Patriarch, humbling himself before his predecessors Ivan III and IV and begging a blessing from the "Angel-Tsar" Feodor. The boyars swear loyalty and Boris invites all to a Coronation feast. Vorotynsky congratulates Shuisky for his foresight; Shuisky, ever the crafty courtier and opportunistic politician, feigns surprise and advises Vorotynsky to forget their earlier conversation.

[5] Night. A Cell in Chudov Monastery [Monastery of the Miracle] (the year 1603)

The old monk Pimen is finishing up his chronicle with "one final tale," which will be the current and criminal reign of Boris Godunov. The novice Grigory awakes and recounts a terrible dream. Recommending fasting and prayer as the proper antidote,

Pimen delivers a lengthy account of Russia's earlier virtuous rulers, bewailing that "we have now angered Heaven by choosing a tsarecide as our ruler." Pimen tells his own hagiographic, and thus anachronistic, version of the Uglich murder (the second account of that event in the play). Grigory swears vengeance on Boris.

By the Monastery Gates [Scene written in 1825, omitted from 1831 published text]
Grigory complains to an "evil monk" about the tedium of monastery life, his desire for adventure, and his dream that the Tsarevich Dmitry would rise from the grave and call upon his servants to avenge Boris. The monk suggests that Grigory assume the name of Dmitry; "our stupid people are superstitious and glad to marvel at miracles and novelties ..." Grigory ponders and then answers: "It's settled. I'm the Tsarevich."

[6] The Patriarch's Palace
In racy and irritated prose, the Patriarch complains to an abbot about the outrageous pretender who claims "he will be Tsar in Moscow." By placing Grigory with the kindly Pimen, the Patriarch had done a favor for the talented young monk, who could read and even compose sacred canons. And this is his unjust reward. "I've had it with all these literate types!"

[7] The Tsar's Quarters in the Palace
Two servants, discussing Boris's passion for soothsaying, withdraw as Boris enters grimly. The entire scene is Boris's famous monologue "I have attained supreme power" – one long diatribe on his unhappiness, his bad luck (in the death of his daughter's bridegroom, in the Moscow fires and the famine, in the suspiciousness and ingratitude of the people); and, finally, on the "single accidental stain on a conscience" that can poison a whole life.

[8] An Inn on the Lithuanian Border
Varlaam and Misail, two vagabond friars, and their civilian companion Grigory Otrepiev take refreshment at an inn. While the friars are drinking and singing, Grigory nervously asks the innkeeper where the road leads; she complains of a roadblock and ridicules official attempts to catch the runaway. Her directions are interrupted by the police. Illiterate and thus unable to read the warrant for "Grishka's" arrest, the police enlist Otrepiev's help – and he proceeds to read out a physical description of Varlaam. In self-defense Varlaam grabs the document, sounds out its syllables (which describe his travelling companion), and Otrepiev, brandishing a dagger, escapes through the window.

[9] Shuisky's House
Concluding a dinner party on a long "loyalty prayer" to Boris, Shuisky retains one guest, Evstafy Pushkin (authentic ancestor of the poet). Pushkin informs Shuisky of news from his nephew in Kraków: a pretender has appeared in Poland-Lithuania.

Both discuss the tyranny of Boris's reign, the omnipresence of informers, and the people's growing discontent.

[10] Palace of the Tsar

A domestic scene: the Tsarevna Xenia laments her deceased bridegroom, and Tsar Boris praises his son Feodor's diligence over a map of Muscovy. Xenia departs when Semyon Godunov, secret police chief, reports that spies had informed on a private meeting between Shuisky and Pushkin. Shuisky is brought in, alerts Boris that the Pretender is using the name of Dmitry of Uglich, and – in response to Boris's furious inquiry – assures the Tsar that the Tsarevich Dmitry had indeed died in 1591 (this constitutes the play's third retelling of the murder). Left alone, Boris gasps for breath: he resolves not to let his bad dreams and an "empty name, a shade" destroy his reign and dynasty.

[11] Kraków. Wisniowiecki's House

The Pretender is discussing with Father Czernikowski his own and the Russian people's conversion to Catholicism when a crowd of Poles and Russians are announced. To each petitioner – a cross-section of his motley support base – the Pretender turns a different and appropriate face: Gavrila Pushkin, Prince Kurbsky (son of Ivan the Terrible's famed opponent), a Pole, a poet bearing Latin verses, a renegade Cossack, and the boyar Khrushchov, a defector from Godunov's side.

Governor Mniszech's Castle in Sambor. Marina's boudoir [Scene written in 1825, omitted from 1831 printed text]

A silent and self-absorbed Marina is being dressed by her talkative maid Ruzia. Ruzia gossips about the Tsarevich, lacing flattery for her mistress with rumor that Dmitry is a runaway monk and rogue. Marina is alarmed and vows: "I must find out everything."

[12] Governor Mniszech's Castle in Sambor

A ball, with Marina and the Pretender leading the polonaise. Marina's father boasts to Wisniowiecki that his daughter will be Tsaritsa; Wisniowiecki boasts to Mniszech that his former servant will be Russia's Tsar. Marina promises Dmitry a meeting the next evening by the fountain. The other dancers remark on the coldness of Marina's beauty and on the regal features of the unprepossessing Tsarevich.

[13] Night. Garden. Fountain

The Pretender waits in dread by the fountain. Marina arrives; she interrupts his lovesick confession with some matter-of-fact inquiries into his political prospects and her future as Tsaritsa. Unable to interest the ambitious Marina in his love and stung to the quick by her arrogance, the Pretender punishes her by telling the truth – that the real Dmitry is dead, and that he is only a poor novice. She is horrified at the ease with which he confessed his deception "for the sake of love." Only when the Pretender scorns her and assures her she will be forgotten or else silenced should she try to expose him, does she come around: "now I hear the words of a man, and not a boy." Overthrow Godunov, she says, and then we'll talk of love.

[14] The Lithuanian Border (the year 1604, 16 October)

The Pretender and Kurbsky, on horseback. Kurbsky sings the praises of his ancestral homeland; the Pretender, less sentimental, regrets shedding Russian blood. But he hopes this sin will fall not on him but on the tsarecide Boris.

[15] The Royal Duma

A council meeting of Tsar Boris, the Patriarch and boyars convenes over the danger presented by the False Dmitry's invasion. The patriarch is first to speak. In a lengthy and lofty speech, he recommends that the sacred remains of the True Tsarevich of Uglich be transferred to Moscow, thus putting an end to all claimants to his name. For emphasis he prefaces this plea with a long reminiscence of a blind shepherd whose sight was restored at Dmitry's grave. (This is the play's fourth full-length narrative on Dmitry of Uglich, and the one most saturated with miracle.) In anguish during the recitation, Boris wipes his face with a handkerchief; Shuisky, always the canny courtier, tactfully dismisses as too inflammatory the Patriarch's idea of a transfer of relics. All notice how Boris had almost lost control, and how Shuisky cunningly saved the day.

[16] A Plain Near Novgorod-Seversk (the year 1604, 21 December)

A battle in three languages: the French mercenary Margeret speaks French and mispeaks Russian; Dmitry's Russian troops ridicule him; and Baron Rosen and Margeret complain about the Russians to each other, each in his own native language. Finally Dmitry appears on horseback, claims a victory and calls a retreat.

[17] The Square before the Cathedral in Moscow

A crowd mills around outside St. Basil's Cathedral. Inside, anathema is being proclaimed on Grigory Otrepiev and a requiem Mass conducted for Dmitry of Uglich. The people are unimpressed: "The Tsarevich has nothing to do with Otrepiev," some utter, and others predict that "Those atheists will get what they deserve, singing a Mass for a living man!" The Holy Fool Nikolka begs a kopek of an old woman; a band of boys teases him and steals the coin. When Tsar Boris exits from the cathedral, Nikolka asks him to slit the boys' throats, "like you slit the young Tsarevich." Boris, utterly humbled, asks Nikolka to pray for him; the Fool refuses to pray for the "Herod Tsar." (The fifth reference to the Uglich murder, this time from the *narod*.)

[18] Sevsk

The Pretender interrogates a Russian prisoner, who coolly relates news of Moscow: all is quiet because torture and informers are everywhere, but the troops are well-fed and numerous. When asked about the reputation of Dmitry, the prisoner laconically remarks: he is considered "a rogue, but a good fellow." The Pretender laughs.

[19] A Forest

The False Dmitry, his troops in utter defeat and disarray, lies sobbing over his dying horse and blaming his losses on Cossack treachery. News of Kurbsky's death in battle. Dmitry decides to camp there for the night, and falls asleep. "Pleasant dreams, Tsarevich," his companion [Gavrila] Pushkin remarks; "utterly defeated, saving himself by flight, he's as carefree as a foolish child. And providence, of course, will preserve him . . ."

[20] Moscow. The Tsar's Palace

Boris complains to his military adviser Basmanov that the Pretender was defeated but is nevertheless still on the march, and now threatens Putivl. Distrustful of his highborn commanders, disillusioned with his subjects ("Treat them well, they won't say thank you; rob and execute them, it won't be any worse for you"), Boris makes Basmanov commander. The Tsar leaves to greet foreign guests. Basmanov's musings are interrupted by cries that the Tsar has suddenly begun to bleed from the mouth and ears, that he's ill, that he's dying. Boris delivers a long, moving, politically naïve farewell to his son; the boyars swear allegiance to young Feodor, and Boris is shorn as a monk before his death.

[21] Military headquarters

The indefatigably pragmatic Gavrila Pushkin tries to persuade Basmanov, now in command of young Feodor Borisovich's troops, to defect to the Pretender. Our forces are miserable, Pushkin admits; the Poles are unreliable and undisciplined, no one knows whether the Dmitry is true or false – but the rebel side is strong in "popular opinion," which sooner or later will topple young Feodor. Basmanov hesitates.

[22] "Lobnoe mesto," The Place of Executions [Red Square]

Pushkin announces to the crowd that the True Dmitry, by heavenly design saved from his murderers (the sixth and final Uglich story, this time "revisionist"), is returning to punish the villain – whom God has already struck down. Basmanov has sworn allegiance to Dmitry, and Pushkin counts on the Muscovites' support as well. Recounting the people's suffering under Boris, Pushkin rouses the crowd, which cries out to "tie up Boris's pup . . . Long live Dmitry! May the Boris Godunov clan perish!"

[23] The Kremlin. Boris's House. Guards at the entrance

Young Tsar Feodor and his sister Xenia are at the window when a beggar is turned away by guards, who permit no exchange with the "prisoners." Voices from the crowd sympathize with, as well as curse, the royal children. Boyars enter the house; someone in the crowd remarks on loud noises and sounds of struggle. Mosalsky, government spokesman, comes out on the porch to announce that "Maria Godunova and her son Feodor have poisoned themselves . . . Shout: Long live Dmitry Ivanovich!" (In 1825, Alexander Pushkin ended the play with a compliant cheer from the crowd, "Long live Dmitry Ivanovich!" In the 1831 printed text, this cheer is removed and replaced by a final stage direction – perhaps the most famous in all Russian drama – *narod bezmolvstvuet* [the people are silent, the people do not respond].)

As the above synopsis makes clear, Pushkin's clipped and episodic drama relies heavily on the audience's previous knowledge of the story. The author himself, sending the tragedy to his friend Nicholas Raevsky in 1829, requested that the latter "skim through the final volume of Karamzin" before reading the play.[21] Indeed, somewhat like illustrations to a novel, Pushkin's seemingly random "windows" that open on to complex historical events serve more to remind people of a familiar plot than to inform them of a new one. This fragmentation is more than a luxury afforded by the proximity of Karamzin's *History*, however. It is clearly also in keeping with Pushkin's ideas on "romanticism" and "tragedy."

As we noted above, innovation, change, unexpectedness were, for Pushkin, the features by which one recognized authentic romantic form. "Verisimilitude of situations and truth of dialogue" were correspondingly the true rules of tragedy. With unnerving intensity, Pushkin combines these two sets of characteristics in his "romantic tragedy." First, the participants in *Boris Godunov* are caught in their own time; forever being surprised by developments, they are utterly without historical perspective on events. Satisfying confrontations or resolutions are rare. The two main heroes, Boris and the Pretender, appear late in the play (in the fourth and fifth scenes respectively), exit early (in the fourth and fifth scenes from the end), and never meet. In place of confrontation and causality, what does link events is rumor – and most particularly the rumor of the murder at Uglich. Everywhere repeated and nowhere proven, Uglich is a pretext that the ambitious manipulate to their own advantage. Literally on the lips of every character and social class, the murder is thrown incessantly in the face of Tsar Boris.

Rumor and slander thus emerge in the play as historical operators, not merely as parameters or vehicles for a disputed event. This is important, for Pushkin's handling of time and the effects of its passing, though frequently compared with Elizabethan "dual time," is in fact more radical. Shakespeare's manipulations and compressions brought people and events closer together; Pushkin's "violations of the unities" accomplishes quite the opposite. Colorful personalities like Pimen, Misail, Varlaam emerge once and are never heard of again. The connections that matter seem to occur in a time and space "between scenes": the last we see of the False Dmitry, he is sobbing next to his dying horse, defeated in battle; the next we hear of him he is triumphantly on his way to Moscow. Mere sequence is never allowed to add up to an explanation for events – which might be one reason why Pushkin ultimately decided neither to number his scenes nor to organize them into acts. He also declined to preface the play with a list of dramatis personae, as if it could not be known in advance who would play which role.

Here we detect an important dialogue with Karamzin. Throughout the *History* but most particularly in its volumes on Boris Godunov, Karamzin's richly authoritative narrative voice speaks for Providence. Transposed into drama, that figural narrative tissue is bound to be weakened. But it is more than weakened in Pushkin's drama; it is dissolved altogether. When Gavrila Pushkin remarks, in the nineteenth scene (the Pretender's last), that "providence, of course, will preserve Dmitry" who has fallen asleep like a "foolish child" after his defeat, Pushkin gives us providence as a product of whimsy and chance. Men, not God, make history – and they do so in isolation, in the heat of their own needs. Pimen is the one figure in Pushkin's play who might be said to "record history" – but his chronicle is far from an objective account. His version of Uglich is permeated with the literary conventions and formulas of a Saint's Life, a document suspiciously fitting the political requirements of the day.

This continual deferral, paraphrase and recirculation of the most important thing – What happened at Uglich? – is, in its way, an identity crisis for the play as a whole. In Karamzin's linear, finite, providential history, Dmitry's rise to power is not highlighted; it is an aberration, a demonic theatrical performance, and the obscurities of its plot are irrelevant. Pushkin, however, devotes more scenes to the Pretender than to Tsar Boris himself, and reworks the False Dmitry's "theatricality" into a positive value. For its time, we should note, Pushkin's Pretender was a radical creation – both in the realm of history and of high theater. His protean personality, at times recalling more the antic heroes of *commedia dell'arte* than the conventions of historical drama, undermines both romantic historicism, with its faith in individual action as significant cause, and the concept of the "stage hero" with his self-assertive monologues, coherent appetites and cumulative biography. The Pretender assumes a different personality in almost every scene. He knows only dialogue, and gets all his ideas from context; as expectations and fortunes change, so does he. Listening to others, he becomes what they need. (Only once, in love with Marina at the fountain, does he lose this transparency and try to tell the truth – and he almost loses everything, his royal future and Marina as well.) A changeling and genius of naïve imitation, Pushkin's Pretender does not sustain a selfish, truly lyrical "I." Already apparent is the challenge that Musorgsky will confront, turning this artful chameleon into solid romantic tenor.

As we have seen, medieval Muscovy linked such theatrical play with the devil. But Pushkin, child of the Enlightenment, was fond of his False Dmitry, calling him an *"amiable aventurier"* and intending a resemblance to Shakespeare's Henry IV.[22] That such a pretender can come to fruition only in Poland is no accident. As opposed to slow-moving, ritualized Orthodox Muscovy, where legitimation was always backwards toward some preexisting icon or traditional value, Catholic Poland was the West: open, initiatory, high-spirited, free.

We must remember how members of Pushkin's cosmopolitan generation distinguished West from East. Russia, whose spiritual sources were in Byzantium and whose image of self was formed on the orientalized borders of Europe, had not experienced the Renaissance or Reformation; humanism had never taken root. The measure of all things was not the human being but a mystical collective, a teleological divine unity. After Ivan the Terrible's most articulate opponent, Prince Andrey Kurbsky, defected to Poland in 1564 and began to abuse his former monarch from across the border, Ivan eloquently defended his mystical, patriotic absolutism and the obligation of individuals to subordinate themselves to it. It is significant that Grigory Otrepiev, when he escapes through a window of the inn toward the West, repeats Kurbsky's challenge. He insists on the right of one person to make history, not – as in Pimen's cell – merely to witness it, record it, submit to it and pray for intercession. Only Boris's "illegitimacy," of course, makes such a challenge possible at all on Russian soil.

What constitutes legitimacy? Boris, the False Tsar, is challenged by a False Dmitry. But even the true Dmitry is something of a false tsarevich, the son of a seventh marriage and technically illegitimate. Everywhere one turns in the play, identity and authority begin to slip; hearsay and theatricality alone hold things together. This sense that the play "shows us characters as actors rather than the other way around"[23] gives the work its eerily modern feel. But Pushkin's contemporaries also made the same complaint, cast somewhat more conventionally: the play *had* no heroes. And indeed, "romantic tragedy" does not really admit of heroes, because heroes are always products of a history, results of historical events. Pushkin's characters might dream of making history, but they lack that control over their own significance. This is as true of the False Dmitry, who wins, as it is of the tragic loser Tsar Boris.

It remains to mention two readings of Pushkin's play that will return us to the genre issues raised earlier in the chapter, as well as help locate this literary text between Karamzin's *History* and Musorgsky's libretto. The first is by the Soviet Pushkinist Valentin Nepomnyashchy.[24] What Pushkin attempted in his "romantic tragedy," the critic claims, was to challenge the ideology of both reigning literary worldviews of his time: neoclassicism and

Romanticism. The former made rational man the center and responsible monitor of the universe; the latter merely reversed the hierarchy, opposing man helplessly to his natural world and condemning him, in Byronic fashion, to futile protest and self-duplication. Both ideologies were equally static and monologic. And, Nepomnyashchy argues, as dramatic principles they were equally unsatisfactory to Pushkin. Drama, after all, is dialogue, and it must transmit a sense of genuine development and unexpected encounter. It cannot merely be recited or unfolded. Thus Pushkin's characters, despite their historical trappings, end up as heroes solely of their own isolated personal fates. Thus this play, about a *Lzhe-*[false] Dmitry who challenges a *lzhe-*tsar, is really about the more general problem of *lzhe-*subjects. As Nepomnyashchy sums up his thesis, "*Boris Godunov* is not a 'historical tragedy' in the usual sense of the term, but a tragedy about History." Again, casting forward to the opera, we see what dramatic tasks await Musorgsky. He will have to find a way to restore to his protagonists the aria-like monologue and the confident, fully embodied "stage presence" that Pushkin had so cunningly stripped away.

A second reading, by the American Slavist Stephanie Sandler, focuses on another aspect of the play: its anxiety about audience. Seeking traces of the fact that Pushkin wrote his *Boris Godunov* during a period of domestic exile, cut off from the capitals and uncertain that his writing would ever reach readers, Sandler documents all those places where the play appears to be deliberately structured so as *not* to produce "the bonding rituals typical of drama." Possessed of "immense centrifugal energy," she claims, the play is a fabric of "successful discontinuities." Things that are supposed to have fixed value are forever being evacuated – starting with the throne and ending, of course, with the people's refusal to respond to the victorious Pretender. In this play, she adeptly notes, "we watch mostly those who watch." And what all the watchers are continually exposed to is the same old rumor-ridden story; "there is no discovery as the play's final reward." [25]

With its indeterminacy, its military battles, its men on horseback, its rapid-fire scenes that nevertheless depend more on talk than on action, was Pushkin's *Boris* ever intended for the stage? Many in Pushkin's time – although not Pushkin himself – doubted that it was, and the lukewarm stage premiere of 1870 only helped to confirm the doubt. This opinion persisted until the mid 1930s, when Soviet theater historians began to suggest that the neoclassical stage is itself the culprit; the dynamic, tripartite stage of Elizabethan drama might better integrate Pushkin's short and mercurial scenes into one dramatic whole. [26] Even if one discounts staging factors, however, obstacles to the play's performance success were immense in the nineteenth century. There was no clear resolution to the plot. There was no genuine love interest. And there was the sense, deeply organic to Pushkin's dramatic plan, that the further the story unraveled the less any story could be trusted, and the more solitary both the audience and the characters felt themselves to be.

Although Pushkin could not immediately publish his play, he did let scenes from it be read. Karamzin – to whom the play was dedicated – must have been one of the more interested listeners. In September 1825, near the end of his life, Karamzin suggested in a letter to his friend Pyotr Vyazemsky that Pushkin give his Boris a "wilder mixture" of emotions – more piety as well as mote criminal passions.[27] "He was forever reading the Bible, seeking in it some justification for himself," Karamzin wrote. "There's dramatic contrast for you!" To this advice Pushkin responded, wryly and indirectly, that he thanked the historian and would make haste to "sit his Boris down with the Gospel, force him to read Herod's Tale, etc." Pushkin's irony is rarely simple. But in this instance it is clear that he did not intend his play as a dramatic corollary to Karamzin's "sacred book of peoples."

History was not that for Pushkin. His heroes – forced to secularize their roles, confined to work within that limited perspective which is all that any individual, even a tsar, can claim on events – clashed with most of the sentiments canonic for the Boris Tale since the time of the early chronicles. A new dramatic contrast was indeed born in Pushkin's play, but not the one Karamzin probably had in mind. Pushkin's Tsar Boris and Dmitry the Pretender come to life only as they strain against Karamzin's providential and figural plot. In so doing, they make problematic the very concepts of heroic personality, historical effectiveness, and the possibility of telling a truth on stage. Musorgsky would rein in these precociously modernist ideas. His revised version of the opera is conventionally dramatic. It nonetheless exemplifies the realism that opera generates best: symbol, allegory, metaphor, myth. Precisely the multi-layeredness of opera opens up to us the possibility of an intuitive, "sense-based" perception, rather than one that is narrowly realistic, cognitive and "fact-based." The following chapter, then, will attempt to tell the story of Musorgsky's revised version of the opera through the interaction of two "sense-based" parameters, narrative plot (part history, part myth) and music.

3

NARRATIVE AND MUSICAL SYNOPSIS OF THE OPERA

The operagoer approaching *Boris Godunov* for the first time confronts a textual problem almost without equal in the standard repertory. As we shall see in greater detail in Chapter 4, Musorgsky himself completed two versions of the work, in 1869 and 1874, that were fundamentally different despite much music in common. Then in 1896 Nikolay Rimsky-Korsakov published an edition of *Boris* based on the composer's printed vocal score of 1874, but heavily cut, reorchestrated, and drastically reworked on the grounds of the composer's alleged technical incompetence. Most of the cuts were restored when Rimsky returned to the opera in 1906–07, and it is this, his second version, that until recently has dominated the world's operatic stage.

Rimsky's changes were controversial and soon became the subject of an acrimonious debate. French writers, in particular, denounced Rimsky for disfiguring Musorgsky while Russians often defended him. Amidst continuing polemic, other musicians also began to lend a hand to *Boris Godunov*. In the 1920s, for a performance at Riga, Emil Melngailis orchestrated the opera from the first edition of Musorgsky's piano–vocal score, in an attempt to circumvent the changes of pitch, rhythm, meter, melody, and harmony that Rimsky had made. About the same time, the firm of J. & W. Chester commissioned Eugène Goossens to prepare orchestrations of excerpts "in accordance with the composer's style" to accompany their publication of a new edition of the 1874 piano–vocal score.[1]

Then in 1928, at the height of the clamor for "authentic" Musorgsky, the Soviet musicologist Pavel Lamm published an edition of *Boris Godunov* which presented both Musorgsky's initial version of the opera (1869) and his own revision (1874). The format Lamm chose, however, further contributed to the confusion surrounding the opera. Even though Musorgsky had considered the 1869 version of *Boris* a finished opera, Lamm designated it "preliminary," as though it were somehow unpolished or incomplete, and presented it in the form of footnotes and addenda to the 1874 score. He thus grafted back onto the revision all the music that Musorgsky had seen fit to cut, obscuring the distinctive individual conceptions embodied in each version and creating apparent continuities never envisioned by the composer. The St. Basil, Death, and Kromy Forest scenes, for example, are combined into a gargantuan final act, and Pimen's narrative concerning the murder of young Dmitry (found only in Musorgsky's *initial* version) is stuffed back into the *revised* Cell scene. In Lamm's conflated score, then, neither the initial version nor the revision unfolds as Musorgsky left them; rather the two are intertwined, and to disentangle them requires careful attention to the vocal score's footnotes and critical apparatus. Working from this edition, Dmitry Shostakovich prepared a fresh orchestration of *Boris* in 1939–40. Then in 1953 Karol Rathaus, a Polish composer who had emigrated to the United States, touched up Musorgsky–Lamm for a new production at the Metropolitan Opera.[2] Finally in 1975, the English conductor David Lloyd-Jones published a new critical edition based on Musorgsky's holograph full score. Although Lloyd-Jones's format is clearer (scenes unique to the initial version are relegated to the appendix), he too has chosen to reinsert into the main text all the cuts Musorgsky took in revising the five scenes common to the two versions.

The work of these scholars and composers gradually has established in the repertory what one recent commentator has aptly named the "super-saturated" *Boris*: all the music that it is possible to include in a single performance without repeating, side by side, separate conceptions of a single scene.[3] Since the "supersaturated" *Boris* is far too long for most houses – ten scenes, each with every available scrap stitched into place – conductors and stage directors are forced to compensate by taking new cuts of their own devising.[4] Of course, such *ad hoc* conflations fail to represent Musorgsky's intentions, and accord with neither of his designs. It is ironic that even today, with Rimsky-Korsakov all but banished outside Russia, the operagoer still is likely to hear *Boris Godunov* in a form that reflects the second guesses of someone other than the composer. It is further ironic that, despite Rimsky's many changes, his 1908 score remains closer in conception to Musorgsky's *Boris* than Lamm's, Lloyd-Jones's, Rathaus's, or Shostakovich's: unlike his successors, Rimsky-Korsakov reinserted none of the episodes from the initial version that the composer had cut.

Although a guide to *Boris Godunov* must deal with both Musorgsky's versions, it would be prohibitively confusing to try to account for all the differences in a linear synopsis, since they range in scale from entire scenes to just a few bars. We shall begin instead with the composer's revision, completed in full score in 1872 and published in piano–vocal score just before the first performance in 1874.[5] Indeed, this first edition has particular

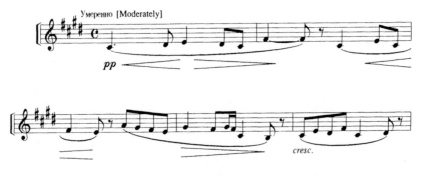

Example 3.1

authority: it was the only score published in Musorgsky's lifetime, it was proofread by the composer, and it represents the last version of the opera to pass through his hands. In the matter of which episodes should be cut and which retained, it represents the final form he gave his revision. It is that final form which is synopsized below.

Prologue, sc. 1: Novodevichy Monastery

The courtyard of the Novodevichy Monastery near Moscow. Near the audience are the entrance gates in the monastery wall, with a turret. The people mill about on the spot; their motions are sluggish.

 Boris Godunov begins with a simple folklike melody stated in unison by the bassoons (Ex. 3.1). This asymmetric five-bar phrase is repeated three times, passing first to violas, then to a solo clarinet, and finally to contrabasses, cellos, and bassoons in octaves. Aside from a single instance of metric displacement and curtailment, the melody itself does not change. But at each repetition, its accompaniment becomes more decorative, more elaborate, and more thickly scored. In the final statement, while the melody unfolds in the lower register, a sixteenth-note pattern is introduced in the violins, which, together with the melody's third and fourth measures, will flesh out the brief connecting passage that closes this short prelude and leads to the rise of the curtain. Such "changing background" variations – in which a melody is simply repeated against a backdrop of varying orchestrations, harmonizations, and decorative counterpoints – are widespread in late nineteenth-century Russian music, and we shall meet several more pieces of this type in *Boris Godunov*. Their source is Mikhail Glinka's *Kamarinskaya*, from which, according to Tchaikovsky, "all subsequent Russian composers (including myself) continue to this day to extract contrapuntal and harmonic combinations in the most obvious way, as soon as they are required to develop a Russian theme of dance character!"[6]

The curtain rises to reveal a crowd of Russian commoners milling about in front of the main gate of the Novodevichy Monastery. A policeman appears, cudgel in hand, and orders the crowd to kneel and beg the boyar Boris Godunov to become their tsar. The short, brutal sixteenth-note theme heard at the policeman's appearance is the first of many reminiscence motives that Musorgsky uses in the opera; it is associated with the police or, more generally, with oppression or brute force (see Ex. 9.2.1, p. 232). As is the case with nearly all the reminiscence themes of the opera, this one recurs infrequently; it appears only in this opening scene, associated with the policeman, and in the scene at the inn on the Polish-Lithuanian frontier, in conjunction with policemen seeking the runaway, Grigory Otrepiev.

The people reluctantly obey the policeman's orders, dropping to their knees to sing a chorus of supplication, the first chorus of the opera:

На кого ты нас покидаешь, отец наш!
Ах, на кого-то ты оставляешь, кормилец!
Мы да все твои сироты беззащитные,
Ах, да мы тебя-то просим, молим
со слезами со горючими;
Смилуйся! смилуйся! смилуйся!
Боярин батюшка! Отец наш!
Ты кормилец! Боярин!
Смилуйся!

Why have you forsaken us, our father!
Why have you abandoned us, protector!
We are all your defenseless orphans,
Ah, we beseech and pray you
With tears, with burning tears:
Have pity! Have pity! Have pity!
Boyar little father! Our father!
You our protector! Boyar,
Have pity!

At once we meet one of the most characteristic traits of Musorgsky's libretto: the "roughening up" (in places) of Pushkin's artful verse into prose. Although these lines evoke the poet's third scene, they incorporate none of his verses and very few of his words. Musorgsky has written the chorus's lines in what he characterized as "simple human speech"[7] and has given them a setting that carefully adheres to the rhythm and pace of the spoken language, freely alternating, for example, between 3/4 and 5/4 meter for this purpose. Such careful attention to declamation was a hallmark of operatic composition as propounded in Musorgsky's circle, the Mighty Handful, or *Moguchaya kuchka*. We shall encounter many passages (even entire scenes) in *Boris Godunov* in which Musorgsky proceeds very much in the manner of a good *kuchkist*, paying scrupulous attention to the declamatory style of individual lines. The melody of the chorus, like that of the prelude, is folklike, incorporating such features as a tonic pedal, frequent falls of a fourth or fifth, and a modally inflected scale (the G♭ in the melody's twentieth measure, for example). Whether self-consciously or not, Musorgsky imitates a style of Russian choral folk singing in which phrases of unaccompanied melody alternate with phrases in block chords. But even folk elements and a careful setting of text cannot disguise the fact that this chorus proceeds in the manner of a set piece to its dissolution in a descending chromatic scale.

Under the watchful eye of the policeman, members of the crowd discuss the situation, revealing that they have no clear idea why they are made to stand about, howling on demand. In the midst of their deliberations, the policeman returns, ordering them to resume their supplications, which they do with redoubled effort. The increased vigor with which they deliver their tune the second time is symbolized, perhaps, by its transposition up a semitone, from F minor to F♯ minor. Although this entire opening *tableau* is exemplary of the ideals upheld by Musorgsky and his circle, it also is redolent of nineteenth-century operatic tradition: soon after the rise of the curtain, we see a chorus of common folk moving about the stage, who inform us of what is happening in their opening number. Viewed from this perspective, this first choral *tableau* fulfils the same dramatic function as many another opening chorus from operas with which Musorgsky was familiar, operas by Rossini, Bellini, Donizetti, Verdi, Weber, and Glinka. Despite his originality, his *kuchkism*, his folklike inflections, Musorgsky knew the works of his predecessors and contemporaries and from time to time used them as models. It does not detract from his genius to realize that he learned from his peers, both Russian and West European. We shall have occasion to return to this point as we proceed.

As the second supplication dies away, the policeman announces the entry of Shchelkalov, clerk of the Duma. His accompanying melody is solemn and stately, as befits his position. He informs the assembled crowd that Boris steadfastly refuses to accept the crown. Foreseeing only misery for Russia unless Boris can be made to change his mind, Shchelkalov urges the people to pray to God to "send heavenly wisdom to strengthen Boris's weary soul." As if in response to this plea, crippled pilgrims are heard advancing in the distance. They approach from offstage, singing, and urge the people to lift up holy icons and go forth to acclaim Boris as tsar. (There is a clear echo in the passage of *La forza del destino*, Act II, sc. I, "Padre eterno, Signor," in which likewise pilgrims approach from offstage singing. Verdi's work, commissioned by the Russian Imperial Theaters and given its premiere in 1862, may have lingered in Musorgsky's memory, providing the model when he came to deal with a similar theatrical situation.) In the revision, the Novodevichy scene ends as the pilgrims enter the monastery. (The initial version of the scene ends not here, but with an additional section in which the people reassemble, receive further orders from the policeman, express their indifference, and finally disperse.)

Prologue, sc. 2: Coronation

A square in the Moscow Kremlin. Directly in front of the audience, in the distance, the Grand Staircase of the Tsar's palace. On the right, near the proscenium, the people, on their knees, fill the space between the Uspensky and Arkhangelsky Cathedrals. The porches of both cathedrals can be seen.

Perhaps the best known scene in the opera, the Coronation scene introduces the title character at the height of his glory. It is the simplest scene of the work in structure, and it presents the most opulent stage picture – common people, nobles, princes, and the Tsar himself in a *tableau* the effect of which, according to Serge Diaghilev, would be compromised by fewer than 300 people on stage. This festive scene begins with one of the most loved moments in all opera: a striking depiction of the bells of Moscow ringing in celebration of the Tsar's coronation. The carillon begins with the single pitch C given to tuba and pizzicato basses, reinforced by a stroke of the tam-tam. Two major/minor-seventh chords, their roots a tritone apart (A♭ and D), then are heard in alternation in the brass; strings and winds join this harmonic ostinato, which moves first in eight notes, then in increasingly energetic rhythmic patterns culminating in sixteenth-note triplets. The curtain rises to reveal the Tsar's procession proceeding from the Imperial Palace toward the Uspensky Cathedral. Boyars and their children, guardsmen and musketeers lead the way. Prince Shuisky, a fatally pivotal character whom we glimpse here for the first time, follows with the fur-trimmed Cap of Monomakh, the coronation crown of the Russian Tsars, on a pillow. More boyars walk behind Shuisky, among them Shchelkalov carrying the Imperial

Example 3.2

scepter. The orchestral evocation of bells is heard again, supported this time by the pealing of real theater bells on stage.[8] Trumpet fanfares ring out as the procession enters Uspensky Cathedral for the coronation, and Shuisky orders the crowd to sing in praise of Boris. The people, who have been kneeling throughout the procession, now stand and comply:

Уж как на небе
Солнцу красному
Слава, слава!
Уж и как на Руси
царю Борису
Слава, слава!

As the beautiful sun
Is above us in heaven
Glory, glory!
So Tsar Boris
Is above us in Russia
Glory, glory!

This, by the way, is one of the few genuine folk melodies in *Boris Godunov* (Ex. 3.2). Published as a text in the collection of Mikhail Chulkov (1770–74) and with music in the collection of Nikolay Lvov and Jan Práč (1790; 2nd edn., 1806), this melody is well known and has been used by several other composers too – for example by Beethoven in the scherzo of the second Rasumovsky Quartet.

The coronation ceremony is concluded offstage during the first half of this chorus, and the procession then reenters from Uspensky Cathedral. The boyars add their voices to the people's acclamation, and in the final measures the Tsar himself finally emerges from the Cathedral, positioning himself to address the crowd. The tumult dies, and a pair of horns are left sustaining the dominant pitch. While another reminiscence theme is introduced in the accompaniment, Boris begins his Coronation monologue, "Skorbit dusha," expressing his anxiety for the future.

This opening monologue falls into three distinct sections, each having its own key and character. In the first, Boris reveals that his soul is troubled by sinister premonitions; indeed, it is the element of anxiety in this text that invites one to label the reminiscence theme introduced in the violins and violas at this point as "Boris's anxiety" (see Ex. 9.2.2). In the second section, Boris prays for divine guidance, and his prayer is echoed in the music by an ethereal orchestration emphasizing high strings and winds with no instruments lower than the viola. Resonance and a firm bass are added only for the final lines of this prayer, in which the Tsar asks for glory. In the third section, Boris breaks out of his reverie and invites everyone to his coronation feast; the music, in turn, breaks out of a remote flat key into C major again.

The people once again take up their chorus of praise, in abbreviated form, during which the procession enters Arkhangelsky Cathedral on the other side of the square. Then having prayed before the tombs of his predecessors, Boris proceeds toward the *Terem* (the royal apartments) while the crowd shouts "Glory!" The curtain slowly falls. (At the premiere, to comply with the official prohibition against representing ecclesiastics on stage, this scene and the Novodevichy scene were played as one in front of a neutral street scene, "Boris's House.')

Act I, sc. 1: Pimen's Cell

Night. A cell in the Monastery of the Miracle. Father Pimen sits and writes in front of an icon lamp. Grigory is sleeping.

Five years have passed since the events of the prologue; the year now is 1603. (Oddly enough, the date appears only in a heading in Pushkin's play, nowhere in the libretto, a detail that was to become controversial after the opera's first production in the West in 1908.) Pimen, an aged monk and chronicler, is writing by lamplight in his cell in the Chudov Monastery inside the Kremlin. The novice Grigory (or Grishka) Otrepiev – whom we later shall know as the Pretender (or False Dmitry) – is asleep on a pad in the cell. The scene begins with a slowly undulating melody in sixteenth notes in the violas, the writing motive, used throughout the scene to depict Pimen's quill moving across the page (Ex. 9.2.3). The old man soon pauses and begins the monologue, "Eshchë odno, poslednee skazanie [Just one more, the last tale]." As is the case throughout this scene, and in sharp contrast to the people's chorus in the Novodevichy scene, these lines are taken directly from Pushkin and are in iambic pentameter.

Еще одно, последнее сказанье —
И летопись окончена моя;
Окончен труд, завещанный от Бога
Мне грешному.

Just one more, the last tale —
And my chronicle is finished;
The task is finished entrusted by God
To me, a sinner.

This smoothly flowing monologue, a fine illustration of Musorgsky's skill in setting blank verse, reveals that Pimen is preparing a chronicle of events that have unfolded during his lifetime. He anticipates the day, far in the future, when an industrious monk will find and transcribe his record, so that "the descendants of the orthodox may learn the ancient fate of their native land." At these words, the orchestra introduces the reminiscence motive associated with Pimen (Ex. 9.2.4); it is immediately repeated as he recalls the turbulent events he has witnessed. The writing figure rises abruptly through the orchestra, perhaps a musical echo of those stormy events, and then subsides as Pimen reflects that now all is calm. The writing motive resumes placidly in the violas, and the monk returns to his work, repeating the phrase "Just one more, the last story."

A chorus of monks is heard chanting offstage; while they sing, Grigory awakens from what we discover is a recurring nightmare. The writing motive is heard again in the violas as Grigory regains his composure and observes that the old monk must have been laboring over his chronicle throughout the night. He asks Pimen for his blessing and receives it while the chorus of offstage monks is heard again. Then, in a passage remarkable for its harmonic daring, Grigory narrates his terrifying dream (which of course turns out to be prophetic). He had climbed to the top of a tall tower from which he could see all Moscow spread below. People on the ground caught sight of him and mocked him; overcome with shame, he fell, and in falling awoke. (Verdi again may have provided models for the short choruses of this passage, added only during the revision. One thinks of the "Miserere" in *Trovatore*,

Leonora's scene before the monastery in *Forza*, the scene in the cloister in *Don Carlos* – all situations in which an offstage choir, serene and aloof, provides a backdrop for an onstage character whose emotional state – anxiety, turmoil, dread – is in sharp contrast. In the 1869 version of *Boris* Grigory also narrates his dream, in a weak passage of ascending and descending chromatic scales that culminate in trills. His agitation is conveyed far more effectively when set against the tranquility of the chorus.)

Pimen counsels Grigory to subdue his youthful blood with fasting and prayer, admitting that even as an old man he is subject to evil dreams of wanton feasts if he should fall asleep without saying his prayers. The orchestra comments on those dreams by playing Pimen's motive *fff*, decorated with wanton trills. Grigory envies Pimen's pre-monastic experience in the world and speaks of his own desire to gain glory in war and at court; the orchestra marks the climax of his speech with further trills. Pimen reminds him, in a lengthy narrative punctuated by frequent appearances of his motive in the orchestra, that the seductions of women and wine are illusory and that even tsars have discovered that worldly glory does not bring contentment.

Grigory then asks Pimen how old the murdered Tsarevich Dmitry would be had he lived. At this crucial question, the reminiscence motive associated with Dmitry is heard for the first time in the orchestra, highlighted by scoring, dynamics, and harmony (Ex. 3.3). Pimen responds, "He would be your age, and the reigning Tsar," whereupon an idea is born in Grigory's brain. The stage direction reveals everything, both the glorious dream of future kingship and the miserable reality of the monastery: "At these words Grigory draws himself up to his full height, then slumps meekly."[9] (In the initial version, just before Grigory's fateful question, Pimen narrates in detail how the Tsarevich was murdered; as we shall see in Chapter 9, Musorgsky may have had several reasons for deleting this narrative in revision.)

Failing to notice the change that has come upon Grigory, the old monk indicates that he will conclude his chronicle with an account of Boris's crime and exhorts Grigory to continue the work. A bell sounds matins, the chorus of monks is heard offstage again, and Pimen exits. As the Dmitry motive is heard in minor key in the winds, Grigory, left alone on stage, rhetorically defies Boris, observing that though none dares remind the Tsar of Dmitry's fate, Pimen has recorded it all. The writing motive, virtually the embodiment of history's dispassionate judgment, is heard one last time in the violas and concludes the scene. (In the 1874 vocal score, the setting for this scene is a cell in an unnamed hermitage, and Pimen and the chorus are described as hermits; Musorgsky chose to use the neutral term *hermit* in this first edition in order to forestall difficulty with the ecclesiastical censor.)

Example 3.3

Act I, sc. 2: The Inn

An inn on the Lithuanian frontier

The short orchestral prelude is built from fragments of melodies and reminiscence motives that will recur later in the scene: Varlaam's "Song of Kazan," Varlaam and Misail's identifying motive, the Dmitry motive, and a "tramping figure" of steadily moving eighth notes heard persistently in the low strings and recurring frequently in this scene as punctuation between the characters' lines. The curtain rises to reveal the hostess of the inn, who sings the "Song of the Drake," a bawdy animal ditty in folk style. As clarinets and bassoons play Varlaam and Misail's motive, the two vagabond monks enter in the company of Grigory, who has escaped from the monastery intending to make his way to Poland-Lithuania and there to establish himself as a miraculously resurrected Dmitry.

Varlaam asks the hostess for wine and upon receiving it launches into the

Example 3.4

well-known "Song of Kazan" (Ex. 3.4). The insertion of this song at this point was perfectly in keeping with the realist aesthetic theories propounded in the *kuchka* while *Boris* was being composed: formal, discrete "arias" were regarded as appropriate only at points in the text where the onstage action required a character to sing a formal song. Pushkin's stage direction at this point is "The monks drink. Varlaam strikes up a song, 'Kak vo gorode bylo vo Kazani' [How it was in the town of Kazan]."[10] The song is another example of changing background variations: two phrases – the first in a Phrygian-inflected F♯ minor, the second in E♭ minor – are repeated in succession through five stanzas of text, each repetition being set apart from the others by changes in tempo, accompaniment, and overall character.

After a brief exchange with Grigory following the song, Varlaam returns to his wine. As he drinks, he begins to sing again; the peculiar mis-pronunciations in the old tramp's second song – *yon* for *on*, "he" – indicate

1   Osip Petrov as Varlaam and Pavel Dyuzhikov as Misail, St. Petersburg, 1874

drunkenness in Russian speech. This second song (changing background variations on a genuine folk melody given to Musorgsky by Rimsky-Korsakov) likewise adheres to *kuchkist* theory, representing singing that is part of the action. But there is more here as well: in interludes between the variations, the hostess reveals how Grigory might make good his escape. This is an ingenious moment and bears a bit more scrutiny. Varlaam introduces the melody, relatively unadorned, in the first stanza. Without pause he sings the second stanza (Variation I), accompanied by pizzicato strings, and Grigory begins to question the hostess about the road to the border. In the first interlude (tremolo harmonies above a bass derived from that of Var. I), the hostess tells Grigory that the police are patrolling the road, seeking a runaway from Moscow. In Variation II, Varlaam – dozing off and then waking up – sings another verse of his song accompanied by a more elaborate harmonization consisting of arpeggios in the upper strings, and thirds, *divisi*, in the contrabasses – the very passage to which the double-bassist on the Imperial Theaters' selection committee had objected at the opera's first examination for performance.[11] In the second interlude, which follows, the hostess complains that the police are only harassing honest folk since the runaway undoubtedly will escape via a little-known path, which she then describes in detail. This narrative obviously is crucial to the drama, and Musorgsky sets it off with new material and a different orchestration (staccato winds, pizzicato strings). The third variation, yet another verse of the song, introduces still another accompaniment – chromatic scales in the bass and suggestions of the motive associated with the policeman in the opera's first scene; then in the short third interlude, the hostess sees the police approaching the inn. In the final variation, the policeman's motive from the Novodevichy scene dominates the accompaniment, and a pair of border guards – only one of whom has a singing role – enters. (For reasons of economy, many productions, including the premiere, assign this role to the singer who sang the policeman in the Novodevichy scene – presumably reassigned to the frontier in the five years between Boris's coronation and Grigory's flight into Poland-Lithuania!)

The two policemen have a warrant for Grigory's arrest. Varlaam and Misail, when questioned, state that they are itinerant monks to the tune of their motive, again given to clarinets and bassoons. Grigory, introduced by the Dmitry motive, identifies himself as a peasant from the neighboring village, who has been guiding the old monks to the border. This raises the policeman's suspicions, and he begins to question Varlaam, who laments the sad state of Christian charity and denies knowing anything about this Grishka Otrepiev whom the police are seeking. The policeman is not convinced and after further interrogation hands the warrant to Varlaam, as though the paper alone is proof of his identity. Since the policemen are illiterate, Grigory – identified again by the Dmitry motive – steps forward to read it for them. Altering the warrant by improvising a description of Varlaam, he convinces them that Varlaam is their man. But the police have interpreted the warrant as an order not just to seize Grishka, but to seize and hang him. Sensing a trick, Varlaam acknowledges that, well, perhaps he can read after all if they will give him time to spell out the letters, particularly since the affair has become a hanging matter. He grabs the warrant and begins to sound the words out syllable by syllable as the first notes of his second song are heard in the oboe. Gaining confidence, he reads the description in a passage that builds intensity by simply climbing the scale. At length, it dawns on all parties that Grigory is in fact the runaway. Amid general confusion, Grigory pulls a knife and escapes through the window while the others, in vaudeville disarray, try to catch him.

Act II: The Tsar's Quarters (*Terem*)

The interior of the Tsar's quarters in the Moscow Kremlin. Luxurious furniture. Xenia is crying in front of her betrothed's portrait. The Tsarevich is occupied with a book of large maps. The nurse is with her needlework. At the left, in the corner, a clock with chimes.

Act II is set in the *Terem*, the family quarters in the palace. The Tsarevna Xenia, Boris's daughter, sings a lamentation for her recently deceased betrothed, while her brother Feodor silently studies a map. Xenia's melody, a tune in Balakirev's "Russian minor" (Dorian mode), is interrupted by Feodor's consoling response, followed by a brief reprise with the two voices singing together. Feodor next tries to cheer up his sister by drawing her attention to the moving figures of their chiming clock, and we hear the music that has entered the consciousness of many operagoers as the very embodiment of Tsar Boris's horror in the hallucination that ends this scene: swirling strings above a sinister tritone ostinato. The effect here, though, is merely to introduce the clock and to show the children's delight in it, the better to underscore the Tsar's terror later. It is a child's toy, after all, that unhinges his mind so completely at the scene's end.

The children's nurse, a rough old peasant woman, tries to comfort Xenia with songs, first the "Song of the Gnat" and then the "Handclapping Game" that she plays with Feodor. At the climax of the handclapping game, when Feodor claps the nurse on the shoulder, Boris enters, terrifying the old woman. He attempts to console Xenia, the orchestra introducing the

2   Ivan Melnikov as Boris, St. Petersburg, 1874

3   Ivan Melnikov as Boris, St. Petersburg, 1874

reminiscence motive that will be associated with her in the rest of the opera (Ex. 9.2.6), and then sends her away. The Tsar then turns to his son in order to examine the map of the realm with him, and as Feodor recites the list of cities and seas, the orchestra introduces the reminiscence motive that is associated with him (Ex. 9.2.7). Boris praises his son and tells him to study diligently, for someday (perhaps soon) he will rule this realm. The reminiscence motive associated with foreboding is introduced (Ex. 9.2.8), followed quickly by a recall of the motive associated with Boris's anxiety in the Coronation scene; this constitutes the orchestral introduction to the Tsar's first great monologue of this act, "Dostig ya vysshei vlasti" (I have attained the highest power). During this introduction, Feodor moves upstage and resumes his work. Boris, downstage, examines documents.

In the first part of the monologue, the Tsar remarks on his six years of peaceful rule. He finds himself unable to draw comfort from the assurances of soothsayers, from the acclamation of the crowd, even from life itself. He recalls the wedding feast for Xenia that he had hoped would bring him consolation and grimly notes that death, "like a thunderstorm," took away the bridegroom. Then the tone changes, and in the second part he begins to brood darkly on his guilt. His mind becomes so agitated that he sometimes fails to complete his thoughts. Fears and agonies are half-formed and then abandoned as he races ahead to another thought, perhaps unrelated to its predecessor. Even sleep escapes him, he says, and in the darkness of the night the child Dmitry rises up before him. This devastating image will not leave him; it possesses him, exhausts him, and leaves him crying to God.

Two important reminiscence themes appear in the monologue for the first time: the motive associated with Boris's majesty and authority (initially at the line "Naprasno mne kudesniki sudyat" [In vain the soothsayers promise me,] Ex. 9.2.9) and the motive associated with his guilt ("I dazhe son bezhit" [And even sleep escapes me], Ex. 9.2.10). As he reflects on his daughter's unrealized wedding, we hear again the theme associated with Xenia. The second part of the monologue begins with the line, "Tyazhka desnitsa groznogo sudii" (Heavy is the hand of the dread judge), and introduces a new and more lyrical theme that is perhaps the most memorable melody of the monologue (see Ex. 9.6, p. 257). (When the monologue was recast during revision, this melody was borrowed from the abandoned opera *Salammbô* – a work from which Musorgsky recycled material into both the initial *Boris* and the revision.[12]) Toward the end of this section the guilt motive appears; we shall hear more of it throughout the rest of the act. As we shall see in greater detail in Chapter 9, Musorgsky has written for this monologue a piece of music in which a character at first relates circumstances and events in a relatively free-flowing *parlando* and then expresses his emotions in more melodious, lyrical, and symmetric music. If this sounds very much like a recitative–aria pair from Italian opera, it probably is no coincidence.

A great commotion now breaks out behind the scene, and Boris sends Feodor to investigate. At the same time, the boyar in attendance enters to announce Prince Shuisky (a powerful boyar and Boris's enemy) and to inform the Tsar that Shuisky has met secretly with a messenger from Kraków. Before Shuisky appears, however, Feodor returns and explains to his father that the squabble was caused by the parrot Popinka, and this provides Musorgsky another opportunity to introduce a folklike genre-song, which has the effect of once again lowering tension (and reinforcing our perception of Boris as a loving parent) prior to the climactic confrontation between Shuisky and the Tsar. Shuisky finally enters and reports, to the tune of the Dmitry motive, the rise in Poland-Lithuania of a pretender calling himself by that name. Overcome with fear, Boris dismisses his son and begs Shuisky to confirm that the child murdered so many years before in Uglich was indeed Dmitry. Seizing the opportunity, Shuisky aggravates the Tsar's dread by giving him a grisly description of the child's body as it lay in state. Boris dismisses Shuisky and falls back into his chair. We are now ready for the other great basso scene in this act, the Hallucination Monologue. To the accompaniment of a whirring symphony of strings, winds, and brass, all erected on a tritone ostinato, the figures on the chiming clock begin to move as the clock strikes the hour. To Boris's disordered mind, the shadows of these moving statuettes seem to be the ghost of the murdered Dmitry. The motive of guilt, introduced toward the end of the Tsar's earlier monologue and heard several times during the interview with Shuisky, appears in rapid-fire sixteenth notes. Near collapse, Boris prays to God for mercy on his guilty soul, and the act ends.

Act III, sc. I: Marina's Boudoir

Marina Mniszech's dressing room in Sandomir Castle. Marina is seated behind her dressing table, Ruzia is dressing her hair. Young girls entertain her with songs.

Both scenes of Act III are set in Poland-Lithuania, the first in the dressing room of Marina Mniszech, daughter of an important nobleman, the second by the fountain in the garden of her father's estate. Both these scenes were added during revision and do not appear at all in the initial version. The first opens with a chorus of handmaidens, who praise Marina's beauty in their song. She is bored with conventional compliments, however, and dreams of greatness, victories, and vanquished enemies. Having ordered all her attendants to leave, Marina begins her aria. She expresses her weariness with ordinary suitors and her burning desire for power and glory, acknowledging that she hopes to gratify that desire by aligning herself with the False Dmitry. The rhythm of the mazurka pervades the entire aria, as indeed do Polish dance rhythms throughout the act.

На престол царей Московских я царицей сяду,
я в порфире златотканной, Солнцем заблистаю,
А красой своей чудесной я сражу тупых москалей,
И стада бояр кичливых бить челом себе заставлю.
И прославят в сказках, былях, небылицах,
Гордую свою царицу
Тупоумные москали!

I shall mount the throne of the Moscow Tsars as Tsaritsa,
And, in gold-brocaded purple, I shall shine like the sun.
And with my wondrous beauty I shall smite the stupid Muscovites;
I shall compel the herd of conceited boyars to prostrate themselves before me.
And the dullard Muscovites shall praise
Their proud Tsaritsa
In tales, songs, and fables!

The Jesuit Rangoni enters, a Machiavellian figure whom Musorgsky's contemporaries compared with Mephistopheles in Gounod's *Faust* and Bertram in Meyerbeer's *Robert le Diable*. He begins his assault on Marina by telling her that the Church is desolate, "the wounds of the martyrs are bleeding in agony . . . [and] the saints themselves are weeping." It is her duty to the Church, he says, to convert the Eastern Orthodox Russians to Catholicism, and when she succeeds, even "the angels of God will praise Marina in heaven." She is enchanted at the thought, but recovers her presence of mind and feigns that she is powerless to accomplish what he desires. Seizing the initiative (to the accompaniment of the descending chromatic triplet scale that functions as his reminiscence motive, Ex. 9.2.12a), the Jesuit counters that she must use all her womanly arts to gain sway over the Pretender. When she has won control of him, she must use that power for the glory of the Church, sacrificing if necessary her own ambition and even her own honor. She is furious at his presumption, berates him, and orders him away. But Rangoni terrifies the superstitious Marina with a vision of Satan hovering over her, spreading his wings above her soul. She collapses in submission; the final words are his, "Give yourself up to the envoy of God; give me your body and soul, your inmost thoughts, desires, and wishes; be my slave!"

Act III, sc. 2: By the Fountain

The Mniszech castle in Sandomir. Garden. Fountain. Moonlight.

The second scene of the Polish act opens quietly with a brief but evocative orchestral portrait of a moonlit night. The Dmitry motive is heard in the clarinet, and Dmitry himself soon announces his presence "at midnight, in the garden, beside the fountain." He eagerly waits to keep a rendezvous with Marina and is disappointed when Rangoni, to the accompaniment of his descending chromatic triplets, steps out from behind a wing of the castle instead of his beloved. In an interview filled with the sly triplets associated with the Jesuit, Rangoni tries to persuade Dmitry that Marina, though hemmed in by opinion and gossip, truly loves him. But the subtle message that quickly emerges from the Jesuit's conversation is that only by accepting the Church, and Rangoni as a spiritual advisor, can Dmitry hope to win Marina. The orchestra strikes up a polonaise, and a crowd of guests emerges from the castle; Rangoni drags Dmitry to one side lest his presence in the garden compromise Marina. The guests then promenade around the garden in stately dance, many of the nobles flirting with Marina the while. After all have gone back inside, Dmitry's thoughts again return to his beloved. Jealous at seeing her on the arm of another, he has almost convinced himself to give her up and to get down to the business of fighting Boris (to the tune of his motive decorated by Polish dotted rhythms) when she at last appears.

A second lengthy dialogue ensues, the counterpoise to that between Dmitry and Rangoni in the first part of the scene. At first sight of her, he expresses only love, having lost his ardor for battle. She will have none of his protestations of love, but wants to know only one thing: when will he be Tsar in Moscow? He asks her what the Tsar's throne can matter so long as they love each other, but this is not what she wants to hear. She dismisses him haughtily; so lost is he in the pains of love, she says, that he has forgotten his struggle with Boris. Finally stung by her taunts, he vows to conquer Russia if only to have the pleasure of spurning her from the Tsar's throne. (The Dmitry motive is heard again at this point, still embroiled in Polish dotted rhythms even as Dmitry is embroiled in Polish schemes.) After this manly display of resolve on the Pretender's part, Marina relents immediately, having won the victory without his knowing of the battle. The act concludes with a lyric love duet (see Ex. 9.12, p. 268), capped by a brief coda in which Rangoni, from the side, observes that both are now in his power.

Act IV, sc. 1: Boris's Death

The Granovitaya Palace in the Moscow Kremlin. Benches on each side. On the right, the entrance to the Red Staircase. On the left, the entrance to the Terem. *Right, near the footlights, a table with writing materials. Left, the Tsar's place. An emergency meeting of the Council of Boyars.*

The curtain rises to reveal the council of boyars, convened in the Granovitaya Palace in the Kremlin and sitting in judgment on the Pretender. To music borrowed from a nearly identical scene of judgment and denunciation in the unfinished opera *Salammbô*, the boyars render their verdict, both basses and tenors expressing their vengeful fantasies. The usurper is to be caught, tortured, and hanged, and his flesh cast to the crows. He is to be burned, his ashes cursed and then scattered. All who follow him, they say, are to die, and their corpses to be hung in public. Finally, this judgment is to be published throughout the land, and all are to pray to God to grant mercy to Russia in her suffering. (In the initial version, this chorus is preceded by a narrative of Shchelkalov, in which the boyars are asked to pronounce sentence on the False Dmitry.) Their verdict complete, the nobles notice that Prince Shuisky is missing. He arrives and informs them that the night before, spying through a keyhole, he saw Boris overpowered with fear before the unseen ghost of the dead Tsarevich. Disbelieving Shuisky, the boyars are stunned into silence when Boris himself stumbles in, reeling in panic before this very phantom. The guilt motive is heard, and subsequently the Dmitry motive, as the Tsar raves, "Begone! Who says I am a murderer? I am no such thing. He lives, the infant lives. And Shuisky shall be quartered for all his lies!" Boris recovers his composure, and as the motive of foreboding sounds in the orchestra, tells the assembled boyars that he needs their advice. Shuisky interrupts to say that an old and holy man, Pimen the chronicler, seeks permission to speak with his sovereign. Boris instructs Shuisky to admit him, and Pimen enters as the orchestra plays his reminiscence motive.

In a complex series of embedded narratives, the venerable monk tells the story of an old blind shepherd to whom the ghost of Dmitry appeared in a dream. Obeying the instructions given him in the dream, the shepherd made a pilgrimage to the Tsarevich's grave in Uglich, where, as he knelt before the grave, his blindness was miraculously cured. Boris listens to this story with increasing agitation and at its conclusion, while the guilt motive sounds in the orchestra, topples from his throne. He sends for his son, who enters to the tune of his reminiscence theme. There is a brief pause, and then begins the final great basso scene in the opera, "Boris's Farewell and Death." In a narration that deftly summons up several important reminiscence themes – foreboding, Feodor, Xenia – Boris instructs his son in how to rule, cautioning him against the boyars and their secret intrigues with Poland-Lithuania, urging him always to listen to the voice of his people, and charging him to care for his sister. The major/minor-seventh chords of the Coronation scene return, this time heralding not the beginning but the end of Boris's rule and embodying his dynastic hope that Feodor will be crowned in turn. A choir of monks enters to administer the *skhima*, a rite of induction into monastic orders that all tsars commonly took at the point of death. The chorus's song strikes a nerve, the words barely audible to the audience but resonating like a great bell in the dying Tsar:

> Вижу младенца умирающа,
> И рыдаю, плачу;
> Мятется, трепещет он,
> И к помощи взывает,
> И нет ему спасенья . . .

> I see the dying child,
> And I weep, I wail;
> He shudders and trembles,
> And cries for help,
> but there is no salvation for him . . .

Boris draws himself to his full majesty for one final shout, "I still am Tsar." Then, pointing to his son, he gasps, "There is your Tsar." Boris collapses and dies as the reminiscence theme associated with his power and majesty is heard one final time in the orchestra.

Act IV, sc. 2: Kromy

A forest clearing near the town of Kromy. To the right, a slope and beyond it the walls of the city. From the slope, a path running across the stage. Directly in front, a woody thicket. At the foot of the slope, a large stump.

The scene in Kromy Forest is remarkably pageant-like and non-narrative. Like the Polish act, it appears only in Musorgsky's revision of *Boris*. The curtain rises on an opening in the forest near Kromy, a village southwest of

Moscow along the pretender's line of march. A shrieking crowd of vagabonds and peasants have risen against Boris and have captured the boyar Khrushchov, a representative of the realm. The crowd drag Khrushchov in, seat him on a log, bind and gag him with a piece of his coat; two men armed with cudgels stand behind him as guards. "Has anyone seen a nobleman without a mistress?" sings the crowd, and they lead forward an old crone. They then begin a mocking chorus of praise, something of an ironic counterpoise to the choruses of the Coronation scene:

Не сокол летит по поднебесью,
Не борзый конь мчится по полю,
Сиднем сидит боряринушка,
Дума думает.
Слава боярину,
Слава Борисову!
Слава боярину,
Слава Борисову!   Слава!

Not a falcon soaring across the sky,
not a swift steed galloping across the field,
our little boyar sits sitting,
thinking his thoughts.
Glory to the boyar!
Glory to Boris's henchman!
Glory to the boyar!
Glory to Boris's henchman! Glory!

Somewhat unnoticed, a *yurodivy* – holy fool – enters surrounded by a group of boys who taunt him and steal his only coin. (This passage, and the fool's lament at the end of the scene, are the only passages from the St. Basil scene – part of the initial version – to survive in Musorgsky's revision.) Varlaam and Misail approach from offstage, singing of Boris's sins and the calamities that have befallen the nation. The melody, collected by Musorgsky from the folk singer Ivan Ryabinin, evolves in changing background variations, like so many of the other folk and folklike melodies. The two tramps deliver the first stanza in octaves, above a sustained tonic pedal F in the horn. The tonic F expands to a dissonant dyad F–G in the second stanza, the rhythm becomes more energetic, and oboes and bassoons replace the soothing timbre of the horn. Strings take up the accompaniment in the third stanza, and the people comment among themselves on these new arrivals, "holy men from Moscow." Unmixed wind timbre returns for the final stanza.

(It is intriguing to note Musorgsky's preference here, and elsewhere in his work, for unmixed tonal colors, a trait he easily could have absorbed from Hector Berlioz, whom he greatly admired and once characterized as the "ur-thinker" in music.)

The people then erupt into their ferocious chorus of anarchy and revolt, "Raskhodilos', razgulyalas' udal' molodetskaya" (Valiant daring has become enraged and broken loose). Varlaam and Misail join in this chorus and urge the crowd to join the forces of the Pretender against Boris. The chorus culminates in the cry, "Death to Boris! Death to Boris! Death to the regicide!"

Two Jesuits, Czernikowski and Lawitski, approach from afar singing a Latin chant. Varlaam and Misail lead the crowd in an attack on these hated representatives of Catholicism. They seize and bind them, then drag them into the forest to hang them, but the priests are saved (in the score at least – they do not fare so well in some productions) by the approach of the False Dmitry. The trumpets of the Pretender's approaching army are heard in the distance. The people, distracted from hanging the Jesuits, reassemble on stage and, in music likewise drawn from *Salammbô*, hail Dmitry as the rightful Tsar. He enters on horseback, calls on all present to follow him in his fight against Boris, and frees the captive boyar Khrushchov. The Pretender, his troops, and all the crowd pass offstage toward Moscow. The *yurodivy* alone is left behind. As he sings a poignant lament for the land and its suffering people, the curtain falls on a scene of desolation unprecedented in opera before *Boris*, and not equalled again, perhaps, until *Wozzeck* or *Lady Macbeth of Mtsensk*.

Rimsky-Korsakov's version of Musorgsky's opera was not the first metamorphosis to which *Boris Godunov* had been subjected. As we shall see in Chapter 4, the composer had conceived the work initially as an *opéra dialogué*, and it was not until this first version had been rejected by the Imperial Theaters that he began the revision that ultimately left the work in the familiar form synopsized above. By far the most extensive cut was the omission of the entire scene before St. Basil's Cathedral, the penultimate scene of the initial version.[13] (A comparison of the two versions, episode by episode, appears in Table 3.1, on pp. 63–65.)

St. Basil's Scene (Initial Version, Part IV, sc. 1)

A square in front of St. Basil's Cathedral in Moscow. A crowd of beggarly people milling about. Women seated sideways looking in the direction of the

Example 3-5

1 Liszt, *Two Episodes from Lenau's "Faust"*: "Procession by Night"

2 Musorgsky, *Boris Godunov*, St. Basil Scene (Initial version, Part IV, sc. 1)

side exit of the cathedral. Policemen move frequently among the crowd. A group of men comes out the cathedral, Mityukh in front. Voices in the crowd.

The scene begins with a short orchestral prelude strongly reminiscent in gesture and orchestration of a passage from Liszt's "Procession by Night," the first of his *Two Episodes from Lenau's "Faust"*, a work admired by Balakirev and probably known to Musorgsky soon after its composition (Ex. 3.5).

A crowd of impoverished Muscovite townspeople has gathered in front of the cathedral. In dialogue exchanged among various subgroups of the choir (a device held in high regard in Musorgsky's circle), the people learn that inside the cathedral, anathema has just been pronounced on the runaway monk Grishka Otrepiev, whom the authorities have identified as the Pretender. This is a matter of little concern to the crowd, however, for they are convinced that Grishka and Dmitry are different persons; they are far more concerned that a requiem mass is being sung for the Tsarevich Dmitry, whom they presume to be alive. They discuss the advance of Dmitry's army on Moscow and happily anticipate the day when "the Tsarevich" will bring "death to Boris and his pups" and ascend the throne which, in their eyes, Godunov had usurped. Fearful of Boris's ever-present police, the older men silence the younger ones and remind them of the rack, whereupon the crowd begins to mill about again. A *yurodivy* enters, surrounded by a group of urchins, who taunt him, steal his coin, and leave him crying. Boris enters from the cathedral, and in a compelling chorus the people beg him for bread. He stops in front of the *yurodivy* and asks, "Why is he crying?" The fool replies that the boys have stolen his only coin and, with a boldness that was a right of *yurodstvo*, asks Boris to have them murdered just as he had murdered the young Tsarevich. Shocked at this *lèse majesté*, Shuisky moves to arrest the *yurodivy*, but Boris intervenes and instead asks the Holy Fool to pray for him. The fool refuses, saying that nobody can pray for a Tsar Herod because "the mother of God forbids it." Boris and his train move on, the people disperse, and the *yurodivy* is left alone on stage. The curtain falls as he sings his lament for Russia.

Only the episode of the fool with the boys and the fool's final lament were transferred, in revision, from this scene to the scene that replaced it, Kromy Forest. But many modern producers, conductors, and singers so regret the loss of St. Basil's that they choose to second-guess the composer and insert it back into the revision, despite Musorgsky's apparent conviction that Kromy and St. Basil's were conceptually incompatible. Such a decision creates an additional appearance for Boris, it is true, but it also creates relationships and apparent continuities that had no part of either of the composer's plans. Not

Table 3.1. *Comparison of Musorgsky's versions of Boris Godunov*

Initial version (completed December 1869)	Revised version (published January 1874)
Part I, sc. 1: Courtyard of the Novodevichy Monastery	Prologue, sc. 1: Courtyard of the Novodevichy Monastery
A Introduction	A Introduction
B Policeman's orders to the crowd	B Policeman's orders to the crowd
C First people's chorus of supplication	C First people's chorus of supplication
D Policeman's return, further orders	D Policeman's return, further orders
E Second chorus of supplication	E Second chorus of supplication
F Shchelkalov's address to the people	F Shchelkalov's address to the people
G Chorus of pilgrims	G Chorus of pilgrims
H Final scene between the people and the policeman	H —
Part I, sc. 2: Coronation	Prologue, sc. 2: Coronation [cut by 5 measures]
Part II, sc. 1: Cell in the Chudov Monastery	Act I, sc. 1: Cell in the Chudov Monastery
A Pimen's monologue	A Pimen's monologue
	B/a First chorus of monks behind the scene
B Grigory's awakening	b Grigory's awakening
—	C/a Second chorus of monks behind the scene;
C Grigory's account of his dream and subsequent dialogue with Pimen	b Grigory's account of his dream and subsequent dialogue with Pimen
D Pimen's story of the tsars	D Pimen's story of the tsars
E/a Pimen's narrative of the murder of Tsarevich Dmitry;	—
b Grigory's question	E Grigory's question
F Chorus of monks behind the scene and conclusion	F Third chorus of monks behind the scene and conclusion

Table 3.1. (cont.)

Initial version (completed December 1869)	Revised version (published January 1874)
Part II, sc. 2: Inn on the Lithuanian Frontier	Act I, sc. 2: Inn on the Lithuanian Frontier
A Introduction	A/a Introduction
—	b Hostess's "Song of the Drake"
B Arrival of Grigory, Varlaam, and Misail	B Arrival of Grigory, Varlaam, and Misail
C Varlaam's first song ("Ballad of Kazan")	C Varlaam's first song ("Ballad of Kazan")
D Varlaam's second song and Grigory's conversation with the hostess	D Varlaam's second song and Grigory's conversation with the hostess
E Arrival of policemen	E Arrival of policemen
F The reading of the warrant and conclusion	F The reading of the warrant and conclusion
Part III: The *Terem* in the Kremlin	Act II: The *Terem* in the Kremlin
A Xenia's lament; Feodor sings at his map	A/a Xenia's lament; Feodor silent at the map
—	b The children with the chiming clock
B Nurse's attempt to comfort Xenia	B/a Nurse's attempt to comfort Xenia
—	b Song of the Gnat
—	c Handclapping Game
C Boris's entry; he comforts Xenia	C Boris's entry; he comforts Xenia
D Boris and Feodor at the map	D Boris and Feodor at the map
E Boris's monologue	E Boris's monologue
—	F/a Tumult of nurses behind the scene
F Boyar's denunciation of Shuisky	b Boyar's denunciation of Shuisky
—	c Feodor's "Song of the Parrot"

G Boris's scene with Shuisky	G Boris's scene with Shuisky
H Shuisky's description of Dmitry's body	H Shuisky's description of Dmitry's body
I Boris's hallucination	I Boris's hallucination, with the chiming clock
	Act III, sc. 1: Marina's boudoir
	Act III, sc. 2: Garden by the Fountain
———	———
Part IV: sc. 1: Square before St. Basil's Cathedral in Moscow	Act IV: sc. 1: Granovitaya Palace (Boris's Death)
Part IV: sc. 2: Granovitaya Palace (Boris's Death)	
A/a Introduction	A Introduction
b Shchelkalov's reading of the ukase	—
B Chorus of boyars	B Chorus of boyars
C Shuisky's arrival and narration	C Shuisky's arrival and narration [cut by 28 measures]
D Boris's entry	D Boris's entry
E Pimen's narrative	E Pimen's narrative [cut by 6 measures]
F Farewell and death of Boris	F Farewell and death of Boris [cut by 13 measures]
———	
	Act IV: sc. 2: A Forest Glade near Kromy [Two of this scene's seven sections are transferred from the otherwise discarded St. Basil's scene: the episode of the fool with the boys and the fool's concluding lament.]

only does the fool's lament become repetitious and anti-climactic when heard a second time at the end of the Kromy Forest scene, but the entire expanded fourth act – consisting of St. Basil's, the Death scene, and Kromy – becomes a symmetric structure with Boris's death at the center flanked by two popular scenes, a false relation that destroys the larger symmetry of the opera overall.

Indeed, once begun, the urge to conflate takes on a life of its own. Once producers have decided to insert the St. Basil scene into the alien context of the revision, they straightway are confronted with decisions concerning the other cuts taken by Musorgsky. Thus some productions show us a Novodevichy scene in which the people return at the end. Others reattach to the Cell scene Pimen's narrative of the murder of the Tsarevich. A few restore Shchelkalov's reading at the beginning of the Death scene; some even reinsert the twenty-odd measures of the Death scene that were cut almost certainly for consistency in the use of reminiscence themes. Thus by degrees producers gradually attain the "supersaturated" *Boris* described above, while audiences cease to be surprised at almost any combination of scenes. There is irony in the circumstance that even the composer's strongest admirers sometimes lack faith in his final conception; it is a fault that the much-maligned Rimsky-Korsakov – whatever his other flaws – did not share.

4

HISTORY OF THE COMPOSITION, REJECTION, REVISION, AND ACCEPTANCE OF *BORIS GODUNOV*

At one of the several performances of Russian opera given under the auspices of Sir Joseph Beecham (Thomas's father) in London just before the outbreak of World War I, a member of the audience was heard to remark that Russian composers, unlike the Germans, always seemed to need help in finishing their works, and that it was lucky for them that Rimsky-Korsakov always had been so willing to lend a hand. With this simple comment, that unknown English theatergoer isolated one of the chief burdens placed on any critic who would attempt to discuss *Boris Godunov*: the problem of clarifying who wrote what, when. The question is complex, and the difficulties begin with the composer himself.

Musorgsky completed the initial version of *Boris* in December 1869; this first conception was an *opéra dialogué*, the style upheld by the composer's circle as the only one viable for operatic composition. After the Imperial Theaters rejected this first version for performance, the composer enthusiastically began a revision at once. Assurances that a few changes (principally the addition of a *prima donna* role) would lead to performance gave Musorgsky the initial impulse toward revision; his own apparent lapse of faith in *opéra dialogué* – wherein the greatest merit was said to lie in an unbroken recitative setting of an unaltered text – sustained that impulse well beyond the bounds of a leading lady's part. For even among those sympathetic to Musorgsky and his circle, *opéra dialogué* was associated with comedy. To weaken these associations of comedy, and perhaps to take greater advantage of music's ability to intensify a text's emotion, the composer recast the opera on a scale far grander than simple performance exigency would have required. Thus, before so much as a single scene had been heard in the theater, *Boris* existed in two quite different versions – initial and revised – sharing much common music but proceeding from different assumptions concerning operatic theater and embodying two different conceptions of the story. Of the two, only the revision was performed publicly and published during Musorgsky's lifetime; a piano–vocal score of it appeared in January 1874, at the time of the premiere. The initial version, though completed in 1869, remained unknown outside the composer's circle for nearly sixty years.[1]

In 1896, just fifteen years after Musorgsky's death, Nikolay Rimsky-Korsakov published his first redaction of the opera. Although based upon Musorgsky's piano–vocal score of 1874, Rimsky took lengthy cuts in the Cell scene, the *Terem* scene, and the Polish act. Then in 1906–07 he returned to *Boris*, restoring most of the cuts he had taken earlier and, at the behest of Serge Diaghilev (whose production of the work was about to appear in Paris), composing additional music to lengthen the Coronation scene. Diaghilev's performance had two results: it established *Boris* in the repertory in Rimsky's version, and it led avant-garde critics to clamor for the restoration of the composer's own score. Few, if any, of these critics could have had the slightest idea that there were *two* distinct auctorial versions of *Boris*, but their polemics served to define the so-called Musorgsky problem, a set of issues concerning the composer's technique, the propriety of revision of his music by alien hands, and the relative merits of original and revised versions.

Polemic continued to dominate the discussion of this opera throughout the first three decades of the twentieth century. The matter finally culminated in 1928 with the publication of the Soviet musicologist Pavel Lamm's conflation of both Musorgsky's versions. As noted in Chapter 3, Lamm created a "supersaturated"[2] *Boris*, retaining all the new music Musorgsky had added in revision but reinserting all the carefully considered cuts he had taken as well. The result is a version of the opera unforeseen by its composer, in which each scene appears in its longest possible form and in which mutually exclusive scenes appear either side by side or in the same "act." The orchestrations of both Dmitry Shostakovich and Karol Rathaus, as we have already seen, proceed directly from Lamm and so perpetuate his conflation; Shostakovich even recommends a further, somewhat bizarre conflation in the *Terem* scene solely on his own authority. Even the most recent editor of *Boris*, David Lloyd-Jones, reinserts into his main text all the cuts Musorgsky took in revising the five scenes common to the two versions.[3] If one wants a copy of the opera in the final form given to it by its composer, one must turn away from modern scholarship either to the first edition of V. V. Bessel & Co. (1874), to Bessel's reengraving of that score (1924, reissued 1954), or the J. & W. Chester score (1926).

The aura of controversy and polemic that surrounds the work has affected our perception of its history. In 1874, when the opera was first performed, Russian musicians and critics greeted it either with enthusiasm or with condemnation. When Rimsky-Korsakov published his final redaction of

Boris in 1908, in the hope of discharging a debt to his friend's memory, he brought upon himself scathing criticism and engendered an argument concerning the value and propriety of his work which continues to this day. With the appearance of Lamm's score, critics began to attack the staff of the Russian Imperial Theaters of the 1870s as well, accusing them too of an inability to recognize Musorgsky's genius because of their rejection of the work in its first version, without the Polish act and the Kromy Forest scene. In their haste to indict tsarist officials, both Soviet and Western writers have made it seem as if Musorgsky had undertaken the revision of *Boris* only for expediency's sake, to satisfy the demands of dull-witted bureaucrats. They have made it seem as if the censor had forbidden the St. Basil scene (leading to its exclusion from the revised version) and had interfered in the Cell scene and the Kromy Forest scene as well. And seizing upon inconclusive evidence, they have made it seem as if the Maryinsky Theater's selection committee had rejected not only the initial version of the opera, but the composer's revision too.[4] Writers on Musorgsky began to repeat that in view of the so-called obtuseness and hostility of the authorities, *Boris Godunov* might never have reached the stage at all had it not been for the intercession of powerful artists.

Reexamination of the available materials suggests that such conclusions are not warranted. There are good reasons to believe that Musorgsky undertook the revision out of artistic conviction.[5] There is no proof of interference on the part of the censor at any stage of composition or performance; indeed, there are compelling reasons for concluding that the censor had nothing to do with the changes Musorgsky made in revision, and nothing to do with the cuts he sanctioned for the first performance.[6] And as we shall see below, there is no persuasive proof of a second rejection or of undue hostility on the part of the Imperial Theaters. There are several reasons, however, for doubting a second rejection: first, the illogic of revamping a work if performance had been unequivocally ruled out (what would there have been to gain? Why not just move on to the next opera?); second, the absence of convincing documentary proof for a second rejection; third, the unreliability of the only contemporary of Musorgsky's – Yulia Platonova – to detail a second rejection; and finally, the silence of Musorgsky's other contemporaries on the issue. Though the sources are sometimes enigmatic, the evidence suggests that the revised *Boris* was not rejected, but accepted by the Imperial Theaters in the normal course of business. For nearly five and a half years, from October 1868 through January 1874, Musorgsky was occupied with *Boris Godunov*. The opera's path to the stage may not have been straight and direct, but then, as the Russian proverb goes, "You can't drive straight on a twisting lane."

In the summer of 1868, three months before beginning work on Alexander Pushkin's *Boris Godunov*, Musorgsky set to music the first scene of Nikolay Gogol's prose comedy *The Marriage*. Adhering to the ideal expounded in his circle, the *Moguchaya kuchka*, or Mighty Handful, he attempted nearly a word-for-word setting of Gogol's text. The work excited him, and he wrote enthusiastically of it to César Cui, Balakirev's lieutenant and the chief spokesman of the *kuchka* thanks to his position as music critic of the paper *Sankt-Peterburgskie vedomosti* (St. Petersburg news). After describing *The Marriage* at some length, and maintaining that various bits had "come out very well," were "not bad," or had "turned out quite comically," Musorgsky states his goal for the work in a few words: "In my *opéra dialogué*, I am trying as much as possible to underscore those changes of intonation, which appear in the characters during the dialogue, apparently for the most trivial reasons and in the most insignificant words, in which is hidden, it seems to me, the force of Gogol's humor."[7]

It is not surprising that Musorgsky would address this letter to Cui. At the time Cui was the only member of the *kuchka* with operatic credentials of a sort. After several years of work he had nearly completed his opera *William Ratcliff*; it would receive its premiere just six months later, early in 1869. As spokesman for the group, he had contributed to the polemics raging around Glinka's second opera, *Ruslan and Lyudmila*, and he had criticized remorselessly the two successful operas of Alexander Serov, *Judith* and *Rogneda*, for their failure to embody *kuchkist* theories of what an opera should be.

More than any other composer of the *kuchka*, Cui was responsible for defining these theories. His writings formulate the conviction, held by the group in the late 1860s, that an opera must be a careful and sensitive setting, in recitative style, of a good text, with each line receiving its own "characteristic" setting, and with little reliance on closed forms or traditional musical logic. (Closed forms are appropriate only in those places where faithfulness to "dramatic truth" requires their use, for example, in the song that a character sings as part of the action.) Cui puts the matter concisely in an essay written in 1889, the late date of which may serve to document how consistent he remained in his theoretical views, even after the *kuchka* had fallen to pieces and two of its members had died.

In [dramatic scenes], feelings, often contradictory ones, swiftly succeed one another; the action is developed without delay; speech becomes impetuous, troubled, irregular. For such scenes all of the above-mentioned [closed operatic] forms are unsuitable; here one must have recourse to another form – the most varied, freest form of all: *melodic recitative*. Here there can be no question of placidly rounded forms, regular melodies or symmetrical phrases. These would contradict the truth, delay the action, dampen and ultimately destroy the impression of the dramatic situation . . . The music [must] flow ever forward without a backward glance, just as the drama itself develops without pause.[8]

Musorgsky's adherence to these principles was at its peak during the composition of *The Marriage* and the initial *Boris*. As he acknowledged later in an autobiographical note, he read Georg Gervinus – most probably *Händel und Shakespeare* – and mixed the German's ideas with Cui's to arrive at a philosophy of text setting to which he expressed allegiance for the rest of his life.[9] He writes to Lyudmila Shestakova (Glinka's sister) on 30 July 1868:

Here's what I would like. That my characters speak on stage as living people speak, but so that the character and force of their intonation, supported by the orchestra which is the musical background for their speech, hit the target head on; that is, my music must be an artistic reproduction of human speech in all its most subtle windings, that is, *the sounds of human speech*, as the outward manifestations of thought and feeling, must become, without exaggeration or coercion, *music* that is truthful and precise, but at the same time artistic, highly artistic . . .

I'm now working on Gogol's *Marriage*. For after all, the whole success of Gogol's speech depends on the actor, on his accurate intonation. Well, I want to fix Gogol to his place and to fix the actor to his, that is, I want to speak musically in such a way that one couldn't imagine oneself speaking otherwise, to speak as Gogol's characters themselves would want to speak. That's why in *Marriage* I'm crossing the Rubicon. This is living prose in music, not the usual neglectful attitude of musician-poets toward simple human speech that isn't dressed in heroic garb – this is respect for human speech, for the reproduction of simple human talk.[10]

Simple human talk notwithstanding, page after page of *The Marriage* reveals *kuchkism* run amok. Apparently preoccupied with creating a "speechlike" setting, Musorgsky writes jagged vocal lines that are filled with dissonant, unstable intervals and goes to great length to avoid melodies having balanced phrases. In an attempt to maintain forward motion, he shuns conclusive cadences, both in the vocal parts and in the harmony. Indeed, the harmony is virtually an unbroken stream of dissonances, primarily seventh chords; some of the most striking discords occur when the text suggests irritation, unpleasantness, or falsehood. Form depends primarily on the sections and subsections of the text.

The result is a disjointed work in which music – to apply Cui's verdict on *The Stone Guest* to Musorgsky's *Marriage* – "is so closely joined to the words . . . that, considered alone, without the words, it loses half its value and occasionally becomes incomprehensible."[11] By attempting to set Gogol's prose virtually unaltered, the composer – though following the *kuchkist* ideal – made the mistake of merely grafting music onto a self-sufficient literary work. At the time he may have believed that such music resulted in "an artistic reproduction of human speech," but it also was superfluous, serving merely to slow the pace of Gogol's humor without providing the degree of emotional intensification of which music is capable. As a piece of musical theater, *The Marriage* is stillborn, and one suspects that Musorgsky may have agreed. In a letter to Shestakova, he described the work as a cage in which he was imprisoned. He was even more explicit in a letter to his friend Vladimir Nikolsky, dated 15 August 1868:

You don't cook a soup without preparation. This means in preparing oneself for work, even though it be Gogol's *Marriage*, a most capricious thing for music, wouldn't you be accomplishing a good deed, that is, wouldn't you be drawing nearer to your cherished and vital goal? It's possible to say to this: And why is everything only a preparation – it's about time to do something! The trifling little pieces were preparations; *The Marriage* is a preparation; whenever will something finally be ready?[12]

Within two months he received the answer to that question when Nikolsky himself suggested that in Pushkin's *Boris Godunov* he would find the subject for which he had been searching.[13]

Nikolsky's suggestion would have been pointless only three years earlier. Not until 1866 did the tsarist censor finally sanction the performance of Pushkin's play, which had been forbidden for stage production since its completion in 1825. Although that approval did not remove all obstacles from Musorgsky's path – there remained, for example, the ruling of Nicholas I forbidding the representation of tsars in opera – the composer had clear reason to hope that other impediments could be overcome as well, and he took to the subject eagerly. His friend Shestakova immediately had a copy of the play interleaved with blank pages and bound, and gave it to him to help him draft his libretto. Recognizing that he could not incorporate all twenty-five of Pushkin's scenes, he chose only those in which Boris appeared, plus the scenes in Pimen's cell and at the inn on the Lithuanian frontier. Since he had not yet rejected the ideals of *kuchkism*, the verbal text of this first version remains quite close to Pushkin, artfully eliding speeches and telescoping scenes. This text volume is dated October 1868; composition may have begun even before the finishing touches had been put on the libretto.

Musorgsky's work on the music progressed quickly. He finished the Novodevichy Monastery scene, in piano–vocal score, on 4 November 1868 and the Coronation scene just ten days later (14 November). The scene in Pimen's cell – textually only a slight abridgement of Pushkin – was completed on 5 December 1868. Though the manuscript is not dated, he must have quickly completed the Inn scene as well since we know that Alexander Dargomyzhsky heard it before his death on 5 January 1869. The *Terem* scene was finished on 21 April 1869.[14] About a month later, on 22 May, Musorgsky completed the St. Basil scene, and within another two months, by 18 July 1869, he had finished the Death scene and thus the entire opera. With composition completed, he turned to the orchestration. That task proceeded even more quickly; on 15 December 1869 he finished the full score.

The initial version thus contains seven scenes, and Musorgsky has grouped them in four parts, as follows. Part I: Courtyard of the Novodevichy Monastery and Coronation; Part II: Pimen's Cell and An Inn on the Lithuanian Frontier; Part III; The Tsar's Apartments in the Kremlin; Part IV: Square before St. Basil's Cathedral and Death of Boris. In the initial version there is no Polish act and no scene in Kromy Forest.

A few months after completing his opera, probably sometime after the end of the 1869–70 season, Musorgsky spoke with Stepan Gedeonov, Director of the Imperial Theaters, about staging *Boris*. Because he finished the work only in December of 1869, in the middle of an ongoing season, he surely must have realized that it would be impossible to produce it immediately. Furthermore, he did not prepare a fair copy of the libretto for submission to the censor until spring of 1870. Since it would have been foolish to have approached Gedeonov without having taken steps toward securing the censor's approval, a meeting with the Director probably occurred between mid-May and early June, at which Gedeonov told him that it would be impossible to stage anything new in the coming season (1870–71) but that once the selection committee had returned from summer holiday, he would summon the composer to play the opera for them.[15]

Musorgsky scarcely could have hoped for more. When he saw the Director, the beginning of the new season was no more than eight or ten weeks away. The repertory for that season had been chosen already and even if there had been an opening in the schedule, *Boris* could not have been accepted before the members of the committee had returned. Under the circumstances Gedeonov was quite encouraging, and, judging by a letter to Rimsky-Korsakov of 23 July 1870, Musorgsky seems to have been satisfied with whatever the Director told him:

Incidentally, I also dragged myself over to Gedeonov's: he was severe but fair and I was severe but fair; as a result they will call me after the 15th of August (?), but *they* cannot put on anything new this year.[16]

In the fall, after the committee had returned to St. Petersburg, Musorgsky submitted his opera. On 10 February 1871, the committee member Giovanni

Ferrero informed Pavel Fedorov, Chief of the Repertory Division, that they had rejected it:

The score of the Russian opera presented for production, *Boris Godunov* by Mr. Musorgsky, [was examined] in the presence of Messrs. *Louis Mauer, Nápravník, Voyáček, Mangin, Papkov, Betz*, and me, who decided unanimously to take a vote in the presence of the above-mentioned seven persons, in consequence of which six black balls and one white were cast, so that I have the honor of returning to Your Excellency the aforesaid score.[17]

Fedorov sent Musorgsky official notification of the rejection one week later, but, according to Shestakova's memoirs, he learned of the committee's decision on the day it was made. She writes:

there was a luncheon at Yu[lia] Platonova's on the occasion of her *bénéfice*. She came to invite me and added that on the morning of this very day the fate of Musorgsky's opera was being decided, and that Nápravník [chief conductor of the Maryinsky] and Kondratiev [soon to become *regisseur* of the Maryinsky] would be at her place. I went and awaited the arrival of these gentlemen with great impatience. Naturally, I greeted them with the words, "Is *Boris* accepted?" "No," they answered, "it is impossible. What sort of opera is it without a female element?! Undoubtedly, Musorgsky has great talent; let him add another scene, then *Boris* would be accepted." I knew that this news would be unpleasant for Musorgsky and did not want to report it to him at once, so I wrote him and V. V. Stasov, asking them to come by around 6:00 in the evening. Returning home, I found them at my place and gave them the news. Stasov heatedly began to discuss with Musorgsky the independent new parts of the opera, and Modest Petrovich himself began to play various motives, and the evening passed in a very lively way. Musorgsky began further work without delay.[18]

Thus we arrive at the delicate and frequently misinterpreted question of Musorgsky's "rejection" by the Imperial Theaters. Throughout the decades of study of the composer and his work, the principal source concerning the reasons why the first *Boris* was not accepted for production has been a passage from the memoirs of Rimsky-Korsakov, written thirty-five years after the events and incorrect in details of fact:

In the course of this very season [1869–70], the completed *Boris Godunov* was submitted by Musorgsky to the Directorate of the Imperial Theaters. It was examined by a committee consisting of Nápravník, the opera conductor; Mangin and Betz, the orchestra conductors of French and German drama; and the contrabass player Giovanni Ferrero. It was rejected. The novelty and singularity of the music nonplussed the honorable committee, who, among other things, upbraided the composer for the absence of a major female role. Indeed, there was no Polish act in the initial version; consequently Marina's part was missing. Much of the committee's fault-finding was simply ridiculous. For example, the contrabasses *divisi* playing chromatic thirds in the accompaniment of Varlaam's second song completely astonished Ferrero, the contrabass player, and he could not forgive the composer for such a device.[19]

Rimsky has dated the meeting and rejection one year too early and has omitted three of the seven members of the committee. The argument that the opera's novelty "nonplussed the honorable committee" originated in this passage, written in 1905–06, though César Cui had accused the committee of hindering originality in Russian art in general both in his notice of the rejection and later in his review of the performance of three scenes from the opera in 1873. The thirds that so astonished Ferrero survived Musorgsky's revision and were performed both in 1873 and in 1874; they may not have been so much the bone of contention that Rimsky makes them out to be. Ironically enough, these same thirds did *not* survive Rimsky's own editorial pen.

Other reasons for the rejection have been found in the passage quoted above from Shestakova's memoirs, written in 1889, and in a passage from Vladimir Stasov's pioneering biography of Musorgsky in which Stasov, one of the composer's admirers and a propagandist for Russian art, asserts that the Directorate found in *Boris* "a prevalence of choruses and ensembles and a too-sensible absence of scenes for soloists."[20] The criticism concerning the absence of a "female element" appears in print for the first time in V. S. Baskin's biography of Musorgsky, published three years before Shestakova wrote her memoirs.[21] No archival documents dealing with the committee's reasons for rejection have been published. There is no record of Musorgsky's having discussed the rejection with any of the committee members, nor is there reference to the rejection or the committee's reasons in his published letters. "Thus was born the durable legend of a *Boris* rebuked and rejected for its modernism when all that was asked, according to reliable testimony, was a prima donna role."[22]

The Theaters had rejected a work that represented, in effect, a step back from the extremes of *The Marriage*. When Musorgsky began *Boris*, only a few months after interrupting work on Gogol's text, he already had abandoned the excesses of the earlier work's idiom, but he had not yet rejected his circle's ideal. Thus one sees in the initial *Boris* such features of *opéra dialogué* as predominantly syllabic *parlando* text setting, an accentuation pattern reflecting that of the spoken language, and *ad hoc* harmony. But the extremes of disjointed recitative, unresolved dissonance, and unperiodic melody that so characterize *The Marriage* are missing from the initial *Boris*. The composer demonstrates that while sectionalization in the text may mark the principal boundaries of the work's form, those boundaries can be clarified and reinforced by patterns of repetition and contrast in the music itself, so that the result, while remaining "closely joined to the words," no longer "loses half its value and occasionally becomes incomprehensible" without them. In short, at the time of the initial *Boris*, Musorgsky already is retreating from the aesthetic that characterizes *The Marriage* and such contemporaneous songs as "S nyaney." During the period of *Boris*'s revision and the first sketches of *Khovanshchina*, he retreats even further, turning with increasing conviction toward greater lyricism; the reason for this probably is his realization that tragedy demands a seriousness of tone that the *kuchkist* idiom could not produce. He gave these convictions forceful expression some years later in a letter to Arseny Golenishchev-Kutuzov, the poet of the cycles *Sunless* and *Songs and Dances of Death*:

The Marriage is simply the best effort possible by a musician, or more correctly a non-musician, wishing to study and grasp the curves of human speech in the unmediated and truthful exposition given them by that great genius, Gogol. *Marriage* was an étude for chamber rehearsal. From the grand stage it is necessary that the speech acts of the *characters*, each with its own nature, habits and "dramatic inevitability," be transmitted to the audience in bold relief, – it is necessary to arrange matters so that the audience can easily pick up on all the artless peripeteia of vital human concerns, while at the same time making them artistically interesting.[23]

This discontent with *kuchkism* may have begun to form as early as July of 1870, the result of a private performance of *Boris Godunov* given at Stasov's summer *dacha*.[24] As the composer himself reports, some of his hearers found the peasants in *Boris* "to be bouffe(!), while others saw tragedy."[25] Such diametrically opposed perceptions in an audience that could be presumed friendly – Stasov's guests – may have forced Musorgsky to recognize the shortcomings of his idiom and to consider even further retreat from *opéra dialogué*. After all, if even colleagues and friends could not distinguish between tragedy and comedy in his music, what hope was there for theatergoers at large?

But even if a thoroughgoing revision of the opera's tone had been on Musorgsky's mind before *Boris* was "blackballed," he still had to begin somewhere and for some reason. The rejection provided the spur to reconsideration and reconceptualization, a process begun with the Polish scenes but ultimately not ended there. Privately he may have been pleased with the committee's veto since it gave him opportunity to recast the work for the "grand stage"; publicly he approached the task with enthusiasm and passion. But he cannot have been so uninterested in putting the work on stage as to have undertaken its reconception without some assurance that once modifications had been made *Boris* would be performed. It is precisely this assurance, recorded by Shestakova, that so many commentators on the composer have chosen to overlook: "Musorgsky has great talent; let him add another scene, then *Boris* would be accepted."

Musorgsky began the revision with the Polish scenes, thereby responding to the committee's objection to the lack of a significant female role, but by the middle of summer 1871 he was deeply enmeshed in a more extensive revision. According to the date on the manuscript, the first Polish scene was completed in piano–vocal score by 10 April 1871.[26] He then seems to have started the scene by the fountain, working on the dialogue between False Dmitry and Rangoni, for he writes to Stasov: "The Jesuit gave me no rest for two nights in a row, that's good – I love it, that is, I love it when I compose this way."[27]

Before finishing the Fountain scene, he began to revise the scene in the Tsar's quarters. Although the basic outline of the action remained the same in this scene, the text was changed substantially and the music thoroughly recomposed. In the first part of the act, through Boris's entrance, the only music remaining virtually unchanged is the setting of the nurse's words of comfort to Xenia. The chiming clock and both the nurse's songs were added, Xenia's lament was set to a different melody and placed in a new key, and Feodor's description of the map was deleted – just another declamatory passage and room was needed for the additions. The Tsar's monologue "Dostig ya vysshey vlasti" (I have attained the highest power) was almost totally rewritten. Only its first part was derived from corresponding material in the initial version. An entirely new middle section was added, with text by Musorgsky and music adapted from his unfinished opera *Salammbô*. Musorgsky recomposed the concluding part of the monologue also, introducing music which later in the scene is associated with the Tsar's madness and hallucination. In the last half of the act, the interview with Shuisky was altered substantially; the "Song of the Parrot," the uproar among the nurses, and that part of the hallucination that includes the chiming clock were added. The final portion of the hallucination is derived from similar material in the initial version.

The net effect of so extensive a remodeling was to elevate the music's tone. If *opéra dialogué* had come to be associated with comedy in the minds of Musorgsky's audience, he would distance himself from the idiom of *opéra dialogué* in the revision. The wholesale rewriting of Pushkin's text, the "criminal *arioso*" for the "criminal Tsar Boris,"[28] the chiming clock, and the retreat from the clichés of "faithful declamation" all point toward an attempt to clarify the tone of tragedy, to introduce, in Abram Gozenpud's apt phrase, a "rude and garish theatricality" into the opera.[29]

The Tsar's monologue and the "Song of the Parrot" were finished by 10 August 1871; the rest of Act II, in piano–vocal score, by 10 September. Also during the summer, while sharing rooms with Rimsky-Korsakov, Musorgsky seems to have decided to replace the St. Basil scene with the Kromy Forest scene, perhaps partly as a result of the insight he had gained from observing his roommate's handling of massed choral crowd scenes in *The Maid of Pskov*,[30] perhaps partly in recollection of the episodic, pageant-like brilliance of the scene in the army camp from *La forza del destino*. At about this time too, he took several important cuts noted in Table 3.1; most of the cuts lead to greater psychological clarity in the use of reminiscence motives and in tonal structure. On 11 September he wrote Stasov that Pimen had been abbreviated and Grigory recomposed, and that the "tramps' scene" (Kromy Forest) was "being thought out."[31] Although no vocal score survives to document the date exactly, he must have continued to work on the Kromy Forest scene through late November 1871, since a private performance omitting only it and the love duet from the Fountain scene occurred early in the month. Soon thereafter he completed the scene; he ended the revision with the missing love duet, finishing the job on 14 December 1871. Before the premiere, Nikolsky suggested concluding the opera with the Kromy Forest scene – a creative act that balanced his original suggestion that Musorgsky turn to Pushkin. (To review the differences between the two versions, episode by episode, see Table 3.1, pp. 63–65.)

With the completion of the vocal score of the scene by the fountain, Musorgsky had finished the composition of new music, and he turned to the scoring. Preparation of the full score continued throughout the remainder of the winter, the following spring, and into the summer. Five scenes simply were transferred, with modifications, from the existing full score of the initial version. The other four, the scene in the Tsar's Quarters, the two Polish scenes, and the scene in Kromy Forest, had to be scored in their entirety. Dates entered on the last page of each of the four new scenes record the progress of the work. The scene in the Tsar's Quarters was completed in full score on 11 January 1872; the first Polish scene on 10 February; the second Polish scene on 29 March; and the Kromy Forest scene on 23 June.

In the first five months of 1872, Musorgsky also worked to secure the performance of his opera. On 4 January, he paid a call on Nikolay Lukashevich, officially the head of the Department of Sets and Costumes but in fact Gedeonov's principal assistant and a friend of Musorgsky's.[32] It is not recorded what the two men discussed, but it is reasonable to suppose that *Boris*, completed in vocal score exactly three weeks earlier, formed part of the conversation. Not long after this, Musorgsky submitted the revised text of the libretto to the censors. Their report of 7 March recommended performance, citing with approval the many changes Musorgsky had made in Pushkin's text and pointing out that the only obstacle to presentation lay in the edict of Nicholas I which forbade the representation of any tsar in opera. Throughout March, this report drifted up through the layers of the Imperial bureaucracy, receiving approval at each stage, and in April it reached the Tsar, who alone could set aside the decree of his predecessor. On 5 April 1872, Alexander II authorized the production of *Boris Godunov*. Within the month notification of His Majesty's approval had come down through the bureaucracy, and on 29 April, the Maryinsky Theater's literary committee authorized *Boris* for production.[33]

Meanwhile, portions of the work had been performed in public. On 5 February 1872, the first performance of the Coronation scene was given at a concert of the Russian Musical Society. Although the performance went badly, Musorgsky was called to the stage twice. In a review published four days later, César Cui praised Musorgsky's evocation of bells and his use of a folk song in the chorus "Uzh kak na nebe solntsu krasnomu" (Like the beautiful sun in the sky) but complained that almost all of Boris's monologue was "completely drab and does not offer bold enough musical thought."[34]

Then, on 3 April, Balakirev conducted the polonaise from the scene by the fountain at the season's final concert of the Free School of Music. Cui had praise for the polonaise's music but condemned its orchestration as "gray and lusterless."[35] According to Rimsky-Korsakov, Musorgsky initially had orchestrated the polonaise "almost exclusively for bowed instruments. [He had] had the unhappy and completely unjustified idea of imitating the 'vingt-quatre violons du roi' – that is, the orchestra of the time of the composer Lully (Louis XIV). What relation this orchestra had to the time of the False Dmitry [1605–06] and to life in Poland at that time is impossible to understand. This was one of Musorgsky's eccentricities."[36]

The second examination of the opera by the Maryinsky's music committee occurred in late spring of 1872. On 24 April, Musorgsky wrote Balakirev requesting him to return the full score of the polonaise "for correction and presentation to the theatrical committee."[37] Then, on 6 May he wrote his publisher Vasily Bessel, "there is a meeting concerning *Boris* this evening at the Maryinsky Theater at 7:30. I await you."[38] A single clause of an item carried nearly six months later, on 29 October, in Bessel's periodical *Muzykal'ny listok* [Musical leaflet] has been cited repeatedly as proof that the result of this second examination was a second rejection.[39] The full text of this crucial item is as follows:

By the way, we have [the following news] to report about a highly remarkable phenomenon: Mr. Musorgsky's opera *Boris Godunov* was not accepted for production, but many artists of the Russian opera are so interested in it that they are studying the parts and concern themselves with its production. One must suppose that there is music in it to justify such attentions from the artists.[40]

This announcement is the primary piece of documentary evidence advanced as proof that the theaters rejected Musorgsky's opera a second time.[41] Closer examination reveals that it may have been misinterpreted. The publication *Muzykal'ny listok* was an ephemeral newsletter designed to provide a guide to musical events in the capital and to advertise Bessel's editions. It was scarcely the official bulletin of the Imperial Theaters.[42] Furthermore, Musorgsky scholars do not quote the announcement's text in full, choosing instead to paraphrase or quote out of context the clause "*Boris Godunov* was not accepted" in an attempt to prove that a second rejection occurred. Even in these circumstances the clause is ambiguous since it fails to mention *when* the opera was "not accepted," and thus easily could be just a reminder of the initial version's rejection. The full text clarifies these matters: it suggests that this item – on which Musorgsky scholars since the 1930s have hung so much – is nothing more than a piece of gossip whose purpose is to take Bessel's readers "behind the scenes" and exert pressure on the Directorate to stop procrastinating in the matter of *Boris*.

We thus have arrived at a detail in the history of this opera that is symptomatic of the many myths and distortions that characterize much modern scholarship on Musorgsky. Beginning in the 1920s, Soviet scholars began to interpret this composer as a prophet of Socialism, emphasizing his affinities with "the people" to the exclusion of other aspects of his creative personality. To rationalize him as a Soviet populist hero, it became necessary to cast him as a victim of Imperial society. Thus, these Soviet scholars maintained that the tsarist censor interfered in the creation and production of *Boris Godunov*; this is not so. They further maintained that the revision of the opera, seen as an enfeeblement, was forced on Musorgsky by dull-witted bureaucrats of the Imperial Theaters; this does not seem to be so. And they maintained as well that even after *Boris* had been revised, it was rejected a second time; this too appears unlikely, as we shall see presently.

The larger question lurking behind these details concerns the false mythology that has been erected around Musorgsky: that he altered his own best visions for expediency's sake, that he was first and foremost a victim, and implicitly that he was unable to learn from other composers, from his own unsuccessful experiments, and to grow. Too often in the past, to paraphrase Marina Sabinina, Soviet critics have placed ideology before fact, contenting themselves with "lacquering over" Russian creative folk heroes and condemning the tsarist formal institutions against which they allegedly struggled.[43] The question of the "second rejection" of *Boris*, to which we now return, illustrates these larger issues.

The hypothesis that there was no second rejection of the opera is consistent with the known facts. In April of 1872 Musorgsky learned that the committee would reexamine his opera near the end of the current season, before leaving St. Petersburg for their summer holiday. Probably sometime after 29 April, when the Theaters' literary committee approved the work, but no later than 6 May, the presentation took place. Musorgsky came to the meeting with a completed piano–vocal score that answered the committee's previous objections, with approval of the censor and authorization of the Tsar himself. *He had not yet finished the full orchestral score.* Apparently expecting to learn of the committee's decision, he asked his publisher Bessel to accompany him to the meeting at the Maryinsky on May 6.[44]

Musorgsky knew that Bessel was a good man to have in his corner. The publisher enjoyed friendly relations with the Directorate and could easily have been expected to use his influence on behalf of a work in which he had a commercial stake. After all, just a year and a half later he was to intervene in order to expedite the performance of Tchaikovsky's *Oprichnik*, another opera in his catalog.[45] Where money was concerned, Bessel was quick to act in his own interest; it seems highly unlikely that he would have failed to exert himself on behalf of *Boris*.

At the meeting of 6 May, the committee probably accepted *Boris Godunov*, but provisionally. Under the circumstances it could do little more. Musorgsky had not yet completed the full score, and the committee scarcely could guarantee the production in the following season of an unfinished work. Furthermore, its members already had accepted Rimsky-Korsakov's *Maid of Pskov*, and they were planning a revival of Wagner's *Lohengrin*. They therefore may have been reluctant to commit themselves to the enormous difficulties involved in preparing two new works and a major revival in the same season. (Rehearsals for Rimsky's work alone were to occupy some four months, never mind the time needed for *Lohengrin*.) The committee thus probably told Musorgsky – and Bessel – that the revision made the opera acceptable and that they would produce it at some future date, perhaps even suggesting the post-Lenten season of the coming year (1872–73) or the main season of the year after that (1873–74).

The results were encouraging enough that Bessel, during his next trip to Leipzig, concluded a preliminary agreement with Karl Gottlieb Röder, his printer, for the engraving of *Boris*. We read in a letter from the publisher to

Rimsky-Korsakov, dated 17 June 1872: "Concerning *Boris*, it is arranged with Röder."[46] Since Bessel's primary purpose in publishing the opera was to sell copies in conjunction with a performance, he scarcely would have considered so great an investment had the result of the meeting of 6 May been another outright rejection. We thus have all the more reason to regard the gossipy item of 29 October – which appeared in Bessel's paper, the reader will recall – as merely a goad to the Directorate not to leave this opera in limbo, a matter that would have made a good deal of difference to a businessman who had gone ahead with publication plans.

None of Musorgsky's published letters mentions a second rejection. On the contrary, in a letter to Lyudmila Shestakova, dated 11 July 1872, Musorgsky writes: "Take my *Boris* under your wing and let him, [thus] blessed, set out from you on his public ordeal."[47] The composer's reference to the "public ordeal" of his opera suggests that even then, two months after the meeting at the Maryinsky and two weeks after the completion of the full orchestral score, he expected a performance of the work.

Further confirmation that no second rejection occurred may be seen in the fact that, with the exception of Yulia Platonova (whose account is unreliable, as we shall see presently), none of Musorgsky's contemporaries details a second rejection. Stasov, Shestakova, and Rimsky-Korsakov all record the rejection of the initial version; none of them mentions a second rejection.[48] Could all of these people have remembered the "first" rejection, but forgotten the "second"? Would the polemical and contentious Vladimir Stasov have allowed a second official examination and rejection of *Boris* to pass unnoticed and unremarked, not only in his public writings but also in his private correspondence?

Platonova's account was set forth in a letter to Stasov of 29 November 1885 and was first published, in part, in an article by him commemorating the fifth anniversary of Musorgsky's death.[49] The entire letter was subsequently published in *Russkaya muzykal'naya gazeta* (Russian musical gazette):

Having for long had the idea of getting *Boris* produced, I decided on an extremely *audacious* step. In the summer of 1873, when Gedeonov, the Director of the Theaters, was in Paris, I, on the occasion of the renewal of my contract, wrote him concerning my conditions, of which the first was: "I demand *Boris Godunov* for my *bénéfice*; otherwise I will depart." There was no answer from him, but I well knew that I would get my way since the Directorate was unable to manage without me.

Midway through August, Gedeonov returned, and his first words, addressed to Lukashevich, who had met him at the station, were: "Platonova demands *Boris* without fail for her *bénéfice*. What's to be done now? She knows that I do not have the right to stage this opera since it has been blackballed! What's to be done now? Perhaps this: we will gather together the committee for a *second* time. Let them examine the opera *again*, as a formality; perhaps now they will agree to pass *Boris*! No sooner said than done. The committee, according to the wishes of the Director, assembles for a *second* time and for a *second* time condemns the opera! Having received this ill-fated reply, Gedeonov sends for *Ferrero*, the chairman of the committee. Ferrero appears. Gedeonov meets him in the antechamber, pale with fury.

"Why have you blackballed this opera a second time?"

"For pity's sake, Your Excellency, this opera is no good at all."

"Why is it no good? I have heard many good things about it."

"For pity's sake, Your Excellency, *his friend Cui* is constantly abusing us in the newspapers; just three days ago . . ." At this he pulls an issue of the newspaper from his pocket.

"I don't want to know of your committee, do you hear! I will produce this opera *without your approval*," shouted Gedeonov, beside himself with rage. And the opera was approved for production by Gedeonov himself, the first instance in which the Director had exceeded his authority in this respect . . .[50]

Platonova enlarged substantially the role she played. According to documents from the archives of the Imperial Theaters, she wrote Gedeonov on 11 April 1873, not in the summer, and asked him only to include a clause in her contract giving her the right to select a *new* opera for her *bénéfice*. The opera was not named. In the contract that she finally signed, no reference at all was made to her *bénéfice* or to her so-called right to choose the opera.[51] In addition there are errors of fact in her account, which, it must be remembered, was written more than a decade after the events occurred.[52]

Then there is the question of Stasov's use of this letter. Although one might think that his quotation of Platonova's letter would have given him an excellent opportunity to launch a polemic against the theater administration, he remains curiously silent, even in this article, on the subject of a second rejection, permitting Platonova to speak for herself without his endorsement. In the remainder of the article, he criticizes those who gave *Boris* unfavorable reviews at its premiere, comments on the cast of the premiere, discusses with rancor the additional cut imposed on the work beginning in 1876, and ultimately launches an attack on the Directorate for its failure to produce Musorgsky's *Khovanshchina* in Rimsky's completion; but he does not return to Platonova's "second rejection." Instead, he laconically writes: "Unusual exertions became necessary in order that this supremely talented opera might be accepted by the theater and presented before the public."[53] This circumstance alone forces one to suspect that Stasov knew she was exaggerating but was unwilling to say as much lest his own polemic lose force.

An autobiography completed by Platonova in September 1886, at Stasov's request, further muddies the waters. In this document, after describing the interest that she and the other artists had "in such remarkably grateful roles," she states, "[The question of] the opera was still not settled, but Kondratiev took the scene at the inn for his *bénéfice*. It had an enormous success. The subsequent fate of *Boris* I've described earlier [in the letter to Stasov]."[54] Now – if we accept this scenario – we are asked to believe that the lurid scenes of confrontation described in the letter to Stasov occurred *after* the successful performance of three scenes in February 1873, an impossible chronology. Moreover to say that the opera's fate was "not yet settled" is a long way from saying that it had been rejected. Although it is true that Platonova was genuinely interested in *Boris* and undoubtedly worked diligently for its production, she was also human and perhaps inclined to exaggerate her own role. To understand why, consider another passage from the memoirs written for Stasov in 1886. After describing the pleasure she had taken in the scenes from *Khovanshchina* that Musorgsky had shown her, she writes: "How we used to dream, he and I, of seeing this opera on stage! It was not to be! He died; me and his opera, *they rejected* [emphasis added]."[55] Still smarting over her dismissal some ten years earlier, she may have sought to portray the theater administration less favorably than herself in the matter of *Boris*.[56] One cannot give credence to the confrontations that she describes so vividly.[57]

There remains the problem of César Cui. The headline of his review of the opera's premiere (which ultimately took place early in 1874) reads: "*Boris Godunov*, An Opera by Mr. Musorgsky, Twice Rejected by the Vaudeville Committee."[58] Furthermore, in his review of Mikhail Santis's opera *Ermak*, Cui rails again at the committee for twice rejecting *Boris Godunov*.[59] We must try to place these data in perspective. Cui easily could be expected to put the Theaters in the worst possible light in the matter of *Boris*, if only as a means of applying pressure for the ready acceptance of the next *kuchkist* opera waiting in the wings – his own *Angelo*, on which he was working at the time of *Boris*'s premiere. First and foremost, Cui was a propagandist, ever ready to bend the truth in the service of his cause. In order to portray the *kuchka* as romantic underdogs, who endured indignity and abuse for the glory of art, he was obliged to exaggerate every injustice they suffered, real or imaginary. His review of *Ermak* – whatever the merits of the music – must be understood in the light of his role as polemicist:

This opera [*Ermak*] has set aside all I previously understood about bad music. It is the worst of all operas ever heard in St. Petersburg, and Petersburg has heard plenty of them. We remember *Natasha*, *Mazeppa*, *The Storm*, *Amalat-Bek*, *Naïda*, and a whole

84

row of Italian operas by various Campanas, Gammieris, and others. And this would be too much said were it not for the circumstance that the vaudeville committee, which halfway rejected *The Maid of Pskov* and twice completely rejected *Boris Godunov*, accepted *Ermak*.[60]

It is a half truth to say *The Maid of Pskov* was halfway rejected; Rimsky was obliged to make certain changes to accommodate the censor, and the opera was accepted. It is likewise a half truth to label procrastination and delay in mounting Musorgsky's opera a second rejection.

And so: although *Boris* was given conditional acceptance on 6 May 1872, by the time Musorgsky completed the full score, on 23 June, the Maryinsky Theater probably had filled its schedule at least through the end of the year. The theaters normally were committed to their schedule at least five months in advance, as we may discover from a letter of Cui concerning his opera *William Ratcliff*. He writes to Musorgsky, 27 July 1868:

Two days ago, I took down to Fedorov the full score of two acts . . . Fedorov sent it along for copying, but he was unable to inform me of a probable performance date for the opera. The time up till January, he said, was all occupied, so that the opera may go on only after the New Year.[61]

Thus, the most management could have promised Musorgsky when he brought them the full score was that they would try to find room for *Boris* after the New Year, after *The Maid of Pskov*, after *Lohengrin*.

This is exactly what took place. Three scenes from the opera were performed at the *bénéfice* of Gennady Kondratiev, Chief Director of the Maryinsky Theater, toward the end of the pre-Lenten season. Rehearsals began in late January of 1873, and on 5 February, the scene at the inn and the two Polish scenes were presented with sets designed by Matvey Shishkov and Mikhail Bocharov left over from the premiere of Pushkin's play *Boris Godunov* two seasons earlier. (In the conventional mythology of *Boris*, the theater artists agree to put on this performance themselves, bypassing the committee. But what would be the point of having a committee whose authority could be usurped so easily?) To coincide with this production, Bessel published a full libretto of the opera sometime after 25 January, the date of censor's approval.[62] Reviews of the performance were generally favorable; public enthusiasm was unusually high.[63] Indeed, the success was so great that the contralto Daria Leonova decided to repeat the scenes from *Boris* for her *bénéfice*. Before this proposed second performance could take place, however, the tenor Kommissarzhevsky fell ill, the performance had to be canceled, and Leonova had to content herself with a potpourri of excerpts from *A Life for the Tsar, Rusalka, The Power of the Fiend*, and *Le Prophète*.[64]

Recognizing in the enthusiasm for *Boris* an opportunity to sell scores, Bessel announced in *Muzykal'ny listok* for 25 March the opening of a subscription list for a complete piano–vocal score. The publisher commented:

Having obtained the rights for all countries to the composition *Boris Godunov* (an opera in four acts with prologue, subject adapted from Pushkin and Karamzin), music by M. Musorgsky, we have the honor to announce the opening of a subscription for an edition of a full transcription of this opera for piano and voice. The subscription price is ten rubles, silver. *In the published transcription will appear even those scenes which, in order to avoid length in the spectacle, will not be performed at the opera's production on stage* [emphasis added], and the score's size, therefore, will be quite substantial . . . In view of the ensuing summer season, just ahead, the subscription will be closed shortly. The piano–vocal score will appear next fall.[65]

This plainly indicates that some thought already had been given to the practical matter of *preparing* the "production on stage" and that Bessel expected a full performance in the near future. (When the score finally appeared, in January 1874, the price to non-subscribers was 15 silver rubles. We may obtain a perspective of this figure by noting that Pyotr Jurgenson was then selling for 50 kopeks apiece "inexpensive complete scores, for piano alone" of such works as *Norma, Lucia di Lammermoor, The Barber of Seville, Don Giovanni, Fidelio,* and *Freischütz*.[66] Even as late as 1882, Jurgenson was selling full piano–vocal scores of *A Life for the Tsar* for 8 rubles, *Aida* for 6, and *Faust* for 4.[67] Bessel apparently foresaw limited commercial appeal in *Boris*, and hoped to do well at the expense of those devoted to "new music.")

A passage in Rimsky-Korsakov's memoirs also suggests that no one in Musorgsky's circle had any reason to doubt that a full performance of the opera would take place in due course: "The [three] scenes enjoyed enormous success. Musorgsky and all of us were in ecstasy, and it was proposed to give all of *Boris* the following year."[68] Hope for producing the work in its entirety before the end of the 1872–73 season lingered awhile, but Stasov, with a certain sense of exasperation, soon realized that *Boris* would have to wait until the next season. He writes his daughter Sofia Medvedeva (17 March 1873):

here now is the trouble I have in view: in spite of everything they still have not given Musorgsky's opera *Boris*, God knows whether they will give it this winter at all. That means for the time being he has received no money; Bessel, it's true, bought from him the right of publication and *has already sent to Leipzig the order for printing* [emphasis added] but when he will give him the money, of this no one sees, no one knows a thing . . ."[69]

Several factors may have been involved in the Theaters' continued procrastination. The main season of 1872–73 had ended on 18 February with a performance of *Lohengrin*. The only remaining opportunity to produce *Boris* in its entirety that year thus lay in the short and much less prestigious post-Lenten season. But the fate of Pushkin's *Boris Godunov*, from which Musorgsky had drawn his libretto, may still have been a vivid memory. The play had received its first performance on 17 September 1870, slightly more than four months before the opera's first version was rejected. It had been a failure. The actors were severely criticized; only the sets were praised uniformly for their beauty and historical accuracy. Some writers – Stasov among them – even questioned whether Pushkin had ever intended the play for stage production at all. Can it come as a surprise, then, that the theaters continued to put off mounting this opera until the height of next year's main season, when it would have a better chance of success?[70]

In addition, most of St. Petersburg's music lovers in the 1870s considered the main opera house to be the Bolshoy Theater, in which works by the likes of Verdi, Meyerbeer, Donizetti, and Rossini were performed in Italian by visiting troupes of foreign artists and stars. Even the Maryinsky, in which opera was sung in Russian, regularly included in its repertory such works as *Il trovatore*, *Rigoletto*, and *Faust*. By combining the repertories of both theaters, we may obtain an indication of public taste: three of every four performances heard in the capital between 1855 and 1881, whether in Italian or Russian, were of an opera by a foreigner. When Adelina Patti first appeared (January 1869), "tickets were obtained with a fight; from 5:00 in the morning, part of the square of the Bolshoy Theater was full of people. Scalpers made enormous sums reselling boxes and stalls at fabulous prices . . . The furor was indescribable."[71] Given such circumstances, the Director may have balked at introducing two "first operas" by unproven Russian composers in a single season.

Finally, there is the practical matter of the travail associated with the production of any new opera. Chorus, soloists, and orchestra had to learn the music and then rehearse it adequately. In *Boris*, the Polish dance sequence had to be choreographed, learned, and rehearsed. Stage action and lighting had to be planned and practiced. Sets and costumes had to be designed and manufactured. Four months – from early September through December 1872 – had been needed to prepare *The Maid of Pskov*.[72] For part of that time, a major Wagnerian revival also had been in rehearsal. Preparing *Boris* simultaneously with *The Maid of Pskov* and *Lohengrin* while also maintaining the rest of the repertory probably was inconceivable; after the two unveilings (Rimsky on 1 January, Wagner on 28 January), the main season was so far advanced that to attempt to produce another entire work was out of the question. The performance of the three scenes was the best that could be done.

Sometime near the beginning of May, Musorgsky seems to have received word that *Boris* would be produced the following season. In a letter to Stasov, dated 3 May 1873, he writes:

> Dear glorious, most glorious, *generalissime*, – How important! "Fomka, Ep*ikh*an! Behind the boyar!" "How important!" *I am completely happy.* Thank you, my dear, I am ready to talk, write, and do all kinds of foolishness. *Our common cause, so dear to us, is safe.*[73]

The euphoria of this letter, the quotations from the text of *Boris*, and the reference to the "common cause" of Stasov and the composer strongly suggest that at last he had received a definite commitment from the Theaters.

The speed with which events moved in the fall further indicates that they had been set in motion the previous spring. Gedeonov arrived in St. Petersburg from Paris on 22 October 1873. On that same date, Musorgsky wrote Bessel: "The Director has sanctioned *Boris*."[74] Clearly, there could have been no time for the lengthy process of reconsideration described by Platonova. A letter of Borodin to his wife (25 October 1873) also emphasizes the speed with which final authorization occurred:

> By the way, here's some news for you – *Boris* is to be given in its entirety. Gedeonov, when he returned from abroad to Petersburg, as soon as he stepped out of his railway car, said in his first words to Lukashevich – "Put on *Boris* without fail and as quickly as possible; send Ferrero the score, I order it passed." Now they are already copying the parts.[75]

In the light of this evidence one may conclude that Gedeonov's approval represented merely the final piece of paperwork in a process which had begun almost a year and a half earlier, in May of 1872, with the provisional acceptance of *Boris* in its revised version.

The preceding hypothesis is consistent with the normal operations of the Russian Imperial Theaters in the 1870s. It was not unusual for months or even years to pass between the committee's acceptance of a work and the work's production, and the Theaters treated the so-called radical composers of Musorgsky's circle no worse than they treated professionally trained musicians like Anton Rubinstein. Cui's *William Ratcliff* was given its first performance on 14 February 1869; it had been delivered to the Theaters the previous summer.[76] Rimsky-Korsakov presented *The Maid of Pskov* to the committee on 11 January 1872.[77] The first performance (1 January 1873) occurred a little less than a year later. The cases of Rubinstein's *Demon* and Tchaikovsky's *Oprichnik* reveal that Musorgsky was not the only victim of the Theaters' bureaucratic procrastination. Tchaikovsky submitted the finished score of his opera in May of 1872, and the following October, the committee accepted it. The work was launched at the conductor Nápravník's *bénéfice* on 12 April 1874.[78] And although Anton Rubinstein enjoyed far greater prestige in the seventies than Cui, Rimsky, Musorgsky, or Tchaikovsky, his opera *The Demon* was subjected to a longer bureaucratic delay between its acceptance and production than any of *Ratcliff*, *Maid of Pskov*, *Boris*, or *Oprichnik*.

According to the report of Giovanni Ferrero to the Director, dated 15 September 1871, the opera was accepted by the committee on the same day that Rubinstein played it for them:

on the fourteenth of September the committee of *Kapellmeister* and conductors, consisting of Inspector of Music Mauer, the composer Minkus, the conductors Betz and Papkov, and assistant conductor Voyáček, was invited to the Repertory Hall of the Maryinsky Theater in order to examine the full orchestral score of Anton Grigorievich Rubinstein's new opera, *The Demon*. But as the author himself played and sang the opera, once the entire opera had been heard, the committee delivered their common conclusion that it[the opera] had great merit both in musical style and in instrumentation; and [the committee] thought it would have a great success on the stage.[79]

But Rubinstein's opera ran afoul of the ecclesiastical censorship, who prohibited the representation of an evil spirit on stage, and so *The Demon* was not performed until 13 January 1875, more than three years after its acceptance.

In view of such evidence, it is difficult to maintain that the Theaters were discriminating against Musorgsky. Even Soviet scholars acknowledge that Stepan Gedeonov was " a man far better educated and more progressive in his thinking than his father,"[80] who had been Director of Theaters under Nicholas I. In general, he staged the works of Russian composers as quickly after their completion as was practical. Even if, as Nápravník maintains, he truly "hated Russian opera [i.e., opera sung in Russian] from the depths of his soul and spoke of it with disdain, while at the same time praising Italian opera [i.e., opera sung in Italian],"[81] he certainly did not use his position to exclude Russian composers from the Imperial Theaters. During his eight-year tenure as Director (1867–75), he produced ten new operas by Russian composers, including four by members of Musorgsky's circle.[82] When he gave final approval, in October of 1873, for the production of *Boris Godunov*, he was doing for Musorgsky no more and no less than he had done, and would do, for several others.

And so, although the opera's path to the stage was not easy, at least it now seems clear that the tale of *Boris* twice rebuked and rejected, born in Stalin's Russia in the 1930s, is itself another of the legends developed to strengthen Musorgsky's credentials as a Soviet creative hero. One of the authors of this volume has attempted elsewhere to dispose of the legend that the censor interfered in the creation and production of the opera, and Richard Taruskin has effectively dealt with the legend that the revision was an enfeeblement undertaken by Musorgsky without artistic conviction.[83] As Soviet and Western scholars begin to reexamine other myths surrounding the Russian nationalist composers, we may confirm further that a just summary of the history of *Boris Godunov*'s composition, rejection, revision, acceptance, and ultimate performance – indeed, a just summary of the history of scholarship itself concerning this opera – is the proverb quoted earlier: "You can't drive straight on a twisting lane."

5

A TALE OF TWO PRODUCTIONS –
ST. PETERSBURG (1874–1882),
PARIS (1908)

The day before the premiere, Musorgsky came by my place in the evening, sat down at the piano (as usual), but after touching only a few chords, stood up, shut the lid, and said with irritation: "No, I can't. I know it's very silly, but what's to be done? I can't get my examination tomorrow out of my mind. How will it turn out?"

ARSENY GOLENISHCHEV-KUTUZOV

On 27 January 1874 *Boris* finally received its premiere, at the Maryinsky Theater in St. Petersburg. The leading roles were taken by several of the most popular singers of the capital's Russian opera troupe. Sets and costumes, left over from the first performance in 1870 of Pushkin's *Boris Godunov*, were designed by two well-known theater artists and a noted historian of old Russian art, respectively. The conductor was Eduard Nápravník, then in the fifth season of a distinguished career as chief conductor of the Maryinsky Theater that would span more than forty years. In some respects the first production was paradigmatic. Starting here we encounter elements that continue to influence performances of *Boris* today – cuts taken to shorten what is seen as an overlong work, declamatory singing by the title character, and historically realistic sets and costumes. When the Metropolitan Opera omits almost half the Kromy Forest scene, when Martti Talvela shouts in terror at the height of Boris's hallucination, or when the Bolshoy mounts *Boris* with decor so stunning that it might have come from a museum, each is following a precedent set at the premiere in St. Petersburg more than a century ago.

Perhaps no subsequent staging was more instrumental in turning these precedents into traditions than that of the opera's European premiere, mounted by Serge Diaghilev in Paris in 1908. Diaghilev's production of *Boris* – utilizing the Rimsky-Korsakov score, omitting two scenes entirely and shuffling the order of the seven remaining – for years influenced how the opera was performed and even synopsized in standard reference works.[1] Feodor

Chaliapin's interpretation of the title role, declamatory and histrionic, became the touchstone by which later artists were judged. And the sumptuous decor – designed and executed by Alexander Golovin, Alexandre Benois, Konstantin Yuon, and Ivan Bilibin, and costing many thousands of francs – created a stage picture that houses struggling to mount *Boris* on a shoestring can reproduce only in mezzotint. Diaghilev's ghost lingers over productions as diverse as the Cincinnati Summer Opera's of 1974, which began with the Pimen Cell scene, and the Salzburg Festival's of 1965, which placed the scene in Pimen's cell between the Novodevichy and Coronation scenes. The goal of this chapter, then, is to examine two prototypical early productions of *Boris Godunov* – the premieres in Russia and in Western Europe – together with contemporary criticism of them. We begin by returning to St. Petersburg for the first run, from January 1874 through October 1882. But since the opera's first production was handed down from the play's, our first task is to glance briefly at the first staging of Pushkin's *Boris*.

Prohibitions against the performance of this play finally had been lifted in 1866, only two years before Musorgsky began work on his opera. Prior to that time any composer wishing to set *Boris Godunov* surely would have been disheartened by the long string of censors' bans on the staging of the work, extending all the way back to 1826, just one year after its completion. In tsarist Russia, dramatic texts approved for print were subject to a second and more severe censorship before they were cleared for public performance. Approval in the first category by no means implied approval in the second. The very first censor's report on Pushkin's *Boris* singles out six problematic passages for deletion or correction and concludes with the remark: "Besides these exclusions and amendments, it seems there is no obstacle to the printing of the play. It goes without saying that it cannot and must not be performed, for we do not allow the Patriarch and monks to appear on stage."[2] But even though Pushkin's first censor had singled out only the churchmen as barriers to performance, subsequent censors routinely denied permission to stage any part of the play at all, occasionally citing the previous refusal as reason enough for their decision.[3]

Only in 1866, in the spirit of tolerance that pervaded the early years of the Reform Decade, was this impasse finally broken. The censor at last gave permission to stage *Boris Godunov*, but still insisted that "the persons of the Patriarch, of the Abbot, and of monks in general, as well as monastery rites and all attributes of ecclesiastic and monastic rank, be excluded from the text of the play."[4] Delays postponed this production until 17 September 1870. Six scenes were deleted, four others compressed into two, and the scene in Marina's boudoir restored. The production thus was mounted in sixteen scenes, drawing upon all but seven of the twenty-five Pushkin had written.[5]

Reviews were mixed, but on balance unenthusiastic. They praised the sets and costumes for their historical accuracy, criticized the weakness of the acting, and questioned the suitability of the work for performance on the stage in the first place. In memoirs published some thirty-five years later, in 1905, the playwright Pyotr Gnedich wrote: "Pushkin's Godunov *failed* triumphantly and brutally, despite the sumptuous production ... The roles were not securely prepared, the performance was so-so. [The well-known actor, Leonid] Leonidov, who played Boris, gave him the color of a melodramatic villain and howled the entire role in the voice of someone deaf. [Feodor] Burdin created a comic character out of the Patriarch, who was transformed on the affiche into an 'Old Boyar.'"[6] The theater historian Alexander Volf confirms Gnedich's judgment: "The performance [of *Boris Godunov*] was facile, even, and conscientious, but no one was remarkably distinguished ... The comedy with couplets *The Claws of St. Petersburg* by Messrs. Khudyakov and Zhulev had an incomparably greater success than [Pushkin's] *Boris Godunov*."[7]

In sum, one must acknowledge that, whatever the literary value of *Boris Godunov*, it had little success at its first production in the theater. Several circumstances seem to have contributed to this failure, among them poor performances by various actors and the complete omission of a number of scenes. The one positive note sounded throughout the literature on this performance concerns the splendor, beauty, and historical realism of the sets, costumes, and properties. It is small wonder, then, that the Imperial Theaters tucked these things safely away for recycling.

As previously noted, Musorgsky had begun work on the libretto of his opera in the autumn of 1868. With only one exception, all the scenes he used were to be included in the production of 1870. The exception was Pushkin's published scene 4, Kremlin Palace, in which Boris addresses the Patriarch and boyars and then departs, leaving onstage only Shuisky and another courtier, who exchange a few words. Musorgsky preserved the coronation monologue in his own coronation scene, but rewrote it so that the Patriarch was eliminated completely, making it possible to present the scene in an ecclesiastically neutral setting – a situation of which the opera's first production took full advantage.

Rehearsals for the premiere started in the fall of 1873, soon after the Director of the Imperial Theaters had approved the production. In November, Musorgsky himself taught the singers their parts in coaching sessions held at the home of the soprano Yulia Platonova, the first Marina. Beginning just before Christmas, Nápravník led eighteen rehearsals at the theater; the first few were for the singers with piano accompaniment, later the orchestra was added, and finally the stage action. Then in early January, Musorgsky and Platonova submitted formal petitions to the Imperial Theaters, which were forwarded to the Director, along with the following summary and report, written by the chief of the repertory division:

Mr. Musorgsky petitions the Directorate of the Imperial Theaters to accept on a fee-for-performance basis an opera in five acts, composed by him and entitled *Boris Godunov*; and a singer of the Russian opera troupe, Mme Platonova, solicits for permission to give the first performance of the opera at her *bénéfice*. Presenting this for Your Excellency's favorable examination and authorization, I have the honor to convey that the libretto of the above-named opera has been approved for the stage by the theatrical literary committee and by the censor and that, according to the regulations concerning the remuneration of authors and translators, this opera belongs to the first class, which gives Mr. Musorgsky the right to receive for each performance payment in the amount of a tenth part of two-thirds of the receipts.[8]

All tickets had been sold by the eve of the premiere, so that the composer, had he been so inclined, could have had the pleasure of contemplating his fee: exactly 125 rubles and 92 kopecks (£19 13s 6d, or $98.40). By contrast, the Russian Imperial Theaters had paid Verdi £2,379 – $11,895 – in 1862 for *La forza del destino*.

The premiere of *Boris Godunov* finally took place on Sunday, 27 January 1874, at Platonova's *bénéfice*. The opera was presented in five acts. The two scenes of the prologue (Novodevichy Monastery and Coronation) were combined into a single continuous scene entitled "The Call of Boris to the Throne," and this scene and the scene at the inn formed the first act. The Kromy Forest scene was presented as a separate fifth act, perhaps to guarantee that the opera qualified as a stage work of the "first class" (yielding its composer maximum revenue), perhaps simply to give stagehands more time for a complex scene change. The scene in Pimen's cell was omitted entirely, as were various bits and pieces from the *Terem* scene, the two Polish scenes, and the Kromy Forest scene.

Although one can only speculate concerning the reasons for these cuts, one thing seems clear: they were not demanded by the censor.[9] Indeed, the scene in Pimen's cell unquestionably was performed at the play's production in 1870, and in 1874 Pimen appeared as a hermit in the opera's death scene. It seems most likely that the conductor, Nápravník, urged the cuts on Musorgsky, justifying them on the grounds of contemporary taste.[10] The poet Arseny Golenishchev-Kutuzov, with whom Musorgsky shared rooms in

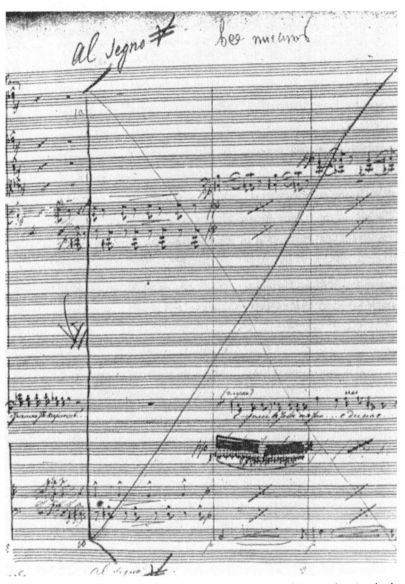

4 A page from the composer's holograph full score of Act II, showing both
Nápravník's cut of the chiming clock and Musorgsky's instructions
("все писать" [write all]) to restore this cut in scores and parts prepared for
rental by his publisher, V. V. Bessel & Co.

the winter of 1874–75, maintains that the composer cut the cell scene as well as the other passages because Nápravník had convinced him that these scenes would be ineffective in the theater.

It was in January of 1874. The rehearsals of *Boris Godunov* were going along rapidly and well. Musorgsky attended every one and always returned happy and full of hopes for success. He could not praise enough the attitudes of all the artists in general and especially that of the conductor, Nápravník, who, in Musorgsky's words, gave much good advice at these rehearsals and according to whose insistence many tedious passages were omitted, passages that did not get to the point, that were not particularly successful, and that spoiled the overall impression onstage. Such passages turned out to be the scene in Pimen's cell, the narrative about the parrot in the scene with the Tsarevich, the chiming clock, and a few others.[11]

Simply put, the uncut *Boris* was too long for Nápravník's audience of the 1870s. In its final form, that of the published piano–vocal score, the opera lasts nearly three hours and fifteen minutes, without intermissions. Taking the cuts of the first performance reduces its length by almost an hour, to about two hours and twenty minutes, a time comparable to that required for such popular favorites as *Il barbiere di Siviglia*, *Il trovatore*, *La traviata*, *Un ballo in maschera*, and *A Life for the Tsar*. Thus, forced to shorten the work by the conditions prevailing in the Imperial Theaters, having good reasons not to exclude the other scenes, and under pressure from Nápravník not to spoil "the overall impression onstage," Musorgsky agreed to sacrifice Pimen. The opera was presented in the arrangement shown opposite.

The most popular singers of the Russian troupe sang the most important roles: Ivan Melnikov sang Boris; Yulia Platonova, Marina; Feodor Kommissarzhevsky, the Pretender; and Osip Petrov, Varlaam. Critics praised both the stars and the minor singers who took the lesser parts. Applauding Platonova, for example, but not without sly criticism of Musorgsky, Hermann Laroche wrote: "[Platonova] was superb: the refined musical taste of her phrasing, the tender nuances of her acting, her feminine grace – all always natural to her – did not abandon her even in the role of Marina."[12] Melnikov received warm compliments from Alexander Famintsyn, a conservative critic whom Musorgsky had lampooned in his song "The Classic":

Melnikov obviously considered his role deeply and in his acting revealed both an extraordinarily subtle comprehension of the role and an enthusiasm that testifies to his great dramatic gift, which he never has displayed before to such a high degree. Melnikov's beautiful voice and handsome figure matched the role of Boris perfectly, and the talented artist was rewarded by loud expressions of pleasure by the audience, who were carried away by his beautiful performance.[13]

The Premiere of *Boris Godunov*, St. Petersburg, 1874

Act I

Scene 1: The Call of Boris to the Throne
[one continuous scene combining the scene at Novodevichy Monastery with the Coronation scene; joined by passing directly from the pizzicato A♭s heard as the pilgrims enter the monastery to the A♭ seventh chord that opens the Coronation scene]

Scene 2: An Inn on the Lithuanian Frontier

Act II

The *Terem* (Tsar's Apartments in the Kremlin)
[omitted: the children with the chiming clock, Boris with the chiming clock, the "Song of the Parrot" and surrounding episodes]

Act III

Scene 1: Marina's Boudoir
[omitted: a few phrases of Marina's monologue]

Scene 2: Garden by the Fountain
[omitted: a section of the polonaise; the final trio of Marina, Dmitry, and Rangoni]

Act IV

Boris's Death

Act V

A Forest Glade near Kromy
[omitted: about three dozen bars from the central chorus "Raskhodilas', razgulyalas'"]

Although Famintsyn singles out the beauty of Melnikov's voice, Ilya Tyumenev (a pupil of Rimsky-Korsakov) reveals that Melnikov in fact initiated the histrionic style of half-singing, half-shouting adopted by later exponents of the role, among them Feodor Chaliapin, Boris Christoff, George London, and Martti Talvela. According to Tyumenev: "[Melnikov] sings scarcely half the time, but speaks and shouts without pitch. In these places (for example, in the scene with the ghost of the Tsarevich), one receives the impression not of opera but rather of melodrama, though not bad. What Modest Petrovich might have said of this, I do not know ... but ... Boris's part itself, in several places, is delivered in pure conversational speech."[14]

Whatever Modest Petrovich may have said of it, the technique produced a powerful effect. Many years later, in 1906, Nikolay Kompaneysky, a friend of the composer's, recalled a conversation he had held with an elderly woman

5   Set design for "The Call of Boris to the Throne" (combining the
Novodevichy and Coronation scenes played without pause), St. Petersburg, 1874

the night of the premiere. Stopping by her box and finding her in tears, he
expressed delight that the opera had moved her so strongly and received the
following reply: "What kind of opera is this? There is no music in it at all. But
I have to say that I never took my eyes from the stage the whole time. How
splendidly Melnikov acts; even now his every word rings in my ears! That's
genius, not just an artist!"[15] Of course, Melnikov may have taken his cue
from Leonidov, the first interpreter of Pushkin's Boris, whose melodramatic
acting we have already noted. If so, there is a sharp historical irony in the
circumstance that Pushkin's sparse and restrained play, created to challenge
his era's declamatory tragedy and bombastic historical melodrama, failed its
author at its first performance through declamation and bombast; and
further irony in the subsequent fact that this very failure perhaps inspired
performers of the opera.

Sets for the production were by Matvey Shishkov and Mikhail Bocharov,
two well-known artists of the day. Except for the Kromy Forest scene, which
occurs only in the opera, these sets had been designed (the reader will recall)
for the first performance of Pushkin's *Boris* in September 1870. An album of
lithographs of all sixteen sets, published soon after the play's premiere,
enables us to gain an impression of both play and opera onstage. In keeping

6   Set design for the Inn scene, St. Petersburg, 1874

7   Set design for the *Terem* scene, St. Petersburg, 1874

with the tendencies of the day, the sets were quite realistic, employing virtually no stylization.

Only six of the sixteen were used in the opera; these included the sets for the inn, the Tsar's quarters, Marina's boudoir, the garden by the fountain, and Boris's death. For the first scene of the opera, that hybrid of Novodevichy and Coronation entitled "The Call of Boris to the Throne," the Maryinsky used Shishkov's set for the final scene of Pushkin's play, "Boris's House."[16] This rather neutral street scene, set in front of Boris's residence in the Kremlin, had two distinct advantages. Not only did it make it possible to combine two scenes that the composer had set in quite different locales, but also it avoided showing onstage the Cathedral of the Assumption, the Cathedral of the Archangel, and the Tsar's ceremonial procession between them. Because Musorgsky had rewritten Boris's coronation monologue to exclude the Patriarch, playing this scene against the secular backdrop of his house prudently evaded the risk of a confrontation with the censorship concerning the scene – the model for which in Pushkin, after all, had *not* been performed in 1870.

The costumes, like the sets, had been created for the play and simply were recycled for the opera. Vasily Prokhorov, an archeologist and an expert in old Russian art, had designed them, and, as with Shishkov and Bocharov's sets, the hallmarks of Prokhorov's costumes were realism and historical accuracy, as we may judge from contemporary photographs of Petrov and Dyuzhikov as Varlaam and Misail, of Melnikov as Boris, of Kommissarzhevsky as the Pretender, and of Platonova and Palechek as Marina and Rangoni.

Properties crafted for the play also reappeared in the opera, and judging from remarks of contemporary critics, the opera's staging too was based on that of the play. We may obtain a picture of at least two of the scenes from the following extracts from the *mise-en-scène* of *régisseur* A. A. Yablochkin, who had staged Pushkin's tragedy: "An inn. Benches here and there. Near the stove there is a tub, oven tongs, and so forth. On the shelves wooden and clay dishes, a washtub, and a torch holder. A small cupboard and in it: wooden plates, bread, salt, a knife, wooden glasses. On the walls hang various peasant garments, collars, and so forth. On the proscenium a simple table near a bench, under the window other benches."[17]

Yablochkin's conception of the scene in the Tsar's quarters provides a striking contrast to the rusticity of the scene at the inn:

The Tsar's rooms . . . Table with geographical maps and globes. On the table a clock in the form of an elephant, made of gold. On the walls portraits in black polished frames of Feodor Ivanovich [Ivan the Terrible's son, who reigned before Boris] and Irina [Tsar Feodor's wife and Boris's sister]. Further down, also on the walls, foreign sheets (engravings by Albrecht Dürer and Otto Venius and others) fastened by tinned nails. On the proscenium a table with a stool, covered with velvet coverings. On the table a sheet of Alexandrine paper, with a map of Russia traced on it. A pencil. At the window lace frames. In them pulled-up kerchiefs of silk, embroidered in gold. In front of the lace frames a stool with velvet brocade. Also near the window a new cage and in it a parrot. The cage is of tin and is supported by little columns; on it brass eagles. On the wall a mirror 38½ inches wide, in a frame covered with crimson or raspberry velvet and held in place by tinned nails. The mirror is draped shut with rose taffeta on rings.[18]

Lighting effects also played a role in the staging. In the first scene, for instance, the sun broke through wintry clouds just as Boris appeared onstage for the first time, its beam playing on the jewels of his coronation robes. Critics generally agreed that sets, costumes, and staging were excellent.

The opera enjoyed great popular success. According to César Cui, "After each of the seven scenes an enormous majority of the public called out the performers and the author."[19] Nikolay Soloviev, a critic who found little to admire in the work, admitted that the audience had summoned Musorgsky to the stage frequently but attempted to minimize the significance of the fact: "We consider as genuine successes those operas that bring good receipts in the course of several years."[20] Four performances of *Boris* were given before the arrival of Lent ended the regular theater season; each was sold out. Even Nikolay Strakhov, a literary critic who strongly condemned most of what Musorgsky had done, was obliged to acknowledge that "the success of the opera was extraordinary. The composer was called out enthusiastically many times at each of the four performances given before Lent."[21]

Although the public responded with excitement to the opera, most critics openly condemned it, or at best, misconstrued what was in it to praise. Vladimir Baskin, guided presumably by the contemporary perception that the *kuchkist* idiom was best suited to comedy, characterized the policeman in the Novodevichy scene and the Jesuits in the Kromy Forest scene as comic, and maintained that Musorgsky perhaps had the makings of a Russian Auber.[22] A week after the first performance Soloviev published a scene-by-scene critique of the opera, finding fault with nearly every page.[23] In an earlier notice, printed only two days after the premiere, he described the opera as a "cacophony in five acts and seven scenes," criticized Musorgsky's alterations in Pushkin's text, said the orchestration was uneven, and commented: "On the technical side of musical art (form, harmony, counterpoint), Mr. Musorgsky is feeble to the point of absurdity."[24]

Several other critics, including Laroche and Famintsyn, also mentioned Musorgsky's alleged technical ineptitude. Laroche wrote: "Perhaps the choruses went very well, but the abundance of dissonances and the unskilful handling of the voices in this new opera reach the point where we could not always warrant the composer's intentions and could not distinguish his wrong notes from the mistakes of the performers."[25] Famintsyn, having begun his review with the epigram "La grammaire est l'art de parler et d'écrire correctement," chastised Musorgsky for what the critic perceived as various lapses in the composer's technique: unresolved discords, parallel fifths, chaotically mixed tonalities, cross-relations, excessive use of pedal point, and nonsensical chord progressions.[26] Famintsyn admitted that the work had triumphed with its audience and, finding this difficult to reconcile with the many weaknesses that he had pointed out, speculated that the opera's subject and the splendor of its staging were responsible for its popularity.[27]

The most shocking review, however, was that of Musorgsky's friend and fellow composer César Cui, who discussed both performed and unperformed sections of the score in a lengthy essay. To a point Cui admired the opera, particularly those pages that adhered to the theories he had propounded in the 1860s as spokesman for the Mighty Handful. But when Musorgsky the artist parted company with Cui the theoretician and polemicist, then Cui had nothing but blame and scorn for his friend and colleague. He found the scene at the inn full of talented declamation and original humor and the Kromy Forest scene very powerful and full of superb music. He considered the "Song of the Parrot" to be the "height of perfection" and deplored its omission at the Maryinsky. And he declared that the opera was "orchestrated with great talent, in sounds that are colorful, effective, and beautiful."[28] Interwoven with this praise, though, was unexpectedly sharp criticism, directed frequently at those places where Musorgsky deviated from *kuchkist* dogma. Cui attacked Musorgsky's failure to adhere strictly to Pushkin's text, commenting that the libretto contained no plot, no character development, and no dramatic interest. He called the Coronation scene the "feeblest" in the opera, declaring that its depiction of tolling bells misfired when transferred from the piano to the orchestra. Cui thought that most of the Pimen scene was

feeble, not because it was incorrectly or impractically handled, not because the declamation was unsatisfactory – on the contrary, here and in other places, this is irreproachable – but because there is very little music in it and its recitatives are not melodious ... No inspiration is needed for the creation of such recitatives, only routine, practice ... It is very good that this long and boring scene is being omitted.[29]

The second act, according to Cui, left an unsatisfactory impression despite a few fine details:

The song about the gnat isn't bad ... The clapping game is far weaker ... Also not bad is Boris's meditation, expressed in the form of an arioso ... The composer quite justifiably wanted to impart a melodious quality to it, but in the end it didn't entirely work out. For the most part, the melodic content is concentrated in the orchestra, to the detriment of the voice, and furthermore, Boris's speech suffers from an overabundance of words ... In its entirety, this act, despite its rather good details, produces an unsatisfactory impression precisely because it is all details, because one impression is immediately replaced by another and they cancel each other out. Besides that, the lack of coordination and the choppy recitative also do their part.[30]

The Polish act was marred by the melodramatic figure of Rangoni. "In the monologue at the fountain we are fascinated with the beauty, the poetic mood, and the enchanting sound of the orchestra, that is, the background, which compensates for the lack of musical ideas in the Pretender's speeches ..."[31] (Both in the *Terem* scene and in the Polish act Musorgsky had moved furthest away from Cui's shibboleths.) He concluded:

Boris Godunov is an immature work (and, truth to tell, may we expect maturity from a first opera?) in which there is much that is excellent and much that is feeble. This immaturity has a telling effect on everything: on the libretto, on the accumulation of detailed effects to the point that cuts become necessary, on the passion for onomatopoeic sounds, on the lowering of artistic realism to anti-artistic activity ... and finally on the mixture of beautiful musical thoughts with worthless ones. The chief defects in *Boris* are two: the chopped recitative and the discontinuity of the musical thought, which makes the opera rather like a potpourri ... These defects result ... from immaturity, from the fact that the composer does not criticize himself sharply enough, and from that unfastidious, self-satisfied, hasty process of composition that has led to such lamentable results in the cases of Messrs. Rubinstein and Tchaikovsky.[32]

Cui's article wounded Musorgsky deeply. Immediately after reading it, he wrote to Stasov:

What a horror that article of Cui's is! ... So it comes to pass that *Boris* had to appear in order for some people to show themselves as they are. The tone of Cui's article is hateful ... And this risky attack on the composer's *self-satisfaction!* Brainless ones have little of that modesty and humility which has not left me and will not leave so long as the brains in my head have not completely burned away. Behind this insane attack, behind this notorious lie, I see nothing, as if soapy water had been spilled in the air, covering all objects. *Self-satisfaction!!! Hasty composition! Immaturity!! ...* whose? ... whose? I'd like to know.

... You have often let slip your true feelings: "I fear Cui in regard to *Boris.*" You are warranted in your loving premonition.[33]

One can only speculate why Cui attacked a fellow member of the Mighty Handful, whose works he usually defended from the criticism of men like Laroche, Famintsyn, and Soloviev. In the 1860s Cui had occupied the position of Balakirev's lieutenant and may have come to regard himself as somewhat more talented than Musorgsky, Rimsky-Korsakov, and Borodin. Then in 1869 Cui's opera *William Ratcliff*, on which he had worked for seven years, failed; his request that the director remove it from the repertory after only eight performances suggests that the failure may have wounded his pride. To see the public give a warm reception to Rimsky's *Maid of Pskov* and an even more ardent one to *Boris* may have been more than Cui could tolerate, particularly since Musorgsky had won this success in part by abandoning the positions which the *kuchka* had held and Cui had defended in the 1860s. Lyudmila Shestakova, not without a certain sarcasm, seems to imply that this was indeed the case:

Suddenly, after the first performance of *Boris Godunov*, when it had been embraced enthusiastically by the public, Cui's review appeared, in which he found very little that was good in the work and rather more that demolished it and its orchestration. I don't know how to regard this action. Many maintained that the review was written out of envy. I myself regard this as inconceivable because after *Ratcliff* it was impossible for C[ésar] A[ntonovich] to envy anyone. Although, if truth be told, *Boris* was received by the public more warmly than Cui's operas in general, should one really pay any attention to that?[34]

In the next season, that of 1874–75, *Boris* was performed eight times; at only one of these performances did the receipts fall below five-sixths of a full house. Even though the work was not performed during the 1875–76 season, indications of its continuing popularity may be seen in the publication of twelve separate numbers from the opera and of a potpourri drawn from it. Then in the season of 1876–77 the Maryinsky Theater revived it, presenting four performances between October and January. Cuts that had been observed before remained in effect; in addition the entire Kromy Forest scene, formerly presented as the fifth act, was omitted.

The reasons for this further cut are unclear. It has long been part of the lore of this opera that the subject matter displeased the Imperial family, who forced its removal. If we may believe the memoirs of Yulia Platonova (who, as shown in Chapter 4, is unreliable elsewhere), the Grand Duke Konstantin Nikolaevich considered the work "*a disgrace to all of Russia*, and not an opera" from the very first performances.[35] But one wonders – assuming that the scene *was* cut at the insistence of the Imperial family – why they waited so long to act. In its first two seasons each performance of *Boris*, twelve in all, included the scene near Kromy. Not until the opera was revived, after a year's absence from the repertory, was the scene omitted.

Considerations other than censorship may have been involved. An extract from the diary of Ilya Tyumenev, though failing to rule out political pressure, strongly suggests that once again, as with the scene in Pimen's cell, Nápravník (and not the Imperial family) was responsible for this cut:

Act 5 [of *Boris Godunov*], to the shame of our directorate (virtually upon the initiative of Nápravník), completely has ceased to be given ... Nikolay Andreyevich Rimsky-Korsakov told me that the pretext, ostensibly, is that the history of Boris ought to conclude with his death, and that the fifth act adds nothing. But on this he remarked, quite reasonably, that the fifth act even can precede the fourth in time. Let the opera conclude with the death of Boris, which Kromy will precede, but to omit completely such a talented scene makes no sense at all.[36]

As we have noted above, the opera's unusual length probably was the principal reason for the cuts observed at the premiere; despite those cuts Nápravník may have believed that *Boris* was still too long for his audience, particularly in view of the four intermissions. Thus for the revival he chose to shorten the work further, justifying this additional cut on the grounds that, to the public, the opera was over when the title character died.[37]

Critics' reaction to the new series of performances was mixed; the public, by contrast, remained enthusiastic. Nonetheless, receipts for *Boris* were notably poorer in 1876–77 than they had been before. None of the four performances was sold out, at only one were more that 90 percent of the tickets sold, and the poorest (the first) achieved only about three-fifths of full receipts. The season of 1877–78 was worse: three performances were given before Christmas, with receipts that fell steadily from slightly more than four-fifths to somewhat less than three-fifths of a full house. The opera was presented only twice in the 1878–79 season, but both performances were nearly sold out. It was not performed at all in the seasons of 1879–80 and 1880–81. Of course, declining attendance eroded Musorgsky's income from the work. For the twenty-one performances given while he was alive (1874–79), he received a total of 2,795 rubles, 41 kopeks (£436 15s 8d, or $2183.90).

All the while the scene in Pimen's cell had never been heard in the theater. It finally was unveiled at a concert of the Free School of Music, 16 January 1879, under the direction of Rimsky-Korsakov. Laroche's review revealed no change in his opinion of the composer.[38] Nikolay Soloviev, who had criticized nearly every page of the score in 1874, found little to admire in this scene as well. Comparing the concert to a banquet, Soloviev wrote:

The first delicacy was a scene from Mr. Musorgsky's opera *Boris Godunov* ... a cell in the Chudov Monastery ... What beautiful poetry and what colorless music! I do not at all exaggerate if I say the very best place in this music is the strokes of the beautiful gong. Imagine that for this scene Mr. Musorgsky has found nothing more clever than to impart to the orchestra a figure from daily piano exercises for five fingers! Knowing the realistic orientation of Mr. Musorgsky, one may think that he wanted to present Pimen not at his chronicle, but practicing at the piano. Against the orchestral background of five-finger exercises, one hears the dreary and melancholy song of Pimen and Grigory. This melancholy scene is somewhat enlivened by the chorus accompanied by sounds of the gong; this chorus is an entirely faithful copy of our church singing. The scene plunged the orchestra and the public into great despondency, which did not encourage them to applaud. To what kind of delicacy may we compare Mr. Musorgsky's scene? I compare it, if you please, to emaciated and somewhat tainted oysters, on which one has spattered a few drops of lemon juice, in the form of a gong and a church choir, in order to choke them down.[39]

An anonymous critic for the *Sunday Leaflet of Music and Advertisement* responded a little more favorably, but with no real understanding:

The scene of Pimen and Grigory (in the Chudov Monastery) . . . is quite interesting. Character and mood are sustained from the beginning to the end of the scene. In a strictly musical sense, the scene does not have great merits and in its entirety provokes weariness by its length. In the theater it might arouse interest . . . but in Kononov's Hall, Mr. Musorgsky's excerpt, with its interminable recitative, passed by perfectly unnoticed . . .[40]

After the composer's death on 16 March 1881, the Theaters revived his opera for the 1881–82 season. The first performance of this revival, the twenty-second since the work's completion, occurred on 11 December 1881. Nápravník entered a single word in his memorandum book to describe this evening: "Success!" And in another notebook he entered the remark: "Revived *Boris Godunov* with great success."[41] Four performances of the work were given in the course of the season; all were either sold out or nearly sold out.

The next season (1882–83) the opera enjoyed only one performance on 8 October 1882, and provoked only a lukewarm response. One theater historian indicated that the audience applauded only "the scene at the inn, the scene of Boris with Shuisky, and the death of Boris," remaining "completely indifferent to the first scene."[42] César Cui was on hand too, summarizing his timeworn views – while affecting not to – in his wearily authoritative voice:

I will not repeat all that has so many times been said about the deficiencies and virtues of this work, about the stiffness and angularity of its writing, the unnecessary and unartistic harshness of expression, and alongside these [negative] qualities the striking lifelikeness of the people's scenes, the inimitable humor, the miraculous declamation, the valuable contributions it makes to our art; I will limit my comments to this performance . . . If in the second act [Mr. Melnikov, as Boris] could have put a bit more singing into his arioso ("Tyazhka desnitsa" [the second section of "Dostig ya vysshey vlasti"]), if he had sung it at a somewhat more leisurely tempo (in Musorgsky it is "Andante"), and if in the final act he could have sung just a little bit, everything would have been inimitably, artistically fine.

Cui also criticized the performance of the chorus in the first scene, praised it in the Death scene, once again lamented the omission of the Kromy Forest scene, but then concluded: "Here is the crucial thing: *Boris Godunov* is not a transitory phenomenon, *Boris Godunov* has serious significance for art. Thus in giving it one must be concerned not with a more or less interesting performance but chiefly with insuring that what is most important in it for art, what is most serious and essential, not be lost."[43]

On 8 November 1882, the Maryinsky Theater's artistic council removed *Boris Godunov* from the repertory by resolution. There is no comment on the decision in the official protocol for that date; the reasons for the action remain unknown. And though the work was performed ten times in Moscow between 16 December 1888 and 12 January 1890, no further performances occurred in St. Petersburg during the reign of the reactionary Alexander III, who had come to the throne upon his father's assassination in 1881, just two weeks before Musorgsky's own death. Indeed, according to Vladimir Stasov, an attempt to bring the opera back into the repertory in St. Petersburg in 1888 met with failure because of the direct intervention of the Emperor. As Stasov explained in a letter to Rimsky-Korsakov, "I do not know if you have heard or not that this winter they are not giving . . . *Boris Godunov* . . . When the list of operas for the winter was presented to His Majesty the Emperor [Alexander III], he, with his own hand, was pleased to strike out *Boris* with a wavy line in blue pencil."[44] Not until 1904, ten years after the death of Alexander III, did *Boris Godunov* in Rimsky-Korsakov's first version finally reappear on the stage of the Maryinsky Theater; within four more years, it had been staged with acclaim in Paris. How the opera came to be resurrected at home and sent on to success abroad is the subject of the next section.

> I both adore and abhor *Boris Godunov*. I adore it for its originality, power, boldness, distinctiveness, and beauty; I abhor it for its lack of polish, the roughness of its harmonies, and, in some places, the sheer awkwardness of the music.
>
> NIKOLAY RIMSKY-KORSAKOV

On 19 May 1908 the first stage performance of *Boris Godunov* outside Russia occurred at the Théâtre National de l'Opéra in Paris. Feodor Chaliapin sang the title role supported by an ensemble of the most talented soloists, choristers, and orchestral musicians of Imperial Russia. Alexander Golovin, Alexandre Benois, and Konstantin Yuon designed the sets; Ivan Bilibin, the costumes. The conductor was Felix Blumenfeld, of the Maryinsky Theater. Dozens of others contributed to the performance. But the organizer of all this talent, and the driving force of the production, was the impresario Serge Diaghilev.

Diaghilev's production of *Boris* marked the beginning of the work's rise to popularity in the West, but it also established – as had the work's Russian premiere thirty-four years earlier – controversial performance practices that are still influential today. For one thing, Diaghilev chose to present the opera in the revision by Nikolay Rimsky-Korsakov rather than in the composer's own final version of 1874. In addition, he presented only seven of the opera's nine scenes and these in an order sanctioned in none of the existing scores, Musorgsky's or Rimsky's. Comparison by critics of what they had read in Musorgsky's vocal score with what they had seen and heard on stage quickly led to the polemics that still echo in discussions of *Boris Godunov*. A few students of Musorgsky – for example, M. D. Calvocoressi – later even maintained that Rimsky's version of the opera never would have established itself in the repertory in the West if Diaghilev had chosen to produce some form of the composer's own score in 1908. But before slipping too deeply into such conjecture, perhaps we should ask ourselves several questions: Did Diaghilev really have a choice? Were there practical considerations, both musical and non-musical, that led him to choose Rimsky's score? In view of the remodeling that he imposed even on Rimsky's score, how sensitive could he have been to questions of authenticity? And finally, despite his infidelity to both composer and reviser, did he succeed in creating an effective stage piece?

Before turning to these questions, however, we must consider how Rimsky came to busy himself with Musorgsky's opera in the first place. In 1871, while sharing an apartment with Musorgsky (who was then hard at work on the revision of *Boris Godunov*), Rimsky-Korsakov was appointed professor of composition at the St. Petersburg Conservatory of Music. Since its founding nine years earlier, the Conservatory had represented the enemy for the *kuchka*, but Balakirev urged Rimsky to take the professorship anyway on the grounds that he would thus get one of his own men into the enemy camp. As things turned out, Rimsky-Korsakov did not infiltrate the Conservatory so much as the Conservatory infiltrated Rimsky-Korsakov. Embarrassed that his students knew more about the technical details of composition than he did, the young *kuchkist* forced himself through a rigorous program of self-instruction in harmony, form, orchestration, and counterpoint. By the end of the 1870s, he had acquired a formidable technique, which in his own words "allowed new living currents to flow into my creative work and untied my hands for further activity as a composer."[45] It untied his hands for activity as an editor too, of other people's finished and unfinished works.

After Musorgsky's death in 1881, Rimsky agreed, at the request of the executor of the estate, to examine his friend's manuscripts and sketches and to "set in order and complete" such works as he should find suitable.[46] He worked at the task throughout the first half of the 1880s, and even presented his redactions to Musorgsky's publisher Bessel without charge or demand for royalties. There can be no doubt concerning the generosity of his motives:

In most cases, these compositions were so talented and so original, and revealed so much that was new and vital, that their publication was a necessity. But publication without a trained hand to put them in order would have made no sense, except perhaps biographically and historically. If Musorgsky's compositions are destined to live unfaded for fifty years after their author's death (when all his works will become the property of any publisher), then such an archeologically correct edition can always be made since the manuscripts went to the Public Library upon leaving me. For the present, though, an edition was needed for performance, for practical artistic purposes, for making his colossal talent known, not for studying his personality and his artistic sins.[47]

His goal initially was simply to realize, and render performable, such unfinished works as the opera *Khovanshchina*. But before completing his first phase of work with Musorgsky's music, he had extended his efforts to certain works left in satisfactory state by the composer himself: *Songs and Dances of Death*, *Pictures from an Exhibition*, *Night on Bald Mountain*, and a few short orchestral works and choruses. He did not at first take up *Boris Godunov*.

Rimsky turned his attention to *Boris* in early 1889 when, under the spell of the first performance in St. Petersburg of Richard Wagner's *Ring des Nibelungen*, he rescored the polonaise from the Polish act for concert performance. For a time in the early 1890s, he considered writing an article about the opera, its merits and faults, but he decided that a revision of the work would be both more instructive and more useful. Rimsky published his version in the spring of 1896, arguing in a preface that his "purification and regulation of [the opera's] technical side will only make clearer and more accessible for all its great significance, and will refute the charges brought against it."[48]

Rimsky introduced many changes into Musorgsky's score, of course, including modifications in tessitura, vocal line, dynamics, harmony, key scheme, and orchestration. In addition, he made lengthy cuts in the Cell scene, in the scene in the Tsar's Quarters, and in the Fountain scene. As a result of these cuts, he was obliged to compose fresh connecting material in various places throughout the work. (Oddly enough, one of these passages, a twenty-one-measure extension of the polonaise to play the chorus off stage, appears in the full orchestral score published in 1896 but not in the piano–vocal score published that same year.) In the Kromy Forest scene, he recomposed the so-called revolutionary chorus, shortening its central section by half and briefly curtailing its closing section. Finally, he reversed the order of the two scenes of Act IV, so that the opera ends with Boris's death.

An opportunity for performing this new version of *Boris* presented itself when Rimsky became chairman of the Society for Musical Gatherings, in spring of 1896. Funds were raised privately, a pick-up ensemble engaged (drawn largely from the recently disbanded orchestra of Count Sheremetev), and soloists hired. Four performances were given between 28 November and 4 December 1896 in the Great Hall of the St. Petersburg Conservatory. Although Rimsky maintains that "the opera went well and enjoyed success,"[49] none of the four performances seems to have sold out, the second in particular having been quite sparsely attended.

Of far greater significance was the production mounted two years later by the Moscow Private Opera of Savva Mamontov, a wealthy patron of the arts. On 7 December 1898, at the Solodovnikov Theater in Moscow, Feodor Chaliapin made his debut in the role of Boris Godunov, a role that would become nearly his exclusive property for more than a quarter century. The work received fourteen performances through the end of the Moscow season in late February, whereupon Mamontov brought his company to St. Petersburg for a short season at the Great Hall of the Conservatory. The work chosen to open the company's stay in the capital, 7 March 1899, was *Boris*, which then was heard four more times before the season ended with Chaliapin's departure in late April for an engagement in Kazan.

Perhaps the most interesting review of these performances was that of César Cui, who, it will be recalled, had rebuked the opera at its premiere in 1874. Now, a quarter century later, Cui acknowledged Rimsky's technical mastery while forcefully expressing a preference for the opera in the composer's original version:

Recollecting and comparing the former *Boris* with the present "corrected" *Boris*, I admit that I sincerely miss the old version. Even if Mr. Rimsky-Korsakov's harmonies are smoother and more natural, they are not Musorgsky's harmonies and obviously not what he wanted. Even if Mr. Rimsky-Korsakov's voice leading is flawless, while Musorgsky's occasionally sins against textbook rules, the latter often better suits the coarse and uncivilized scenes of the opera. Even if Mr. Rimsky-Korsakov's instrumentation is incomparably more perfect than Musorgsky's, it is nonetheless

8   Feodor Chaliapin as Boris, Mamontov Private Opera, Moscow, 1898

9 S. F. Selyuk-Roznatovskaya as Marina, Mamontov Private Opera, Moscow, 1898

obvious that its coloration is not entirely what the author tried to achieve. The reorchestration of a work more normal, less off the beaten track is a feasible thing, but the reorchestration of so extraordinary a work as *Boris* – hardly possible to consider as a rational act – only makes the opera insipid.[50]

Other critics, by contrast, considered Rimsky's work essential. "There is no doubt," writes Yuly Engel, "that all these corrections affect the opera for the better."[51] This critic also recycled the opinion that great acting went a long way toward redeeming Musorgsky's score. Indeed, one may almost see the ghost of Nikolay Kompaneysky's "elderly woman" in Engel's characterization of Chaliapin:

In a musical sense, the part [of Boris] is not the best in the opera, despite many startling details, but what this talented artist did with it! Beginning with makeup and ending with each pose, each musical intonation, this was something amazingly alive, vivid, brilliant. Before us stood the tsar ... in a word the very Boris Godunov created by Pushkin and regenerated musically by Musorgsky. The scene of Boris's hallucination, in Mr. Chaliapin's interpretation, produced an unusually powerful impression; after it, a startled public called out the artist without end.[52]

These performances, with Chaliapin in the title role, launched the work once again. The Imperial Theaters staged it (again with Chaliapin) at the Bolshoy in Moscow on 13 April 1901; at this performance the Kromy Forest scene was heard for the first time in Moscow. Finally, after an absence of twenty-two years, *Boris Godunov* returned to the stage of the Maryinsky Theater on 9 November 1904; nine performances were given through 26 February 1905, with receipts falling off dramatically once V. S. Sharonov had replaced Chaliapin in the title role. All these performances continued to reinforce the stage tradition that was beginning to emerge with this opera. All the cuts Rimsky had taken in his 1896 score remained in place, to shorten what otherwise might have seemed an overlong work. The star Chaliapin, like Melnikov before him, employed a declamatory style of half-singing, half-shouting in such overtly dramatic scenes as Boris's hallucination and death. Costumes were historically accurate; sets were secondhand and realistic.

Rimsky-Korsakov returned to *Boris Godunov* in 1906 in order to restore most of the cuts he had made ten years earlier, and his labors with it might have ended with these restorations had it not been for Diaghilev. At the impresario's request, and for the production in Paris, he composed in late 1907 insertions of forty and sixteen bars before and after Boris's coronation monologue in order to lengthen the spectacle of the Coronation scene. In 1908 the firm of V. Bessel & Co. published a new piano–vocal score incorporating these changes, and it is primarily by this score that the work has been known ever since. Most opera lovers learned the work in Rimsky's version, with or without the cuts of 1896, and many still love it best in this form. Rimsky's own final word on the subject, written in 1906, appears in his memoirs:

> I remained indescribably pleased with my reworking and orchestration of *Boris Godunov*, which I heard for the first time with a large orchestra [at the Maryinsky, in 1904]. Musorgsky's fierce admirers knitted their brows a bit, regretting something . . . But having prepared a new version of *Boris Godunov*, I had not destroyed its original form, I had not painted over the old frescoes forever. If ever the conclusion is reached that the original is better, more valuable than my revision, mine will be tossed out, and *Boris Godunov* will be performed according to the original score.[53]

No such consensus had emerged by the time that Diaghilev decided to bring *Boris* to Paris.

Serge Diaghilev had known *Boris Godunov* at least since the early 1890s, when he was a student in St. Petersburg. According to Alexander Benois, "We [Diaghilev's schoolmates] had heard a lot about Musorgsky, but at that period it was not so easy to get to know his music . . . We accepted on credit the fact that he was the real genius of the 'Great Five,' for he was considered as such by 'old Stasov' . . . [Diaghilev], on the other hand, actually *knew* Musorgsky's music and not only his songs but even the piano score of *Boris Godunov*."[54] Indeed, the young man was so taken with *Boris* – both Pushkin's and Musorgsky's – that in 1894 he composed a new setting of the Fountain scene which his biographers describe as a blend of Musorgsky and broad Italian melody.[55] His friends sharply criticized the scene, and Diaghilev gave up composition, but he did not abandon music. According to the Soviet scholar Abram Gozenpud, he and Walter Nouvel often performed piano duets together, devoting particular attention to opera.[56] He regularly attended the Imperial Theaters, where he heard such works as Tchaikovsky's *Queen of Spades* and Borodin's *Prince Igor*, and when Mamontov brought his private company to St. Petersburg, Diaghilev finally had the chance to experience *Boris* in the theater.

The tale of Diaghilev's success in bringing Russian art and music to Western Europe has been told many times.[57] In 1906, supported by the patronage of the Grand Duke Vladimir, the Tsar's uncle, Diaghilev brought an exhibition of Russian paintings to Paris. He returned in 1907, again with the Grand Duke's blessing, with a series of concerts devoted to Russian music, and even before this series had ended, he had begun to think of producing opera the next year. He was considering *Boris*, Rimsky-

Korsakov's *Sadko*, and at least one work by Tchaikovsky, but his aide, the French critic Michel Calvocoressi, ultimately convinced him to "stake his all on *Boris Godunov*."[58]

In a letter to Rimsky-Korsakov dated 17/30 July 1907, Diaghilev reveals that he was even then considering how to rearrange the work in order to increase its effect. At this early stage of deliberation he was willing to sacrifice the opening scene in the courtyard of the Novodevichy Monastery, the scene in Marina's boudoir, and the Kromy Forest scene, and he plainly already regarded the Coronation scene as an opportunity for lavish spectacle. He writes:

Not so much, it would seem, is lost from the omission of the scene in Marina's boudoir, and without it there are still many pages of genius in *Boris*. Why weaken the impression with this alien element, perhaps not of the very highest quality?

Concerning the first scene of the prologue [the Novodevichy scene], my considerations are of an entirely different character, outside the province of music and of a purely theatrical nature. The scene begins brilliantly with the quarrels and lamentations of the people, then falls into Shchelkalov's recitative and further slips into the chorus of cripples, which is short and concludes the scene with a perfectly vague theatrical impression. After this, and *this is most important*, an entr'acte of not less than fifteen minutes, for it is necessary to prepare the Coronation scene so that the French will go mad with its grandeur; that means, besides its sets, one must place on stage no fewer than 300 people, and this can delay the spectacle for more than a quarter of an hour. Thus, right away the effect of the opera goes limp, and it would be very difficult to smooth this away in what follows ...

The gravest of my doubts concerns Kromy. The scene is splendid but unendingly difficult to produce and, chiefly, interrupts interest in the act ... There is such an upsurge of genius in it, however, that one loses heart, not knowing what to do with it ... In a word, here is an exceptionally large question mark.[59]

The impresario continued to think about the opera for the next several months and sought the advice of his old friend and associate, Walter Nouvel. The two of them, according to Gozenpud, "were acquainted with the manuscripts of Musorgsky,"[60] but Nouvel writes:

We were not always of the same opinion. Diaghilev was ever drastic in cuts and revisions. He had entirely suppressed the tavern scene as being too *ambulant* in tendency, also he had changed the order of many scenes ... Diaghilev always laid stress on dramatic effect, was terrified of boring his audiences, and on that account never hesitated to make cuts that musicians and critics might consider sheer vandalism.[61]

After spending many hours with both Musorgsky's original score and Rimsky-Korsakov's arrangement, he finally selected seven of the nine scenes

10   Boris's exit from the Uspensky Cathedral after his coronation. A sketch by
L. Faure executed at the time of the opera's production in Paris, 1908

of Rimsky's revision, arranged in the following order. Act I: Novodevichy
Monastery, Pimen's Cell, and Coronation; Act II: Garden by the Fountain
and the Tsar's Quarters in the Kremlin; Act III: Kromy Forest and the Death
of Boris. Rimsky's shorter versions of 1896 were used in the Cell scene and the
Fountain scene, and all but one of his cuts in the scene in the Tsar's quarters

were taken as well. The scenes at the inn and in Marina's boudoir were omitted entirely (see Table 5.1).[62]

Several French critics and musicians, among them Calvocoressi and Claude Debussy, protested the loss of the Inn scene, but there is no agreement in the sources concerning the reasons for its omission. Calvocoressi maintains that the scene was sacrificed to prevent the opera from lasting too long.[63] Alexandre Benois indicates that it was omitted "in a fit of nervousness, a reluctance to show to the elegant, squeamish Parisian audience something so coarse and 'messy.'"[64] He adds that when the protests began, Diaghilev could not restore the scene since he lacked both a set for it and a singer for the hostess's role. But Chaliapin writes that "the inn scene could not be included due solely to the fact that no singers of stature were available – and that in spite of all the talent to be found in Russia. In my youth I often sang both Boris and Varlaam in the same performance, but I didn't dare do it [in Paris]."[65]

The opera's European premiere finally occurred on 19 May 1908; six more performances followed within two and a half weeks.[66] The work itself, according to Prince Peter Lieven, "was well received. It was even a striking success, but . . . it appealed rather to the advanced Press and the *élite* than to the general public."[67] French critics gave high praise to Chaliapin and the Russian chorus, reveled in Musorgsky's so-called realism, and pronounced the work a masterpiece, comparing the composer with Shakespeare and Tolstoy. The English author Rosa Newmarch wrote:

Those who in the face of some preliminary opposition persevered in their efforts to see Musorgsky's music drama *Boris Godunov* produced at the Grand Opera have reaped the reward of their wise temerity. The house was practically sold out for every one of the seven performances given since May 19th. The approval of the Press has been almost unanimous, and the display of public enthusiasm unprecedented.[68]

Despite such comments, one suspects that many, as Prince Lieven suggests, were not yet true believers. Only one year earlier, after all, when excerpts from *Boris* had been given at one of Diaghilev's concerts of Russian music, a critic for *La revue musicale* had written:

After a charming symphony (Op. 21) by Alexander Taneyev, impregnated with Russian folk song, we heard Mr. Chaliapin in two fragments by Musorgsky (from an opera entitled *Boris Godunov*): the first [was] very expressive but monotonous, without rhythm, probably chosen in order to show off the dramatic qualities of the interpreter much more than the genius of the composer; the second "Song of Varlaam" was much more lively but less vocal, recalling the manner of Weber in certain pages of *Freischütz*.[69]

Table 5.1. *Comparison of Musorgsky's, Rimsky's, and Diaghilev's Boris*

Musorgsky's published score (1874)	Rimsky's published score (1896)	Diaghilev's arrangement
Prologue, sc. 1: Novodevichy Monastery	Prologue, sc. 1: Novodevichy Monastery	Act 1, sc. 1: Novodevichy Monastery
sc. 2: Coronation	sc. 2: Coronation	sc. 2: Pimen's Cell (cut)
		sc. 3: Coronation (expanded)
Act 1, sc. 1: Pimen's Cell	Act 1, sc. 1: Pimen's Cell (cut)	
sc. 2: Inn	sc. 2: Inn[a]	
Act II: The *Terem* in the Kremlin	Act II: The *Terem* in the Kremlin (cut)	Act II, sc. 1: Garden by the Fountain (cut)
		sc. 2: The *Terem* in the Kremlin (cut)
Act III, sc. 1: Marina's Boudoir	Act II, sc. 1: Marina's Boudoir[a]	
sc. 2: Garden by the Fountain	sc. 2: Garden by the Fountain (cut)	
Act IV, sc. 1: Boris's Death	Act IV, sc. 1: Kromy Forest	Act III, sc. 1: Kromy Forest
sc. 2: Kromy Forest	sc. 2: Boris's Death	sc. 2: Boris's Death

a omitted by Diaghilev

In 1908 the same journal took scant notice of Musorgsky's opera, devoting only a single paragraph of about 200 words to it.

Examination of the box office receipts also fails to confirm the assertion that the house was "practically sold out" at each of the seven performances. The arithmetic average of the seven nights' receipts was 26,340 francs. Four of the performances brought in receipts above this average, three below. The final performance generated the highest receipts: 29,992 francs, 60 centimes. The third produced the lowest: 20,213 francs exactly.[70] These figures suggest that Arnold Haskell's evaluation of the production is near the truth. He writes:

Boris was a success, but by no means the immediate and striking triumph that the Russians had expected. The first performance was crowded with an elegant public, but for the next two or three there were many gaps, and it was only at the last two . . . that the work was fully appreciated.[71]

Soon after the performances, several French critics attacked Rimsky's redaction, basing their criticism on examination of Musorgsky's piano–vocal score of 1874, copies of which Diaghilev had given them in compensation for his failure to produce the composer's score. In these polemics are the origins of what came to be called the "Musorgsky problem": a group of questions concerning the composer's technical ability, the propriety of the revision of his music by other musicians long after his death, and the relative merits of original and revised versions. For example, Gaston Carraud writes:

Rimsky-Korsakov's alterations are the most needless, incomprehensible, and revolting thing ever done in a similar line. Like an insect pest, he has gnawed away every characteristic detail in the work – everything that struck him as irregular because he was incapable of penetrating its logic.[72]

Many other critics expressed similar views in other publications, but none of them, of course, was able to base his opinion on familiarity with the composer's version in the theater or even on examination of his full score.

Despite the indignation of critics such as Carraud, few members of the public at Paris, indeed at any performance of the work in this era, seem concerned with Rimsky's participation in Boris. After all, when Newmarch implies that the orchestration heard at Paris was Musorgsky's own,[73] and when Calvocoressi, an acknowledged authority on Russian music, minimizes the significance of the revisions,[74] why should ordinary theatergoers protest? Indeed, concerning a subsequent performance, in Russia, we have the evaluation of just such an ordinary theatergoer, Eugene Simpson, an American music lover who traveled in Russia in 1910 and 1912 as correspondent for the *Musical Courier*. His remarks suggest that he enjoyed *Boris Godunov* without being the least aware of the dimensions of Rimsky's involvement in it:

The opera otherwise includes impressive choruses, *unceasing invention for the orchestra*, beautiful numbers for the vocal principals, and the whole in a wide range of mood, as of the sad, of Oriental or barbaric, ecclesiastic, and of Russian folk . . . Only once, late in the evening, *is there a bit of Wagnerian color brought out by the cellos, before the beginning of the polonaise*. As this opera was first given in 1874, when the composer was thirty-five years old, *it is not improbable that he had already observed something of the Wagnerian instrumentation* [all italics added].[75]

Quite apart from critical polemics and public indifference to them, the fact remains that Rimsky's edition was Diaghilev's only practical choice. When the idea of staging *Boris* first arose, Calvocoressi had attempted to convince him to produce the opera in Musorgsky's own scoring, but the impresario declined to do so, arguing that his singers knew the opera only in Rimsky-Korsakov's version and that they would be "not only unwilling, but positively unable to learn the genuine text."[76] Of perhaps equal importance was the simple problem of where to obtain performing materials for the composer's version, a matter that brings us to yet another issue in the polemic surrounding the opera. So long as Rimsky's version was the only one easily available in both score and parts, there was little hope that Musorgsky's would dislodge it from the repertory.[77] Critics might argue for the authentic version with all the zeal of a crusader defending a piece of the True Cross, but in the end something has to be put on the music stands, and neither Diaghilev nor any other performer could control the commercial decisions of Musorgsky's publisher. Indeed, it seems likely that already by 1908 Diaghilev would have found it quite difficult, though perhaps not impossible, simply to procure score and parts of Musorgsky's orchestration. Consider the problems.

In 1874, when *Boris* was staged at the Maryinsky Theater in St. Petersburg, Musorgsky sold the rights to his opera to V. Bessel & Co., and Bessel then apparently prepared for hire, in accordance with standard publisher's practice, full score and parts that coincided with the firm's published piano–vocal score.[78] In 1896 Bessel published both full and piano–vocal scores of Rimsky-Korsakov's revision of *Boris* and then attempted to divest himself of the remaining manuscript copies of Musorgsky's score by selling them for whatever he could get. Thus in the firm's catalog of 1898, in the section devoted to full scores of operas, one finds two listings for *Boris*. One is for the full score of Rimsky's redaction of 1896; the other reads as follows: "*Boris Godunov*, opera in five acts. Libretto according to Pushkin and

Karamzin (full orchestral score in manuscript, price by agreement)."[79] The designation of the opera as in five acts, the phrase "libretto according to Pushkin and Karamzin," and the fact that this score was in manuscript all suggest a rental score prepared in the 1870s, at the time of the premiere. We do not know whether all copies of this score were sold, but in a catalog issued after 1908, the entry no longer appears.[80] Thus, Diaghilev might have been unable to obtain the authentic score and parts from the publisher simply because Bessel, having chosen to replace Musorgsky's score with Rimsky's, no longer had copies himself. And even if Diaghilev had had access to Musorgsky's holograph, most of which lay in the library of the Maryinsky Theater, he could not have used it or copied it without the publisher's consent. An agreement concluded by Bessel and the Imperial Theaters in June of 1874 prohibited the Theaters from issuing to anyone copies from full scores constituting Bessel's property without his permission.[81] Perhaps the firm would have granted permission; perhaps, having scrapped Musorgsky's score and invested in Rimsky's, they would have encouraged the latter's use (and popularization). In any event, it would not have been easy for Diaghilev to have produced the original – without calling on the aid of the Grand Duke – even if he had wanted to try.[82]

Apparently he did *not* want to try. Calvocoressi maintains that he "neither knew nor cared" whether performance materials for the composer's score were available.[83] The production itself demonstrates that his conception of the opera emphasized spectacle and brilliance; perhaps finding Rimsky's view of *Boris* closer than Musorgsky's to his own, Diaghilev may have seen no reason to wrestle with the problems of producing the composer's score. In addition, like most Russian musicians of the time, Diaghilev had no axe to grind over Rimsky's revision. (One must discount heavily his latter-day description of Rimsky's score as a "disastrous enterprise which should never have been attempted."[84] The impresario was never one to display himself in an unfavorable light, and by the year 1928, when that statement was written, one of the most fashionable stances in music was for "authentic" Musorgsky.) His performers knew only Rimsky's version, belief in the inviolability of a composer's text was not as strong in 1908 as it is today, and few in the audience were even aware of the issue. Rimsky's score clearly was the logical choice. Moreover, as his friend Nouvel has indicated, Diaghilev was ever ready to alter *any* composer's score in order to produce a powerful theatrical impression. Our final task is to consider whether he indeed achieved in *Boris* the effectiveness he had been seeking.

Diaghilev apparently viewed the opera as the story of the struggle for power between Boris and Dmitry. As noted above, he presented only seven scenes in an order of his own devising. His arrangement, omitting both the scene at the inn and the scene in Marina's boudoir, reversing the order of the Coronation and Cell scenes, and placing the scene by the fountain ahead of the scene in the Tsar's quarters, would seem to emphasize the interconnected destinies of the two rulers. In each act we see first a scene concerning the Pretender's fortunes, ever rising, and then one concerning Boris's, ever falling. Thus, in Act I, after the introductory folk *tableau* at Novodevichy Monastery, we see first the Pretender as a poor monk in Pimen's cell and then Boris in the splendor of his coronation. The second act reveals that the Pretender has obtained support from Poland and that Boris is going mad. The third act shows the Pretender's victory and Boris's death. The people, in Diaghilev's scheme, serve primarily as the backdrop against which this game of power is played.

Diaghilev's cuts, despite the serious objections one may advance against them, do serve to lessen the sense of diffuseness which this episodic opera can sometimes produce, particularly upon non-Russian audiences. Though attractive musically, such passages as Feodor's "Song of the Parrot" and Pimen's narrative about the tsars who reigned before Boris (both omitted at Paris) are unnecessary to the plot. By omitting the scene in Marina's boudoir and curtailing the Fountain scene, Diaghilev lost the Jesuit Rangoni entirely. He thus sacrificed one of the most subtle of Musorgsky's transformations of Pushkin (as we shall see in Chapter 8), but he may have reasoned that a foreign audience acquainted with the conventions of operatic intrigue would understand the relationship between Marina and Dmitry well enough without Rangoni. As for the loss of the Inn scene, together with the details it adds concerning the Pretender's escape from Russia, perhaps Diaghilev felt that it was enough to see that he *had* escaped – fate willed it – and had established himself among the Polish nobles, thereby beginning his climb toward Boris's throne. (In 1913, when the opera was revived in Paris and then brought to London, the Inn scene replaced the Fountain scene. Either arrangement results in a second act in which we see first the Pretender gaining ground, then Boris losing it.)

The sequence of scenes chosen by Diaghilev also has a logic of its own. In reversing the order of the two final scenes, he was simply following faithfully Rimsky's score of 1896. As we saw above, Rimsky himself had recommended such a change in 1876, when the Russian Imperial Theaters began regularly to omit the Kromy scene on the grounds that the opera properly should end with Boris's death. Rimsky had argued then that it was perfectly logical for the uprising in Kromy forest chronologically to precede Boris's death and that reversing the order of the scenes was preferable to omitting one of them entirely. It is equally possible, as Diaghilev apparently noticed, for the scene by the fountain to precede the scene in the Tsar's quarters. The only link between them is Shuisky's declaration, in the latter, that a pretender has arisen in Lithuania. It is not unreasonable, however, to see this pretender before we hear of his activities.

Perhaps Diaghilev's most controversial transposition was his inversion of the Coronation and Cell scenes. Nadezhda Rimskaya-Korsakova, the composer's wife, expresses a point of view encountered often in the literature of the time. She writes: "To present the scene in Pimen's cell between the scene of Boris's refusal [of the crown] and that of his acceptance and coronation is absurd: how could Pimen write of Tsar Boris in his chronicle when Boris was not yet tsar?"[85] To an audience well-schooled in Pushkin, there can be no question that this is a serious breach, for Pushkin clearly indicates that the events of the prologue occurred in 1598, the Cell scene in 1603. But Musorgsky omitted the year 1603 from his stage directions for the Cell scene, and Diaghilev took advantage of this circumstance to arrange the first three scenes in what to him was a more effective order for an audience that was largely ignorant of the fine points of Russian literature and history. He later rebutted the criticism of his "absurd" chronology by arguing that he had made inquiries and had learned it was "chronologically possible" for the Coronation scene to follow the Cell scene.[86] And history bears him out in the following particulars. As noted in chapter 1, the historical Boris Godunov was offered the crown in February of 1598, maneuvered to consolidate his position throughout the summer, and celebrated his coronation only in September. To an audience that did not know its Pushkin, if not to Mme. Rimskaya-Korsakova, Pimen could easily be represented at work during the summer preceding Boris's formal coronation.

What then can we conclude about this production? In a more nearly perfect world, perhaps Diaghilev would have presented Musorgsky's own final version of the opera, and, as Calvocoressi puts it, "Musorgsky's music would have carried the day without the help of palliatives."[87] Largely for practical reasons, but perhaps partly for legal reasons as well, he was unable to do this. Setting aside Musorgsky's versions, then, and thinking only of arrangements prepared by other artists, we find that Diaghilev's was surprisingly effective. Sacrificing from Rimsky's edition only two scenes (the Inn and Marina's Boudoir), the impresario created a version of Boris notable for its directness, brevity, and balance between the two main characters. Thinking of his French audience, he minimized the episodic nature of the work by cutting extraneous material, no matter how charming, and by placing the dramatic core of each act in a pair of scenes – the first devoted to the Pretender and the second to Boris. Finally, he provided the title character with three superbly effective "curtain" scenes.

In a letter to Rimsky-Korsakov concerning that composer's *Sadko*, Diaghilev described his stance in the sentence: "The question is not of cuts, but rather of remodeling."[88] But remodeling, once one decides to do it, can be done either badly or well. This production thus was paradigmatic in yet another sense – transcending singing style, sets, costumes, and *mise-en-scène*. In revamping the opera, Diaghilev anticipated modern producers and stage directors, who to this day continue to second-guess Musorgsky in such matters as version, orchestration, scene sequence, and cuts. Unlike many of them, however, he created a version of *Boris Godunov* which retains both logic and clarity, qualities that arrangements pretending to greater authenticity have sometimes failed to achieve. "We've done something tonight," Chaliapin told Diaghilev as they returned to their hotel after the premiere, "I don't know what, but we've really done something!"[89]

PART II

ENTR'ACTE

6

BORIS AND THE CENSOR: DOCUMENTS

In Russia under the Old Regime, as under the Soviets, there was both positive and negative censorship: that is, Russian subjects were instructed *what* to do as well as informed of what they could not do. The frequent legal result, as we saw in Chapter 5 with Pushkin's *Boris*, was the assumption that everything not explicitly permitted was thereby prohibited. The starting point was cultural unfreedom; thus the peculiar sense we have that the censorship documents in this chapter often enable the artist largely by waiving restrictions.

One of the most serious censorship problems with *Boris Godunov* – play or opera – was the appearance in it of churchmen. According to the Imperial Law Code of 1857, "At domestic theaters it is forbidden to dress in monastic or ecclesiastical garments and to walk along the street in these or other theatrical garments." [1]

This prohibition is also to be found in the law codes of 1845, 1842, and 1832, and may be traced to the following edict of the Empress Elizabeth, dated 21 December 1750:

Concerning permission to have evening parties with decorous music for amusement at home, and concerning a prohibition to walk or drive along the street in indecent clothes.

Her Imperial Majesty is pleased to indicate, according to petitions of local citizens, who want to have evening parties with decorous music for the amusement of an honest company, or Russian comedies for the present forthcoming holiday, that permission is given to them in this, and prohibition not put in the way, only with such confirmations that at these parties there will occur no disorders, actions contrary to law, noise, or fights of any sort, likewise at Russian comedies they will not dress up in black garments or other garments having to do with ecclesiastical persons, nor will they walk or drive along the street in such attire or in other attire appropriate to comedies. [2]

Punishment for violation of this prohibition, in 1857, was a fine of from 10 to 100 rubles.

Alexander Pushkin completed his play *Boris Godunov* in 1825. In the autumn of 1826, he was ordered to submit it directly to the Emperor Nicholas I, who had appointed himself Pushkin's personal censor. Nicholas apparently did not read the play, but forwarded it to a subordinate, Faddey Bulgarin (a minor novelist, cutthroat journalist and the personal butt of Pushkin's scorn), who prepared the first censor's report on the work, "Remarks on the Comedy of Tsar Boris and Grishka Otrepiev":

> In this play there is nothing complete: it is separate scenes, better to say excerpts, from the tenth and eleventh volumes of *History of the Russian State*, by Karamzin, transcribed into *conversations* and *scenes* ...
>
> Characters, events, opinions – everything is founded on the work of Karamzin, everything is borrowed from there. To the author of this comedy belong only the narrative, and the disposition of action on stage ... The spirit of the entire work is monarchical, for nowhere are introduced visions of freedom, as in other works of the author ... The literary merit [of the play] is much lower than we expected. This is not an imitation of Shakespeare, Goethe, or Schiller; for with these poets, in works compiled from various epochs, one always finds coherence and wholeness in stage plays. In Pushkin there are conversations that remind one of the dialogue of Walter Scott. It would seem as though these pages are dragged out of a novel by Walter Scott ...
>
> Several places must be excluded without fail. [Bulgarin cites six such places in all, of which no. 5 has particular interest to students of Musorgsky's opera.] ... No. 5: The scene at the inn must be softened; the monks are portrayed in too dissolute a guise. The proverb "Each to his own taste, and safety is mine," is changed to "Each to his own taste, and drinking is mine." Although these monks have in fact run away from the monastery, and although this circumstance is found in Karamzin, nonetheless it seems this same depravity and debauch must necessarily be ennobled in poetry, especially with respect to the vocation of monks.
>
> [...] Besides these exclusions and amendments [i.e., the six passages], it seems there is no obstacle to the printing of the play. *It goes without saying that it cannot and must not be performed, for we do not allow the patriarch and monks to appear on the stage* [emphasis added].[3]

Although Nicholas probably did not read all of Pushkin's tragedy, Bulgarin's remark concerning Walter Scott seems to have lingered in memory. On 14 December 1826, Alexander Benckendorff, Head of the Third Section (the Russian secret police of the day), wrote to Pushkin: "I had the joy of presenting to His Majesty the Emperor your comedy about Tsar Boris and Grishka Otrepiev. His Majesty deigned to read through it with great pleasure and wrote the following in his own hand on the note which I had presented to him on the subject: 'I believe that Mr. Pushkin's goal would be fulfilled if, *with the necessary refinement*, he were to transform his comedy into a historical tale or novel, on the lines of Walter Scott.' I am notifying you of this Imperial remark and, returning your work along with it, consider it my duty to add that the places which attracted the attention of His Majesty and which demand a certain refinement are noted in the manuscript itself and consist of short excerpts enclosed with it."[4]

In 1831, Nicholas I permitted the play's publication. But in tsarist Russia approval for publication by no means implied approval for performance. Material to be read in private did not have to meet the more rigid restrictions applied to material to be performed in public. Thus, just two years after Nicholas permitted the play to be printed, censor Evstafy Oldekop denied a request to perform only one scene, the Polish scene by the fountain, even though it contains none of the passages cited by Bulgarin – *de facto* proof of a two-tiered system.

> Forbidden / 23 March 1833 / No. 89 / Night, The Garden, The Fountain / An excerpt from *Boris Godunov* by A. S. Pushkin / For the Moscow Imperial Theater. [Censor's report in French:]
> Monsieur Pushkin, in creating his *Boris Godunov*, had wished to create a stage play. His Majesty the Emperor not having authorized it, the author has published his work in the form of detached historical scenes. Since the decision of His Imperial Majesty clearly shows that this play must not be represented on the stage, I have refused to accept all the excerpts from this book that the actors of St. Petersburg had for the Imperial Theater in Moscow. [The play] must be suppressed. [Signed] Evstafy Oldekop.[5]

We come now to the celebrated prohibition of 1837, a single sentence whose effect on nineteenth-century Russian opera was profound:

> This is to inform Gedeonov that His Majesty permits the production of Rosen's drama *The Daughter of Ivan III* and, in the future, the acceptance of dramas and tragedies, but not operas, in which are represented on stage Russian tsars who ruled before the Romanovs, but excluding those who have been canonized, as for example, Alexander Nevsky.[6]

Plainly forbidding the representation of *any* tsar on stage in opera, the ruling was issued by Nicholas I in 1837 in response to a request for clarification of his position concerning the depiction of tsars in theatrical productions. Uncertain about whether to proceed with the staging of Baron Georgy Rosen's drama *The Daughter of Ivan III*, Alexander Mikhailovich Gedeonov, the Director of the Imperial Theaters, wrote to Prince P. M. Volkonsky, the Minister of the Court, for guidance. (The Director already had received assurances from the Minister of Education that the play could be staged, but ever the cautious bureaucrat, he went to higher authority to learn whether the minister of Education's "view corresponds to that of the Emperor.") Prince Volkonsky placed the above resolution on Gedeonov's letter and returned it to him.

The prohibition was never published formally as law but had the effect of law nonetheless. Rimsky-Korsakov was obliged to secure an exemption from it in order to stage *The Maid of Pskov*. Musorgsky was obliged to secure an exemption from it in order to produce *Boris Godunov* (see below). And because of this single sentence, he would have been unable to bring on stage in *Khovanshchina* the figure of Peter the Great even if he had wanted to do so.

Four years after the death of Nicholas I, who had steadfastly refused to permit any portion of Pushkin's play to reach the stage, another attempt was made to secure the performance of the Fountain scene. If the organizers of this attempt hoped that the censor's attitude had softened under the new tsar, Alexander II, they hoped in vain. This request also was refused. The full text of the censor's report follows; it is perhaps most remarkable for its total omission of any reasons for the suppression of the performance.

Forbidden / 30 October 1859 / Adjutant General Timashev / No. 464 / A Scene from the Drama / Boris Godunov / by A. S. Pushkin. / For the Imperial Theaters.

This scene, drawn from Pushkin's drama *Boris Godunov*, contains the secret rendezvous of Dmitry the Pretender with Marina Mniszech, scheduled by her at night in the garden by the fountain. At this rendezvous, Dmitry reveals to his proud beloved that he is not tsarevich, but a poor monk, and together with this, tells her of his ambitious hopes, but Marina promises him her hand only under the condition that he achieve the tsardom of Muscovy.[7]

In 1862 a group of amateurs requested permission to perform the scene by the fountain. They too failed to secure approval, on the grounds that the scene had been examined just three years earlier and prohibited!

On the basis of the resolution / of the year 1859, FORBIDDEN / 12 December 1862 / Iv. Nordström / No. 305 / A Scene from the Drama / Boris Godunov / by A. S. Pushkin. / For performance by amateurs in St. Petersburg.

This scene was under the scrutiny of the censorship before, in 1859, and was forbidden for performance. [Signed] E. Keiser.[8]

The long-awaited change finally occurred in 1866, the result of an earlier period of *glasnost* in Russian history following the reforms of Alexander II. Even so there were still to be prohibitions and exclusions.

Pushkin's *Boris Godunov* at last has been approved for production. Until this time it was forbidden fruit for the Russian stage. The play will appear in Petersburg in the fall. The Directorate has decided to present it with every possible splendor. Costumes and sets supposedly will be new.[9]

The persons of the patriarch, of the abbot, and of monks in general, as well as monastery rites and all attributes of ecclesiastic and monastic rank, are to be excluded from the text of the play.[10]

With the removal of the ban on staging Pushkin's drama *Boris Godunov*, a formidable obstacle was removed from the path of anyone contemplating a musical setting of this play. Although the prohibitions against the appearance of ecclesiastics remained in effect, shrewd construction of the libretto could easily eliminate most of them, and clever staging might do the rest.

Pushkin's play was performed on 17 September 1870. All the scenes incorporated by Musorgsky in his libretto were performed with one exception, Pushkin's Coronation scene, which was omitted because of the appearance in it of the Patriarch. Musorgsky had addressed this obvious problem by rewriting Pushkin's text so that Boris addresses his monologue to God, rather than to the Patriarch standing beside him. Thus, what certain critics sanctimoniously have characterized as a garbling of Pushkin's holy writ was in fact a deliberate reshaping of text calculated to avoid the suppression of this most regal means of introducing the title character.

The only obstacle now in the composer's path was the long-standing prohibition against the representation of any tsar in opera, a policy that originated, as we have seen, in a note jotted down on the back of a letter in 1837 [see above]. Solving this problem seems to have been merely a formality, but nonetheless the papers had to drift up through the bureaucracy and then drift back down. Here is the report of the censor for dramatic works, Keiser von Nilkheim, dated 7 March 1872:

The content of this opera is adapted from Pushkin, with the preservation of several scenes and verses but with the removal, in general, of the clergy: there appears on stage neither the patriarch, the abbot, nor the other clerical characters with the exception of Pimen. As a literary object, the libretto, deviating significantly of course from its chosen model, is a mutilation of Pushkin; and in these very deviations the historical characters of the original are vulgarized. Furthermore, the end of the opera is incoherent and compressed to an extreme degree. But in opera even a poor libretto, in the presence of good music, has its merits. From the censor's point of view, there would be no existing difficulties if only it were not forbidden by Imperial decree of 1837 to introduce tsars on stage. In view of the stated obvious musical virtues of the opera *Boris Godunov* and in view of previous examples, as well as the recent Imperial permission to examine the opera *The Maid of Pskov* (which had been forbidden by the aforementioned Imperial decree of 1837), the Council *decides* to leave to the discretion of the Minister of Internal Affairs whether His High Excellency would like to solicit for Imperial permission to produce the present opera on stage.[11]

Von Nilkheim's report served as the basis for the following recommendation of the chief of the Bureau for Printed Materials, Ministry of Internal Affairs, dated 31 March 1872:

> From the censor's point of view, the present opera presents no difficulties; from the artistic point of view, it is noted for especial musical merits, according to the testimony of specialists in music. In consideration of this, and being influenced by the following list of similar operas which already have been given Imperial authorization for production (*Ruslan and Lyudmila*, *The Battle of Kulikovo*, *Rogneda*, and *The Maid of Pskov*), and with the aim of encouraging authors to create operas on historical subjects, I, in agreement with the Council of the Bureau for Printed Materials would presume the possibility at the present time of authorizing the production of this opera, *Boris Godunov*, on the stage.[12]

On 5 April 1872, the Emperor Alexander II approved the production. By the end of the month, notification of his approval had come down through the bureaucracy, and on 29 April the Maryinsky Theater's literary committee authorized the opera for production. Exactly one week later, on 6 May, the music committee probably accepted the opera for production, at least provisionally. (See above, Chapter 4, pp. 81–85.)

The new censorship law, promulgated by Alexander II in 1865, required that published works of fewer than ten printer's sheets (80 pages in quarto, 160 in octavo) be submitted to the censorship for scrutiny and approval prior to publication.[13] Works longer than ten printer's sheets were freed from preliminary censorship, but were subject to prosecution after printing if the government found them in violation of the law. The first edition of the libretto, published in February of 1873 to coincide with the performance of three scenes from the opera, had to be submitted and approved since it contained only 68 pages octavo. There follows a diplomatic copy of both recto and verso of the title page of this libretto:

> [Recto:] *Boris Godunov* / Opera in four acts with a prologue / by M. Musorgsky / Compiled according to Pushkin and Karamzin / by M. Musorgsky / Price 50 silver kopecks / Property of the publisher for all nations / St. Petersburg, V. Bessel and Co. / Copies from full scores of operas constituting the property of the music / publisher V. Bessel and Co., in accordance with agreements with their authors, / must be obtained

from the publisher; copies of full scores obtained / in other ways will be prosecuted as illegitimate.

[Verso:] Passed by the censor, St. Petersburg, 25 January 1873.[14]

Copies of the first printed edition of the piano–vocal score contain no additional censor's approval, apparently for two reasons. First, as a volume of 250 pages quarto, the piano–vocal score was not subject to preliminary censorship. Second, quite apart from any considerations of length and format, the law gave the publisher one year to print the work under the approval of 25 January 1873.[15] The piano–vocal score of *Boris* "came out of the press" on 15 January 1874, just in the nick of time.[16]

7

THE OPERA THROUGH THE YEARS:
SELECTED TEXTS IN CRITICISM

The premiere

(VLADIMIR STASOV, CÉSAR CUI, HERMANN LAROCHE,
NIKOLAY STRAKHOV, ARSENY GOLENISHCHEV-KUTUZOV)

Vladimir Vasilievich Stasov (1824–1906), art and music critic, cultural historian and polemicist for the New Russian School of Music, was one of Musorgsky's closest friends and advisers. (It was Stasov who coined the phrase *Moguchaya kuchka* or "Mighty Handful" for the five composers of the nationalist school.) A passionate advocate of *Boris Godunov*, Stasov cooled toward Musorgsky in the latter half of the 1870s, finding in *Khovanshchina* – an opera for which Stasov offered much advice, most of it ignored – a falling-off of talent. Nevertheless Stasov was fierce in condemning the Imperial Theater Committee for its reluctance to stage Musorgsky's work, and until the end of his life he championed, often narrowly and stridently, the musical innovations of Glinka, Dargomyzhsky, and the "Handful" against the academic practice of Anton Rubinstein and the official conservatories.

[1881] Musorgsky followed the text of Pushkin's drama closely in only a few places. For all its many beautiful features, that dramatic text could not be transmitted completely nor in its entirety, since it is comprised for the most part of scenes that are excessively short and too compressed (a misapplied imitation of Shakespeare). Musorgsky composed most of the text himself. Later, people (especially the worst music critics) reproached him severely for this, not understanding that there was nothing else he could have done. Musorgsky had at his disposal neither Pushkin himself nor even some mediocre versifier; and even if he had, doubtless he would have had a terrible time with him (as happened earlier with Glinka and Dargomyzhsky, who were also obliged to insert quite a few of their own verses into librettos adapted from Pushkin). It is worth noting that Musorgsky, although not a poet by profession, wrote for *Boris Godunov* – as for many of his previously composed romances – a good number of talented and poetic verses, full of power, conciseness, precision, expressiveness, and rich imagery. At the same time, true to the system he had tested in *The Marriage*, Musorgsky composed music directly to prose, in this instance to Pushkin's prose in one place and to his own in another. And the music did not suffer in the least because of it; on the contrary, the music sometimes won. Generally speaking, our profound art critics did not notice that Musorgsky, of all those composers who set their own texts, wrote verse and prose far better than the others (including, of course, Berlioz with his pompous verses and prose, and Wagner with his insufferably pretentious and befogged rhetoric). [. . .]

The opera *Boris Godunov*, which achieved its full and final form after the reworkings and additions of 1870–1871 [sic], is one of the most powerful works not only of Russian but of all European art. The common people are portrayed here in forms of truth and realism such as no one had ever attempted before (in Dargomyzhsky's *Stone Guest*, the people do not appear on stage at all). [. . .] The monks Varlaam and Misail, the innkeeper, the Tsarevich's nurse, the border police, the holy fool, and finally the many nameless people in the folk scenes and especially the popular masses of peasant men and women in the first and last acts – all these are types quite unprecedented in opera, both in Russia and throughout Europe. Compared with them, even the best popular choruses of Meyerbeer (to say nothing of Glinka or Wagner) are idealized, impersonal, conventionalized, and not national in spirit. The closeness to reality that we find in Musorgsky's music one can find only in the best folk scenes of [the prosewriters and playwrights] Gogol and Ostrovsky. In those scenes Musorgsky is indisputably their equal. A grasp of history, a profound rendering of the innumerable nuances of the people's spirit, of their mood, intelligence and stupidity, strength and weakness, tragic quality and humor – all this is unparalleled in Musorgsky. The people, as submissive and stupid as sheep, electing Boris to the throne under the policeman's cudgel, and then, as soon as the policeman has moved away, fully ready to turn their humor against themselves (Act I); a crowd of people gathered from all parts of Russia, inflicting savage reprisals on their domestic and foreign enemies, on their cruel superiors, and on Catholic Jesuits, but first viciously playing with their victim and mocking him; the vicious and greedy Varlaam with the police officers at the Inn; the humble monk Pimen, a chronicler and pious soul, a genuinely epic Russian personality – what profound, authentic historical pictures these are! And what deeply truthful Russian speech one hears from all these Mityukhs, Fomkas, Epifans, holy fool Ivanyches and Afimyas, innkeepers, bands of little rascals and dozens of other nameless persons! What Russian voice intonations! With good reason did the historian Kostomarov, who had studied well the Russian people's Time of Troubles, exclaim in ecstasy to the author after seeing and hearing *Boris Godunov* on the stage: "This is like a page from history!" [...] No other results were possible from a person, and from an artist, as truly "of the people" as Musorgsky was. [...]

I cannot analyze here all the perfections of this opera, but I firmly believe that as the artistic and historical intelligence of our society grows, the more frequently and deeply will people study this masterpiece, one of the greatest pearls of Russian nationalist art. If the Germans study the operas of Wagner, which seem to them truly national and great, so painstakingly and with such love and attention to detail, then the same should be expected for Musorgsky's opera in the future – for it is an opera not seemingly but authentically, equivalently national, historical, and infinitely truthful in its every turn of speech, phrase, and word.[1]

César Antonovich Cui (1835–1918), of French-Lithuanian parentage and by profession a military man, was both the weakest musician among the Nationalist composers and their most prolific publicist. Over his long life he composed fifteen operas, more than two hundred songs, several dozen choruses, orchestral music, and three string quartets – as well as a huge body of music criticism for leading Petersburg newspapers and journals. Almost none of his music is remembered, but the assessments he penned of his fellow composers, a curious mix of patronizing narrow-mindedness and astute insight, were very influential in their time. His judgments have continued to echo in Musorgsky studies (at times uncritically), for he had a gift for turning any utterance into an instant "classic opinion." Throughout his writings, wearily authoritative repetition of first impressions – such as the contention below that the Polish scenes mix "wonderful inspired episodes" with "feeble phrases" – contributed to confirming Musorgsky as a brilliant eccentric and musical incompetent among both music professionals and members of the composer's own circle. As noted in Chapter 5, an element of envy cannot be ruled out. Although Cui considered himself more talented than Musorgsky or Rimsky, his own mediocre opera *William Ratcliff* had failed with both critics and public in 1869, and was removed from repertory at Cui's own request.

On 5 February 1873, three scenes from *Boris* – the Inn and the two Polish scenes – were performed at the *bénéfice* of Gennady Kondratiev, Chief Director of the Maryinsky Theater. Reviews were favorable, and public enthusiasm was high. The lengthy review by Cui excerpted here appeared several days after the performance, and called for a full performance of *Boris* as soon as possible. Cui's opening comparison of Musorgsky with Rimsky-Korsakov (interesting for its relevance to Rimsky's subsequent "editings" of *Boris*) was doubtless occasioned by the fact that the latter's *Maid of Pskov* had received its premiere a month earlier, on 1 January 1873.

[1873] Before I say anything about [these scenes], I remind the reader that we are not speaking here of the whole opera *Boris Godunov* but only of three excerpts from it; *Boris* in its entirety might turn out to be more remarkable than these excerpts, or perhaps weaker. [. . .]

Musorgsky, like [Rimsky-]Korsakov, is one of the most talented representatives of the New Russian Opera School; [but] by their natures and talents the two men are diametrically opposed to one another. Korsakov is primarily a symphonist, Musorgsky primarily a vocal composer; [. . .] Korsakov is so much the musician that for the sake of well-rounded form and the musical development of the phrase he is sometimes capable of not attending sufficiently to scenic demands or dramatic truth; Musorgsky is so much the dramatic composer that, satisfying himself with a truthful expression of the word, with irreproachable declamation and an accurate communication of the scenic situation, he sometimes is capable of not paying proper attention to the quality of his music.

The scene in the inn at the Lithuanian border follows Pushkin with only the most insignificant changes: here and there a phrase is omitted, which would have slowed down the musical speechline, here and there a word is left out, here and there one word substituted for another for the sake of rounding out the musical phrase. [. . .] All these insignificant changes are reasonable and legitimate, since Pushkin wrote his *Boris* not as an opera text. [. . .]

The music of this whole scene is astonishingly good. It is written in the style of *The Stone Guest* and is worthy of the music of *The Stone Guest*. [. . .] The music fuses with the text to such a degree that having heard the phrases it is no longer possible to separate the text from the music; in all these phrases there are infinite resources of typicality, of rhythmic and, once again I repeat, of melodic wealth. [Here Cui inserts a footnote: "To this day, many hidebound conservatives acknowledge as melodies only crude Italian eight measure cantilenas, and for these people recitative phrases are not melody. But melody is musical thought; any form is good for its expression. Not to acknowledge melody in recitative phrases is like not acknowledging the presence of thought in ordinary, brief conversational speech and assuming that thought is confined solely to complex Karamzinian constructions. And all the while it is clear that short, concise speech rich in content and ideas produces a much stronger impression than if the same thoughts were expressed in diffuse constructions, garnished by many superfluous words for the sake of the roundedness of the form and the fluid flow of speech."] [. . .]

Everyone knows how good the Inn scene is in Pushkin, how vividly it is played on stage. With Musorgsky's music the scene produces an even stronger impression. [...]

In the scenes at the Mniszechs', [however,] Musorgsky departed from Pushkin; both scenes – in Marina's chambers and at the fountain – are done in an entirely different way. In Pushkin these scenes are too rational, and poorly suited for music. [...] It is apparent that in its basic plan this [Polish] act, when compared to the Inn scene, is weaker and more coarse. To many this may seem paradoxical, that scenes with drunken monks are more subtle than scenes at a noble magnate's house. But after all, the most elegant subjects can be expressed crudely, and vice versa. A certain relative crudeness of conception in this act is revealed in the poorly motivated polonaise: Mniszech's guests enter and exit the stage solely so that Musorgsky may provide his public with the opportunity to hear his sparkling polonaise, and the Pretender exits and enters in order not to get in its way. The character of the Jesuit and his appearance at the very end of the act also seem somewhat stilted and melodramatic. [...]

The other scenes – Marina with the Jesuit and the Pretender with the Jesuit and Marina – are written not entirely evenly; there are wonderful inspired episodes but also feeble phrases, with the melody insufficiently defined, which lapse in two or three places into completely meaningless sounds. [...] I point out one technical failing: the Jesuit has too many words. Thus they are hardly audible and their rapid pronunciation is registered negatively on the strength of the voice. (To listen to *Boris*, one must have a libretto in hand.) [...]

Boris is orchestrated with great talent. If in places the orchestration reveals a certain technical inexperience – which expresses itself primarily in a constant thickness of color, in a massiveness unfavorable at times to soloists, and in an excessively frequent use of pizzicato – nevertheless there is much independence, creative craftsmanship, and completely new effects in it. Especially new and noteworthy in *Boris* is the use of the brass, even the trumpets, in soft places, which gives the sound a special roundness and beauty. The orchestration of *Boris* is purely operatic, colorful throughout, and thoroughly effective; the personalities of the characters and the dramatic situation are marvelously set off by it. [...]

And so the New Russian Opera School has been enriched by one more splendid work. The school arose only recently and has already given us such operas as *The Stone Guest*, *The Maid of Pskov*, *Boris Godunov*. [...] This new movement is being reproached for its supposedly destructive intentions. The reproach is completely unfounded: the new movement is not destroying but trying to broaden the realm of music, to blaze new paths, to add new thoughts, new forms, new sources for musical enjoyment to those that we already have.[2]

[Cui's obituary of the composer, 1881] Few have been the composers with so distinctive a set of characteristics, so sharply-etched an individuality, as the just deceased Musorgsky. Few have been the composers whose works were distinguished by such highly artistic qualities and by such powerful shortcomings as Musorgsky's. His nature, talented to the highest degree, generously endowed with the abundant gifts necessary for musical creativity, at the same time contained a certain anti-musical ferment often and unpleasantly appearing in his creations. I will not presume to judge whether this strange mixture is met in other areas of art, but in music Musorgsky is not the only example of such an incomprehensible, abnormal phenomenon [Cui mentions in this context Berlioz, Dargomyzhsky, and Serov]. [...] As an opera composer Musorgsky belonged to a group of musicians known under the mocking names "the Handful" and "the Gang" – names that have today completely lost their caustic ring.

[Cui then lists four principles common to the group's musical aesthetics:]

Opera music must be good music. Strange as this might seem, opera composers always ignore this principle with astonishing boldness. In no other sort of music can one find as much banality, repetitions, straight-out copying, slavish imitations. Things that would be intolerable in symphonic music receive full rights of citizenship in operatic music. An opera with three or four successful scenes and, excepting these, filled to overflowing with trivial and vacuous sounds, enjoys glory and success. The New Russian Opera School too highly honors the sanctity of art to allow that; it strives to achieve operatic music that is "musical" through and through. *Fear of the past* and of platitude is perhaps the most characteristic trait of this school.

Vocal music must strictly correspond to the meaning of the text. Again, an elementary rule that is violated at every step by opera composers, who have so often forced their heroes to suffer and die against the background of happy dance tunes. The New School strives for a fusion of two great arts, poetry and music; it desires for the two arts to supplement one another. [...]

Opera forms are the most free and most varied musical forms. They are not subject to routine rules and depend solely on the scenic situation and on the text, i.e. on the general plan of the libretto and its details. This elementary truth is also unceremoniously flouted at every step by opera composers ... Recall the catastrophes that are interrupted by lengthy ensembles with the cast of characters arranged along the footlights in rows according to height, catastrophes that continue only after the successful completion of the ensemble. Recall the arias, duets, trios cut to conventional pattern and consisting of the required two parts, preceded by the required recitatives. All this is utterly false; only that which takes place on stage must guide the musician. [. . .] Our New School is no enemy of choruses or ensembles, but the ensembles must be rationally motivated and not slow down the course of the drama – since choruses represent not choristers but the people with its own life and passions.

If one adds to this [a special attention to] *distinctive features of characters, of the locality and the epoch,* then here are the main ideas for which Musorgsky was the most ardent, passionate and progressive advocate.

In its realization of these ideals, the New Russian School could not always keep within the proper boundaries. But these one-sided and, one must say, rather rare enthusiasms were a natural and inevitable consequence of the newness of the task, the isolation of the position of the school, and the cruel, not always fairminded struggle it was forced to wage against the general coalition of the press of that time. Of all the composers of that circle, the most exaggerated enthusiasms are met in Musorgsky. [. . .]

Boris Godunov was written by Pushkin more for reading than for the stage. On the stage, as drama or as opera, it reveals serious defects stemming from the fragmentariness of its scenes – scenes which have, to be sure, a certain tangential relation to known fact but which are in no way organically linked. Despite that, the choice of *Boris Godunov* as a subject for his opera does Musorgsky a great honor. It is considerably more honorable and alluring to be inspired by a great work of a great poet than to work with a second-rate libretto, however more suitable from the point of view of staging. What is more, many scenes in *Boris Godunov* present the musician with new and very productive tasks (the folk scenes, the scene at the Inn, the death of Boris). Where one can seriously reproach Musorgsky as regards the libretto of *Boris Godunov* is his substitution, without any real need, of his own very dubious verses for several marvelous verses of Pushkin's, and also for the Jesuit Rangoni – a new, unnecessary, crudely melodramatic character. [. . .]

No other composers of the New Russian Opera School and no other works were subjected to such mockeries and attacks as were Musorgsky and his *Boris Godunov* ("garbage music," etc.) [*Musor* in Russian means "trash," "garbage"], even though *Boris* enjoyed great and uninterrupted success. Its last, and as I recall twentieth performance, was given to a completely full house. [The opera received twenty-one performances while Musorgsky was alive and five more after his death, before being removed from repertory in 1882.] And if this opera was removed from repertory, that was the result of the numerous actions of our Theater Directorate, to whom it is impossible to ascribe any logical motive regardless of the perspective one brings to the matter, artistic or commercial. Now that the author has died, now that it is no longer necessary to pay him by single-ticket sales, *Boris Godunov* will probably again appear on the stage, and its success will prove great and permanent. [...]

Summing up the above, it is clear that Musorgsky, in spite of his early end, accomplished a great deal for art. [...] Musorgsky's merits are great; of all our deceased composers, he ranks directly after Glinka and Dargomyzhsky and occupies a place of honor in the history of our music. To be sure, in Musorgsky's creations there are powerful inadequacies and defects; without these defects, Musorgsky would have been a genius.[3]

German Avgustovich Larosh [Hermann Laroche] (1845–1904), a graduate of the St. Petersburg Conservatory, was professor of music history at the Moscow Conservatory and a gifted, prolific music critic of conservative tastes. On principle he was unfriendly toward the aspirations of the Nationalist School. A translator of Hanslick and student of Bach, Laroche also wrote substantial studies of Glinka and Tchaikovsky (who was a personal friend).

The three excerpts of Laroche's criticism offered here illustrate the curious evolution of his views regarding *Boris Godunov*. At first captivated against his will by the three scenes presented in 1873, he subsequently laundered his own enthusiasm as he heard more of the opera, and as he pondered the implications of such music for Russian culture in its "liberal" and "realist" phase. It is worth noting, however, that both Cui and Laroche (for all their eagerness to point out defects) comment on Musorgsky's effective orchestration – a useful antidote to the widespread contrary consensus that became prevalent at the time of the opera's revival in Rimsky-Korsakov's edition.

Despite its acerbic opening comments, Laroche's lengthy review of the three scenes performed for Kondratiev's *bénéfice* at the Maryinsky Theater on 5 February 1873 is serious, candid, and surprisingly sympathetic.

[1873] Strictly speaking, those of [Mr. Musorgsky's] works that have already appeared in print are not appropriate for any sort of concert performance; it would be difficult to explain for whom and for what reason they were published. They have consisted chiefly of a moderate number of songs or "romances" (about twenty) – or, more accurately, of fragments written in three staves (one for the voice and two for the piano) and labeled "romances," even though these fragments present the most radical departure from all romances known up to now and in fact from all that we are accustomed to call music. They are, for the most part, a series of unmelodic exclamations, tricky for the ear and inconvenient for intonation, accompanied by something in the way of chords or chordal figurations, the cacophony of which, whether naïve or intentional, surpasses all description. With regard to musical technique, this accompaniment presents a spectacle unprecedented in the chronicles of art. The most elementary, schoolboyish blunders leap into the eyes of the performer and torment the ears of the listener: parallel octaves, parallel fifths, unresolved dissonances, the appearance of new tonalities without modulation, orthographic errors in sharps and flats, incorrect designation of meter. [...] By these mistakes it is easy to determine the musical age of the composer: only a child could write like that. But various fanciful flights of chromaticism and dissonance, attempts at complexity, startling effects and so-called "new paths" have revealed in this child an unusually precocious perversity. [...] In a word, under a thick crust of ignorance and pretences to originality one could sense a musical nature, one not devoid of intuition and talent. But these flashes were extremely rare and disappeared amid the rubbish that surrounded them.

That is how Mr. Musorgsky appeared to me in his romances. The reader will not be surprised if I say that on 5 February I set out for the theater with a most powerful prejudice against the new music which I expected to hear. In advance, I had applied to Mr. Musorgsky an epigram written in the middle of the preceding century on the French composer Rameau:

> Distillateur d'accords baroques
> Dont tant d'idiots sont férus,
> Chez les Thraces et les Iroques
> Portez vos opéras bourrus.
> Malgré votre art hétérogène
> Sully de la lyrique scène
> Est toujours l'unique soutien.
> Fugez! laissez-lui son partage,
> Et n'écorchez pas davantage
> Les oreilles des gens de bien.

But the composer, whom in my thoughts I had already advised to take to flight, stunned me with the completely unexpected beauties of his opera excerpts, so that after hearing the scenes from *Boris Godunov* I was forced to change rather considerably my opinion of Mr. Musorgsky. True, one does encounter certain things in these excerpts that vividly recall those romances which instil in me such sincere terror of Mr. Musorgsky's muse; true, the utter lack of technique and schooling makes itself felt wherever the author attempts to write in a rounded form, and the indefatigable quest for novelty and piquancy further fractures and mangles this form; but the proportion between these defects and the spiritual power that forces its way out from under them is entirely different from that which I saw in the romances. [. . .]

Of the [three] scenes, the middle one ("[Marina's] Boudoir") seemed to me the most insignificant. The protracted mazurka which Marina sings in it is a sort of twofold extract from Chopin, overly refined and ungraceful, awkwardly written for soprano (too low) and, in the ugliness of its melody, worthy to stand alongside the published works of Mr. Musorgsky. [. . .] But the remaining two scenes of the opera, the Inn scene and the Fountain scene, struck me by the brilliant musico-dramatic talent that everywhere speaks in them. The scene at the inn is a brilliant study in the comic mode; its action is so unmediated that at the performance a good part of the public laughed with that cheerful laughter that good comedy provokes. [. . .] [In Varlaam's song about Kazan] the harmonic twists are marked by an elasticity and brilliance, which I least of all expected from Mr. Musorgsky, and in the mood of the entire number there is something wild and awesome, which is communicated by the author with great poetic animation.

The same animation prevails in the Fountain scene. This scene is full of sumptuous sensuality and languor, which could not have been expected from the author of *Boris*, again judging by the published samples we have of his creative work. Also very remarkable is the bold, heroic melody in the high notes that the Pretender sings at the end of the scene. This melody is folklike in the highest sense of the word; apparently Mr. Musorgsky is not only sympathetic to but also well acquainted with the Russian folk element. I should add that he could realize the ideal of the Russian folk idiom in his music far more often if (apart from contrapuntal clumsiness) he could free himself from his own uncommon passion for mannered augmented and diminished intervals in declamatory melody and for intervals based on the augmented triad, and from a number of other dissonant chords that he loves. All these nasty habits are about as antipathetic as possible to the spirit of Russian folksongs, and also one cannot say that intervals of this sort are indispensable for correct declamation.

[Laroche then criticizes the "strained and incoherent" polonaise in the fountain scene.] Here in the dance number Mr. Musorgsky revealed that he has little competence in instrumental music, and absolutely no technical preparation. However, if the art of instrumental composition were limited to the art of orchestration, then Mr. Musorgsky would have to be recognized as a master in this kind of composition. All three scenes performed on 5 February and especially the third (at the Fountain), are orchestrated sumptuously and with variety, vividly and effectively, so that involuntarily you ask yourself why the artist, who apparently spent much time and labor on learning the resources of the orchestra and the rules of writing for it, did not devote at least some time to familiarizing himself with harmony, counterpoint, and the theory of forms. But expressing my frank opinion about the virtues and defects of Mr. Musorgsky's music, I do not at all have in mind offering him any sort of advice. I look on him as a ready-made and completed fact, and assume that for him to move off the false path and fill in the gaps in his education would be incomparably more difficult than it would be for Mr. Rimsky-Korsakov [...] because the author of *Boris* possesses a much greater distinctiveness and originality of imagination, and thus it would be harder for him to submit to some external oppression, for example, to the rules of strict contrapuntal style. [...]

  Boris Godunov is a phenomenon of great significance. The opera has revealed the fact that in the group which forms the extreme left of our musical world there is a quality by which that circle heretofore has not been distinguished: originality, inventiveness, independent content. [...] Now this defect has been corrected by Mr. Musorgsky [...]. Nothing could better delineate the strivings and spirit of the circle: what we must take as preponderate in the group is not fullness of knowledge, not many-sided development, not artistic elegance, not breadth of horizon, but crude and powerful nature. The circle has always aspired to the emancipation of instinct and arbitrary will, to the triumph of spontaneous forces over tradition, over history, over knowledge, over aesthetics. Now, apparently, the circle has achieved that triumph. Perhaps we will live to see the day when all the remaining members of the circle, convinced of the uselessness of that slight academic ballast which they have been able to acquire up to now, will cast it all overboard and turn themselves into slavish imitators of Mr. Musorgsky.[4]

In his review of the full premiere, Laroche again mixes praise and blame, but attaches the whole to his larger critique of "liberalism," adjusted here to apply to music. Two items are of special interest: Laroche's comments on Musorgsky's "pianistic" style of writing, and his prescient discussion of the internal contradiction in *kuchkist* theory and practice between the setting of actual speech patterns to music (which requires maximum flexibility) and the drive to utilize Russian folksongs, often highly stylized in form and accent.

[1874] The success of a new staged work is rarely as great as it seems at its first performances, but the success of Mr. Musorgsky's *Boris* can hardly be called transitory. The writer of these lines is far from an enthusiast of the composer, but he unhesitatingly recognizes that Mr. Musorgsky is capable of pleasing and even of captivating many. He has talent; but even if he had no talent at all, he would still possess many other qualifications for success. He is utterly a man of the times, and yet he is still a Russian. Out of the many varieties of the "authentically Russian," he personifies precisely that type in which there is more liberal instinct than there is knowledge, skill, or intellectual development. Such personalities are well known to the experienced observer of Russian life: a man who has taught himself "little by little, somehow and any which way" [a line from Canto One, 5 of Pushkin's *Eugene Onegin*, describing the education of the hero – a foppish, disillusioned "superfluous man" of the 1820s], who feels the constriction of his surroundings and is unconsciously struggling toward the light, toward broad open spaces – such a man is an agreeable phenomenon, fully understandable and for the most part honorable. [. . .] He is not only a musician, he is also a poet. Like Richard Wagner, he creates his own libretto and combines in himself competencies that are usually separated out in persons with no understanding of each other at all. In both spheres, Mr. Musorgsky commands our attention by the abundance of his progressive spirit and by the paucity of his development. [. . .]

I forgot to mention that I do not understand liberals of Mr. Musorgsky's sort. Such liberals look at the soaring poetic line of [Pushkin's] *Boris* as oldfashioned rhetorical rubbish that it's time to do away with. In the opinion of the liberals, the real-life Boris, the real Pretender, the real Marina did not speak anywhere near as eloquently as Pushkin forced them to speak. The realism with which Mr. Musorgsky is permeated has compelled him to perform a merciless operation on Pushkin's poetry. Our present-day poet has in places completely destroyed the verses of the poet of bygone days; in places he has chopped these verses up into little pieces and mixed them in with pieces invented by him; he has torn big strips out of the living flesh of Pushkin's poetry, and patched the gaping wounds with plasters from his own home apothecary. I could cite many examples of this domestic cure to which Pushkin was subject at the hands of doctoring realism . . . [there follows an example of Musorgsky's "vulgar prosifying" from the Fountain scene.] This is far from being Pushkin, but we can console ourselves with the fact that it is life itself.

One way or another, in language and in verse, Mr. Musorgsky is undoubtedly a realist. What that means for me is that he cultivates liberal instincts and aspires to liberate himself from any sort of shackles, among which must be numbered a high style and classical versification. Mr. Musorgsky's liberal spirit is not limited to external effects, however; the new poet looks on history itself through the eyes of progress. [. . .] [Here Laroche criticizes Musorgsky's Jesuit Rangoni as a melodramatic historical shorthand for the enemies of liberalism, and warns against the danger of portraying on stage a single representative "of a whole party, of a whole tendency of thought" – a device, he claims, that inevitably leads to cardboard characters and crudely false motivation, in both liberal and conservative artists.]

I have just spoken of Mr. Musorgsky's declamation; this side of vocal music is one of the favorite hobbyhorses of that liberalism which aspires to reform our art. Mr. Musorgsky's recitative is the apex of liberalism: there is no conventional form, no melodic, harmonic or rhythmic law that might constrain or stop him in his goal of transmitting the accents of simple speech by means of musical accents. But it is not this ["liberal"] orientation alone that sustains him: it is clear that he also has talent. In his manner of illustrating the rise and fall of the human voice, its stops, hesitations and rapid patter, one is aware of an indisputable keenness of observation; one sees a person capable of noticing how people speak and gifted with an intuitive sensitivity that can guess out the special accent of the moment and the individual accent of a personality. [. . .] This is the brightest side of realistic opera, but precisely here the education of the realist gives itself away in the most unambiguous fashion. The musical gusts in which Mr. Musorgsky lives cast him in two different directions at once, and he swings between the two without finding a point of support in any firm system. On the one hand, he would like the long and short, the low and high notes to correspond literally to the prosody of the words. On the other hand, he draws on the melodic turns of Russian folk songs, whose style bursts forth in the recitative passages of *Boris* at times in small, at other times in large segments. There is no declamation freer and more irregular than that found in folk songs; this circumstance results from a verseline that is not strictly regular with respect to number of syllables, so that the same musical rhythms fall on verselines with different distributions of accent. And this is so even when the songs' refrains are repeated in couplet form. That is why one sometimes encounters in Mr. Musorgsky's romances such curious declamation. [. . .] But despite these deviations and hesitations, the new opera reveals, in patches, both talent for recitative and sensitivity to Russian folk singing. [. . .]

It is most regrettable that our musical realist is gifted with great ability. It would be a thousand times more pleasant if his method of composition were practiced only by untalented dullards, if feebleness of education were never masked by an inborn flair. [. . .] All his compositions are worked out on the piano: take away his piano today, and tomorrow he will cease to be a musician. *Boris Godunov* is, first and foremost, an improvisation for the piano. It is remarkable with what love the author cleaned up, smoothed out and dressed up the piano–vocal score of his opera before releasing it for publication, not to mention the subtlest markings of intensity, legato and staccato, the pedal, etc.; not to mention the virtuoso passages of the second scene of the Prologue, with the portrayal of the bells; not to mention, finally, how Mr. Musorgsky, as a subtle and sensitive pianist, ofttimes carefully marks what to play with the right hand, what with the left – his entire opera, despite all its harmonic blunders, is laid out from a pianistic perspective very sonorously and elegantly: chord sequences are wild and scandalous, but a given individual chord is distributed in such a way that it is comfortable to reach [on the piano keyboard] and sounds distinctly, effectively. In places it seems as if the author were reckoning primarily on piano "salon performances." [. . .] The choice of tonalities, the modulations and voice-leading of this strange composer are so pianistic that they can only be explained as an incessant noodling about [on the keyboard] with an abundant use of the right pedal.[5]

After a year's absence from repertory, *Boris Godunov* was revived at the Maryinsky in the 1876–77 season, but without the Kromy scene. Criticism of this new series of performances was mixed. Laroche now appears maximally intolerant of the work, the composer, the New Russian School and the frailties of the Russian public.

[1876] *Not to give* [the works of] Mr. Musorgsky, Mr. Cui, and Mr. Borodin (when will we hear from Mr. Borodin?) is ill-advised. It would mean bestowing on these gentlemen a martyr's crown, which they do not at all deserve. But I suppose there's no reason even to raise the question: under the current arrangement of Russian opera as a private club, it's precisely the Mighty Handful that has all the chances on its side, and its works will always be performed in preference to others. A good example of this very thing, it seems, is *Boris Godunov*; this "soft-boiled boot" is being given for its *fourth* season! [It was in fact the work's third season: it had not been given in 1875–76.]

Whenever I hear that in Petersburg they are giving or will give *Boris Godunov*, there awakens in me an inexplicable tenderness toward Italian opera, toward French quadrilles, toward *teatro buffo*, and especially toward barrel organs. Barren simplicity, barren vulgarity! [. . .] From the "soft-boiled boots" of the new Russian school I feel a need to run away and hide somewhere, anywhere, but primarily (according to the law of reaction) under the canopy of unpretentious music.[6]

Nikolay Nikolaevich Strakhov (1828–96). Literary and art critic, journalist, librarian, and Hegelian philosopher of ideas with training in the natural sciences, Strakhov became associated with two of Dostoevsky's journals in the early 1860s. As a leading *pochvennik* (advocate of a romantic–nationalist fusion between Slavophile and Westernizing tendencies in Russian intellectual life), he deeply admired Dostoevsky and Tolstoy, publicized their works, and polemicized with their ideas. Strakhov's 1874 review of Musorgsky's opera appears in the form of three letters to the editor (Dostoevsky) of the conservative periodical *The Citizen*, and constitutes a spirited defense both of Russian historical experience and of the literary interests of Pushkin against the indignities of operatic transposition.

The case could be made that Strakhov poorly understood the historical Time of Troubles, Pushkin's drama, and the dynamics of the libretto. But we should remember that Musorgsky's contemporaries perceived *kuchkism* largely as an idiom suitable only to comedy; they considered declamation and "naturalism" generically unsuitable for transmitting the themes and elevated emotions of serious opera. In the context of our Chapters 2 and 10, it is worth remarking that Strakhov fully understands – and fully condemns – Musorgsky's deeply pessimistic historical vision.

[Second letter, 4 March 1874] Let us return to our opera. I would like to tell you its content, so you can judge what sort of music might be written on such a remarkable subject. As I said earlier, the composer intensified Pushkin's drama; apparently he found everything in Pushkin pale, weak, unclear, and he tried to embellish it, elevate the tone, place more emphatic accents. A huge brouhaha takes place on stage. The public looks on and finds it all very entertaining.

So see where Shakespeare has taken us! Yes, the present opera is a fine little example of how we understand art in general and Shakespeare in particular. As is well known, Shakespeare's dramas present a constant, almost regular mix of tragic, solemn scenes with vulgar comic ones. The [English] poet employed this device apparently for contrast, in order to set off one by the other, so that the tragic element would stand out all the more vividly alongside the trivial and vulgar, and trivial vulgarity would be more markedly conspicuous against a tragic background. Pushkin imitated this aspect of Shakespeare, and in *Boris Godunov* he alternated serious scenes with comic ones. But the composer understood the matter in his own way: he took the comic scenes as primary; he developed them, reworked them and made them the main content of the opera. His first and last scenes are comic through and through; the scene at the Inn is the chief pearl of the opera; just judge for yourself what sort of a whole can come of all this! [. . .]

[Strakhov then cites approvingly and at length one of César Cui's reviews of *Boris*, in which Cui criticizes both the opera's shapelessness and Musorgsky's unfortunate replacement of Pushkin's verses with "other, very mediocre and often tasteless" lines of his own. Strakhov replies to Cui:]

Mr. Cui grants too much to Mr. Musorgsky. He says that only the opera as a whole lacks interconnection, integrity of impression, and he speaks about the separate scenes as if there is connection and integrity in them; but one must say about each scene what is said about the opera as a whole. Each scene, taken separately, is incoherent, contradictory, full of incongruities. [. . .] It's impossible to call Mr. Musorgsky's verse *mediocre and tasteless poetry*, as Mr. Cui does. It is not poetry at all and not even prose, but rather some sort of ugly pile of words.

[. . .] And if this is indeed the case, what sort of music can be written to such content? Isn't it clear to everyone, even to someone who has not heard the opera, that the composer could not create anything integral or consistent in music either, that he did not even bother himself about such a task? Ugliness and monstrosity – that's the surprising result of all this striving toward truth and realism!

[Third letter, 18 March 1874. Strakhov opens this final letter with a discussion of the particularly disastrous performance of Pushkin's *Boris Godunov* several years earlier, crudely acted and trivially interpreted. Musorgsky, he adds, only reinforces that disrespect for the people, for the boyars, and for Russian history itself.] In general, if one considers all the particulars of Mr. Musorgsky's opera, one receives a very strange overall impression. The mood of the entire opera in *accusatory*, [among us] a longstanding and well-known mood. Ancient Rus emerges here in those dark colors in which many of our scholars see it. The background of the opera is composed of the common people: they are presented as crude, drunk, oppressed, and embittered. Against such a background some sort of proper movement could still have been constructed. But the people turn out to be, in addition, utterly stupid, superstitious, devoid of sense, and capable of absolutely nothing. What indeed could be constructed out of this? Against the dark background of these senseless commoners appear characters who for some reason are able to manipulate and control the people: Boris, the Pretender, Marina, the Jesuit, the Boyars, etc. The clashes, passions, actions of these characters have no relation at all to the people, no connection with them (and there would be nothing to connect with in any case, since the people are devoid of any content). For this reason, the spiritual movement of these characters loses any sense of relation to the dominant background of the opera. It's all a matter of their personal affairs, which have private, egoistic significance; on the sea of the people are borne figures in the grip of terror, ambition, love, religious feeling, greed for money, and so on. These aspirations have no connection among themselves, no interest for the author, and make no overall sense. It is impossible to find in the opera that central point or basic contrast which would constitute its guiding thread, its dominant interest. The people: here is the sole such general rallying point. But because the people are presented as utterly trivial, the opera itself merely unravels in scraps.

This is not at all like the individual scenes of, say, Glinka's *Ruslan* and Pushkin's *Boris*. In Glinka and Pushkin there is a general background that is very broad and reliably stable. In Glinka, for example, [the constant factor] is the beauty of life, the beauty of the passions, youth, love, boldness, the extravagance of power and sensuality in its elemental freshness. Individual scenes can be drawn against such a background. In Pushkin the general background is our ancient Rus and the entire foundation that sustained her: deep religiosity, family and monastic life, loyalty to the government, the ideal of the tsar, fidelity to the dynasty, the Time of Troubles arising out of a vacillation and confrontation of these elements – against such a background, too, one can write separate scenes. But what serves as background for Mr. Musorgsky? Of all the dramatic scenes chosen by him for the opera, which evoke his sympathy? What inspires him? What does he celebrate? In vain will you seek an answer.[7]

Count Arseny Arkadievich Golenishchev-Kutuzov (1848–1913). A poet and playwright of middling gifts, close friend and housemate of Musorgsky's (1874–75), Kutuzov provided the poetry for two of Musorgsky's song cycles, *Songs and Dances of Death* and *Without Sun*. In the 1880s, after Musorgsky's death, Kutuzov received a high position at court, shifted his politics to the right, and downplayed his relationship with the radical musician-realists of the 60s and 70s. Both the correspondence between the two men and the poet's "Reminiscences of M. P. Musorgsky," from which this excerpt is taken, were not discovered until 1932.

In these memoirs, composed in the late 1880s in response to the "Stasov line" among Musorgsky biographers, Kutuzov attributed the composer's decline and miserable last years to an incomplete renunciation of his earlier misguided infatuation with radical populism and thus to a self-eroding betrayal of his true lyric gift. According to Kutuzov, Musorgsky's final words to him were: "You know, I feel like doing something completely new, something I've not yet touched on, I feel like resting from history and in general from all this excessive prosiness (*prozishche*) which even in life doesn't give one a chance to catch one's breath" (p. 29 of the memoirs).

In the two excerpts here, Kutuzov sharply polemicizes against several widely-held beliefs about the composer: Stasov's claim that Musorgsky felt his opera had been "castrated" by cuts during performance (and especially by the omission of the Kromy scene), and then Strakhov's (and others') insistence that Musorgsky's prose adjustment of Pushkin's text was not artistically motivated but the result of mere inept naïveté.

[1888] In the last years of his life, Musorgsky almost entirely renounced his enthusiasms and false paths of that [earlier realist] period, and, had he lived longer, his talent doubtless would have triumphed in its struggle against the influence of the sixties, against the oppressiveness of its surroundings, and would have raised him to great heights. But I will speak of all that in its proper place; for now let me turn to the performance of *Boris Godunov* and try to explain both the good and the deplorable effect of its success on Musorgsky's later creative work.

It was January 1874. Rehearsals of *Boris Godunov* at the Maryinsky Theater were going smoothly and well. Musorgsky was present at each one, and returned joyful and full of hope for the opera's success. He could not praise enough the attitude of all the artists and especially of the conductor Nápravník, who, in Musorgsky's words, offered much good advice at the rehearsals and upon whose insistence many things were omitted that were too long, not relevant, not especially successful and ruinous to the general on-stage impression. These cuts were: the scene in Pimen's Cell, the story of the Parrot in the scene with Boris and the Tsarevich, the Chiming clock, and several others. Musorgsky fully and sincerely agreed with Nápravník, and heatedly argued with those who accused him of weak character or a willingness to give in. "All that is absolutely impossible on stage," he often said to me after such quarrels. "And these gentlemen don't want to know anything about it. They don't care about the quality of impressions, only the quantity. They say that I'm weak-willed, but they don't understand that an author himself is never able to judge the impression a stage performance will make on the public before an opera is actually staged. Meyerbeer crossed out whole pages mercilessly – he knew what he was doing, and he was right!"

Later on, when (I don't know on whose initiative) they began to omit the final act from performances of *Boris*, Musorgsky not only approved of the abridgement but was even greatly satisfied by it. [...] I nevertheless much regretted its complete omission, since I found much that was musically good in it and therefore told Musorgsky that I would prefer to see *Boris* with that act included, only moved forward, so that entry of the Pretender into the Kremlin [sic] preceded the death of Boris. Musorgsky disputed this opinion of mine and once, in some heat, told me that its full omission was required not only by the flow of the drama itself and by the conditions of the stage, but also for the sake of his – Musorgsky's – auctorial conscience. I was surprised, and asked him to explain.

"In this act," Musorgsky answered me, "I, for the sole time in my life, lied about the Russian people. The crowd's mockery of the boyar – that's an untruth, that's a non-Russian trait. An enraged people kills and condemns to death, but does not make fun of its victim."

I had to agree. [...]

I especially emphasize these words that Musorgsky spoke to me, because they directly contradict the opinion expressed in [Stasov's] biographical sketch mentioned by me above: that the abridgement or, as he put it, the castration of *Boris* by the Directorate deeply saddened and embittered Musorgsky and even hastened his death. [...]

Thus Musorgsky [in the second half of the 1870s] suddenly found himself outside the musical realm, surrounded by people who were God knows what: artists, architects, university professors, government officials, lawyers – all of them perhaps very honorable people – but alas! not only not musicians, but people who understood absolutely nothing at all about music. Musorgsky came to trust their opinions utterly, and for him it was easier this way, for their opinions flattered his auctorial vanity. From their words Musorgsky concluded that the public welcomed him precisely for his "novelties," for that musical radicalism which he displayed in *Boris* [...] – for all those impossible innkeepers and Jesuits, tramps and holy-fool Ivanushkas with which he from time to time filled the stage, interrupting the flow of the drama, violating its unity and integrity – in a word, for his adding that which did not need to be added to Pushkin's great and immortal creation. Musorgsky and I disagreed on this point, and we frequently had heated quarrels. At the time I was an ardent admirer of Pushkin and considered any distortion of his works to be impermissible sacrilege. When, as I recall, the newspaper *The Citizen* ran Strakhov's article censuring Musorgsky seriously and severely for his "corrections" in Pushkin's text of *Godunov*, I, despite my devotion to Musorgsky, was entirely on Strakhov's side. But it was a strange thing: Musorgsky least of all tolerated comments concerning any [verbal] text that he had composed. About the music he would speak very willingly, without irritation, and he often agreed with the comments, but any criticism of a verbal text written by him irritated him and he always stayed with his own opinion.[8]

Rediscovery in Rimsky-Korsakov's edition

(NIKOLAY RIMSKY-KORSAKOV, FEODOR CHALIAPIN, CLAUDE DEBUSSY, ARTHUR POUGIN, JEAN MARNOLD)

Nikolay Andreevich Rimsky-Korsakov (1844–1908), prolific composer and music pedagogue, composed fifteen operas of his own in addition to resurrecting – some would say eviscerating – the two historical operas of his deceased friend. Much of the polemic surrounding *Boris Godunov* in the twentieth century centers on the status and legitimacy of Rimsky's two editions of the opera: an 1896 score heavily cut and extensively recomposed and a 1908 score with most – but not all – of the cuts restored. Rimsky's "corrections" in Musorgsky's music soon became a focus of controversy, and it is interesting to note in this regard that César Cui was still on hand to take part – characteristically mixing praise and censure, repeating opinions that by the end of the century were decades old, and expressing a curious nostalgia for the original un-Rimskified *Boris* (see Chapter 5, p. 110).

The term "folk musical drama" first occurs in conjunction with *Boris Godunov* as a subtitle on the frontispiece of the 1896 Rimsky edition; it was a label that Musorgsky himself reserved exclusively for his second historical opera *Khovanshchina*. Musorgsky always referred to *Boris* as an opera, which, we might surmise, he regarded as a work with individual personalities, not historical groups, as heroes. This retroactive genre confusion has been exploited by Soviet critics to portray Musorgsky's populism as politically more progressive than it was.

[Preface to Rimsky's first edition, 1896] The opera or folk musical drama *Boris Godunov*, written twenty-five years ago, provoked two contradictory opinions among the public upon its first appearance on the stage and in print. The great talent of its author, its permeation by the folk spirit and by the spirit of the historical epoch, the liveliness of its scenes and the skill with which its characters are drawn, its life-like truth in both the dramatic and comic mode, the vividly grasped "everyday" side of life realized through a wealth of originality in musical ideas and devices – all this evoked delight and astonishment in one part of the public. On the other hand, impractical difficulties, the fragmentation of melodic phrases, clumsiness in vocal writing, harshness of harmonies and modulations, errors in voice-leading, feeble orchestration, and in general the weak technical side of the work evoked a storm of derision and censure in another part. For some, the above-mentioned technical shortcomings eclipsed not only the lofty virtues of the work but also the very talent of the author; others, on the contrary, elevated these very same shortcomings almost into virtues and merit.

Much time has passed since then. The opera either has not been staged at all or else staged exceedingly rarely; the public has not been in a position to verify these well-established contradictory opinions.

Boris Godunov was composed before my very eyes. Since I was on intimately friendly terms with Musorgsky, no one could be as well informed as myself of the author's intentions regarding *Boris*, and of the process of their execution.

Highly valuing Musorgsky's talent and this work, and honoring his memory, I decided to undertake a revision of *Boris Godunov* as regards its technical side and its reorchestration. I am convinced that my reworking and orchestration have not in the least betrayed the unique spirit of the work and the bold ideas of its composer, and that the opera, although reworked by me, nevertheless fully belongs to the creative achievement of Musorgsky. The cleaning-up and ordering of the technical side will only serve to make its lofty significance clearer and more accessible to all, and will put a stop to all sorts of censure against the work.

During the revision I made several cuts in light of the opera's excessive length. This length had necessitated cuts – in material that was too essential to the opera – even during stage performances mounted while the author was alive.

The present edition does not, by its presence, eliminate the first, original edition; Musorgsky's own work continues to be preserved in its integrity in its original form.

1 May 1896. St. Petersburg. N. Rimsky-Korsakov.'

[Preface to Rimsky's second edition, 1908] For this proposed edition of *Boris Godunov*, the scenes and aspects reworked and orchestrated by me that were omitted in the previous edition in view of the great length of the work, are; (1) Pimen's narrative about the tsars; (2) the scene of Boris and the Tsarevich Feodor over the map of the Muscovite lands; (3) The story of the parrot and the scene of Boris with Feodor and Shuisky; (4) the chiming clock; (5) the scene of the Pretender and Rangoni; and (6) the Pretender's monologue.

Although they do not have essential significance for the work as a whole, these scenes nevertheless present great musical and dramatic interest. In compliance with the wishes and choice of the performers, they may be inserted, each separately, during any given performance of the work. Thus in the present edition Musorgsky's folk musical drama appears in its full form, without any cuts [not true: the episode of the children with the chiming clock, at the beginning of Act II, is still omitted]. 12 May 1908. St. Petersburg, N. Rimsky-Korsakov.[10]

Feodor Chaliapin (1873–1938), great Russian bass and operatic actor of genius, was the primary vehicle through which Musorgsky's two historical operas reached the West. His professional theatrical life began in the 1890s, on the stage of Mamontov's Moscow Private Russian Opera (where he pioneered the revival of *Boris* in Rimsky's edition). He then worked with Serge Diaghilev in Paris between 1907 and the war years, creating sensationally successful "Saisons Russes" in that city and eventually in other great houses of Europe. In 1922 Chaliapin, with part of his family, left post-revolutionary Russia, never to return.

Chaliapin wrote two memoirs. One began to appear in 1926 in Soviet editions, heavily "edited" and supplemented by his friend, the Bolshevik activist and writer Maxim Gorky; the other (1932), from which this excerpt is taken, is entitled *Maska i dusha*, which was reprinted in full unlaundered form only in 1990. To our knowledge, no English translation has been made of the entire original Russian text of *Maska i dusha*. A quite different version of the excerpt below can be found in Chapter 40 of *Man and Mask: Forty Years in the Life of a Singer*, trans. from the French by Phyllis Megroz (New York: Alfred A. Knopf, 1932), pp. 160–63.

My great distress in life is that I never met Musorgsky. He died before my appearance in Petersburg. My misfortune. It was like arriving late for a fateful train: you come to the station and the train is pulling out right in front of your eyes – forever!

Our coterie [of composers], however, treated the memory of Musorgsky with love, with loving pride. Long ago they had understood that Musorgsky was a genius. Not in vain had Rimsky-Korsakov, with truly religious fervour, worked to perfect *Boris Godunov*, the greatest work that Musorgsky left us. Today a number of people inveigh against Rimsky-Korsakov for having "disfigured" Musorgsky, as they call it. I am not a composer, but in my humble opinion such a reproach is profoundly unjust. Even the *material* labor that Rimsky-Korsakov contributed to this work is astonishing and unforgettable. Without this work, the world would still not be acquainted with *Boris Godunov*. Musorgsky himself was modest; the fact that Europe might be interested in his work never so much as entered his head. He was possessed by music. He composed because he could not do otherwise. Wherever he might be, he was always composing.

In the Petersburg tavern Maly Yaroslavets, the one on Morskaya Street, alone in a private room, he drinks vodka and writes music. He writes it on napkins, on bills, on greasy bits of paper ... He was a magnificent rag-picker. He picked up everything that was music. He was a discriminating rag-picker. Even a cigarette-stub exhales a perfume in his hands. And he had written so much for *Boris Godunov* that had the opera been produced as Musorgsky had written it, it would have had to begin at four o'clock in the afternoon and would have ended at three in the morning. [Of course Chaliapin greatly exaggerates here.] Rimsky-Korsakov understood this and condensed it, but everything valuable he preserved. Well, yes. There were some errors. Rimsky was a pure classicist, he disliked dissonances, he had no feeling for them. Or, rather, he did feel them, and they hurt. A parallel fifth or parallel octave was already enough to upset him. [...] On the whole our musical classicists, although they bowed to Musorgsky's genius, in their heart of hearts were all somewhat repelled by his "realism," which was too crude for them.

Indeed, Musorgsky is usually described as a great realist. His warmest admirers often talk about him in this way. I am not authoritatively enough versed in music to give a confident opinion on this score, but relying on my simple feeling as a singer, someone who perceives music with the soul, this description is too limited for Musorgsky and in no way embraces the whole of his greatness. There are some creative peaks so high that formal epithets lose their sense or assume only a secondary value. Certainly Musorgsky is a realist, but his power lies not in the fact that his music is realistic but in the fact that his *realism is music* in the most staggering sense of the word. Behind his realism, as behind a curtain, there is a whole world of insights and emotions that simply cannot fit into the realistic plane. [...]

As a composer, Musorgsky so keenly sees and hears all the scents of a given garden, of a given tavern and so forcefully and persuasively describes them, that the audience actually hears and feels all these scents ...

This is realism, of course. But it is a particular kind of realism. Russian peasants take up simple beams, they take up simple axes (they have no other tools) and build a temple. But with these axes they carve out lace of a sort that the most subtle and delicate inlay artist could not have dreamed.[11]

Claude Debussy (1862–1918). Perhaps the best known assessment of Musorgsky by a French musician, this article by Claude Debussy isolates precisely those qualities in Musorgsky that the French avant-garde found appealing. Russian music had been gaining ground in France since 1878, when Nikolay Rubinstein conducted four concerts, including works by Alexander Dargomyzhsky, Rimsky-Korsakov, and Tchaikovsky, at the Trocadéro. Just over a decade later, Rimsky-Korsakov and Glazunov conducted their own works, as well as music by Glinka, Borodin, and Musorgsky, at the World Exhibition of 1889; Russian music became even more popular after the forging of a political alliance between the two nations in 1893. As the nineteenth century drew to a close, French composers – if one may borrow Satie's characterization of Debussy – were "quite deliberately seeking a way that wasn't very easy to find," out from under Massenet and Wagner. Russian music seemed to offer a path. Spurred on by the lecture-concerts of Musorgsky's songs given by Pierre d'Alheim and his wife, the singer Marie Olénine d'Alheim, many French musicians began to see Musorgsky as the one Russian who had accomplished most successfully what they wanted to do: break through established rules into uncharted territory. Thus, what Russian musicians criticized in Musorgsky's music, these Frenchmen saw as virtues. Despite the tantalizing promise in the last sentence, this article represents the only time Debussy wrote of Musorgsky at length for publication.

> [1901] No one has spoken to the best within us in tones more gentle or profound; he is unique and will remain so because his art is spontaneous and free from arid formulas. Never has a more refined sensibility been conveyed by such simple means; it resembles the art of a curious savage, uncovering music at each step through his emotions. Nor is there ever a question of any particular form; in any event the form is so varied that by no possibility whatever can it be connected to any established, one might say official, form. It depends on and is composed of successive minute touches mysteriously linked together through his gift of luminous clairvoyance. [. . .]
>
> Musorgsky was content with a chord which would have seemed impoverished to Mr. — (I forget his name!) or with so instinctive a modulation that it would be quite unknown to Mr. — (the same fellow!). We shall have more to say about Musorgsky; he has many claims to our devotion.[12]

Arthur Pougin (1834–1921) was a French critic and violinist trained at the Paris Conservatory. His discussion of Musorgsky serves as a valuable corrective to the misconception that all France admired the composer's music. Pougin, an unqualified admirer of Rimsky-Korsakov, regarded Rimsky's music as "the loftiest and most original in all the modern Russian school." In the selection quoted here, he argues at length that Musorgsky lacked the technical means of realizing his vision and thus remained – like Berlioz, he says – only half a composer. As he put it, Musorgsky had something to say but was content to stammer. Furthermore, the letter he cites, from an anonymous "friend in St. Petersburg," demonstrates an essential point: most Russian critics and musicians at the turn of the century acknowledged no "Musorgsky problem" because they saw no harm in what Rimsky had done – quite the contrary.

[1897] If [Musorgsky] has a place apart from the Russian composers of his time, as we are told that he had; if in his isolation he escaped all other influences and displayed audacity of every sort; it was not so much because he had a specially artistic temperament, as that, by continuing deliberately to ignore the principles and even what may be called the orthography of music, he ceased to be conscious of the liberties he was taking and simply put down his ideas as they entered his head, without troubling to give them any particular kind of form. [. . .] It would be rank injustice to pretend that when Musorgsky spoke he had nothing to say; the misfortune was that he too often was content to stammer. [. . .]

In the case of a complex work on a large scale, it is not enough to spin a few lovely tunes out of one's head, or even to utter cries of passion and anguish; one must be able to co-ordinate and present one's ideas; one must dress them and give them shape so that they stand out in relief. It is no use hurling contemptuous sarcasms on such criticism, as had been done by an enthusiastic biographer of Musorgsky, Pierre d'Alheim, who cannot find abuse enough for those who are unwilling to kneel, like him, before the genius. This writer excuses Musorgsky's mistakes in the following words: "He did not want to increase his means of expression; he simply tried to translate into sound the soul's cries which struck upon his ears from without or rose from within himself. In very truth he trampled on the rules and crushed the life out of them by the sheer weight of his thought." That may be. Nevertheless, if someone wishes to trample underfoot the laws of a language in such a way as not only to be excused but even to win admiration, he must know the laws first and also the language he wants to use. [. . .] As to Musorgsky, he was ignorant of the language of music, and the mistakes he made are not the mistakes of genius but of ignorance. [. . .]

I once wrote in a similar vein to one of my friends in St. Petersburg, telling him exactly what I thought of Musorgsky, and saying that in my opinion he was musically illiterate. He replied as follows:

What you say of Musorgsky could not be fairer, and it explains why he is unrecognizable in the posthumous works which have been corrected and revised by Rimsky-Korsakov, in whom the sense of form is very strong. [. . .] Some have spoken of the popular character of this composer's music, but anyone who has closely looked into the matter knows that not a single musical thought of Musorgsky has become or can become part of the people's heritage, and that when his ideas clarify themselves and begin to look attractive, it is because they are drawn from the people's muse itself or have been inspired by the essentially Russian style of Glinka. Everything is strange and formless except what has been tidied up and straightened out by Rimsky-Korsakov. [. . .]

What is chiefly remarkable in the score of *Boris Godunov* is its sense of character and its general feeling for color; in that lies its real originality. As to the orchestration (which is not symphonic, but is exactly what it ought to be), if I mention it, I do so in order to compliment Rimsky-Korsakov; for anyone who is familiar with Musorgsky is well aware he was incapable of writing in that way.

In *Boris Godunov*, then, we are confronted with a very interesting work, but one whose importance must not be exaggerated; above all we need not hail it as an absolute masterpiece, as some insist on doing. Let us give it the high and honorable place that is due to it without attempting to deceive ourselves.[13]

Jean Marnold (1859–1935), an apologist for Musorgsky, eloquently expresses the opposite point of view from Pougin; he and critics like him were instrumental in establishing the dimensions of the so-called Musorgsky problem. To these critics, most of whom supported the French avant-garde, Musorgsky could do no wrong; Rimsky-Korsakov, on the other hand, by forcing his friend's music into a conservatory frock coat, had betrayed its essential genius. Marnold and his colleagues, having compared Rimsky's version of *Boris* with Musorgsky's vocal score of 1874, noted many changes of tessitura, vocal line, dynamics, chord, key, and rhythm; and they berated Rimsky without mercy. Although Marnold may state the case against Rimsky too fervently, it is nevertheless a fact that only about 15 percent of the measures found in Rimsky's piano–vocal score of 1908 take the same form in Musorgsky's piano–vocal score of 1874.

[1908, some four months after Diaghilev's production of *Boris* in Paris] Rimsky-Korsakov has corrected the score of *Boris Godunov* as a schoolmaster corrects the homework of a bad student. [. . .] But Rimsky-Korsakov did not content himself with unceremoniously altering rhythm or melos in order to eliminate delectable and manifestly intentional fifths; *he has also corrected the harmony* in the bargain, making it conform, without doubt, to his *Treatise*. Since this latter probably forbids the tritone, Rimsky-Korsakov prunes it from the polyphony as often as he can. Throughout the entire scene in Pimen's Cell, the Dorian mode is adulterated into banal D minor to the point of travesty. The interval of the augmented fifth is frequently the object of equilateral ostracism – wherever it appears – because the implacable corrector hesitates no more to rectify the melody than the chords. Almost at every moment, Rimsky-Korsakov changes something for the sole reason that it is his good pleasure, quite frankly, to replace that which Musorgsky wrote with that which pleases him. [. . .] To [Rimsky-Korsakov], it is good to correct everything – harmony, melody, modulation, tonality – with neither caution nor appreciable cause. [. . .]

It is false that Musorgsky was destitute of technique and that *Boris* would not be performable save for Rimsky-Korsakov's changes. Without a doubt, Musorgsky did not write as one learns in conservatories, and this was good fortune for him and for us [. . .], but he did not write any the more "incorrectly," if that word means anything musically. An instinct more certain than rules guided his sensibility and his genius.[14]

After the Bolshevik Revolution, at home and abroad

(ANATOLY LUNACHARSKY, BORIS ASAFIEV, ALEXANDER GLAZUNOV, DMITRY SHOSTAKOVICH, M. D. CALVOCORESSI, WILLY SCHMID, CARL DAHLHAUS)

Anatoly Vasilievich Lunacharsky (1875–1933), old Bolshevik, Marxist literary and music critic, minor dramatist, and cultural historian, served from 1917 to 1929 as the first People's Commissar of Enlightenment. Energetic in protecting Russian national culture during the Revolution and Civil War, Lunacharsky worked tirelessly to save artists' lives and to establish a "Communist basis to culture" by promoting modernism and radicalism in the arts. Even Lenin – who was, as a rule, indifferently tolerant of artistic experimentation – often expressed dismay at Lunacharsky's pluralism; Stalin, naturally, removed him from his post in 1929.

Lunacharsky's several essays on Musorgsky combine much keenness of observation with an unnerving Bolshevik mix of aggrieved nationalism and class consciousness. His eulogy to Musorgsky in this essay might be seen as an early Soviet move to make this rebellious opera – and its rebellious source text, Pushkin's play – socially respectable within Marxist ideology. He begins conventionally, by declaring the common people to be the opera's primary hero. Faced with the people's irresponsible behavior (in turn ironic, inarticulate, and deceived), Lunacharsky defends them much as Lenin defended the contradictions of the Christian anarchist Leo Tolstoy: as a "mirror of the Russian revolution," that is, as persons whose ideologically retrograde behavior was unfortunate but appropriate to their historical condition. Perhaps oddly, Lunacharsky designates as the mature mouthpiece for the popular conscience the representative of a reactionary class and ideology, the old monk Pimen.

Lunacharsky also reinforces both the "myth of the malign directorate" and the view that Musorgsky prepared the revision of *Boris* under protest, and he reaffirms the imputed class war between Musorgsky, committed populist, and the institutions of the imperial bureaucracy.

[1920] Musorgsky pursued two great ideas, fully consciously, in his creative work.

First of all he wanted to be *truthful*, he wanted to be a *realist* in that area which seemed to be least of all accessible to realism. With inimitable boldness and the freshness of genius he demanded from music that it speak concretely and convincingly, on behalf of living life, that it serve as carrier of those spectacles which, having come out of life, would directly return to life, like a force that cultivates and educates human souls.

When I formulate this task of Musorgsky's realism, in essence I approach his other great idea – outside of which he would not have been a musician and perhaps not an artist at all. A mere copy of reality least of all has claims to being musical. And I repeat, in general even the most skillful copying can hardly create an artist.

The heart of the matter is not to be found in naturalism alone, for Musorgsky's second idea was *greatness of content*, depth of psychological penetration, [two qualities] which made the truth portrayed by him *complexly significant*, raising it above the everyday truth that we can meet in life. [. . .]

And only very recently, in Russia as well as in France, thanks to musicians such as Debussy, Musorgsky has become generally recognized as a great among musicians, not only as a person who marked out new paths in opera and who does not have a single worthy successor, but also as a person who created new horizons for music itself [. . .]

Among Musorgsky's operas, the highest degree of completedness belongs to *Boris Godunov*. Pushkin's historical drama is itself a great work. [. . .] But remarkably, Pushkin's text did not fully satisfy Musorgsky; he did not limit himself, as so many do, to cuts in the text, but made a whole series of extremely important additions.

Why?

Pushkin touched upon the crowd in a masterful way, but he only touched upon it. The simple remark "The people remain silent" [the final stage direction of Pushkin's play], is memorable, it stuns us; and in other places small exclamations arising from the crowd characterize this unfortunate, beaten, agitated mass that nevertheless ultimately creates history. But this great muteness is what interested Musorgsky most of all. In his music drama he decided to make the people his main hero. Did he make the people great, did he invest them with the features of a fairy-tale hero, did he celebrate their virtues? Nothing of the sort! Internally true to Pushkin's masterful analysis, he made them just as abandoned, beaten, cowardly, cruel, weak – the crowd as it was and had to be under the conditions of an anti-popular regime that for centuries had fettered any vital activity of the democratic forces. And all the same, this people evokes immense sympathy – not pity, but profound compassion, connected with an involuntary premonition of the potential strength and greatness of the popular masses. [. . .]

Musorgsky's libretto itself, in its remaining [non-folk portions], adheres more or less to Pushkin. In this connection we must note that in the original construction of the opera there was no Marina Mniszech and no scene at the fountain, but the theater directorate of the time categorically announced that an opera without love simply could not exist, and Musorgsky, not without resistance and gritting his teeth, inserted this scene, which in general he did not like, although it is written in a sufficiently competent way so as not to spoil the opera. [. . .]

The first scene of the first act coincides with the most masterful pages of Pushkin's dramatic poem, bringing the chronicler Pimen on stage as a representative of the popular conscience. The people are not silent: by the church elder's withered hand, everything that lives in the people's heart as a deaf protest is transferred to pages that will survive centuries. The people themselves are eternal and write their own commentary for the coming years of their maturity. And there, alongside the greatness of the collective – expressed in Pimen, who has renounced his own personality – is the rebellious individualist, the adventurer Grigory.

The second scene, the Inn, gives Musorgsky the opportunity to create some unusually vivid pages. [. . .] The figure of Varlaam dominates over everything. This is a genuine rollicking, broad, absurd, chaotic Russian nature. [. . .] From Oblomov to Ilya Muromets, all is contained in the supremely rich nature of Varlaam, who, in another time, perhaps would have been the great son of a great people, but in the given circumstances becomes merely an obscene do-nothing rogue and debauched old man. [. . .] If Pushkin had lived to see this musical-scenic embodiment of his concept, most likely he would have triumphantly greeted this union of his own genius with the genius of Musorgsky. [. . .]

We repeat: more vividly than in Pushkin, a contrast is sustained throughout the entire opera between the seething, suffering but predatory powers-that-be and the blindness of a still more suffering infant-people, for whom everything is in the future.[15]

Boris Vladimirovich Asafiev [pseudonym Igor Glebov] (1884–1949), musicologist, theorist, composer, was author of half-a-dozen essays on *Boris Godunov* and one of the most respected and prolific music critics in the inter-war Soviet Union. In his *Boris* essays of the late 1920s, Asafiev passionately propagandized for *Boris* in the de-Rimskified edition of Pavel Lamm – a conflation of Musorgsky's two versions. Supporting his case with lengthy socio-psychological arguments, Asafiev noted Musorgsky's peculiar intonation and his "improvisatory" style (he even drew comparisons with impressionist painters). The later essays from the 1930s and 40s are more sober and conservative. While incorporating much obligatory Stalin-era cliché about Musorgsky's revolutionary populism, Asafiev now reassesses more positively the services of Rimsky as an editor. The times had changed: by 1948 the fad of "Musorgsky's original" had passed, the Bolshoy was mounting a new production of *Boris* in Rimsky's editing, and a neo-Romantic cult of buoyant folksongs and consonant sounds had long enjoyed a central place in the aesthetics of Socialist Realism.

Our excerpts sample both periods. First, there is the early zealous defense of Musorgsky's original score as an ascetic, "anti-Wagnerian" work more resembling Monteverdi than any nineteenth-century operatic norms (1928). Then we include a brief passage from a later and very lengthy essay (1945–48) that stresses Musorgsky's commitment to a national operatic music based on the intonational peculiarities of Russian speech; the excerpt also contains provocative – if initially somewhat counter-intuitive – comments on the laconicism and "absence of commotion" that, according to Asafiev, characterize the opera. This later essay, written for inclusion in a projected volume of "Scholarly Papers of the Moscow State Conservatory," never appeared in Stalin's Russia.

[1928] "Why is it necessary to perform Musorgsky's *Boris Godunov* in its authentic form?" It would seem that the question makes absolutely no sense. Over fifty years ago in Russia, the epoch of populism produced the conditions necessary for the creation of the opera *Boris Godunov*. [...] Musorgsky's experiment was so far ahead of its time that almost twenty years after its realization, the editorial interference of Rimsky-Korsakov was required to accommodate Musorgsky's score to the tastes of the theater public and to the luxuriant baroque style of the "last empire." To this end the entire score of *Boris* was subject to severe pedagogical review and was *smoothed out* and polished up in accordance with the musico-theoretical views and technical devices of Rimsky-Korsakov – a composer with a vivid and strong individuality of his own. [...]

All this was done in the name of convenience and for ease in execution and performance, and for the sake of the popularity of Musorgsky's music – whose talent had always been acknowledged but whose right to speak in his own language had been taken away due to doubts concerning his alleged illiteracy. And what was the result? A brilliant historical theater performance with the figure of the repentant villain Boris right up front, with his sumptuous coronation and no less sumptuous end. Folk drama retreated to the background and the people, as an urgently immediate element, were softened and ennobled. Thanks to changes in the nature of Musorgsky's choruses, thanks to the non-staging of the Kromy scene, much that is essential but severe in the opera's music was overshadowed by beautiful writing. Most important, the intonation was completely changed. Without noticing it himself, Rimsky-Korsakov turned *Boris Godunov* into *his own* opera. [...]

This situation was further helped by the fact that one of Chaliapin's most powerful roles, that of Tsar Boris, was learned by the artist precisely in the Rimsky version. Chaliapin's tours abroad promoted the success and popularity of the opera. But little by little, interest in the performing artist was replaced by interest in the composer, and then, linked with the growth of that interest, there arose a desire to get to know Musorgsky's *Boris* in its authentic form. [...] The tenth anniversary of the October Revolution opened up new paths to an awareness of Musorgsky's music: the Music Sector of the State Publishing House issued a piano–vocal score under P. A. Lamm's editorship and is now preparing for publication a score of *Boris Godunov* which will bring together everything that Musorgsky created under that title. [...]

[It is now clear that in Rimsky-Korsakov's edition] we have a peculiar example of the shortsightedness of a great master: on the one hand, faith in the rightness of his theory up to the point of merciless "censor's" reprisals against "muddy voice-leading." On the other hand, all this correcting turns out to be so harmless and formalistic that, you see, nothing at all is changed in the music and it all corresponds to the author's wishes. How is this possible? Could it be that all this theory and the "purge" that results from it is so *external and formal* that no matter to whose work these methods are applied, and no matter how, the essence of the work does not suffer? We must deliver a death sentence to such formalism, because in music there should not be such a separation between *what* and *how*, between that which is expressed and the means of expression. [...]

Let's assume that Michelangelo "edited" Raphael, that Wagner "corrected" Debussy, [...] that Stravinsky "fixed up" Schoenberg or Skryabin. Try to apply Turgenev's language to Gogol's language or Tolstoy's syntax to Dostoevsky's – what will you get? And the Russian language, after all, is one and the same for all of them. Only a soulless and moribund formalism in music can reconcile itself to a single "theory" for all ages, times, nations and people ... [...]

I repeat: it is time for Musorgsky's music to answer for itself. Our epoch has no need to soften and prettify the severe and astringent language characteristic of Musorgsky, just as we do not need sumptuous orchestral finery, deeply alien to the ascetic texture of the original. By its nature, *Boris Godunov* is a vocal opera (not in the sense of virtuoso Italian vocal art, but in the sense of Musorgsky's main idea: melody created by the sound of human voices). Under no circumstances should the orchestra play a dominant or externally decorative role. In this sense, and also by the nature of its deeply Russian musico-speech intonations, *Boris Godunov* is an anti-Wagnerian composition. And without doubt, its success in the West is connected with a falling-off of interest in Wagnerian symphonic-instrumental dramas. "The music of the future" is yielding to the truthful emotional music of the Russian musician-dramatist. [. . .] As is the case with Musorgsky's other work, I repeat, the vocal quality of *Boris Godunov* does not answer to the conception of "operatic vocality" in an Italian-*cantilena* or a virtuoso "concertizing" style. In principle, *Boris Godunov* stands much closer to the musical and dramatic experiments of the Florentines at the beginning of the seventeenth century, closer to Monteverdi.[16]

[1928] The Coronation scene, as it now sounds [i.e., in Musorgsky's orchestration], once again underscores Musorgsky's astonishing sensitivity with regard to the psychology of the people. Boris's coronation flows directly from the crowd's words in the opening scene, [which appear only in the concluding *tableau*, cut by Musorgsky in revision]: "If they want us to howl, we'll howl at the Kremlin"; this coronation is by no means the subject for an independent scene with all the pomp of "grand opera." Rimsky-Korsakov moved in an entirely wrong direction by turning it – in conformity with the taste of the public of his time – into a courtly spectacle or an episode from a historical novel.

[. . .] If we may judge by [Musorgsky's] severe and ascetic music, by the passive character of the chorus's song [. . .], and by the composer's instrumentation, there are ample grounds for thinking that Musorgsky's conception speaks of an *involuntary* festivity and an *involuntary* coronation. The people praise the tsar reluctantly. The boyars quickly are compelled to take up and underscore the people's voices. Shuisky conducts himself as an experienced stage manager. But every effort born of command quickly fails. [. . .] And not only for Boris, but also for the people, the coronation is full of gloomy feelings and characteristics.[17]

[1945–48] From these few comments [on Chaliapin and on the degree of sumptuous gesture necessary in the title role], it is clear how difficult it must have been to resolve problems of performance in *Boris Godunov*, and how the truth of Musorgsky's music demands a rejection of scenic extravaganzas, including both the extremes of gesticulation and the overloading of the action with visually "mute" witnesses. "It's a remarkable opera," one astute foreigner remarked, "when in Verdi you would always sense noise, drama right out front, here there reigns silence – and the clanging of the chimes which disturbs this silence is huge, the way the beating of your heart seems huge during insomnia: in *Boris*, these are the footsteps of conscience."

One more curious aspect to the music in *Boris* is the sedate and measured quality of its flowing, which transmits a sense of the sedate and measured passage of time rather than the hustle and bustle of a human gait. From this also follows a corresponding rhythm in the on-stage action. The rare individual flashes do not disturb the basic impression of the opera's gait or "opera time" as one of sedateness, measuredness, an absence of commotion and human vanity.

Life really passed that way in those times. Musorgsky sensed, through nuances in rhythm and tempo, the subtle shifts in the psychology of the history of the epoch, and he did so with a sensitivity that is inaccessible to novelists. [. . .] A laconicism and a refined precision of intonation in the dialogues against a background of sedate, measured tempos and rhythms: here is where the intuitive sensitivity of the opera dramatist really shows, in opposition to the elements of cantata-like and oratorio-like writing that occur not infrequently in Glinka and Borodin. Moreover, when the tempo and rhythmic patterns are suddenly wound up or loosened up by Musorgsky (as when we work up to Varlaam's song in the Inn, or in the whirlwind beginning of the Kromy scene), then it seems as if life has "spiralled off somewhere," as if a tornado has struck. And there rises up before us, in full height, the mastery of Musorgsky's command over the theatrical nature of music. Only we are not accustomed to observing these phenomena, nor to studying them. [18]

Alexander Konstantinovich Glazunov (1865–1936), Russian composer, pedagogue, and student of Rimsky-Korsakov, became a professor at Petersburg Conservatory in 1899 and remained active well into the Soviet period. In his eight symphonies as well as a wide variety of chamber works, Glazunov succeeded in combining, in his own lyrical style, the folk and national principles of the Mighty Handful with the rich melodiousness of Tchaikovsky.

Glazunov was the leading composer of stature in the 1920s to resist the "restorationism" of Lamm and Asafiev. The Lamm–Asafiev score was used for a conflationist new production of *Boris* mounted in the 1927–28 season of the Leningrad Academic Opera Theater. Apropos of this performance, under the general rubric "Controversy over *Boris Godunov*," the article below appeared in the *Red Gazette* together with an article by Igor Glebov [Boris Asafiev] arguing the opposite position. Asafiev's anti-Rimsky stand was clearly favored by the editorial board of the paper – which caused Glazunov considerable bitterness – and after one more exchange the debate was brought to a close.

Note that Glazunov defends Rimsky's orchestration on the grounds that it more closely resembles the effects Musorgsky achieved in his own performed piano realizations of the score. Glazunov also laments, and properly, what has since become notorious practice: an arbitrary conflation of the "best" scenes from both Musorgsky's versions under the single label "original version."

[1928] Musorgsky's *Boris Godunov*, presented for consideration to the Directorate of the Imperial Theaters in 1870, was at first rejected. The reasons, apparently, were "an abundance of choruses, ensembles, and the absence of solo numbers." The opera was first performed on 26 January 1874 [sic]. Not long before the premiere, a full piano–vocal score of *Boris* was published, and *precisely from this moment is it proper to consider [that we have] an original edition of the author's.*

At first *Boris* enjoyed success, but due to ever diminishing box-office returns it was subsequently removed from repertory.

I was present at the final performances of *Boris*. Knowing its music perfectly, and in ecstasy over it, I carried away the impression at the time that in comparison with its sonority on the piano, the opera lost a good deal with an orchestra: in an orchestra neither the power, nor the fullness, nor the intensification of sound is felt. To be sure, a certain intuitive feeling for color is present, but all the same there is a hint of the orchestrator's inexperienced hand, which manifests itself in impracticality and some-times even in unperformability. Rimsky-Korsakov, a passionate admirer of Musorgsky and a witness to the creative conception and growth of *Boris*, took all this into consideration when approaching the revision of a work greatly valued by him. He had no selfish aims, in fact no aims at all except the desire to open a path to a forgotten work. Not only did Rimsky-Korsakov not intend to oblige anyone's tastes, but for his selfless work he, as co-author, did not even receive an honorarium, neither from the publisher nor from the theaters . . .

Rimsky-Korsakov attended to three aspects of Musorgsky's imperfect music writing: (1) to the general technical side of the score, which suffered from carelessness; (2) to the orchestration, which Rimsky-Korsakov created anew under the influence of the graphic and orchestrally-colored keyboard performances [that he had heard] from the author Musorgsky himself, who was a first-class pianist; and (3) to several departures of the libretto from Pushkin's text.

Without denying that Rimsky inserted a certain measure of his own individuality into *Boris*, I point out that Mozart did not hesitate to undertake an independent reworking of the oratorio *Messiah* by so great a master as Handel, citing as his reason insufficient sonority and an orchestration twenty years out of date. For this he was roundly censured. But I am convinced that Handel's creation only gained in Mozart's edition.

In an analogous situation, *Boris Godunov* in Rimsky-Korsakov's reworking – to which Rimsky binds no one – is a work that is in all respects artistically integral, true to the traditions of Musorgsky, and I would have thought that we could show greater trust in the inspired and expedient labor of an artist who endowed his best friend with world fame. *That is why I insist that* Boris Godunov *be performed, as before, in Rimsky-Korsakov's edition.*

In conclusion I point out that *Boris Godunov* is performed at the Academic Opera Theater not in Musorgsky's original [1874] edition to which I have referred. A whole series of episodes are omitted and the St. Basil's scene, which musically presents nothing new, is even re-inserted. It is common knowledge that Musorgsky himself, after he had written a sketch [sic] for this scene, removed it with the Kromy scene in mind.[19]

Dmitry Dmitrievich Shostakovich (1906–75), one of the very great Soviet composers, is the author of fifteen symphonies, two major operas, and abundant chamber work. His decision in 1939–40 to rework *Boris Godunov* marks a new phase in the debate of "Rimsky versus the original," namely, that neither version is satisfactory and thus restoration and reorchestration should be attempted anew.

To be sure, Shostakovich inherited the assumption that dissatisfaction with someone else's published piece of music can be taken as license to rework it in the author's name. (Note his curious defense that "Musorgsky himself changed many things on the advice of Stasov, Rimsky-Korsakov and others.") More surprising than mere technical correction, however, is Shostakovich's apparently earnest goal to impart to Musorgsky's opera "features of the Soviet epoch," just as Rimsky had allegedly imparted "the ideology, thoughts and mastery of an earlier century." Part of this attitude might be due to the conventions of Soviet newspaper interviews; part, however, is no doubt due to the general ethos of updating and rewriting literary and musical classics in the interests of the new society – a practice so taken for granted in Stalinist culture that it needed no special defense.

[1941] Almost simultaneously with the creation of my Piano Quintet [i.e., at the end of 1939], I was busy working over a new edition of Musorgsky's opera *Boris Godunov*. I had to re-examine the score, somehow smooth over the roughness of the harmonization, the unsuccessful and bizarre orchestration, separate harmonic progressions. A whole series of instruments were introduced into the orchestration that were not used by Musorgsky himself nor by Rimsky-Korsakov when he edited *Boris Godunov*.

I revere Musorgsky, I consider him the greatest Russian composer. To penetrate as deeply as possible into the original creative concept of this composer of genius, to uncover this concept and bring it before his listeners – such was my task. After all, Musorgsky himself changed and reworked a good deal under the influence of advice from Vladimir Stasov, Nikolay Rimsky-Korsakov, and others. Rimsky-Korsakov himself changed many things in the opera in the process of editing it.

The Rimsky edition of *Boris Godunov* reflects the ideology, thoughts, and craftsmanship of the past century. One cannot but react to Rimsky-Korsakov's immense labor with a feeling of the greatest respect. But I wanted to edit the opera on another plane, to reflect in it, as much as possible, the features of the Soviet epoch. I strove to achieve a greater symphonic development in the opera, to give the orchestra a greater role than merely to accompany the singers.

Rimsky-Korsakov was despotic, he strove to subordinate Musorgsky's score to his own creative style, he recomposed a great deal and added some things. I only changed a few individual measures and recomposed very little.

In Musorgsky's score, some things sounded very poorly: the tolling of bells and the coronation (in the beginning of the opera), the Polonaise in the Polish act. But precisely those were the scenes of immense symphonic intensity! Some musicologists insist that these scenes do not sound bad at all, but sound good. It's just that the composer, in order to show the whole paltriness of the Polish gentry, in order to stress the fact that the people were dissatisfied with the coronation of Boris Godunov, wrote those scenes on that level. [Though his paraphrase is exaggerated, Shostakovich refers here, it would seem, to remarks of Boris Asafiev; see above, p. 165.] This argument is very easy to refute. The late Glazunov often said that Musorgsky himself played the bell-ringing scenes at the piano. They sounded splendid, as did the coronation scene. Glazunov recalled that Musorgsky performed for his friends the most successful excerpts with special pleasure.

The bell-ringing in the opera *Boris Godunov* sounds like a pitiable parody. And yet from the transcription made by Musorgsky for piano four hands, it's clear to what extent these pages were richly executed by the composer.

In my new edition, the folk scene "Near Kromy" occupies a more significant place than it did earlier. This is one of the most important scenes. In the score it's orchestrated very poorly, timidly. It had to be redone.

It was by no means my principle to change every note no matter what. Take, for example, the scene in the Cell: its beginning is orchestrated splendidly. Naturally there was no reason to change it. It would have been silly to replace the violas in this scene with cellos, or clarinets, or bassoons. I didn't even touch this scene.

Those who think that I didn't leave a stone standing in this orchestration are cruelly mistaken. I worked over the new edition in the following way. Before me lay Musorgsky's and Rimsky's orchestral scores, but I didn't look at them. I only glanced now and then at Musorgsky's piano–vocal score, and did the orchestration whole acts at a time. Only afterwards did I compare what I had written with the orchestral scores of the two composers. If I found that one or another place was done better in their scores, and it had come out worse in my version, then I immediately restored the better one.

I worked with great excitement over this edition of *Boris Godunov*. I literally sat whole days and nights over the score. For the past few years it has been one of my most engrossing projects. Now it is basically finished, but during rehearsals there will probably crop up a series of corrections, changes, and additions. [The forthcoming performance implied by Shostakovich in this last sentence did not take place.][20]

Michel Dimitri Calvocoressi (1877–1944), one of Musorgsky's most important Western biographers, was a French music critic of Greek parentage. Although his first book (published in 1902) was about Liszt, he quickly was attracted to Russian music and served as Diaghilev's French lieutenant during the years prior to World War I. In that capacity, he was involved in the production of *Boris Godunov* at Paris in 1908, and ultimately received the Tsarist Order of St. Anne in recognition of his services to Russian music.

Calvocoressi is perhaps best known for his three books on Musorgsky, the latter two of which remain standard references. He also wrote numerous periodical articles on the composer, translated the libretto of *Boris* into English for the Oxford University Press, and championed the cause of performing the composer's music in auctorial editions. Many points of view concerning Musorgsky that remain current in the West trace their authority to Calvocoressi and, through him, to the Soviet scholars of the 1920s and 1930s on whom he relied. Although his work has been superseded in several particulars, he remains the leading Western European scholar of Musorgsky of the period between World War I and World War II.

Our first text, despite the disclaimer at the end, shows Calvocoressi ready to believe in the superiority of Musorgsky's initial *Boris* even before he had seen Lamm's edition. Once the score was in print, Calvocoressi argued unfalteringly in support of the conflation of the composer's two versions – the "supersaturated" *Boris*. With varying degrees of passion, he maintained consistently throughout the rest of his career that both the idea of revision and all the cuts had been forced upon Musorgsky by "the managers, conductor, stage-manager, and so forth" of the Imperial Theaters, thereby helping to entrench what we have called "the myth of the malign directorate." Though expressing gratitude for some of the presumably involuntary revisions – "How very much poorer we should be," he writes, "if the revolution scene had not been written" – he never abandoned the belief that the supersaturated *Boris* was the best *Boris*, often supporting his position with arguments borrowed from Asafiev and his disciples. Our second text illustrates this aspect of his work.

[1927] It was known, through the Russian biographers of Musorgsky, that the version performed in 1874 was not the very first, but an after-thought and in some respects a compromise, certain parts being altered, others introduced by way of a sop to the managers of the Petrograd Opera and upon the advice of Musorgsky's friends. But it is only of late that Prof. Paul Lamm, of Moscow, started work on the first, hitherto unpublished and unknown version, which is shortly to be published with all variants and additions made by Musorgsky himself.

The time to write the full history of the genuine *Boris Godunov* has not yet come. [. . .] This much, however, I wish to say forthwith: the first draft, the outcome of Musorgsky's unhampered, enthusiastic, swift work, shows from the purely musical point of view, how very sure and apposite his methods were. There has been so much talk of his lack of skill that certain people might now and then be tempted to imagine him as proceeding by a series of random shots, hitting or missing the mark, as the case might be – although he very seldom, if ever, missed it. But a comparison between the first genuine *Boris* and the second will reveal the actual intuitive logic that co-operated with his imagination, and will account for many things that in the second *Boris* may appear to be just incredibly lucky "bull's-eyes."

I do not wish to imply that the 1874 *Boris* is to be considered in any way inferior to the primitive. This is a question whose solution may wait. [. . .][21]

[1928] I have referred more than once in these columns to an astounding piece of news that came from Russia in 1924, or thereabouts: that a collation (the first ever attempted) of the original manuscripts of Musorgsky's *Boris Godunov* had revealed the fact that Musorgsky's masterpiece had never been published as he had written it. [. . .]

Already in 1869 Musorgsky, after completing *Boris Godunov* according to his own conception, had been compelled to recast it because the management of the Imperial Theatres would have nothing to do with it as it then stood – a direct, mercilessly sombre drama, all dialogue and choruses, lacking practically every feature of grand opera, in which there was hardly any "singing," and only a couple of very small female parts. So he set to work, altered and considerably enriched *Boris Godunov* [. . .].

Very fortunately the manuscripts of both versions were preserved. And today, thanks to the patient, well-judged, and admirably carried-out labour of Prof. Paul Lamm, of Moscow, the full and genuine text of *Boris Godunov* is made available. The edition, containing all known variants, reveals in their entirety both the initial and the final versions. Footnotes show exactly what was cut in the 1874 edition, so that it is possible to compare the complete version not only with the 1874 abridgement, but also with the despised and rejected initial version. Generally speaking there can be no doubt that by recasting *Boris Godunov* after 1869, Musorgsky improved his work in many respects, giving us a great deal of beautiful music that was not in the first version. [. . .] But Musorgsky also did away with much that was altogether admirable. [. . .]

As for the curtailments, they are purely and simply deplorable. [. . .] Practically every bit of the music that was cut out contributed to the compactness of the whole – a compactness which can be felt even in the 1874 version but is far more apparent, and certainly more easily demonstrable by concrete proof, in the unabridged text. [Calvocoressi here inserts a footnote, which reads in part: "Could any of us have guessed that the 1874 text was incomplete? I think not. And yet we can see now – and see very clearly – how far it fell short of what Musorgsky had actually achieved. *Never again can it fully satisfy anyone who knows the full text* [emphasis added]." He next turns to an examination of the music. We rejoin him at his discussion of the *Terem* scene.]

[. . .] There are big differences in the monologue of Boris, in his dialogue with Shuisky, and in the final hallucination.

At first blush, when one is accustomed to the later version of the monologue, the music of the earlier version may strike one not only as starker (which is a gain if anything) but as rougher, more angular. One may be disconcerted a while, as one would be by suddenly encountering any familiar work in altered form. But even then one can hardly fail to realise the pregnancy and force of Musorgsky's first inspiration. What it lacks in romantic colour and sensational contrasts it more than makes up for in terseness and austere grandeur. The music is founded on one theme only – one of several mutually related themes that accompany Boris – and the Dimitri theme appears towards the end.

The psychological differences between the two versions are most clearly brought out by the Russian critic M. Igor Gliebof [Boris Asafiev] in a pamphlet on *Boris Godunov*, just published at Moscow, which contains the finest criticism ever written on the subject:

> In the second version, Musorgsky adopts a more sentimental tone. He shows Boris no longer under an aspect of unmitigated grimness, but as a repentant sinner whom he pities. He accordingly imparts to his music a warm, lyrical quality, touching upon distress, repentance, prayer, and qualms of conscience in turn . . . The music of the first version was far better suited to the original conception of the whole opera, that of a social and political tragedy, not the tragedy of Boris's conscience. I consider it as more coherent and better thought out.

[. . .] Now that we have the whole text of *Boris Godunov*, can there be any reason for not producing the work in its entirety? The only one which might be adduced is, it seems to me, the length of the score. It is not a very good reason. *Boris Godunov* is no longer than the *Götterdämmerung*, the *Meistersingers*, or *Parsifal*. Surely, what is done for Wagner's masterpieces can and must be done for Musorgsky's. The complete version is longer than the primitive version, but makes up for its length by affording opportunities for relaxation and points of repose which, far from breaking or unduly delaying the course of the action, co-operate in it. [. . .]

To sum up, in *Boris Godunov* the interest is extraordinarily sustained, balanced, and well distributed. The effect of the cuts practised so far was to illustrate the truth of the old paradox that "cuts make plays and musical works longer" [. . .]. The only *Boris Godunov* which should be performed from now on is the unrevised and complete *Boris Godunov* which appears at a time when many of us had almost given up all hope of the original manuscript ever being published.[22]

Willy Schmid (1876–1944) was one of the few authors to question the consensus that began to emerge concerning *Boris Godunov* in the late 1920s and early 1930s. With the appearance of Pavel Lamm's edition of *Boris Godunov* (1928), the critical contention gained force that Musorgsky's initial version, completed in 1869, had been a stronger work than his own revision, published 1874, and that the revision had been forced upon an unwilling composer by dull-witted bureaucrats and performing musicians in the Imperial Theaters. As we have seen above, the foremost Russian exponent of this view was Boris Asafiev, who wrote under the pen name Igor Glebov.

In the West, M. D. Calvocoressi accepted Asafiev's opinions uncritically, giving them wide circulation. In arguing for the integrity of the composer's final version, Schmid was swimming against the tide in 1928, but his views have been vindicated in our own time.

Both [Mr. Calvocoressi and Mr. Glebov] show a tendency to pass off the version of 1869 as more authentic than that of 1874. And, playing on the words "authentic" and "integral" – two adjectives that may in all justice be applied to the Chester Edition since it integrally reproduces the authentic edition and the only one made by Musorgsky himself – Mr. Calvocoressi gives us to understand that the authentic edition can only be the integral edition comprising, together with the two versions of *Boris*, the small or large fragments discarded in the course of revision. [. . .]

Mr. Glebov insists with good reason on the fact that the first version of *Boris* formed a unity that was valuable in itself and conformed to a definite dramatic conception. That we knew before; but we also knew that Musorgsky, when he undertook to revise his work, modified the conception of the drama itself. He displaced its axis, as it were, and in rewriting his score adjusted the music to his new viewpoint. He created a new work that was sanctioned as definitive by the edition of 1874 no less than by the production of the same year.

That in deciding to retouch his music drama he should have allowed himself to be persuaded by practical considerations – but tending to facilitate its comprehension and to enrich its means of expression – is only natural. It by no means follows that such a revision, undertaken, as we have seen, with the fullest freedom and with such enthusiasm, had of necessity to become no more than a distortion of his first plan. That the score of 1869 is the older of the two is not enough to warrant the inference that it is therefore the more authentic. The fact that Musorgsky relinquished [*The Marriage*], begun with such masterful command of his resources, shows that he was just then passing through a phase of research, that he was feeling his way in the domain of dramatic music; but it also proves that he knew what he wanted without being able to find it immediately and that he was not so greatly influenced by his friends as some people would like to make out. As we know nothing about Musorgsky's feelings with regard to the first version, but are aware of the ardour with which he worked at the second, it is the latter [. . .] that we may reasonably consider as authentic and accept as a criterion whereby to judge the former. [. . .]

[Publication of Lamm's edition] will make it possible for us to follow

Musorgsky down to the minutest detail in his process of creation and elimination that led to the edition of 1874. But it is impossible to see why the re-modelling of these portions should be attributed to nothing more than a desire on Musorgsky's part to conform to expediency and obey the dictates of his friends. [. . .] His reasons for composing this or that portion anew cannot be imagined to have been other than a desire to give them a higher perfection or perhaps to attune them to the new orientation imparted to the drama on its revision. This is very much what one would expect of an artist who was incessantly sailing "towards new shores," nor is this view invalidated by an ambiguous sentence of Mr. Calvocoressi's where, dealing with the two versions of the scene in the Tsar's apartment, he asserts that "the first version . . . is rich in certain beauties worthy of being admired without afterthought – just as one may, and should, admire the definitive version without reference to the first."

[. . .] One cannot help thinking of the successive recastings to which *Fidelio* had to submit and of the ruthless cuts made by Beethoven. Some twenty-five years ago the primitive score was reconstructed and published under the original title of *Leonore*. As a document showing the struggles against himself, endured by Beethoven when he wrote for the stage, this score is highly instructive; but I know of no opera house where *Leonore* ever supplanted *Fidelio* [. . .].[23]

The late Carl Dahlhaus (1928–89), one of the most influential of twentieth-century musicologists, wrote infrequently of Musorgsky and Russian music. The loss is ours, for when he chose to examine this composer, his insight was keen. Here he discusses one of the monk's choruses near the beginning of the Cell scene, and it is worth noting that the music under discussion represents Musorgsky's second thoughts. In the initial version, the monks sing only once, at the very end of the scene.

The off-stage chorus of monks chanting a prayer (Fig. 9 [in the Cell scene]) uses harmonies which convey the effect of a church mode, in other words provide some musical local colour, or what Marxist aesthetic theorists would call 'milieu realism'. The last chord, c♯ minor in the sixth bar from Fig. 9, is simply inexplicable in terms of the rules of tonality as they were understood in the nineteenth century, except as the blunder of a dilettante. The progression V–III in A major takes the place of a cadence, without performing its function, according to the criteria of major-minor tonality. But the archaicizing modality is also somewhat problematical as an instance of stylistic imitation: it is certainly not a case of simple reproduction of church-mode harmony as originally understood. While a 'Dorian' Sixth was just one degree among others in the sixteenth century,

175

by the nineteenth it was recognized as a deviation from the minor scale and the 'characteristic' degree of the Dorian mode: it was solely by a reference to the minor scale, which the sixteenth century did not make but the nineteenth could not help making, that the concept of the 'Dorian' Sixth existed, as it had not in the sixteenth century. The alterations to which modal harmony was subjected in the nineteenth century were, so to speak, 'composed out' by Musorgsky. The conspicuously modal final chord, C♯ minor, is the unexpected conclusion of a chord progression, B minor – E major, which raises expectations of a tonal continuation and indeed was continued tonally earlier, in the choir's first lines (B major – E major – A major = II – V – I). The juxtaposition of a tonal and a modal version of the progression means nothing less, however, than that the C♯ minor chord, the modal element, is there because the composer deliberately decided against a tonal cadence, and his avoidance of the expected cadence is plain for all to see. The modality – the means whereby the realist, historical local colour was achieved, should therefore not be interpreted as a naïvety; it must have been chosen by Musorgsky as a precisely calculated deviation from the tonal norm, and with full consciousness of the historical distance separating the nineteenth century from the sixteenth. Schoenberg would diagnose a lack of musical logic, because Musorgsky did not, at the end of the chorus, draw the musical consequences implicit in its start, but side-stepped into the unexpected. But this apparent sign of clumsiness is in fact a skilful device intended to create not only modal harmony but also the impression of the exotic, and thus to make the historical element of 'milieu realism' tangible. Musorgsky was a self-taught composer, but he was also undoubtedly an intellectual one.[24]

Epilogue

(SERGEY SLONIMSKY)

The March 1989 issue of the leading Soviet music journal, *Sovetskaya muzyka* [Soviet music], was devoted to the Sesquicentennial of Musorgsky's birth. This entry provides a taste of *glasnost*-age speculation on Musorgsky's meaning for both performers and cultural historians of the twenty-first century. Sergey Slonimsky (b. 1932) is a prolific Soviet composer of symphonies, vocal cycles and operas.

Slonimsky's irreverent opening sentences about the probable fate of Musorgsky's *Boris* had it been composed in the twentieth century might serve to put the debate over various editions in some perspective. His later ruminations on the sad significance of the Boris plot for Russian history capture well the mood that has become routine in the late 1980s for Russian intellectuals reconsidering the cultural monuments of their nation's past.

I risk opening these very subjective comments with a contentious and unprovable assertion. If the opera *Boris Godunov*, and even more so *Khovanshchina*, had appeared in the seventies not of the last but of the present century (not to speak of the forties or fifties), I make bold to assert: Musorgsky would not have the academic status of a classic. More likely these works would not be permitted on the stage at all, nor into print – in any case, not in the form in which they were created by the composer, who was the author of the libretto of *Boris* and of the entire literary text of *Khovanshchina*. And those who would be setting straight the ideological concept, the dramatic content, and many individual scenes, dialogues and rejoinders (and consequently the music as well) would not be any Rimsky-Korsakov or Shostakovich but rather those censors and office overseers, very familiar but in no way noteworthy, modestly hidden away in literary committees and bureaucratic departments, acting according to instructions. (Their activity over the past several decades has been felt on all of our hides, and on Shostakovich and Prokofiev more than on any others.) [...]

Even today, Musorgsky's creations are not simple, but full of riddles. They help us to contemplate human fates, the history of our fatherland, without glossing over any of its difficulties or the roughness of life as it really is. Involuntarily, various allusions to later epochs arise – right up to the Stalinist, Khrushchev and Brezhnev years. [...] Musorgsky foresaw and predicted a great deal. He saw the past not only in the present but also in the future.

These operas, without an apotheosis of any kind, are remarkable for the ambivalent, unpredictable behavior of people and whole masses – who do not submit to any peaceful, systematic accounting or control. Unexpected characters and whole groups burst out of the thick of the people and disappear back into it. The crowd grows or disperses in front of our eyes; squabbles and conflicts blaze up fanned by news, rumors and gossip. You feel yourself to be not in an auditorium or reading musical notes on a page but in today's living crowd, on the street among raging and blustering little groups or standing in some immense, inevitable line, waiting for essentials. For the non-aggressive person, the popular scenes in *Khovanshchina* (and of course in "Kromy" as well) hold no little danger. There are considerably more little groupings in these scenes than there are social strata or classes of society. And each one of them, hitherto obedient to the authorities, wants to subject or frighten the others. Inside these groups, practically everyone is ready, should the chance arise, to seize leadership and sit on the necks of everyone else. Each against all and all against each! [...] In *Boris*, the people often unite grief, need, rage, and a simple desire, understandable to anyone, to live like human beings. But I repeat, each group wants to become an oligarchy, to rise to the top, to enrich itself. In *Khovanshchina* these groups of the people are themselves already warring with one another. That's what's so terrifying. [. . .]

Having experienced Stalin and Beria, we are compelled to conclude that tyrants and hangmen are not vulnerable to pangs of conscience. Not one single murdered child but thousands, millions (there are no statistics yet, as indispensable as they are . . .) were cast into fatal tortures; interrogated men were blackmailed through the fate of their children and wives. And it was not the tormentors who were tormented by visions and nightmares, but each one of their victims! For this reason, it seems to me, the repentant Boris Godunov is touching but, alas, not very true-to-life – even if he really weren't a villain by nature but had only acted pragmatically, in a way that was advantageous to him and his family . . . Shakespeare's Macbeth and Richard III superstitiously fear only their own death (in this they resemble Stalin), but they do not feel sympathy for the murdered. It's possible that Pushkin's (or more accurately, Karamzin's) Boris was in part an allusion to the living tsar: don't be a tyrant, don't transgress through blood! The main idea of Pushkin and Musorgsky is indisputable: the path to autocratic power, even for an initially decent person, is possible only through murder, violence, cruelty. Speaking frankly, the role of Boris – so supremely effective, so supremely popular since Chaliapin's time – moves me personally much less than many other images of Musorgsky's. Boris's role is precisely too operatic, too deeply theatrical, too actor-ish. [. . .]

In no way do political leaders in Musorgsky crystallize the interests of their subjects and dependents. [. . .] In the finale of *Boris* one hears an intentionally false glorification of the pretender by fugitive monks, somewhat resembling a tearful lament, and later, an absurd quasi-canonic combination of a Russian "Glory!" with a Latin *Gloria*. Heterogeneous mobs at odds with one another do honor to the False Dmitry – whose first deed is to free the Jesuits and Godunov's boyar Khrushchov, who had been seized by the rioting peasants. But Boris himself, after all, is just as much of a pretender as Grigory – both seized power in a criminal way and both were far from the needs and thoughts of simple people and even of their own nearest kin. [. . .] No, neither the leaders nor the main heroes of these folk musical dramas express anyone's interests except *their own*! And solely by this inner loneliness and everyday solipsism do they symbolize the spiritual profile of each and of all in society, a society divided not only into classes, social strata, groups, but also into myriads of individual people each stubbornly going his own way, forcing his way upward. All these people are tied to one another against their will, and they struggle to rip apart the rope or chain holding them fast.

But there is one person, the most lonely, the most unfortunate, who is more base than the most low-born group, who has nothing at all – no home, no family, literally not a kopek. And he is the only one who understands everything, predicts everything, and who is compassionate to all. Not only does Musorgsky's holy fool boldly speak the truth to the tsar (as happens in Pushkin) according to the rights of a fool in Christ, he is also elevated to the level of a universal national voice. [Like so many other Russian commentators on the opera, Slonimsky is thinking of a conflated version of Musorgsky's two scores: the holy fool "boldly speaks the truth to the tsar" only in the St. Basil scene, which appears in the initial version; the "quasi-canonic combination of a Russian 'Glory!' with a Latin *Gloria*" occurs only in the Kromy Forest scene, from the revision.] And his elevation is accomplished above all through the very music of his remarkable little song. The purest diatonicism of the first four measures is undercut, imperceptibly but swiftly, by chromatic modal modulations into remote pitch areas, their flickering tonics veiled. A chain of unstable sonorities comes to rest on an augmented triad. The intervallic shape of the melody narrows from fifths at the beginning, through "chant-like" seconds in the middle, to hesitant semitones outside the modality, which distinctly imitate untempered, natural pitch. Having begun strictly diatonically, the naïve little song ends outside all tonality.[25]

PART III

INTERPRETATION

8

THE *BORIS* LIBRETTO AS A FORMAL, LITERARY, AND HISTORICAL PROBLEM

Chapter 3 attempted to capture the storytelling pulse of the opera through a mixture of genres: stage directions, plot summary, details of orchestration and glimpses of score. Reading that synopsis is in fact good preparation for the present chapter – because reading a libretto arouses many of the same suspicions. We suspect that both plot summary and libretto, however well-crafted, are impossibly reduced versions of the real thing. Both make sense only as partial transcriptions and as reminders of a larger, more integral aesthetic experience.

Indeed, as a literary genre the libretto is a vexed entity. Expected to carry the narrative plot, published and read independently of its music yet deemed by most readers to be a ludicrous literary experience without its music, it has long been considered an unsatisfying hybrid.[1] If the librettist takes too many liberties in adapting the literary source (especially if the text is a beloved classic), then accusations of "infidelity" are routine. If, however, attempts are made to be scrupulously faithful to the literary source, then the result is usually judged inappropriate for music – since music, as we know, is forever on guard against too many words, and has proved on the whole a poor vehicle for such essential literary subtleties as semantic ambiguity, paradox, and a sense of past and future. What is more, in all but the most conventional numbers opera, the verbal text must successfully accomplish several tasks at once. It must deliver a well-motivated dramatic narrative on stage. It must aid characters in developing onstage personalities that are integral enough to communicate persuasively even though charged with opera's inevitable stylizations. In addition, the distribution of voice-parts in a libretto must ensure an aural texture that is both pleasing and provocative: virtuosi must be given their show pieces, sopranos should balance basses and tenors, ensembles must be coordinated with solo arias and recitative. Little wonder, then, that the "literary integrity" of a libretto is so often disregarded. The genre serves too many masters.

Disregard for libretti is thus easy to come by in any culture. But such an attitude was especially widespread in nineteenth-century Russia. Among the educated classes, literature enjoyed an almost sacred status, and many considered any tampering with literary texts on behalf of musical form to be akin to blasphemy. What is more, Russian secular music was still in its infancy. "Russian operas" had begun to appear only late in the eighteenth century and professional librettists of the calibre of Metastasio or Scribe were unknown. Musorgsky, however, would not have engaged a librettist in any case. Committed from the beginning of his career to embodying the Russian word in musical form, always fastidious in his attention to verbal texts, his very compositional technique mandated that he be his own librettist. Yet for all this solicitude, Musorgsky could not have been wholly surprised by the ridicule heaped on the *Boris* libretto in reviews of the premiere (see Chapter 7). His verbal texts – and the libretto of *Boris Godunov* in particular – were uncommonly vulnerable to misunderstanding in the 1860s and 70s. In this chapter we will examine that mix of dramatic innovation, sacrilege to Pushkin, and utopian visions about language that made the *Boris* libretto a landmark in the history of Russian opera.

I

Let us begin at the most general level, "utopian visions about language." We must not forget that a crucial half-century separates Musorgsky from those earlier famous tellers of the Boris Tale, Karamzin and Pushkin. In that earlier period, the 1810s and 20s, progressive literary figures in Petersburg and Moscow were deeply influenced by Enlightenment and Sentimentalist ideas. They had celebrated the possibility of Russian culture becoming part of Europe. (In the heated debates between "archaists" and "Westernizers" over Russia's literary identity, both Karamzin and Pushkin had belonged to the cosmopolitan "Westernizing" camp.) By the 1860s, however, polemics had taken a different turn. Now there was a concern over *too much* Europe in Russian culture. Tolstoy was writing his massive *War and Peace* as a challenge to the comfortable, canonic European novel; a decade later, Dostoevsky would predict the collapse of a soulless and commercialized West before a resurrected Russian Orthodox Christianity. And most importantly, the Emancipation of the serfs in 1861 had inspired the nascent Russian populist movement to idealize the potential of the Russian peasantry and its role in the nation's history.

Debates raged anew over the status and future direction of Russian culture. Thanks in large part to the accomplishments of Karamzin and Pushkin a generation earlier, Russia now possessed a mature, flexible literary language adequate to many genres. But the relationship of this literary system to a *musically* distinct language for Russia did not become a major issue until the 1860s, the decade during which an ideology and institutional base for Russian national music was born. The *Moguchaya kuchka* – "Mighty Handful" – set out to create musical and vocal forms that would not be mere Russian approximations of genres that had originated in Western Europe. This task was unusually difficult, however. For reasons relating to church bans on polyphony and instrumentation, Russia lacked a well-developed domestic tradition of secular art music until well into the eighteenth century. Even the so-called "nationalists" were dependent on Western forms. If the Conservatory taught counterpoint, fugue, and classical symphonic form, then the Balakirev Circle analyzed Schumann, Lizst, and the irregularities of a Berlioz symphony. It was one sort of Western heritage against another – as indeed had been the case during earlier reigns, which had witnessed oscillations between Italian-style and French-style opera. Inspired by native material, the musical nationalists hoped to take from other cultures the forms and techniques needed to develop it. But they differed among themselves on the scope of the borrowings and on the musical realization of verbal text. Musorgsky was the most radical of the *kuchkist* composers, both as a musician and as an ideologue of the Russian word, but even he was not immune to the West.

This radical peculiarity of Musorgsky as musical dramatist is in large part due to the eccentric mix of romantic, realist, and neoclassical mimetic impulses in his work. The romantic aspect of his aesthetic, which is to say its opposition of life's emotional spontaneity to cold technical training that produces mere "copy," Musorgsky shared with most populist artists of his time. In their spirit, he was a careful student of Russian folk rhythms, modalities, and popular songs. But Musorgsky was also a realist, in the urgent, almost journalistic sense that the epithet acquired during the 1860s. He set to music as "art songs" – most often to verbal texts of his own devising and even to unreworked overheard speech – the cries of beggars, orphans, young children, holy fools, shrewish wives cursing their drunken husbands, impoverished peasants. Musorgsky in his early period had only a minor talent for writing romances to the standard, exalted "love text" (as we will see, this fact is germane to the evolution of *Boris*). And, although he may have learned from Wagner's scores in certain particulars (see Chapter 9), he was no special fan of Wagnerian opera – which, he believed, was too symphonic and mythic, too distant from the inspiration of everyday life. In the militant prosaicism of his vision, then, Musorgsky departed from both the conservative and the reformist musical practice of his time.

Here we must confront Musorgsky's "mimeticism" – the third, most elusive component of his creativity, often subsumed under his realism. The trait might best be understood in contrast to the work of Alexander Dargomyzhsky, a man much revered by the *kuchkisty* for his pioneeringly faithful musical setting of Pushkin's micro-drama, *The Stone Guest* (1869). Altering scarcely a word, Dargomyzhsky strove to embody the literary text in a continuous, flexible, strikingly lyrical arioso so that each line received individualized expression. But we should note that merely "not to change the words" is an easy sort of fidelity for a musician to observe, especially if exercised on a poetic text. Pushkin's texts, whether poetry or prose, are so supremely balanced and well-crafted that setting them to music word-for-word can only reinforce their lyricism and, as it were, their readymade librettistic qualities. Pushkin in the raw already sounds and feels like what high art music does best.

The youthful Musorgsky wanted music and words fused together in a very different aesthetic. At its base was a new, "realist" understanding of the relation between art and life, which entailed a redefinition of beauty. As Richard Taruskin has shown, this aesthetic had much in common with seventeenth-century mimetic theories of musical art (and especially of recitative) as revived by European theorists in the 1860s.[2] These theories began with the word – whose proper realization, in both art and non-art, was understood to entail inevitably musical components: rhythm, pitch, timbre, volume, tone. Musorgsky was much taken by these ideas. In the spirit of the German aesthetician Georg Gottfried Gervinus (whose *Händel und Shakespeare* had just appeared in Leipzig in 1868), the composer surmised that the meaning of a word, and thus its potential musical exposition, could not be found in dictionaries or etymologies but only in concrete unrepeatable utterances. As a musician, he hoped to contribute to research on his native language by fixing in sound the essential "musicality" of ordinary Russian speech patterns. But Musorgsky's search was inspired by more than the uncomplicated Rousseauian aim of equating music with honest, unstructured emotional response. His was to be a more scientific route, one that documented the dependence of speech on such performative categories as grammatical stress, rhetorical emphasis and intonation. He believed that speech, although infinitely varied, was governed by musical laws that in turn could be discovered by human intellect.

Such faith in the mechanistic matching up of individual expression with "laws" was, of course, part of the optimism of that positivistic era. Utilitarian and monistic theories of art flourished in the Russia of the 1860s, and the enthusiastic subjugation of art to a mimetic reading of reality was much in vogue across all the creative arts.[3] In contrast to Dargomyzhsky's passion for literal fidelity to a poetic masterpiece, then, Musorgsky legitimized his musical realism by an appeal to language as a web of communicative "speech acts." To test his musical skill in amplifying these speech acts, he chose for his first serious operatic experiment not a lyrical text but one that was aggressively prosaic and colloquial: Gogol's dramatic farce *The Marriage*.

As we relate in Chapter 4, Musorgsky devoted the summer of 1868 to the "mimetic experiment" of setting Gogol's play. He interrupted this task to start work on *Boris*, and the techniques applied in *Marriage* – a syllabic, *parlando* setting of the text and empirically derived harmony – marked the new project as well. Although subsequently attenuated, they remained important for Musorgsky throughout his life. "Art is a means of conversing with people and not an end in itself," he wrote in an autobiographical sketch a year before his death. "The task of the art of music is to reproduce in musical sounds not merely modes of feeling but above all the modes of human speech."[4]

A brave credo. One might properly ask, however, what it means in hard practice to base a libretto on dialogic speech and then produce an opera around it. Since speech is forever changing in response to new contexts, it would seem to follow for Musorgsky, at least in his early radical period, that any music written to speech would forgo autonomous, purely musical development. This commitment goes some way toward explaining the composer's early and angry polemics against conservatory-style theory and technique. For Musorgsky at this time, research into the word had priority. He believed that Russian speech had been distorted by borrowings and dilutions, and as a result its intonation, and thus its communication potential, had been crippled. Beginning the *Boris* revisions, Musorgsky put the problem this way: "Modern Russian speech is like a person wearing high-heel inserts and tight shoes, which make his toenails grow all crooked and cause outgrowths of proud flesh; one must cut these growths away and shoe the sick man, if only for a time, in bark sandals."[5] Perhaps, Musorgsky conjectured, the proper sort of vocal music could point the way back to health; perhaps it could rehabilitate and even resurrect his native language. But the composer hoped that capturing in music the authentic intonations of Russian speech would do more than merely rescue a nation's linguistic treasure from the dissipation threatening it. If, he wrote, we could register an emotional intonation with absolute accuracy and "artistic instinct," then perhaps we could "capture our thought processes as well."[6] It is clear that during these years the composer held altogether utopian ideas about the power of spoken language to reveal the workings of the mind.

Before attending to the specifics of the *Boris* libretto, we might wish to consider this issue in its larger context. The task Musorgsky had taken on was difficult and in many ways profoundly counterintuitive.[7] From the perspective of musical form, of course, creating an effective operatic "communication act" is not merely a question of crafting a series of mimetically amplified speech-curves. Nor does successfully integrated musical form naturally generate an expectation of individuated, spontaneous response. (To be sure, music does employ subtle echoing and recapitulation strategies – but these are technically closer to mimicry or to formal "development" than to the dialogue Musorgsky had in mind.)

In short, we must come to terms with the hyperbolic but widely shared opinion recently voiced by the late Carl Dahlhaus: "If modern European spoken drama – as distinct not only from opera but also from mime – rests on the premise that everything important which happens between people can be expressed through speech, then opera . . . has at its core a profound distrust of language. It is not arguments exchanged in recitatives, but affects expressed in arias – i.e., in soliloquies – that reveal the true substance of relationships between characters in musical drama."[8] If this generalization is even partially true, how might a composer with Musorgsky's commitments bridge the contradiction between what dialogue and music each do best?

One place to begin might be to note what linguists have long known about spoken dialogue, namely, that it is inefficient, repetitious, full of phatic reassurances, and extremely sensitive to what might be called "dialogic clamps" at those points where speech subjects change. As we can all attest from experience in everyday spoken dialogue, the interest and energy of real-life communication is sustained through continual monitoring: are you there? do you hear? what is your reaction to what I've just said? As students of Musorgsky have noted, music can do this too.[9] In a musically expressed question, for example, the setting can reflect (through a tentativeness and instability in melody or harmony) the larger context in which all questions occur – the expectation of an answer, the uncertainty of resolution, an avoidance of cadence. Dissonance and chromaticism can be employed to reflect agreement, disagreement, even to reflect that special sort of dialogue grounded in hypocrisy and the lie that is so crucial to *Boris*.[10] In more neutral exchanges on stage, a simple "clamp" or monitoring of the contact ("Yes, we heard each other") can be accomplished by repeating the rhythmic, melodic, or harmonic parameters of a previous phrase. Since music tolerates absolute repetition so much better than words, the possibilities here are many.

Always central to true dialogue, and in tension with a strict sense of musical form, is the preservation of a sense of *spontaneity* – perhaps the single factor most indispensable to active, ongoing speech. We approach here the whole problematic of improvisation, and its application to so highly stylized an aesthetic system as opera is understandably complex. Mid-nineteenth-century operatic art had few conventional means for registering this impulse toward spontaneous form. Musorgsky's letters (so prescient and precise on others' work, so metaphoric, evasive, and impressionistic on his own) are a record of his often painful search. He came up with many techniques. For example, in places Musorgsky abruptly directs the audience's attention to non-foregrounded events, or allows for important action to emerge unexpectedly from the back of the stage or the back of a chorus. Dialogic scenes must always be open to an element of surprise.

The libretto of Musorgsky's new project was thus freighted with significance far beyond the usual for nineteenth-century opera. For global pretensions, perhaps only Wagner's texts can compete. But the fact that two world-class talents, Musorgsky and Pushkin, came together to produce a masterpiece is an event that we appreciate as such only in retrospect. In 1868 Musorgsky was an untried musical amateur, and Pushkin enjoyed nothing like the rapturous nationwide cult that developed around him in the 1890s – a cult that declared him the supreme embodiment of Russian poetic genius, a position he still holds today. To be sure, a small group of aesthetic critics held Pushkin up as the ideal lyric poet of formal perfection. But during the utilitarian 1860s, the much noisier radical critics were busy reducing art to concrete social commentary, or to little more than an imitation – always inferior – of nature. In that decade, a debate was launched over the value of Russia's Golden Age of Poetry (1820s–30s). According to one irritable participant, "no one else among Russian poets can inspire his readers with such limitless indifference to the people's sufferings, such profound contempt for honest poverty, and such systematic rejection of useful work as Pushkin."[11] In order to distance themselves from the leisured aestheticism that Pushkin's aristocratic generation seemed to represent, the radicals called themselves "thinking realists."

Significantly, this was the very term later applied to Musorgsky by the conservative music critic Hermann Laroche, in a review of the 1874 *Boris* premiere (see Chapter 7, pp. 145–47). The challenge was clear. When Vladimir Nikolsky, professor of Russian history and close friend of the *kuchkisty*, suggested to Musorgsky in 1868 that he turn Pushkin's *Boris Godunov* into an opera, the composer had the tantalizing chance to make a unique contribution to the debate. He could bridge the gap between Pushkin and the real world. He would take a mixed prose–poetry work by the very poet who was being idolized by the aesthetic critics, and realize its "realistic" potential by roughing it up into declamatory prose amplified by music.

The libretto of the first, or 1869, version of *Boris* contained seven scenes condensed out of ten of Pushkin's. As Richard Taruskin has observed in his comparison of the two auctorial versions, Musorgsky's principle of selection was sensibly draconian: he incorporated two scenes almost without change, setting them in two orthodox *kuchkist* styles (the "loftily poetic" Cell scene [Pushkin's no. 5, cast in blank iambic pentameter] and the "prosaic" Inn scene [Pushkin's no. 8, written in rhythmic prose]); then, out of the remaining twenty-three scenes of Pushkin's play, "Musorgsky simply threw out all the scenes in which the title character failed to appear."[12] After these massive cuts were made and the necessary linkages fashioned, the remaining text was moved more or less intact into the libretto.

Thus in the first version of the verbal text, the poet's surviving lines were viewed, as it were, through a small window, true to themselves but only in microcosm. Musorgsky had extracted from the panorama just enough to illustrate the guilt-ridden conscience and fate of the Tsar; Pushkin's larger sense of the historical event and the complex relation among his scenes were lost. The Pretender, for example, was altogether eliminated as a physical presence once he passed beyond the Polish border. No trace can be found of Grigory/Dmitry's erotic awakening, of his struggle with Marina, of his appetite for war or the actual invasion of Russia, all of which figure prominently in Pushkin's play. And the People, that ideological staple of later productions, are present as no more than a colorful backdrop. Such a reduction of Pushkin's wide-ranging narrative to the inner conflict of the Tsar was congenial to Musorgsky for several reasons.

First, Musorgsky was still very much in his "mimetic" and "chamber" phase. A convincing symbolic juxtaposition of Catholic Poland and Ortho-dox Russia, as well as the dynamics of a genuinely mass scene, were dramatic techniques he would master only several years later, in part under the creative influence of his apartment mate at the time, Rimsky-Korsakov.[13] In the opera's first version, the geographical spread of the action was much more constricted. This detail we know from recent Russian research into Musorgsky's earliest drafts – for among the many marvels promised by the projected thirty-two-volume Academy Edition of Musorgsky's Works is a closer look at the genesis of the 1869 plot.[14] Since productions of the first auctorial version have come back into vogue in the 1980s and 90s (see Chapter 10), a sampling of this commentary-in-progress is of some interest.

The earliest stage directions, for example, indicate that the opening scene was originally conceived on a rather small scale. The dramatic action took place not in front of the Novodevichy Monastery but inside it. Likewise, the geographical distance separating Tsar Boris from his "biographer" and nemesis, the chronicler Pimen, was minuscule – in fact, the two men were within earshot of each other. It was widely known at the time (but since forgotten) that Chudov Monastery – the Monastery of the Miracle – was situated in a corner of the Moscow Kremlin, looking out on Cathedral Square and located literally across the street from Boris Godunov's quarters. As the Moscow Kremlin's oldest monastery (founded 1365, dismantled 1929), it had special privileges; to be a monk in the Monastery of the Miracle was a high state honor. And as the commentators point out, "the birth of a clergy opposition ... within a few steps of the tsarist palace" adds a treasonous coloration to the Cell scene we do not sense today. One of the goals of the Academy Project is to ascertain what nineteenth-century operagoers took for granted and thus what no one wrote about – and in this way to begin reconstituting the cultural literacy of nineteenth-century theater audiences.

In addition, the educated elite in both Pushkin's and Musorgsky's audience would have known that in 1568 Ivan the Terrible, at the height of his reign of terror, forbade the writing of chronicles, a ban that lingered by inertia until 1630. Thus Pimen puts himself at some risk in recording the story – which, as he tells us in his opening monologue, he expects to be found only by some future anonymous monk who will "shake the dust of centuries off the parchment and recopy these true tales." The chronicler Pimen thus shares the status of "criminal in hiding" with his own subject matter, the Tsar. For the rulers of both secular and sacred realms, then, irrepressible truth is pitted against the cunning of politics, and all within a space commensurate with a theater stage.

This first libretto adaptation of Pushkin's drama thus played to Musorgsky's chamber strengths, yielding a compressed, symmetrically balanced moral drama. But that was not all. It also spared the composer that obligatory operatic ingredient, an ill-starred romantic plot and its virtuoso singers. As we noted earlier, Musorgsky was not very good with love. Whereas *power* in his operas and song-cycles is always subtly delineated and psychologically astute, erotic love is usually underdeveloped, melodramatic, and stunted. Critics have speculated, for the most part irresponsibly,[15] on the links between this creative deficiency and the details of the composer's lonely, disjointed bachelor life. More germane to the shape of *Boris Godunov*, however, is the fact that romantic love itself was under considerable and quite sophisticated attack in the 1860s.[16] Among the Russian intelligentsia, the "woman question" was everywhere in the air; traditional attitudes toward marriage, courtship, and sex roles were being rethought in the radical press and tested in experimental urban "communes." It is reasonable to assume that an opera without the prescribed love interest appealed to Musorgsky as a daring innovation, and one with liberal overtones as well. Pushkin, we recall, had already stripped his Marina Mniszech of almost all romantic overtones, making her into an ambitious powerbroker; in his first version of the opera, Musorgsky omitted her altogether.

This lean 1869 plot and its musical realization were not acceptable to the Imperial Theaters (see Chapter 4). Musorgsky began to rework the opera, and the result – paradoxical at first glance – was a libretto that both more closely resembled Pushkin's text and departed more radically from it. On the large scale, Musorgsky drew closer to Pushkin by incorporating additional scenes from the drama. But on the small scale, the revised libretto drastically altered Pushkin's actual verse line, and consequently refashioned the personalities of the characters engendered by that line. Musorgsky trimmed the monologues in the Cell scene, and he eliminated altogether the St. Basil's scene where Tsar and Holy Fool confront each other. He returned to Pushkin and created the Fountain scene out of Pushkin's scenes 12 and 13, preceded by a scene in Marina's boudoir that drew on an episode Pushkin had written in 1825 but had not included in his initial published edition of the play. The most important structural change in the opera's plot came at the end, where Musorgsky added an entirely new scene after the death of Boris: popular insurrection and the reappearance of the Pretender in a forest near Kromy.

The remainder of this chapter will concentrate on the verbal text of the revised opera, prefaced by a discussion of the composer's special understanding of the prose libretto. We have chosen three episodes to illustrate Musorgsky's talents both as literary adapter and as librettist working with raw historical accounts: Boris's famous monologue and hallucination "arias" in Act II; the relationship between Marina, Dmitry and the Jesuit Rangoni in the Polish Act; and the Kromy scene – the last example also serving to introduce the more general topic of Musorgsky's historical vision. As we hope to show, Musorgsky's skills as a dramatist and librettist were formidable. But the welter of re-editings, pastiche performances, and Musorgsky's highly eccentric commentary on his own creativity have worked to obscure them.

II

What are the constraints and potentials of a libretto in prose? At the outset we should emphasize that for Musorgsky in his early period, with his orientation toward artworks as "speech acts," a prose libretto was not just a non-verse text. It was a prose text *spoken in dialogue*. This factor has immediate structural significance, as will become clear if we briefly review some of the basic competencies of a libretto as narrative.

Most libretti are composed of texts destined to be performed in two fundamentally different types of time: aria and recitative. Recitative is the dynamic, social and dialogic component; it knows real duration and expects a response "within the story" from those who hear it, or are implicated in it, on stage. Aria, on the other hand, stops or marks time: it is often a meditation sung to oneself, or to the audience, outside the public bounds of the story. Its relative autonomy is marked by decontextualization, melodiousness and rounded musical form. When "heard" at all by other onstage characters, aria is heard "as a song."

Of course the boundaries here are not absolute. When the plot calls for it, arias can become part of the dramatic action. And recitatives can be cast as stage asides intended solely for the audience. (Musorgsky gives us an example in *Boris* of a "stage aside" sung by the chorus: in the opening scene the crowd, threatened by a cudgel, placates the police officer to his face – "Don't get angry, Mikitich, my good man, we'll howl again in a moment, just let us rest a bit" – and then, off to the side and supposedly out of earshot, the crowd sings: "He won't let us catch our breath, damn him!").[17] To further complicate the task of reading opera, there are, in addition to boundary-crossing between aria and recitative, various intermediate ensemble genres that exploit a special type of "librettistic complexity." For unlike spoken drama, where verbal complexity is linear and as a rule developed by one voice at a time, the text of a libretto (for all its tendency to exaggerate emotion and flatten out verbal nuance) can exhibit *simultaneous* complexity. Several voices – and, of course, any number of orchestrally realized themes – can sound at once, each with its own words, melodic profile, and degree of vulnerability to neighboring voices. An experienced opera-viewer is expected to sense intuitively when to apply the proper convention. That is part of the literacy required by the genre.

Reformers of opera who campaign for a more "deconventionalized" realism, therefore, often begin by insisting on what might be called a "fused-time" libretto. Composed entirely in recitative (social time/public space), such a libretto depicts actions that cannot be stopped or internalized; both the actors on stage and the audience in the hall see and hear the same thing, and the libretto is lived through in imitation of real life. Not surprisingly, such an operating procedure greatly appealed to Musorgsky. When he added to the revised version of *Boris* those winsome incidental songs (the Innkeeper's "Song of the Drake," the Tsarevich's "Song of the Gnat," the "Handclapping Game" and "Song of the Parrot") to lighten its austere recitative texture, he made sure that each song made sense as a song within the logic of the dramatic action – and that the surrounding recitative responded to it. Again predictably, these songs were based not on imported opera models but on native Russian "musical-speech genres": folksongs, children's ditties, laments. In this too, Musorgsky was an innovator; the most celebrated composer to follow him on this path would be Igor Stravinsky.

In addition to the fused-time libretto and a softened aria–recitative distinction, Musorgsky also refashioned other boundaries in the nineteenth-century libretto. One was the chorus–solo distinction. Masses on the Russian operatic stage were not a theatrical novelty, to be sure; Mikhail Glinka had provided a large onstage role for the people in his *Life for the Tsar* back in 1836, and European opera provided many more models. Crowd scenes in Glinka, however, function as the traditional antiphon chorus, a sort of amplifying vocal backdrop that glorifies the heroes and literally repeats their words. Musorgsky at his most innovative deliberately opposes himself to this lyrically exultant echoing practice. Choruses in *Boris* quarrel, beg, and sing constantly and indifferently of violence. Rather than reinforce the heroes or the solo parts, choruses – both secular and sacred – routinely misapprehend, distort, threaten and ridicule the leading roles.

Musorgsky employed a variety of choral-writing techniques. They range from solo scenes with simple choral backdrop (as in, say, the monks' choruses) to mass scenes where the people themselves function as a sort of collective protagonist. In such mass scenes, the people often appear as prime movers of dramatic action, interacting either in compact ensemble choruses or in "dialogue choruses" patterned, as is melodic recitative, after natural speech intonations. These techniques – in which the type of choral setting chosen reflects the degree of cohesion, ideological commitment, or historical effectiveness of the people – must count as one of Musorgsky's great contributions to musical dramaturgy.

In the opening scenes of the opera, for example, the fearlessly cynical, "Shakespearean" attitude of the crowd toward the bullying policeman is portrayed by means of energetic "speech sketches" where individualized exchanges predominate. The crowd is in equal parts obedient, resentful, and indifferent. (In the initial version, which has a lengthier opening scene, the crowd actually flaunts its ignorance of, and indifference to, the imminent coronation. Many in the crowd do not even know why they have been herded together and whom they should glorify; when they do find out, they agree apathetically: "If they order us to howl, we'll howl in the Kremlin too" [*BGLibr* 74, 63]). Each type of choral setting has its corresponding political implications. The more the chorus differentiates, the less it can be controlled, and the more aggressively it can parody and undermine the image of a unified official authority.

Here Musorgsky – and we repeat, for all his limitations as a singer of love, as a student of power he was unexcelled – clearly grasped a political as well as a dramatic truth. The people are most attractive and vigorously autonomous in their anarchic "dialogic aspect," that is, when they resist ossified ritual with a voice (or many voices) of their own. Such is their opening choral profile, which is characteristic of Musorgsky's early *kuchkist* idealism toward the word. In the initial version of the opera (quite in the spirit of Pushkin's play), "the people" do not confront Tsar Boris in any aggressive or coherently unified way.[18] In those two versions of the tale, Boris's nemesis is the Pretender. By 1872, however, with the addition of the Kromy scene, Musorgsky's own dramaturgy as well as his historical awareness had clearly evolved into a more complex unity. As we shall see below, this rather stylized final scene, full of large self-contained musical numbers minimally adorned with declamation, is something of a dramatic anomaly in the opera as a whole.

As a statement on the political potential of dialogue, however, the Kromy scene complements and consummates what the opening mass scenes had begun – and, we note, to rather pessimistic effect. When the crowd is at its most atomized, alert and dialogic, as during the "staged" coronation, it is hopelessly ineffective as a political force. When it finally does sound a unified choral note, as in the Kromy Forest scene, it is the most thoroughly deluded. This debasing "prosification" of the ostensibly heroic chorus – which works to deflate regal pretensions through comic declamation in the opening scenes, and works against historical optimism by blindly endorsing a Pretender in the closing scene – is one of the more startling aspects of the opera's new dramatic frame.

This outer frame of crowd scenes is not, however, the only symmetry the opera exhibits. Here again Richard Taruskin has suggested a helpful way to look at the revised opera.[19] He sees its nine scenes, now grouped in a prologue and four acts, as a progression neatly mapping the Fall of Boris and the launching of the Pretender. Flanked on their outer rims by choral support, scenes 2 and 8 (the inner frame) are given over to Boris's formal rites of passage: coronation (already omen-ridden) and death. The middle rings (scenes 3-4 and 6-7) develop the Pretender's two faces, one transitional and the other totally fraudulent: a monk-turned-traveller in the Cell and Inn scenes, and an ambitious impostor-courtier in the two Polish scenes. The dramatic core or "keystone of the arch" then becomes the *Terem* scene, which occurs at the precise midpoint of the opera. There Tsar Boris is portrayed in the paralytic grip of history, his power infected fatally from within.

Thus did Musorgsky soften the militant *kuchkism* of the opera's first version and create a genuinely unified drama. But in this commitment to a prosaicized libretto for the revised *Boris*, the composer faced the additional serious problem of theatrical convention.[20] In *The Marriage*, we recall, Gogol's prose (as well as the accompanying plot) was colloquial, everyday, miniaturistic. That, in fact, was what most people thought orthodox *kuchkist* prose-setting was all about: *bouffe* and comic humor. In the revised version of *Boris*, Musorgsky strove to maintain the dialogic aspect, the attention to prosaic detail that had always marked his musical settings, but he wished to add a tragic and serious sweep. His goal was to portray, in its historical dimension, the prose of life – but this was to be, by and large, *tragic* prose. Such a project contradicted a lengthy European tradition that associated tragic seriousness with poetry. To accomplish this adjustment on Pushkin's lean and whimsical play, Musorgsky developed a whole set of musico-verbal strategies.

The task was complex, because Pushkin's *Boris Godunov* was too poetic in some scenes, too light-hearted and matter-of-fact in others. (In its own day, we recall, Pushkin's "romantic tragedy" had been criticized for its levity and insufficient loftiness of diction.) Predictably, the Cell and Inn scenes presented no serious problem, for they were already written in forms that *kuchkist* composers had learned to set: melodic declamation and comic recitative. But even there – and this point must be stressed – Musorgsky made many subtle alterations, often to disrupt Pushkin's regular meter (with its hint of rounded intonational periods) and to employ more rigorously declamatory devices. One such device was the "mute ending" (see Chapter 9), a musical setting of words that end on unaccented syllables through the use of two eighth notes, or a triplet, followed by a rest. (An example in the Inn scene would be Musorgsky's replacing of Pushkin's amphibrach phrase, spoken by Father Misail to the Innkeeper: "*Spasíbo, rodnáya*" [Thank you, my dear] with "*Spasíbo, khozyáyushka!*" [Thank you, my dear innkeeper!][21]) In the same scene, Varlaam's speech is subtly abridged so that words with the vowel "o" predominate – thus displaying Varlaam's *okanie* or failure to reduce the unstressed "o," which in spoken Russian produces a comic effect.[22] Elsewhere in the scene Musorgsky fastidiously replaces Pushkin's phatic particle *zhe* with a nonsyllabic *zh* of his own, or reverses the order of words in a line, or alters a punctuation mark.[23] Musorgsky was anything but careless in his fine tuning of Pushkin for his own purposes.

Paradoxically, these changes often resulted in a smoother and more metrically rhythmic line. From this we might surmise that in the Inn scene, one of several that Pushkin (inspired by Shakespeare) had composed in prose, Musorgsky made these minuscule adjustments in order to disrupt expectations – that is, to reconstitute a verselike rhythm against the grain of a prose norm. And this in turn suggests a larger hypothesis: that for Musorgsky, "prose" awareness signified not so much a formal stylistic category as it did a sense of the unexpected, of spontaneity, of constant readiness for possible interruption. True dialogue, as we intimated early in this chapter, presupposes a genuinely autonomous speech partner and thus must "write in" an element of precarious improvisation. This insight was surely one starting point for Chaliapin's great and nervewracking embodiments of Boris.

Other scenes required a restructuring considerably more radical than the minor adjustments of the Cell and the Inn. Soviet musicologists have offered various typologies for understanding the rhythmic and stylistic shifts that Musorgsky wrought on Pushkin's line – shifts that consequently affected the images of the heroes and the shape of their developing plots. Among the more interesting of these typologies is by Aleksey Ogolevets, who suggests four basic types of adjustment: toward a more regular meter ("verselike"), toward a more dialogic and colloquial style ("prosaicized"), toward an enhanced, loftily monologic, pulsating line such as Pimen's ("archaicized"), and then a "singing" line which could accommodate more rounded musical structures.[24] With these shifts and overall priorities in mind, we now turn to our three textual examples.

III

Our first example, which occurs in Act II at the dramatic midpoint of the revised version, is perhaps the most famous scene in all of Russian opera: Tsar Boris's hallucination of the slain Tsarevich Dmitry.[25] The change Musorgsky effected on Pushkin's text (scenes 7 and 10) poses several questions crucial to Musorgsky's dramatic vision, in both initial and revised versions of the opera. How might the composer unfetter Pushkin's disciplined and strong-minded monologues, the better to communicate the *tragic* prose of life? Toward this end, how might Tsar Boris be invested with a larger, less ambivalent sense of guilt? And finally, what does this sort of character adjustment do to the whole nature of the historical hero, as Pushkin (and later as Musorgsky) understood it?

Except for a bit of opening gossip, Pushkin's scene 7 is essentially Boris's monologue.[26] It is one long catalog of complaints:

1   Достиг я высшей власти;
Шестой уж год я царствую спокойно.
Но счастья нет моей душе. Не так ли
Мы смолоду влюбляемся и алчем
5 Утех любви, но только утолим
Сердечный глад мгновенным обладаньем.
Уж, охладев, скучаем и томимся?..
Напрасно мне кудесники сулят
Дни долгие, дни власти безмятежной —
10 Ни власть, ни жизнь меня не веселят;
Предчувствую небесный гром и горе.
Мне счастья нет. Я думал свой народ
В довольствии, во славе успокоить,
Щедротами любовь его снискать —
15 Но отложил пустое попеченье:
Живая власть для черни ненавистна,
Они любить умеют только мертвых.
Безумны мы, когда народный плеск
Иль ярый вопль тревожит сердце наше!
20 Бог насылал на землю нашу глад,
Народ завыл, в мученьях погибая;
Я отворил им житницы, я злато
Рассыпал им, я им сыскал работы —
Они ж меня, беснуясь, проклинали!
25 Пожарный огнь их домы истребил,
Я выстроил им новые жилища.
Они ж меня пожаром упрекали!
Вот черни суд: ищи ж ее любви.
В семье моей я мнил найти отраду,
30 Я дочь мою мнил осчастливить браком —
Как буря, смерть уносит жениха...
И тут молва лукаво нарекает
Виновником дочернего вдовства
Меня, меня, несчастного отца!..
35 Кто ни умрет, я всех убийца тайный:
Я ускорил Феодора кончину,
Я отравил свою сестру Царицу,
Монахиню смиренную... всё я!

198

Ах! чувствую: ничто не может нас
40 Среди мирских печалей успокоить;
Ничто, ничто... едина разве совесть.
Так, здравая, она восторжествует
Над злобою, над темной клеветою.
Но если в ней единое пятно,
45 Единое, случайно завелося,
Тогда — беда! Как язвой моровой
Душа сгорит, нальется сердце ядом,
Как молотком стучит в ушах упрек,
И всё тошнит, и голова кружится,
50 И мальчики кровавые в глазах...
И рад бежать, да некуда... ужасно!
Да, жалок тот, в ком совесть не чиста.

1 I have attained the highest power;
For six years now, I've reigned in peace.
But there's no happiness for my soul. Isn't this
What happens when we're young?
5 We fall in love, and thirst for
Love's pleasures, but as soon as we've appeased
The hunger of the heart with momentary possession
We cool, grow bored, and languish ...
In vain the sorcerers have promised me
10 Long life, and peaceful years in power –
But neither power nor life delights me;
I sense the coming wrath of heaven, and calamity.
Happiness is not for me. I thought
To soothe my people with prosperity and glory,
15 To win their love with generosity –
But that vain hope I've put aside.
The mob despises living power.
Only the dead they love.
We are mad to let the popular applause
20 Or furious outcry move our hearts!
God sent a famine on our land,
The people howled, perishing in agony;
I opened up the granaries, scattered gold,
Found work for them – and, raging,
25 They cursed me!

Then fire destroyed their homes,
I built new houses for them all.
I was the one, they said, who set the fires.
The judgment of the mob: seek love in it!
30 I thought to find solace in my family,
I thought to please my daughter with a wedding –
When, like a tempest, Death took off her bridegroom . . .
Then the rumor spread that
I was guilty of my daughter's widowhood.
35 Me, me, the miserable father!
Whoever dies, I am the secret murderer:
I hurried Feodor to his grave,
I poisoned my own sister the tsaritsa,
A humble nun . . . It's always me!
40 Ah! Now I know: there's nothing can
Console us mid the sorrows of the world
Except our conscience. Nothing else.
If healthy, it can triumph
Over malice, evil slander.
45 But if a single spot is there,
One accidental stain,
Then woe! The soul flares up
With pestilential sores and pours
Its poison on the heart.
50 Reproaches hammer in the ears,
And one is nauseous, the head spins, and
Bloodstained boys before one's eyes . . .
And I'd be glad to run, but where? It's awful!
Yes, he's pitiful whose conscience is unclean.

Three scenes later, the Tsar is again visited by bad memories. He has just endured an interview with Prince Vasily Shuisky – who has recounted, yet another grisly time, the death in Uglich. As Pushkin's Boris remarks in this second and much briefer monologue (scene 10):

1 Ух, тяжело!.. дай дух переведу...
Я чувствовал: вся кровь моя в лицо
Мне кинулась — и тяжко опускалась...
Так вот зачем тринадцать лет мне сряду
5 Всё снилося убитое дитя!
Да, да — вот что! теперь я понимаю.

Но кто же он, мой грозный супостат?
Кто на меня? Пустое имя, тень —
Ужели тень сорвет с меня порфиру

10 Иль звук лишит детей моих наследства?
Безумец я! чего ж я испугался?
На призрак сей подуй — и нет его.
Так решено: не окажу я страха —
Но презирать не должно ничего...

15 Ох, тяжела ты, шапка Мономаха!

1 Ach, how difficult it is! ... Let me catch my breath ...
I felt my blood was rushing to my face,
And then it painfully subsided ...
So that is why, for thirteen years,

5 I've constantly been dreaming of the murdered child!
Yes, yes, that's it! So now I understand.
And who is he, my threatening opponent,
Who is attacking me? An empty name, a shade –
But could a shadow really strip the purple from me,

10 Can a sound deprive my children of their rightful due?
I'm mad! For what's to fear?
Just blow upon this ghost, he'll disappear.
So it's decided: I'll not show my terror –
But neither must I miss a thing ...

15 Oh, heavy thou art, crown of Monomakh!

After a fashion, these two monologues do function as "confessions." But their tone is more truculent than repentant: the Tsar spends most of his time dismissing others' authority and testimony (the soothsayers, public opinion) and reproaching himself for faint-heartedness. He is distraught that no one credits his accomplishments. As noted in Chapter 2, there is every reason to believe that Pushkin endorsed Karamzin's account of a historically guilty Boris. In reworking the historian's material into a "romantic tragedy," however, Pushkin changed its emphasis. The Tsar's two monologues in the play are not really about the effects of guilt; they are primarily about the destructive power of *rumor*.

Anachronistically, Pushkin gave his Tsar a cool and rational eighteenth-century mind. The Tsar of the drama is a pragmatic politician; he understands that what matters to the world is not what is true, only what is *believed* to be true. For him innocence is the best policy – not because of any moral absolutes, but because only a healthy conscience can triumph over the "malice and evil slander" that is the stock in trade of the ungrateful mob. As Boris views the matter, the mob already considers him the secret murderer of all his kin; had he done no more than entertain the thought of murdering the Tsarevich (and the first monologue insists on no more), he would still be guilty in the people's eyes. Pushkin's Boris, in short, cannot understand why he has been so victimized by fate, and his is a personality that insists not merely on exorcising but on understanding.

In his *Terem* scene (Act II), Musorgsky works an immense change on this self-righteous, stubbornly embittered personality. (The original 1869 version of this act was extensively rewritten for the revision: we deal here only with the later text.[27]) The hallucination itself is tantalizingly slow in coming. To string out suspense, the Tsarevich Feodor's prattle and then Shuisky's retelling of Uglich are slotted in between the Tsar's two gloomy meditations. The first monologue-arioso expounds on Boris's guilt; then the actual apparition at the end of the act embodies it. Together, the two episodes refashion Tsar Boris from a strong, ambitious but embattled ruler – the original Pushkinian model here is Shakespeare's Macbeth – into a helpless and desperate repentant, closer in spirit to King Lear.

Musorgsky wrote to Vladimir Stasov in August 1871, in his mocking, archaicized letter-writing voice, "the criminal Tsar 'Boris' creates a bit of a scandal with a certain *arioso* . . . this criminal *arioso* is verily quite pleasing and tickles the ear most entertainingly, and the words of this *arioso* have been concocted by me."[28] He was almost right. Only twelve lines of Pushkin's monologue from scene 7 survive, and even those not precisely or consecutively. In keeping with Musorgsky's new and greater tolerance for formally segmented musical structure, this "Pushkinesque" portion becomes the first part of a three-part *arioso* that is both sectional and symmetric. In the second part, whose textual inspiration comes from Pushkin's scene 10, Musorgsky – as per his letter to Stasov – adds criminality with a vengeance. The third part, though more declamatory in style, is nonetheless linked with the second by a common rhythm (see chapter 9).

Here are Boris's two monologues, in Musorgsky's revised Act II:

Достиг я высшей власти.
Шестой уж год я царствую спокойно.

(Оживленно.)

Но счастья нет моей измученной душе!

5 *(Спокойно.)*

Напрасно мне кудесники сулят
Дни долгие, дни власти безмятежной.

(Оживленно.)

Ни жизнь, ни власть,
10 ни славы обольщенья,
Ни клики толпы
меня не веселят.

(Спокойно.)

В семье своей я мнил найти отраду.
15 Готовил дочери веселый брачный пир.
Моей царевне, голубке чистой.

(Оживленно.)

Как буря, смерть уносит жениха...
Тяжка десница грозного судии,
20 Ужасен приговор душе преступной...
Окрест лишь тьма и мрак непроглядный!
Хотя мелькнул бы луч отрады!
И скорбью сердце полно,
Тоскует, томится дух усталый.

25 *(Шепотом.)*

Какой-то трепет тайный...
Все ждешь чего-то...
Молитвой теплой к угодникам божьим
Я мнил заглушить души страданья...
30 В величье и блеске власти безграничной,
Руси владыка, я слез просил мне в утешенье.
А там донос: бояр крамолы,
Козни Литвы и тайные подкопы,
Глад и мор, и трус, и разоренье...
35 Словно дикий зверь, рыщет люд зачумленный;
Голодная, бедная, стонет Русь!..

И в лютом горе, ниспосланном богом
За тяжкий мой грех в испытанье,
Виной всех зол меня нарекают,
40 Клянут на площадях нмя Бориса!
И даже сон бежит, и в сумраке ночи
Дитя окровавленное встает...
Очи пылают, стиснув ручонки,
Просит пощады ...

45 *(Глухо.)*

И не было пощады!
Страшная рана зияет!
слышится крик его предсмертный.

(Вскакивает и тяжело опускается в кресло.)

50 О, господи боже мой!

1 I have attained the highest power;
For six years now I've ruled in peace.
(With agitation.)

But there's no happiness for my tormented soul.

5 *(Calmly.)*

In vain the sorcerers have promised me
Long life, and peaceful years in power.
(With agitation.)

But neither life, nor power,
10 Nor the temptations of glory,
Nor the calls of the crowd
Delight me.
(Calmly.)

I thought to find solace in my family,

15   I prepared for my daughter a joyful wedding feast,
For my tsarevna, my pure dove.

    (With agitation.)

Like a thunderstorm, Death carried her bridegroom away.
Heavy is the hand of the threatening judge,
20   Terrible is the sentence over a criminal soul ...
All around, only darkness and impenetrable gloom!
If only there were a ray of comfort!
And the heart is full of sorrow,
The weary spirit grieves and languishes.

25   *(In a whisper.)*

Some sort of secret trembling ...
All the time awaiting something ...
With a fervent prayer to God's saints
I hoped to muffle the sufferings of my soul ...
30   In grandeur and in the glitter of unlimited power,
I, the ruler of Russia, begged for tears to console me ...
But then, denunciations:
Boyars' plotting, intrigues in Lithuania,
Secret machinations,
35   Famine and plague, cowardice and devastation ...
Like a wild beast, ransacking a plague-infested people;
Poor, hungry Russia groans ...
And in this savage misery sent by God
As punishment for our severe sins,
40   They name me the guilty cause of all these evils,
On the public squares they curse the name Boris!

And even sleep flees,
And in the twilight of the night
The bloody child rises up ...
45   His eyes blazing, his little hands clenched,
He begs for mercy ...

    (Hollowly.)

But there was no mercy!
The terrible wound gapes wide!
50   His pre-death shriek is heard.

    (Jumps up and falls back heavily into the chair.)

O, my God!

Gone from this first monologue are the ill-tempered complaints against the people. Also absent is any assignment of the Uglich murder to the category of rumor. In Pushkin's drama, Boris had seen the Russian people as ungrateful tormentors of a well-meaning but maligned tsar; in the mouth of Musorgsky's Boris, in contrast, the people become the victim – and the Tsar, eternally reliving his crime, becomes their tormentor. Thus the second version of the opera restores Karamzin's sense of Divine Providence to Pushkin's "enlightened" text. And Tsar Boris becomes a static, obsessed, symbolic figure, rooted in his guilt and his fate.

The hallucination is the external sign of this obsession. In his revision Musorgsky added many childish songs and antics to this scene, in part to relieve its menacing atmosphere and in part to highlight Boris's love for his own son and heir – as ominous counterpart to his earlier (but never absent) murder of another tsarevich. The Tsar's passionate love for his son Feodor is an essential part of the scene. For the ghost of Dmitry appears to prefigure what history will later confirm, that Boris Godunov's death is not enough; the death of the Uglich Tsarevich Dmitry Ioannovich will require the death of Tsarevich Feodor Borisovich. (In Chapter 10 we discuss Jubilee productions of *Boris* where this conflation of murdered tsareviches is realized on the opera stage through spectral walk-on appearances of white-robed children.) For Tsar Boris, a profoundly dynastic thinker, this unthinkable possibility is one of the factors unhinging his mind.

If Pushkin's Boris was determined to resist such grim logic and "blow upon this ghost" to make it disappear, then Musorgsky's Boris collapses before it utterly. His sentences are incomplete, his thoughts disjointed. In the libretto, the text for the hallucination begins with the opening lines from Pushkin's scene 10 – and then takes off on its own, with a free variation on the theme of "a single accidental spot on the conscience" from the Tsar's earlier monologue.

1 Уф, тяжело! Дай дух переведу...
  Я чувствовал, вся кровь мне кинулась в лицо
  И тяжко опускалась.
  О совесть лютая, как страшно ты караешь!

5 (*Часы с курантами приходят в движение.*)

  (*Глухо.*)

  Ежели в тебе пятно единое...
  Единое случайно завелося,

Душа сгорит, нальется сердце ядом,
10 И тяжко, тяжко станет,

(Глухо.)

Что молотом стучит в ушах укором и проклятьем...
И душит что-то,

(Глухо.)

15 Душит... и голова кружится...
В глазах... дитя окровавленное!
Вон... вон там... что это?.. там, в углу?
Колышется, растет... близится...
Дрожит и стонет...

20 *(Говорком.)*

Чур, чур...
Не я... не я твой лиходей...

(Постепенно ускоряя, говорком.)

Чур!.. чур, дитя!.. Народ... Не я...
25 Воля народа!.. Чур, дитя...
Господи! Ты не хочешь смерти грешника,
Помилуй душу преступного царя Бориса!

Занавес падает

1 Oof, how difficult it is! Let me catch by breath ...
I felt my blood was rushing to my face,
And then it painfully subsided.
O cruel conscience,
5 How terribly you punish!

> *(The chiming clock goes into motion.)*
> *(Hollowly.)*

If there's a single spot in you ...

One accidental stain,
10 The soul flares up,
Pours its poison on the heart,
And it becomes depressing, so depressing,

(Hollowly.)

Reproaches, curses hammer in the ears ...
15 And something is stifling you,

(Hollowly.)

Stifling ... and the head spins ...
And in one's eyes ... the child ... covered with blood!
There ... over there ... What is it ... There in the corner ...
20 It's swaying back and forth, growing ... coming closer ...
Shuddering and groaning ...

(In a speaking voice.)

Get back, back [*Chur!*] ...
It wasn't me ... Your malefactor wasn't me ...

25 *(Gradually gaining tempo, in a speaking voice.)*

Get back, get back, child! ...
It was the people, it wasn't me ...
It was the will of the people! ... Get back, child! ...
God! You don't want this sinner's death,
30 Have mercy on the soul of the criminal tsar Boris!

Curtain falls

This famous hallucination scene occurs neither in Karamzin nor Pushkin, and was most likely prompted by Holofernes's hallucination in Alexander Serov's opera *Judith*, which had its premiere in 1863. Musorgsky's enhancement of his literary sources at this point works a curious change on Boris's royal biography. On the one hand, the confrontation between tsar and ghost embodies the "inner life of tsars" that Karamzin had hinted at darkly and had hoped to explicate. On the other, the gaudy hallucination exemplifies the "pure theatricality" that Pushkin had continually tried to prune out of his spare, emotionally lean drama. Does Musorgsky – with his subtle musical realism, his superb sense of history, and his talent for penetrating psychological states – sacrifice all those strengths in a simple appeal here to melodrama? And, in a related question, is this culmination point of the opera necessarily untrue as a historical portrait?

Let us begin with the first question, on melodrama. Here we might recall one of the issues important to current researchers of the Academy Edition, namely, nineteenth-century "theater literacy," the sense of "what a cultured audience was assumed to know." With our postmodernist sensibilities, we now look on gothic melodrama as low culture, as kitsch. But a century ago the genre had both status and serious influence in the high arts. We must not forget that during the mid nineteenth century, that stretch of time between the death of Schiller (1805) and the rise of Ibsen and Chekhov, formal tragedy experienced an eclipse on the European stage. In its place, melodrama ruled the theaters – a sensibility so immensely popular that it leaked into mass novels and into novelistic masterpieces (Victor Hugo, Dostoevsky) as well. Horror and the Romantic grotesque were not the excess as much as they were the norm of the dramatic stage.

And now to our second question, the legitimacy of so "melodramatic" a tsar as a historical portrait. Here we return to an idea first intimated in Chapter 2. The sixteenth-century Tsar Boris, even if responsible for the death of Dmitry, would scarcely have felt any guilt. His hallucination might thus seem inappropriate, a piece of gothic theater designed to deliver a political warning to all Napoleonic parvenus who unseat dynasties and thus come to a bad end. But alongside these images, anachronistically retrofitted into Boris's biography from a much later set of literary conventions and political expediencies, we might consider a third and historically quite valid explanation of Boris's breakdown in the second act. It is this: that the hallucination, regardless of immediate cause, is a real and fully logical event for the sixteenth-century medieval mind.

In all probability the historical Boris did not feel personal guilt; he felt terror. Always a superstitious man, he is known to have practiced black magic in his final years. Along with most of his contemporaries he believed in prophecy and consulted witches, soothsayers, and holy fools. One detail of the hallucination text that non-Russian audiences might easily miss is Boris's incantational use of the word *chur!* (Get back!) when addressing the advancing ghost of Dmitry. *Chur*, related to the Russian words for "drawing a line" (*chertit'*) and "devil" (*chort*), is literally a magic circle drawn around oneself that an unclean force cannot cross.[29] *Ne stupay za chur!* (Don't cross the line!), the Russian children's game goes, but what is at stake in the Hallucination scene is no game. As one student of Russian folklore writes: "Once the magic circle has been drawn, anybody inside it will supposedly be unable to get out and anyone outside will be unable to get in."[30] The half-pagan Boris, who unconsciously recasts the advancing spirit as the devil, might protect himself in this way from the ghost of Dmitry – but at the cost of his own absolute alienation. Paradoxically, it is not the archivist Karamzin nor the neoclassicist Pushkin but the "realist" Musorgsky, with his deep interest in the occult and his affinity with folk forms, who restores to the scene its historically proper horror.

Our second example does not examine a word-for-word "text transfer" from drama to libretto. Rather, it considers a larger question: how a compact opera detailing the collapse of a single personality was altered by adding a bold cultural contrast, the two Polish scenes (Act III), and how this addition might be understood as part of a new dramatic whole. If Tsar Boris's hallucination scene is an exploration of the medieval Russian mind, then the Polish scenes are a strange, historically imprecise evocation of *non*-Russia. As our documents in Chapter 7 attest, many critics of Musorgsky's time and later were dissatisfied with the dramatic plot and music of this act. One reason, perhaps, is that the revised version of *Boris* appeared to mimic a "home–away–back home" operatic model, but then, on the level of character and plot resolution, disappointed these expectations.

In such operas, the central "away" portion is often exotic and attractive. This is the case even if (or especially if) the middle Act is located in enemy territory; consider Borodin's *Prince Igor* or Verdi's *La forza del destino*. In those two works, however, non-continuity of cultural space is compensated for by a continuity of characters; they move across barriers and then back again, bringing their experience home. If, however, we apply such a model to *Boris Godunov* – both Pushkin's drama and Musorgsky's opera – it is clear that the emotional (that is, the romantic) culmination of the "away" portion does not reintegrate into the opera at the level of plot. After Act III, we never see or hear of Marina again – and this episodic quality to her role is increased when the Boudoir scene is omitted in performance, as it often is. Dmitry reappears briefly, albeit crucially, at the end of the Kromy scene, presenting himself as "the Tsarevich of all Russia" on a campaign to win back "the sacred motherland, Moscow, the gold-domed Kremlin." He brings with him Polish soldiers and Jesuit priests, but there is no trace of a Polish fiancée – except, perhaps, in the dotted rhythm that accompanies his entrance, just as it had accompanied his leavetaking. What happens to romance in this opera? In an attempt to answer that question, and keeping in mind the bleak male bravado of the final scene, we offer a reading of the Polish act that integrates it into the Muscovy plot, in a craftier way than mere continuity of signature motifs or "character survival" across national boundaries.

Let us first recall the content of the two Polish scenes in Pushkin (12-13) that take place in Mniszech's Castle in Sambor. In scene 12, Marina's father and an old friend sit out an elegant ball recalling their own (idealized) youth; comments on Marina's conquest of the young Tsarevich are heard through the music of a polonaise. Scene 13 is the famous episode by the fountain, the layout and dramatic development of which Musorgsky closely followed. There Dmitry, bold enough in pretendership and in war, prepares for his tryst with Marina in some agitation ("Is this desire? . . . No – it is terror . . . Love has confounded my imagination …"). Uncertain in genres of romance, Dmitry speaks bad love poetry to her (as bad, that is, as Pushkin could manage to write); Marina, on the other hand, answers him with clipped, practical-minded pieces of advice. She has one firm request: "reveal to me the secret hopes, intentions and even fears of your heart" so that a Polish princess will know the risks of following a royal scion to the throne of Moscow. Her nonstop needling and indifference to her lover's passionate courtship finally registers. Stung, Dmitry does indeed tell her the whole truth: that he is an impostor, that "her Dmitry perished long ago, was shoveled into the earth and will not rise again," and that he, a poor monk, "had deceived everyone and prepared a miracle for the world."

This rash confession has its calculated effect. Marina is humiliated, not in matters of love (to which she is impervious) but in her ambition. Forgetting that she herself had demanded the truth, she threatens to expose him; this stings him all the more, and only when he is rejected a final time in his plea for love does he counterattack by assuring her that no one will listen to her "exposure": "Neither the king, nor the Pope, nor the Polish magnates even think about the truth of my words. Whether I'm Dmitry or not, they couldn't care less. I'm a pretext for discord and war … And as for you, you little rebel, they'll shut you up fast enough." This final onslaught wins her over. "At last," she says, "I hear the words of a man and not a little boy." With that she calmly takes her leave, ordering Dmitry to send for her "after the Kremlin has been cleaned out." Exhausted, Dmitry then closes down the scene with some grim thoughts on the topic of Woman as Serpent. "It's easier for me to do battle with Godunov or to outwit a court Jesuit than to deal with a woman: to hell with them, I haven't the strength. She misleads, twists, crawls, slips out of your hands, hisses, threatens, stings. A serpent! With good reason was I trembling. She practically did me in."

We retell Pushkin's masterful scene in some detail because it seems so ready-made for Musorgsky's talents. There is a great deal of deception going on, but no danger of reciprocal love – that is, little risk of romantic cliché. As Pushkin wrote a friend in 1829, "a tragedy without love appealed to my imagination … Most certainly [Marina] was a strange, beautiful woman. She had only one passion and that was ambition, but to such a degree of energy, of frenzy, that one can scarcely imagine it."[31] Accordingly, shifts in power in this scene are carefully nuanced and fatal. And above all, words come first. The whole scene is a duel of appearances and conflicting verbal claims. What a person should be feeling, given the setting and dramatic precedent, is not what is spoken about; and what is spoken about, in turn, is continually revised on the basis of what "one calls oneself" – the literal translation of the Russian word *samozvantsvo*, "pretendership."

For reasons we will now try to discern, however, Musorgsky did not develop the potential of the scene in this way. To be sure, the basic duel between lovestruck Pretender and ambitious Polish princess remains in place. But almost none of Pushkin's actual lines survive, and little of Pushkin's self-conscious irony. By the early 1870s, Musorgsky's *kuchkist* literalism had ceased to be so dogmatic. The insertion of a piece of the secularized West into medieval Muscovy was destined to play a much larger role in the revised opera than it would have in a miniaturist character study. Musorgsky had little choice in the matter in any case; as we saw in Chapter 4, the one thing demanded of the composer by the selection committee of the Imperial Theaters was that he add a female romantic lead – and then his opera would be produced. It is also possible that the composer had come to respect the simple dramatic effect of a love duet on stage.

In the libretto version of the scene, Marina does not request that the Pretender "reveal the secret hopes and fears of his heart." He is not goaded to confess his origins, only made to feel the fool for his pathetic love talk; when he turns on Marina and rejects her (thus rekindling her respect), he acts solely as a lover spurned. The scene ends with a passionate bit of triumphant play-acting by both parties: Marina declares her love for the Tsarevich but urges him to "forget about her and hasten to the throne"; Dmitry, raising Marina from her knees, calls her his wondrous Tsaritsa. To be sure, beneath this coming-together of fantasies, Pushkin's duel of competing cynicisms is still visible. But opera singing in the high style must inevitably transmit some degree of emotional conviction, and for the moment the cynicism of Pushkin's plot is dramatically overshadowed by what really looks, and sounds, like love. How did Musorgsky turn those two calculating duelists into a romantic couple that could, if only at the climaxing musical moment, fall appropriately into each other's arms? He extracted the intricacies of politics from the two "lovers" in Pushkin's scene 13 and projected them onto a totally new character, the Jesuit Rangoni.

Count Claudio Rangoni, a genuine historical figure of some influence, does not appear in Pushkin at all and is mentioned only briefly in Karamzin's *History* (XI, 79). As papal nuncio he was formally responsible for Dmitry's conversion to Catholicism; the historical Dmitry courted this dignified personage very carefully. According to one account, Rangoni was a powerful and subtle figure, "both a cleric and a courtier ... with an abundance of banalities appropriate to every situation."[32] As such he was clearly the perfect vehicle for those political sentiments and pragmatic reservations that had so distracted Pushkin's characters from falling in love. As we will see, he also serves as foil and dramatic counterweight to the Muscovite cleric, Pimen.

In Musorgsky's revised libretto, Rangoni is a very prominent presence. (All the more distressing, then, is his complete or partial omission from so many productions of the opera, on the pretext that his personality is mere melodrama.) It was not enough to enmesh Rangoni with the Pretender, to feel the full weight of his political machinations; he also had to be brought into direct and discrete contact with Marina. The dramatic genesis of the Polish act is uncertain (its early drafts have not survived), but we might surmise that it was partially in order to place Rangoni in private audience with Marina that Musorgsky returned to Pushkin's drama and retrieved a scene, "Marina's Boudoir" (between scenes 11 and 12), written in 1825 but omitted by Pushkin from the published text of the play in 1831. This episode provides the setting for the first scene of the Polish act.

In Pushkin's scene, Marina is alone with her talkative maid Ruzia. Ruzia blurts out rumors that the Tsarevich Dmitry is a fraud. Marina, grim and almost totally silent throughout, is determined to "find out everything" – and this cold determination works to demystify her seduction-and-rejection strategies in the Fountain scene. (Pushkin's ultimate decision to omit this scene from his play suggests that he wished the courtship between the two to remain more ambivalent.) In Musorgsky's treatment of the Boudoir episode, Rangoni absorbs all the heroine's manipulative coldness. By this maneuver Marina is freed to develop, both in this scene and in its sequel, somewhat more operatically, with passionate feelings she can invest in the necessary arias. Let us now look more closely at Rangoni's role in the two Polish scenes.

Scene 1 of the Polish act shares with its prototype in Pushkin little more than the setting of the boudoir. Musorgsky replaces the gossipy maid with some pretty female choruses glorifying the unwilling and impatient heroine (a tactic he will reemploy in *Khovanshchina*, where the bullying boyar Ivan Khovansky forever insists on being "glorified" in song and then dismisses the singers in disgust). Marina tells her serving girls that songs praising her beauty are tedious to her; what inspires her are ballads of Poland's past military glory. Left alone, Marina then delivers a major aria on her hopes for the future, in which a deep-felt patriotism is fused with personal ambition (". . . on behalf of the infant Tsarevich, the victim of that evil-doing Tsar Godunov's insatiable power, I'll arouse the sleepy Polish magnates, tempt them with the glitter of gold and booty"). This national-messianic impulse is combined with what sounds like a genuine passion for Dmitry ("my Tsarevich, my predestined bridegroom, I'll smother you in my embrace . . .") (*BGLibr* 74, 90).

Marina's aria is interrupted by the unexpected, unannounced arrival of Rangoni. The papal nuncio is the perfect insinuating diplomat. As Marina's "spiritual father," he occupies an ambivalently intimate space in her life; he is not out of place, even in her dressing-room, although he is careful to interrupt her self-absorbed solitude with the appropriate secular formula ("Can God's humble slave beg an audience from the Panna, radiant with unearthly beauty?"). Marina immediately assures him that she is an "obedient daughter" of the Catholic Church, and the trap is laid. For only one energy can effectively unite and tame the two powerful forces already aroused in Marina – the erotic and the national-political – and that is religion.

Pushkin's Marina, we must remember, is a completely secular coquette. Her robust and utterly self-serving appetites delighted the irreverent Pushkin, whose interest in the psychological dynamics of male–female attraction was subtle and profound, almost "Mozartian." Musorgsky lacked that subtlety, and was drawn more to the one-dimensional, static treatment of women typical of Gogol. For both, woman was embodied in a single and simple reflex – whether comic, or evil, or virginally pure, or betrayed and yet loyal until death. In creating an operatic Marina from Pushkin's portrait, then, Musorgsky flattened her out, making her (and the Pretender when under her sway) less self-aware, less intelligent. Rangoni's role here is clear. He serves to complicate and, as it were, "choreograph" the lovers – Marina first, and then the Pretender – by transposing their trivial passion to a realm where Musorgsky was already a proven master dramatist: political intrigue.

The duel played out between Marina and Rangoni in scene 1 is fully as desperate and erotically charged as the more familiar duel between Marina and Dmitry in scene 2. Rangoni first paints a mournful picture of the Catholic Church in decline ("the pure sources of our faith have faded . . . the wounds of our sacred martyrs are gaping . . . there is desolation and groaning in the monasteries") (*BGLibr* 74, 91). When Marina shows alarm, Rangoni presses further: "My daughter, Marina! Convert the Muscovite heretics to the true faith!" But here Marina, who has much more naive integrity in the opera than in the play, hesitates: she feels "ignorant," "frivolous," "helpless," not qualified as an emissary to "glorify God's church." Rangoni has a ready answer. Don't use your faith, he commands her, use your beauty: "bewitch the Pretender . . . subdue his reason with a passionate glance . . . and when he lies exhausted at your wondrous feet, in speechless ecstasy . . . demand full allegiance to Rome!"

Marina resists indignantly. Then Rangoni gets abusive: "So you're daring to defy the Church? . . . You must be ready to sacrifice even your honor!" At this point Marina shows her mettle: "I curse your depraved heart . . . be gone!" Rangoni plays his final and indispensable card: he claims to see the Devil incarnate hovering over Marina in her pride. Crying out, the superstitious Marina faints at his feet, and Rangoni (in Musorgsky's stage

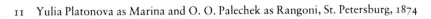

11   Yulia Platonova as Marina and O. O. Palechek as Rangoni, St. Petersburg, 1874

direction, "as if crouching over his prey") instructs her, as the curtain falls, to "humble herself before God's emissary ... be my slave."

As literature, it need hardly be said, this portion of the libretto is sorry indeed – and the character portraits are very crudely drawn. But this initial Rangoni episode is poorly served if judged by its poetry alone. Dramatically it has important structural resonances with the two acts that flank it. The whole scene, in fact, can be read as a manipulated and debased variation on Boris's hallucination scene. Back home in Orthodox Russia, crimes are experienced from within and exorcised by suffering and penance. Abroad in Catholic (that is, infidel) Poland, the land of mere appearances and hypocritical pretenders, the very concept of a "guilty conscience" is corrupted, externalized, and politicized in the person of a crafty Jesuit.

The second (and more famous) scene from the Polish act, Dmitry's "courtship" of Marina by the Fountain, recapitulates this theme. It opens with a long exchange, often cut in performance, between Dmitry and Rangoni. Just as Rangoni had stolen into Marina's boudoir and urged her to prostitute herself for the Church, so now he steals into the tryst spot and offers to act as go-between for the inexperienced Pretender. (Much in Rangoni recalls Shuisky's manipulation of Tsar Boris in the *Terem* scene; one might say that Rangoni plays the Shuisky to the Pretender's worst fears.) Dmitry calls out for his beloved, and who should come forth but this everpresent Jesuit, pretending to be sent by Marina. But the Pretender trusts Rangoni even less than Marina had trusted him in the previous scene. Calling the Jesuit an "evil demon" and a liar to his face, Dmitry is calmed only when the unflappable Rangoni reassures him of Marina's passionate love, and of her suffering at the hands of envious women and jealous suitors. Dmitry now resolves to declare his love openly, and imperiously tells the Jesuit that if he would bring Marina to him "no price would be too much" (*BGLibr* 74, 95).

Rangoni exacts his price – the right, as he puts it, of a father "to follow after the Tsarevich's every step and thought" – and then orders Dmitry to hide: Marina is approaching (on the arm of an elderly nobleman), accompanied by a crowd of guests. As they sing boisterously of taking Moscow and capturing Tsar Boris, Dmitry falls into impotent despair. The famous polonaise masks continual scheming. "That crafty Jesuit has me in his accursed claws ... How often I've wanted to shove aside that unwelcome protector of mine, my spiritual father! While he was babbling all his unbearable and cunning insolence, I saw my haughty beauty Marina go by on the arm of some toothless old nobleman ... whispering tender caresses ..." (*BGLibr* 74, 96).

Marina finally emerges, alone, in search of the Tsarevich – and the "Scene at the Fountain," so familiar from Pushkin, begins. By this time in the libretto, however, we are no longer dealing with Pushkin's razor-sharp couple. By having their most manipulative traits transferred to Rangoni, both Dmitry and Marina have been cleansed of their irony and most of their ambivalence. The contested love scene unfolds, then, on a much simpler plane. It raises no questions of identity, only the question of love versus ambition, an ancient operatic theme.

All goes according to the Jesuit's plan. Dmitry persists in noising his love while Marina insists that military strategy must come first. But when he lies helpless at her feet, as Rangoni had predicted, Marina does not mention the Church or its imperial project at all. Instead, in Musorgsky's marvelous stage direction, "she shoves the Pretender away with her foot." Ridiculing his confession of love, she calls him a slave and a "brazen tramp" (*brodyaga derzky*) – not, however, in reference to his lowly origins but solely to his helplessly paralyzing passion. This insult stings Dmitry into resistance. In his retort (which makes only indirect reference to her "cruelly taunting him with his past life") he promises to despise her once he is crowned in Moscow. Quickly the love is restored on both sides in an appropriate duet. But significantly, the final lines of the duet are in fact a trio. In a masterful *piano*, the two lovers each sing quietly and simultaneously of their primary intention:

Марина:	О мой Димитрий!
	Войско давно ждет тебя,
	Спеши в Москву, на царский престол!

Самозванец:	Моя Марина!
	Скоро ль блаженства миг настанет,
	Скоро ль счастья желанный день придет!

| Marina: | "O my Dmitry, the troops have long awaited you, hurry to Moscow, to the royal throne!" |
| The Pretender: | "Will the moment of bliss come soon, will the longed-for day of happiness arrive?" |

Beneath both of them, marked *pianissimo*, Rangoni sings from a distance in an undulating line: "O my little doves! O, how simple you are, how tender! With langorous glance, in a passionate embrace, my trusty prey!"

The libretto enters Rangoni's lines last, immediately before the curtain. Using the simplest of emotional ingredients, then, the Jesuit has "framed" his two lovers. And true to Musorgsky's deepest talent, the political has absorbed the erotic.

We end discussion of our second example with some speculation on the relationship between this crafty Jesuit and the chronicler Pimen, who is the equivalent clerical presence in the Orthodox Muscovite scenes. If, in the spirit of current research on the libretto, we assume that Musorgsky and Pushkin intended their audiences to appreciate the risk Pimen took in pursuing his criminal chronicle-writing in the bosom of the Kremlin, then both Pimen and Rangoni are bold activists on their respective political fronts. Pimen, however, is a much more prominent figure in the opera than in the drama. In Pushkin's play, we recall, Pimen appears only in the Cell scene. In the libretto (in part because state law forbade the representation of high-ranking ecclesiastics on the dramatic stage), Pimen is, as it were, "recycled" in the first scene of the fourth act, to deliver a speech which in Pushkin (scene 15) belongs to the Patriarch.

In this aria, the operatic Pimen narrates to Boris the miracle that occurred at the site of Dmitry's grave in Uglich. It is this story that directly triggers Boris's collapse. Several bars after the point in Pimen's narrative where the blind shepherd hears the angel-Dmitry's voice in a dream, Boris gasps for air and tumbles unconscious from the throne. In his expanded role, therefore, Pimen's skillful manipulation of miracles – to the novice Grigory in the Cell scene and to Boris in the Death scene – enables both the Pretender's rise and Boris's fall. Unlike his debased Catholic counterpart Rangoni, who is the wrong sort of storyteller, Pimen's stories serve the just cause of history. The Jesuit can engineer only an opportunistic betrothal.

Rangoni is best measured, it would thus seem, not by his demonic and banal characteristics alone but by his value as a counter-character to other, more complexly spiritual personages in the Russian world. These figures include the chronicler Pimen with his denunciation of political ambition, and later the holy fool with his painfully accurate prophecy of Russia's disintegration and fall from grace. From the perspective of Orthodox believers, these are the right sort of storytellers. They relate divine narratives – whereas Rome, which rules by the sword, cares only for territorial success in this world. Musorgsky's anti-Polonism is well documented. In Old Muscovy as Musorgsky presents it, state power answers ultimately to the spiritual realm, and matters of state are never above moral judgment.

The contrast that Musorgsky draws between Pimen and Rangoni is therefore much larger than might appear from their stage roles alone. Their differing worldviews were codified in seventeenth-century chronicles and polemics as the struggle between *khitrost'*, "Western cunning, guile, technical skill," and *blagochestie*, "the pious fidelity" of the Orthodox. As James Billington remarks in his discussion of these two terms in his monumental cultural history, *The Icon and the Axe*: "When Boris Godunov became Russia's first elected Tsar in 1598, he had to quiet popular misgivings about the procedure by publicly proclaiming that he had been chosen 'in faith and truth without any kind of guile *(bezo vsiakie khitrosti)*.'"[33] Pimen is suffused with Orthodox virtue, Rangoni with Catholic guile. Only Tsar Boris is forever in a no-win situation, an innovator longing for traditional legitimacy, at home in neither East nor West.

We might conclude, therefore, that the purpose of Rangoni in the Polish scenes is twofold. He serves to ratchet up the romantic plot beyond mere love, and to taint the Western Church with an erotic trivializing of its mission that is magisterially absent from the stately rituals and political risks of the high-minded Orthodox. (The antics of those drunken monks Varlaam and Misail, of course, occur on another plane altogether.) But there is an additional benefit to be had from Rangoni's maneuverings. His interventions in the plot suggest that the real confrontation of the "romantic heroes" in this opera – Dmitry's fraught courtship of Marina in Poland – is not primarily personal and sexual at all but rather cultural, dynastic, political. And thus the operatic plot cannot be consummated by means of a single romantic gesture, as so often happens in operas with otherwise identifiable historical subtexts: by a Leonora reunited with her Florestan, by a Yaroslavna greeting her Prince Igor home from captivity, or even by the death of one of those beloveds. The fate of beloveds is not particularly important in *Boris Godunov*. For this reason Marina does not have to return in the final act; she is genuinely "episodic," central neither to the opera nor to its resolution. It is enough that the Pretender reenter Russian territory to spin a further web of pretense. That final scene, A Forest Glade near Kromy, is our third and last example of Musorgsky's libretto-building.

The final act of *Boris Godunov* is one of the great problems in operatic literature. With the order of its two scenes frequently inverted, with the Kromy scene of "popular rebellion" often staged aimlessly (ignoring its harrowingly abrupt alternations between carnival and violence), and with the holy-fool episode usually duplicated earlier in the opera through a conflation of Musorgsky's two versions, Act IV makes a strangely disjointed impression. It also combines the most conventional with the most unconventional ending devices. In the first scene of the act the title role dies, and even delivers an appropriately lengthy and tragic aria while dying, but the opera is not over. The subsequent Kromy scene promises robust sonic closure with a series of energetic choruses, but at the last moment everyone leaves. The opera ends on an empty stage, a holy fool, a single musical pitch. The genesis and reception of the Kromy Forest scene, as well as its non-*kuchkist* musical "numbers" and its almost pageant-like formal structure, have received detailed treatment by Richard Taruskin.[34] These issues are also discussed elsewhere in this volume (pp. 271–75). In the context of this chapter, as our one libretto example based not on a literary text but compiled by Musorgsky out of raw historical accounts, we will note only the overall resonance of its episodes as part of the opera's philosophy of history.

The siege of Kromy during the ferocious winter of 1604–05 was a real historical event, a victory (although a pyhrric one) for Boris. Soon after the siege was lifted, Boris died, and his teenage son Feodor Borisovich assumed the throne under the most terrible conditions. Thus Musorgsky's ultimate decision to enact Boris's death in scene 1 of the act, before Kromy, violates strict historical chronology. Literal rendering of historical time is frequently ignored in historical opera, however, and in this instance there is good additional justification for the composer's final preference in ordering the two scenes. The revised version of the opera is no longer a personal but a national tragedy. And as with Pushkin's drama, which also tucks the death of the Tsar into the inner frame of the work (it occurs in scene 20 out of 23 scenes), the end of the title role does not imply the end of the story.

As we noted in chapter 1, Boris's ambitions, as portrayed in both drama and opera, are less individual than they are dynastic. A ruler with deeply conservative instincts despite the "popular election" he was forced to arrange, Tsar Boris consents to pay for his own misdemeanors if his gifted, cherished son can inherit the throne. As he puts it in his deathside aria to young Feodor – following, incidentally, Shakespeare's regal hero in *Henry IV Part 2* – "Don't ask how I acquired the tsardom . . . that you don't need to know. You will reign by right, as my heir . . ." (*BGLibr* 74, 105).

Had the social and military situation been less threatening, of course, Boris's death would have stabilized the country's politics by returning Russia to dynastic rule. But since Boris's crime was also dynastic – cutting down the last scion of Ivan IV's royal house – his own death, as we suggested earlier, is not enough. In a parallelism worthy of Greek tragedy, Boris must pay for Dmitry by sacrificing his own son. This dynastic subtext to the opera, calibrated to the Tsar's faith in the occult, has been splendidly realized in stage productions, most famously by Martti Talvela at New York's Metropolitan Opera: Boris topples from his huge throne upon hearing

Pimen's story of miracles wrought by St. Dmitry, and, as the curtain falls on scene I of Act IV, a tiny Tsarevich Feodor sits helplessly in one corner of that huge throne with the cunning bulk of Prince Shuisky standing by.

Boris's dying is important, therefore, not only as a just and justified end to his own torment. It is the *timing* of his death in history that matters, the *dying-out of his hopes for a dynasty that would provide vigorous new stock around which the nation might rally.* These blasted hopes and a prefiguration of the coming national chaos are given voice by the holy fool in the final words of the Kromy scene, and thus of the opera:

> Лейтесь, лейтесь, слезы горькие,
> Плачь, плачь, душа православная!
> Скоро враг придет и настанет тьма,
> Темень темная, непроглядная.
> Горе, горе Руси!
> Плачь, плачь, русский люд,
> Голодный люд!..

   1 Flow, bitter tears! Weep, Orthodox soul!
>   Soon the enemy will come, and darkness will fall.
>   The darkest of darknesses, impenetrable.
>   Grief, grief to Russia:
>   5 Weep, Russian people, hungry people.

In Musorgsky's stage direction – always carefully penned and crucial to his sense of a scene – we read: "Shouts of the crowd offstage ... the hollow beating of the tocsin continues. The holy fool shudders, glancing around at the glow from the fires" (*BGLibr* 74, 112).

It is right that the opera end on conflagration and the brink of civil war, on national history and not personal history. For as we have seen, in the 1874 version of the opera, personal biography – even in contexts as intimate as a father doting on his children or a lover's tryst – is always a captive to political history. With the removal of Tsar Boris in the penultimate scene, the theme of "guilty conscience" has all but disappeared. It is succeeded by the much more substantial and frightening theme of a deluded populace as historical nemesis. What Musorgsky appears to give us in the final Kromy scene is an overview of extant historical forces, a generalized panorama based on select documented events from the final few rebellious months of Boris's reign.[35]

The sequence of Kromy events is an eerie and disjunct variation on the opera's opening scenes. Again ragged masses crowd the stage, but this time deep in a forest rather than in front of an urban monastery. Gone is the *bouffe* quality of the crowd, its extended individualized repartee which, in orthodox *kuchkism*, had been linked to private everyday life and the comic. The episodes in Kromy, presaging as they do national tragedy, are more unanimous, more overtly theatrical, musically better developed and balanced. And the people themselves now play the role of the police.

A band of tramps has caught and bound the boyar Khrushchov, a supporter of Boris. He is taunted with a "Glory to Boris's boyar" chorus and then forced, with much obscene jeering and an undercurrent of real cruelty, into a mock "marriage" with a hundred-year-old crone. This grim warm-up to torture is interrupted by the arrival of a holy fool, followed somewhat incongruently by a group of young boys who tease him and steal his kopek (Musorgsky pasted this event into the revised score from the discarded St. Basil's scene of the initial version). This episode, in turn, is interrupted by those two clowning vagrant monks from the Inn scene, Misail and Varlaam, who had accompanied Grigory to the border and now loudly denounce Tsar Boris. (This detail in the libretto is an interesting variant on historical fact: the historical Varlaam, ordered to Poland to expose the Pretender, was arrested at the Russian border for his pains. Only after the False Dmitry's death in 1606 did the Muscovite government welcome his deposition on the events of 1603–04.) As Misail and Varlaam chant about Boris's sins, the tramps break into their own spirited song calling for Boris's death – again, an anachronism indicative of the temporal "suspension" in which this scene lives.

This song is cut short by a Latin chant offstage, sung by arriving Jesuits. Calling them "accursed ravens" and "heathen sorcerers," the tramps bind up the Jesuits just as they had bound poor Khrushchov, and drag them into the forest. But at that moment a trumpet sounds, horsemen and foot-soldiers with torches appear, and the Pretender himself enters on horseback. All these disparate endangered groups (the boyar, tramps, monks, Jesuits) immediately forget their mutual antagonisms and gather round to glorify the Pretender and usher him offstage, giving full voice to a "Slava" chorus sung without a trace of irony. Without, that is, any irony from the perspective of the *characters*: for on the plane of history, as any audience of Musorgsky's opera would have been well aware, the unification of two cultures and all social classes around a fraudulent claimant to the throne was the beginning of "the darkest of darknesses," the Time of Troubles.

We suggested at the end of Chapter 1 that Musorgsky, despite the efforts of Soviet scholarship to make him into a progressive materialist and populist, was "by every indication a profoundly mystical and pessimistic historical thinker." The politics of this final act is indeed deeply ambivalent. So much so, in fact, that one close friend of the composer claimed that Musorgsky himself later disavowed the scene, on the grounds that "an enraged people kills but does not make fun of its victim" (see Chapter 7, p. 152). If Musorgsky did express this reservation – and the witness is not entirely reliable – there are good reasons why he might have been alarmed at his own vision. Accompanied by a series of manipulated "Glory" choruses, one false tsar replaces another. But compared with the opening scenes and their "Glory" choruses, there is this important difference: the people at Kromy have become more herd-like and cruel, more aggressively malicious, less discriminating. By the end of the opera the popular masses have unlearned that irony toward power, that "Shakespearean" intonation, that had characterized their irreverence toward all politics at Boris's coronation seven years earlier. Amid their violent mockery and deluded merrymaking, the sober voice of history is heard from only one onstage character: the holy fool.

The Kromy Forest scene, then, has carnival overtones; it might even be said to celebrate, in some sense, the strength of the unofficial masses over the official structures of state power. But in no sense does it communicate any hopefulness about the role of those masses in history. Rather, Dmitry's "polonized" reappearance in the middle of the Russian forest sets up the sort of spectacular no-win confrontation between whole generations, worldviews and cultures at which Musorgsky as dramatist excelled. That, in fact, was his mature historical imagination: put people together and watch them not understand one another, sing past each other, or better yet, deceive one another. As in the desperate plot of *Khovanshchina*, where representatives of several utterly incompatible worldviews and historical time-frames are continually forced to occupy the same space, it is not clear which (if any) group has access to the truth. In *Boris*, this tension is resolved only at the quasi-mystical level of a fool predicting full disaster for Russia. His authoritatively prophetic voice does serve to clear the stage of all falseness, and this move is significant: as nihilist views of history demonstrate, the acknowledgment of a void can itself have moral content. But the holy fool provides absolutely no new grounds for legitimacy. In an opera where all important confrontations are reduced to politics – Tsar Boris's hallucination, Rangoni's stage-managing of Dmitry and Marina's love, the deluded pageantry of the Kromy scene – this void at the end is painfully felt, and must have been so designed.

Musorgsky, as this chapter has tried to show, was deeply committed to finding a musical language for Russian popular and collective experience. In this task he was not alone. The elite among Russia's literate public took historical drama and opera very seriously during the 1860s and 70s, hoping to find in the theater as well as in the journals some satisfying clues to Russia's national identity. But in historical opera, as in his early *kuchkist* experiments setting the prose word, Musorgsky belonged to a category of his own. He was certainly no conservative, but he could not share his populist contemporaries' positivist and optimistic temperament. In the next chapter we will see how Musorgsky's understanding of musical technique also set him somewhat apart from the established schools and categories of his time. In fact, Musorgsky might be said to embody Arnold Whittall's comment: "admiration of and stimulation by the major Romantic masters was a more crucial factor in the development of the best Russian composers than willingness to shackle their musical instincts in the abject service of texts." [36] The man, and his work, were more complexly cosmopolitan than has often been assumed.

9

THE MUSIC

But *maestro Senatore Verdi* is quite another matter! This one pushes ahead on a grand scale, this innovator doesn't feel shy.

MODEST MUSORGSKY

In 1928, when most music critics were celebrating Pavel Lamm's conflated edition of *Boris Godunov* as a restoration of Musorgsky's intentions and deploring the composer's own revision as an impoverishment that had been forced upon him, a little-known Swiss critic, Willy Schmid, argued instead for the supremacy of the revised *Boris* of 1874 over the *opéra dialogué* completed in 1869:

It is impossible to see why the re-modelling should be attributed to nothing more than a desire on Musorgsky's part to conform to expediency and obey the dictates of his friends. [. . .] His reasons for composing this or that portion anew cannot be imagined to have been other than a desire to give them a higher perfection or perhaps to attune them to the new orientation imparted to the drama on its revision. This is very much what one would expect of an artist who was incessantly sailing "toward new shores."[1]

Though Schmid was decidedly in the minority when these lines were written, his view has been vindicated in our own time: Musorgsky very likely revised *Boris* because he was dissatsified with it, even though external circumstances might have prompted him to begin. The composer was not one to continue working on projects in which he had lost interest, as we may see in the cases of both *Salammbô* and *The Marriage* – two operas abandoned before *Boris* was begun – yet he undertook the revision of *Boris* with enthusiasm and high spirits. He displayed no irritation that the work had to be done, complied eagerly with the demands placed upon him, and in reality went far beyond the addition of a mere scene or two for the *prima donna*.[2] By contrast, when he turned to the collaborative *Mlada* – a project in which he had no real interest – he chafed under the demands imposed by the Directorate and grumbled to Stasov, "My kind and dear friend, you know that I cannot carry trash within me and fuss with it . . . *In the matter of our labor*, I will prescribe, not listen; I will ask the questions, not give the answers. . . . And as for the contractor [the Director of Theaters], let him do as he chooses."[3]

In addition, despite the prevailing mythology concerning the composer, Musorgsky was neither incapable of defending his works nor too eager to accept advice concerning them. Even before he began to compose *Boris*, he had demonstrated that he could be adamant if he felt changes were unwarranted. In 1867, when Balakirev refused to perform *St. John's Night on Bald Mountain* without revisions, the composer responded:

I considered, I consider, and I will continue to consider this piece [*St. John's Night*] to be decent; in it, after independent trifles, for the first time I came forward in a large-scale work. [. . .] Whether or not you agree, my friend, to perform my witches [Musorgsky's nickname for the piece], that is, whether or not I hear them, I will alter nothing in the general plan or in the treatment, tightly bound to the content of the picture, and carried out sincerely, without sham or imitation.[4]

The author of this letter is neither pliant nor docile; quite the contrary, he is willing to sacrifice performance of the work rather than comply with his mentor's wishes. These various considerations further support the view that Musorgsky revised *Boris Godunov* out of artistic conviction, not against his will and despite his better judgment.

Why he saw fit to revise so many other works too is a more difficult question. As Roland John Wiley has suggested, Musorgsky and other members of the Mighty Handful at times may have been hindered in the realization of their aims by their proud "repudiation of formal training in order to preserve their originality. They were mavericks in this regard, and suffered the vagaries of a peevish and fickle muse. They paid dearly for their originality with small outputs, agonizing creative process, and unfinished works."[5] That several important works of Musorgsky remained unfinished is undeniable. Four of the five operas that he began were left incomplete – *Salammbô*, *The Marriage*, *Khovanshchina*, and *The Fair at Sorochintsy*. Many of his works exist in two versions.[6] The creative agonies that lurk behind these facts remain a matter of speculation even when we accept as motivation the composer's unspoken wish to improve each work he chose to revise. We imperil the full truth, however, by refusing even to consider that what came easily to, say, Tchaikovsky (as a result of the time and discipline he had invested in Anton Rubinstein's "German Conservatory") might have come with greater effort to Musorgsky, Balakirev, Borodin, Cui, and the young Rimsky-Korsakov. In Musorgsky's case sheer genius and a keen ability to learn from the stage works of his contemporaries – particularly Verdi –were able to make up the difference most of the time. Yet even he faltered on occasion: the "mischievous technical demands" of writing for an alto, a tenor, and three basses seem to have frustrated his intention to conclude the second act of *Khovanshchina* with a quintet – an ensemble that remained unwritten at his death.[7]

Boris Godunov suffers from no such difficulty. Put into its final form when Musorgsky was at the peak of his powers, the revision shows plainly the "higher perfection" that Willy Schmid sensed in it. But for many years it was Rimsky-Korsakov's "purification and regulation of [the work's] technical side" that captured the critics' attention and provoked their indignation, to the detriment of a just assessment of Musorgsky's achievement.

Of the 4,245 bars in Rimsky-Korsakov's final piano–vocal score of *Boris Godunov*, only 665 were transferred from Musorgsky's piano–vocal score of 1874 without change of any sort.[8] This simple statistic, though ignoring the altruism of Rimsky's motives, eloquently documents the extent of his "corrections," and it helps to account for page after page of the literature on the work. Confronted with such wholesale alteration, critics and scholars often responded with shrill polemic concerning the propriety of the revision and the relative merits of original and revised versions. The following diatribe, written in 1925, is typical:

The same drastic and senseless process [of revision] was applied to many other works of his, with the curious result that Musorgsky nowadays is a composer whom most of us admire, while knowing very little of his music as he actually wrote it. *Boris Godunov*, as performed at present, is a weird and wonderful commixture of things written by Musorgsky and things which Rimsky-Korsakov thought Musorgsky ought to have written. [. . .] Will the inertia of publishers and the indifference or impotence of producers enable a few pundits to go on repeating that Musorgsky's music would never have endured but for Rimsky-Korsakov's intervention?[9]

The indignation of this passage, and others like it, leaves one wondering what changes Rimsky could have wrought that would provoke such deep sarcasm. It thus may prove instructive to examine a specific passage, drawn from Boris's second-act monologue "Dostig ya vysshey vlasti."

The passage shown illustrates characteristic alterations in harmony, melody, tessitura, choice of key, rhythm and meter, and – though not

1 (Rimsky–Korsakov)

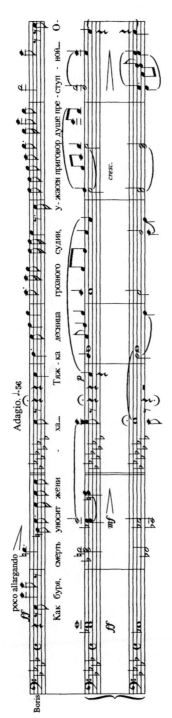

2 (Musorgsky)

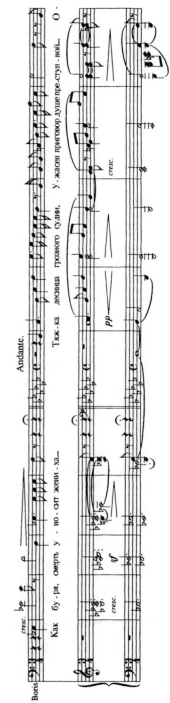

Example 9.1

revealed in the piano–vocal format – orchestration as well. Rimsky alters each of the chords preceding the double bar and concludes the progression in a key a fourth higher than Musorgsky's (A♭ minor, rather than E♭ minor). Perhaps the main reason for this transposition is Rimsky's decision to carry the voice into the more brilliant upper register, reaching as high as g♭', whereas Musorgsky's vocal line throughout the entire monologue rises no higher than e'. To emphasize even more strongly the heroic tones of the upper register, Rimsky adjusts the voice part so that in places (for example, the fourth measure after the double bar above) it lies a full seventh above Musorgsky's melodic line.

Rimsky's change of key obscures an important structural relationship as well. Musorgsky centers Boris's hallucination monologue, the climactic conclusion of Act II, on the pitch-class A♭, the act's primary pitch center. He centers "Dostig ya vysshey vlasti" on E♭, the dominant of A♭. Musorgsky's choice of pitch center for these two monologues thus reinforces the psychological relationship between them, a relationship of anticipation and release. By contrast, even though the pitch E♭ is prominent in Rimsky's version, his choice of key as A♭ minor produces a sense of local resolution that weakens the composer's structure.

Throughout the lyrical phrase commencing at the double bar – borrowed, by the way, from the unfinished opera *Salammbô* – Musorgsky sustains ambiguity between relative major and minor (G♭ major/E♭ minor), tilting toward E♭ minor only at the end, with the appearance of the dominant on the seventh eighth-note of the phrase's last measure. Rimsky fails to preserve this effect, even transposed upward, but instead anticipates the voice's entrance in the next phrase (and gives the singer his pitch!) by sounding E♭ as the fourth quarter-note of the seventh measure. Rimsky's metric and rhythmic changes in the measures preceding the double bar arbitrarily modify the composer's declamational pattern, removing, for example, the equal agogic stress Musorgsky chose to give to the accented first syllable of *burya* and to the word *smert'* and altering the pace of the unaccented syllables in the phrase *unósit zhenikhá*. Finally, Musorgsky accompanies the first statement of the lyrical idea with cellos and contrabasses; Rimsky accompanies it with winds. Not one measure in the example quoted is left untouched by Rimsky-Korsakov.

The sweeping nature of the many changes of this sort, the bitter outrage they provoked from critics and scholars, and the apparent indifference to them of both performers and the general audience created a situation in which, for years, the principal issue in Musorgsky criticism was the question of editorial intervention by alien hands. In 1948, coincidentally the year that

Moscow's Bolshoy Theater mounted a new production of Rimsky's *Boris*, one writer summarized the matter as follows:

Rimsky-Korsakov's injury to Musorgsky was not merely that he made Musorgsky's works known to the world in outrageously altered versions, but that he got the world to accept the idea which justified not only his falsifications but anyone else's – the idea of Musorgsky as a clumsy dilettante whose insufficient technical equipment prevented him from achieving more than partial realizations of his conceptions, which other people were, therefore, and still are justified in helping him to complete.[10]

With such drums to thump, few writers have taken the time to examine *Boris Godunov* in detail.[11] Perhaps because they often felt compelled to defend Musorgsky from charges of incompetence, many have concentrated on details of style observed throughout the composer's work at the expense of a more thorough analysis of *Boris* alone.[12] To examine such questions as the opera's structure and tonal plan, the integration of its text and music, and influences on it from unexpected quarters is the goal of this chapter. As we shall see, tonality functions as an opposition of colors in much of *Boris Godunov*, with opposing characters or ideas receiving their musical expression in opposing keys. One may associate these various keys with the literary themes of the drama by identifying common ideas in the texts sung when a certain pitch center prevails, so that keys become musical symbols for aspects of the drama. The resulting key scheme, rich in traditional functional relationships, gives structure to both the music and the drama. And Musorgsky may very well have hit upon this idea, and others equally fruitful, as a result of his absorbing not just *A Life for the Tsar*, *Ruslan and Lyudmila*, and *The Stone Guest*, but also *Rigoletto*, *La forza del destino*, and *Don Carlos*.

> We fell to talking about leitmotivs and how they had found their way into Russian music as early as Cui's *Ratcliff* and Musorgsky's *Boris Godunov*. Rimsky-Korsakov is of the opinion that the idea of the leitmotiv came not so much through Wagner as it did through Berlioz and his *Symphonie Fantastique*, that it was already in the air and Richard Wagner himself might not have hit upon it had it not been for Berlioz.
>
> VASILY YASTREBTSEV

In a perceptive essay that provides a fresh reckoning of whom we may legitimately regard as Musorgsky's musical creditors, Roland John Wiley writes: "It is, moreover, precisely within the realm of opera that Glinka and Dargomyzhsky (to say nothing of Liszt and Berlioz) perform least satisfactorily their roles as teacher to the later generations [i.e., Musorgsky, Rimsky, Borodin]. To be sure, the music of *Ruslan*, *Susanin*, and *The Stone Guest* contains a repertoire of devices – orchestral combinations, fragments of melody, techniques of text setting, harmonic audacities – upon which the generation of the seventies and eighties drew. But these operas did not teach what those of Verdi, Meyerbeer, and Wagner did – about theatricality."[13]

Consider the matter of reminiscence music. At least twelve recurring motives (see Example 9.2) appear throughout *Boris Godunov*, serving to identify and recall character, situations, and even certain abstract ideas, to evoke pathos, or merely to pantomime physical action. Thus the theme of Ex. 9.2.4 identifies Pimen and recalls his virtue; that of Ex. 9.2.12 identifies Rangoni and recalls his scheming. The theme of Ex. 9.2.1 is associated with brute force, both in the scene at Novodevichy Monastery and in the scene at the inn. Ex. 9.2.9, used in Act II in conjunction with Boris's majesty and authority, reappears at the end of the Death scene, moving us to pity and tenderness. Ex. 9.2.10 is associated throughout the opera with Boris's vision of the murdered Tsarevich and thus with the Tsar's guilt. Ex. 9.2.3 is used merely to suggest the physical act of writing and appears only in the scene in the cell. The theme recalled most often in *Boris Godunov* (Ex. 9.2.5) represents both the murdered Tsarevich Dmitry and the False Dmitry (Grigory); it appears in six of the work's nine scenes. We may judge how carefully Musorgsky has calculated his second thoughts by noting the subtlety with which he uses the Dmitry motive in the opera's final version. There (in the revision) this motive always signifies to Boris the spectre of the murdered Tsarevich. To all the other characters the same tune refers to Grishka Otrepiev, the Pretender. By contrast, in the opera's initial version, the motive at times represents the Pretender even to Boris and the real Dmitry to characters other than Boris – a psychological misstep which the composer was careful to correct in the revision.[14]

Musorgsky's use of these recurring motives, as Rimsky-Korsakov hinted to Yastrebtsev, is not particularly Wagnerian. Although both composers sometimes associate recurring motives with intangibles (brute force, anxiety, guilt in *Boris*; resentment, renunciation, redemption in *The Ring*), Musorgsky never attempts to generate an elaborate symphonic texture from them. Perhaps this is not too surprising since dislike of Wagner was virtually an article of faith in Musorgsky's circle. For example, when *Lohengrin* received its Russian premiere at the Maryinsky Theater on 4 October 1868, Vladimir Stasov wrote to Berlioz:

Possibly part of the audience will like this brutal heavy-handed music. But *we all* do not believe that Wagner is a prophet: we hold that he marks a retrogression from the music of Weber. We find in him a lack of taste and measure, vulgarity, noisy scoring, no gift for the recitative, [and] horrible modulations.[15]

Example 9.2   Recurring motives of *Boris Godunov*

Example 9.2   (*cont.*)

Yet there was something in Wagner that appealed to Musorgsky. He writes, significantly *not* to Stasov, but to Rimsky-Korsakov, his friend, colleague, and co-equal in the circle: "We often rail at Wagner, but Wagner is powerful, powerful in that he grabs hold of art and yanks it around. . . ." Then lest he reveal too much, he adds, "If he were more talented, he would do much more."[16] Later in his career, Musorgsky "played and sang Wagner's *Siegfried* on the very day that the printed music arrived in St. Petersburg and, when asked to repeat Wotan's scene, played through all of it from the beginning from memory."[17] In the privacy of his workroom, Musorgsky must surely have noticed how adept Wagner was at placing and highlighting a significant leitmotiv – the unveiling of the sword motive in Act I of *Die Walküre*, for example. He may have absorbed from Wagner important lessons in dramatic pacing; he certainly is equally adroit, say, in introducing the Dmitry motive at the second climax in Shuisky's narrative in Act II. Yet despite his apparent interest in and respect for Wagner's art – running counter to one of the most cherished dogmas of his circle – and despite the occasional lesson he may have taken from him, Musorgsky cannot be said to have followed Wagner. He had no need to; other models were closer to hand: Glinka, Berlioz, and – perhaps most surprising of all – Verdi.

If dislike of Wagner was part of the Credo in Musorgsky's circle, adoration of Glinka was one of the Commandments. Consider, for example, the opening paragraph of César Cui's review of the 1864 revival of *Ruslan and Lyudmila*:

> At last, after a few weeks' delay, we again have had the opportunity to hear *Ruslan*, the foremost opera in the world in musical beauty; a work in which we find that so rarely encountered harmonious confluence of thoughts of genius expressed in forms of genius; a work for which there is no equal in richness, diversity, freshness and originality of ideas; a work from whose scraps it would be possible to construct five or six superb operas.[18]

Musorgsky himself, toward the end of his life in a deeply emotional letter addressed to Glinka's sister, referred to *Ruslan* as "the greatest creation of [Glinka's] genius – the honor and pride of the Russian land and of the entire Slavic world."[19] In *Boris* he follows Glinka's lead in several particulars. He stitches a number of motives (Foreboding, Feodor, Xenia, Boris's Authority) into Boris's farewell and death, probably modeling the passage on Susanin's final monologue in *A Life for the Tsar*. He uses the themes associated with Shuisky and Rangoni as calling cards, just as Glinka uses the whole-tone scale as Chernomor's calling card in *Ruslan*. The "Coronation chords," surely the most characteristic sonority in *Boris*, also apparently were borrowed from *Ruslan*, perhaps by way of Alexander Serov's *Rogneda*.[20] Changing background variations, a device patented by Glinka for the development of folksongs in an orchestral texture, are heard in the prelude, the two songs of Varlaam in the scene at the inn, and in the genre pieces of Act II (Song of the Gnat, The Handclapping Game, and Feodor's Song of the Parrot). Such passages undoubtedly illustrate the "repertoire of devices" passed along to the *kuchkisty* by their Russian forebears, but they do not, by themselves, give *Boris* its raw theatrical power.

In Berlioz we encounter a figure whom Musorgsky greatly respected and from whom he adapted specific technical procedures. He expressed his admiration for the Frenchman on a number of occasions, perhaps most forcefully in the following terms: "In poetry there are two giants: rough-hewn Homer and elegant Shakespeare. In music there are two giants: the thinker Beethoven and the ultra-thinker Berlioz."[21] Less than a year later he again endorsed the French composer: "The colossal *Te Deum*, bearing on the immense second mass of Beethoven, as the Roman St. Peter's on our St. Isaac's, could only have been built in the head of the brave European Berlioz."[22] Berlioz's music was widely admired in Musorgsky's circle: not only did Musorgsky know it, he imitated it – as anyone familiar with the composer's *Night on Bald Mountain* would be forced to admit.[23]

Berlioz's shadow is most visible in *Boris* in the use of the Dmitry Motive (Ex. 9.2.5). After its introduction in the scene in Pimen's cell, it appears in all but one of the opera's remaining scenes. It frequently undergoes transformation: it appears in minor key near the end of the Cell scene, it is rhythmically jaunty in the Inn scene, and it is accompanied by dotted rhythms *à la polacca* in the Fountain scene and the Kromy Forest scene. It appears in conjunction with references to the murdered Tsarevich in the scene in the Tsar's quarters and in the Death scene; it accompanies Grigory's escape into Poland-Lithuania, his posturing in the Fountain scene, and his address to the mob in the Kromy Forest scene. Thus associated with both the murdered Tsarevich and the Pretender, the theme comes to represent the forces arrayed against Boris. It becomes his – and the opera's – *idée fixe*. As Rimsky-Korsakov explained to Yastrebtsev, "the idea of the leitmotiv came not so much through Wagner as it did through Berlioz and his *Symphonie Fantastique*."[24]

But perhaps the most unexpected model for Musorgsky is Verdi; like Wagner, he is rarely linked with the Mighty Handful. Whether by design or coincidence, Musorgsky treats many of his recurring themes in a manner similar to Verdi's, "introducing a musical phrase already associated with a certain dramatic situation into a later situation with the purpose of underlining the similarity – and also perhaps, by implication, the contrast – between the two."[25] Like Verdi, he recalls most of his themes no more than two or three times. The Xenia theme, for example, first appears in Act II when Boris comforts his daughter, reappears in the Tsar's monologue "Dostig ya vysshey vlasti" as he recalls his hopes for a happy family life, and occurs for the last time when the dying Tsar instructs his son to care for his sister. Boris's farewell begins with the motive of Foreboding (Ex. 9.2.8), which first is heard in Act II when the Tsar tells Feodor that the day will come, perhaps sooner than he thinks, when the Tsarevich must begin to reign. The motive of Anxiety introduces both Boris's Coronation monologue and "Dostig ya vysshey vlasti" in Act II. And the reappearance of Pimen's theme in the Death scene reminds us that Pimen is the catalyst for both Grigory's rise and Boris's fall. The principal differences between Musorgsky's and Verdi's uses of recurring motives lie in Musorgsky's repeated use of one of his themes (Dmitry), in the large number of such themes in *Boris*, and in the shorter length of the themes themselves.

The larger question of Verdi's overall influence on Musorgsky is more difficult. Yet despite the circumstantial nature of much of the evidence, the case for Verdi's presence in Musorgsky's thinking is persuasive. A well-known memoir of Borodin reminds us that Musorgsky was well acquainted with *Trovatore* and *Traviata* while still a young guards officer, and Igor Stravinsky relates that, according to his parents, Musorgsky was a connoisseur of Italian operatic music and accompanied concert singers in it quite adeptly. He had many opportunities to observe Verdi's skill at firsthand, for during Musorgsky's career as a composer, Verdi's works were among those performed most often in St. Petersburg, at both the Italian and Russian opera theaters. Indeed, at the Italian opera in this period, one in every four performances was devoted to Verdi; the works heard most often were *Rigoletto*, *Il trovatore*, *La traviata*, and *Un ballo in maschera*. In addition, *La forza del destino* was commissioned by the Russian Imperial Theaters and received its first performance in St. Petersburg in 1862, a few months before Musorgsky began work on his first operatic project, *Salammbô*. Although Verdi's work received mixed reviews – foreign critics found more to admire than did native Russians – and although the leading members of Musorgsky's circle viewed Italian opera with disdain, it is hard to imagine that Musorgsky himself, an aspiring opera composer, would have ignored such a significant premiere. It is even harder to dismiss the parallel between the chorus of pilgrims in Act II, scene 1 of *Forza* and the chorus of crippled pilgrims in the opening scene of *Boris*, or the similarity between Leonora's "Madre, pietosa Vergine" (Act II, scene 2) – projecting agitation against the backdrop of a chorus of monks offstage – and the revision of Grigory's dream (Cell scene). Nor can one ignore the similarity in pacing between the Kromy Forest scene and the scene in the army camp in *Forza*. Both unfold in clearly marked contrasting sections; both provide diverse scenic incidents; both make extensive use of chorus; and characters seen earlier in quite different circumstances turn up unexpectedly in each (Preziosilla, Melitone, Varlaam, Misail, Dmitry).

In addition, there are intriguing similarities between the revised *Boris* and

Verdi's *Don Carlos*, which received its first Russian performance, sung in Italian, on New Year's Day 1869. Though one recent commentator already has noted that both Verdi and Musorgsky begin their respective garden scenes by having the tenor sing what amounts to a stage direction,[26] the parallels in fact go further than this. Both the scene in Marina's boudoir and the scene before the monastery of St. Juste begin with a decorative chorus of handmaidens, who set the scene in triadic harmony while preparing the appearance of an important character. Both choruses incorporate syncopation. In Verdi, this syncopation remains accompanimental and decorative, whereas in Musorgsky it is transformed into the central feature of the chorus's melody. King Philip's aria "Ella giammai m'amò!" must surely have lingered in Musorgsky's ear when he came to write the revised "Dostig ya vysshey vlasti"; each, in Budden's phrase, is "an aria of loneliness sung by a man of power."[27] A tone of profound melancholy informs both pieces; both begin with recitative-like writing that nonetheless is surprisingly melodic for recitative; both conclude with more melodious – indeed, memorably melodious – music that is formally symmetric while skirting conventional patterns. Furthermore, each of these scenes is followed by a scene of confrontation with a sinister character from which the ruler emerges defeated, Philip by the Grand Inquisitor, Boris by Shuisky.

But what direct evidence can one bring to bear? Although none of Musorgsky's letters reveals his opinion of Verdi's early operas, there is a significant endorsement – subtle, oblique, and punning – of *Aida* in a letter to Stasov dated 23 November 1875.

But *maestro Senatore Verdi* is quite another matter! This one pushes ahead on a grand scale, this innovator doesn't feel shy. All his *Aida* – ai-da! – outdistancing everything, outdistancing everyone, even himself. He had knocked over *Trovatore*, Mendelssohn, Wagner – and almost Amerigo Vespucci too.[28]

These are the words of someone who clearly admires Verdi; the praise is couched in the codewords of progressivism that Musorgsky and his circle used to express approval: "pushes ahead on a grand scale," "innovator," "outdistancing everyone, even himself." Furthermore, translators of Musorgsky's letters in the past have failed to point out that the playful reiteration of the opera's name constitutes an enthusiastic – if somewhat sly – endorsement of the theatrical force of Verdi's latest work: *Aida* – ai-da! *Aida* – oh-yes! It is quite likely, moreover, that Musorgsky would hide behind puns precisely when writing to Stasov, for Stasov railed loudly and incessantly at "Italian music." Stasov (Musorgsky feared) might misconstrue an acknowledgment of the genius of any Italian composer as evidence of "weak

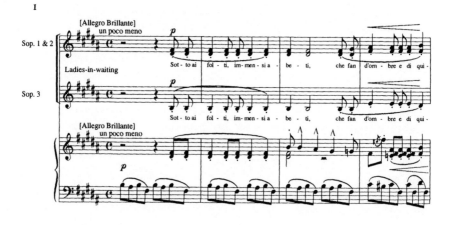

Example 9.3
1 Verdi, *Don Carlos*, Act II, sc. 2
2 Musorgsky, *Boris Godunov*, Act III, sc. 1

brains." And Stasov, though perhaps no longer the composer's most
important confidant, was still someone whose support Musorgsky did not
wish to lose. He therefore puns, plays, conceals his private thoughts, and even
permits himself to cavil, in the letter's next sentence, at Verdi's portraying
"hot African blood' with reminiscence music – all probably to mollify his

contentious correspondent. But the tribute is there all the same, hidden in the words of his letter, in the music of the revised *Boris*, and in the music of *Khovanshchina* as well.

We thus have witnesses (Borodin, Stravinsky's parents), opportunity (the many performances of Verdi given in Musorgsky's St. Petersburg), motive (Musorgsky's ambition to transcend the limitations of *kuchkism* and *opéra dialogué*), and even an apparent confession (the letter to Stasov). We turn now to an examination of one of the lessons Musorgsky may have absorbed from Verdi, concerning the ways in which tonality can contribute to the overall *tinta* of an operatic work.

> And to want F♯ major *à la* Liszt's *Divina Commedia* for the vile glorification of Satan? *Corpo di bacco!*
>
> MODEST MUSORGSKY

Scattered comments in letters to Rimsky-Korsakov of 1867 and 1868 suggest that Musorgsky was well acquainted with the technique of organizing programmatic and dramatic music by associating certain keys with specific concepts or characters. Commenting upon Rimsky's *Sadko*, Musorgsky approves his friend's choice of D♭ major for Sadko and D major for the Sea King.[29] A few months later, he expressed astonishment that Balakirev would want him to use for Satan in *St. John's Night on Bald Mountain* the same key that Liszt had used for the love of Paolo and Frencesca in his *Dante Symphony*.[30] But Musorgsky's last and most extensive statement concerning these matters occurs in a letter dated 15 August 1868, shortly before he began work on *Boris*. The subject is Rimsky-Korsakov's *Antar*, a program symphony in four movements completed in 1868, revised in 1875, and published in 1880. According to a note in the published score, Antar, having saved the peri Gul-Nazar from capture by an evil spirit (Movement I), is given as his reward first the joy of vengeance (Movement II), then the joy of power (Movement III), and finally the joy of love (Movement IV). Concerning this work Musorgsky writes:

As for your intentions in "Power," I do not argue and I think that oriental power, understood externally, does not contradict artistic demands, for this power loved and loves to express itself *primarily in pomp*. But concerning the last scene, "Love," I argue against the introduction; frankly I think [the scene should be] as you had it, without introductions. More artistic, simpler, and more unaffected. After the D major pompous character, is the A in the horns really necessary for aesthetic taste, for D♭

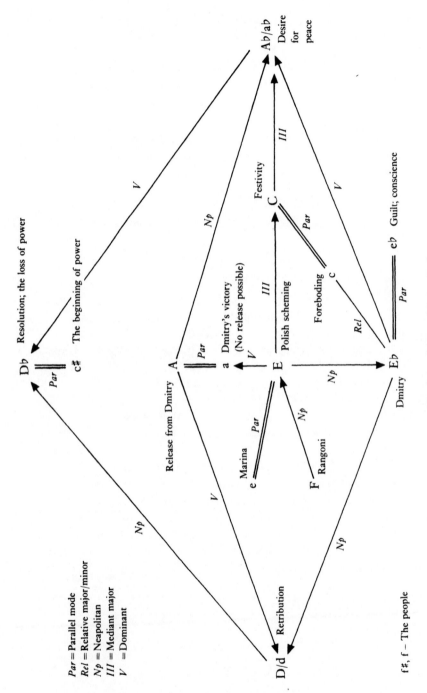

Figure 9.1 The key scheme of *Boris Godunov*

Par = Parallel mode
Rel = Relative major/minor
Np = Neapolitan
III = Mediant major
V = Dominant

f♯, f – The people

major's melancholy-pathetic character? . . . What could be more poetic after the *forte pomposo* D major (as I remember you conclude the scene of "Power") than the melancholy Db major, straightway, without any preliminaries? [. . .] You know that after Antar's C# minor and D major, Db major *straightway* carries Antar beyond the clouds, into the world of houris, peris, and generally sweet people, a world that purifies and temporarily calms (reconciles) Antar and poetically ennobles him. O preliminaries! How many good things you have spoiled![31]

In this letter, Musorgsky plainly accepts at face value Rimsky's expression of the contrast between power and love in the contrasting tonal colors of D and Db. His remarks on Rimsky's *Antar* provide the paradigm by which tonality functions in *Boris Godunov*: opposing characters or ideas in the opera receive their musical expression in opposing keys, with the work's dramatic conflicts reflected in the underlying opposition of tonal colors. Confirmation that Musorgsky indeed thought in these terms comes to us from Rimsky-Korsakov himself. Many years later, when questioned about Musorgsky's use of Eb major for the Fountain scene of *Boris*, Rimsky replied that "although, of course, E major would have been preferable, in this case Eb major is not at variance with the coloring. 'Now if this scene had been written in F,' he said, 'that wouldn't have done at all, so far as the color is concerned. But don't forget – *Musorgsky was by nature also a colorist and he certainly would never have made such a blunder*' [emphasis added]."[32]

We propose that throughout *Boris Godunov* Musorgsky employs specific keys in association with specific aspects of the drama, and that the resulting key scheme helps to clarify the opera's form and to integrate its text and music. Of course, in the absence of documentation from the composer, one must regard any analysis, including the present one, as a hypothesis. David Lawton further cautions:

The determination of dramatic associations for particular key areas in an opera is to some extent, no doubt, a subjective process. The analyst or critic must base his decisions upon the sense of the text, or the meaning of a dramatic situation as he understands it, together with his perception of large-scale tonal relations. Just as it is undesirable to pin down a Wagnerian *Leitmotiv* to one simple label, so it is unwise to attempt to interpret tonal and dramatic associations in a rigid way. Opera is theater, and good theater is constantly in a state of flux; associations established early in an opera are likely to acquire new shades of meaning as the drama unfolds. Nonetheless, it is widely understood that increasingly during the nineteenth century opera composers employed tonality for dramatic effects of various kinds.[33]

The principal tonalities of *Boris Godunov*, together with their primary dramatic associations, are shown in Figure 9.1. With few exceptions the keys shown on the diagram are related either as dominant to tonic or as

Neapolitan to tonic. Thus the strife in Boris's mind between the ideas of Dmitry (E♭) and release from Dmitry (A) leads to his exhaustion and his desire for peace (A♭), expressed most powerfully at the end of Act II. In the Death scene, exhaustion and longing (A♭) finally lead to resolution (D♭). Polish scheming dominates Dmitry (E → E♭), but Polish scheming also leads to Dmitry's victory (E → a). In two cases, Musorgsky associates opposing modes with opposing ideas: D♭ major, the fundamental key of the work, is associated with the resolution of conflict and the loss of power, and C♯ minor is associated with the beginning of power. Likewise, A major is associated with release from Dmitry, A minor with Dmitry's victory. Moreover, there is exactly one large-scale authentic cadence, connecting A♭ at the end of the *Terem* scene with D♭ at the end of the Death scene – a circumstance that exemplifies the following observations of Guy Marco:

> At the [Aristotelian] reversal scene of the plot ... tonality ought to reflect greatest tension; at the end of the drama it ought to embody response and reconciliation, the dialectic catharsis. In an opera of the eighteenth or nineteenth century we would expect the tension–release cycle to sound like an authentic or possibly a plagal cadence, so the end of a tragic opera could only be in the tonic key (with reversal in the dominant or perhaps the subdominant domain). And since there is really no other point of high tension and release in the tragic plot, there ought to be no other macrolevel cadence formed by operatic key relations ... tragedy's tonic, unlike that of a sonata, needs to be reserved, in its full flowering, for the catharsis.[34]

Musorgsky's way of defining tonalities within the opera varies, but remains remarkably close to methods recently attributed to Verdi: "Depending on the dramatic situation, related musico-dramatic events may be articulated by a fully worked-out key, generating its own substructure, or perhaps merely by a gesture or a chord, backed up by a vocal or orchestral sonority."[35] In the Cell scene, for example, when Pimen inadvertently gives Grigory the idea of posing as the False Dmitry, Musorgsky focuses attention on the moment in several ways. He shifts the music abruptly from d/D to E♭ (Dmitry's key), introduces the Dmitry motive in flute and clarinet (highlighted by a change to string tremolo in the accompaniment), instructs Grigory in a stage direction to "draw himself up to his full height, then to slump meekly," and finally permits the music to fall back into D minor even as Grigory slumps on stage. The moment passes in two measures; yet to fail to identify it as the source of one of the opera's tonal poles is to err. We might further note that the model for the moment easily could have been the passage in *Rigoletto* (Act I, scene I) in which Monterone pronounces his curse on Rigoletto and the Duke, thereby setting in motion the fundamental dramatic events of that opera. In *Rigoletto*, the basic context of Db major/minor is interrupted at the precise moment of the curse by a momentary deflection to D (the Neapolitan, the same relation Eb bears to D in the example from *Boris*), only to settle immediately back into Db minor for the run to the curtain. To reinforce the significance of D as the "curse key," Verdi later in *Rigoletto* puts two numbers in D that are central to Gilda's destruction: the Duke's cabaletta "Possente Amor," in which the Duke decides to *act* upon his desire to ravish Gilda, and thus sets in motion her downfall, and the trio in the final scene, in which she is murdered. And, as Roland John Wiley has observed, the progression from Db to D and back to Db that lay at the heart of the curse (what Parker and Brown would call a "gesture or chord, backed up by a vocal or orchestral sonority"), recurs at the end of the opera when Gilda dies.[36] By contrast, the Polish act in *Boris* is "articulated by a fully worked-out key," E major, which does indeed generate "its own substructure," including frequent digressions to mediant major (spelled enharmonically as Ab) and to flat-submediant major.

Musorgsky has further organized the music of *Boris Godunov* in sections similar in some respects to Wagner's poetical-musical periods. The Russian composer employs a hierarchy of what we shall term *periods, segments,* and *parts*, with text the main underpinning of this sectionalization scheme. The largest of the three structural units is the *period*; it corresponds to a complete episode in the text and is articulated by major events in the music, including changes in key, texture, or orchestration and the recall of previously heard material. *Segments* form the principal subdivisions of a period, corresponding to the larger units of text within an episode. Their boundaries are marked by such occurrences as the introduction of a new topic, alternation between characters in dialogue, a shift of direction in a monologue. Musically a segment is marked by such devices as strong cadences, temporary excursions into related tonal regions, sometimes even a modulation. *Parts* are the building blocks of segments; they usually correspond to not more than a line or two of text and are defined musically by cadences. The textual hierarchy of lines, paragraphs, and episodes corresponds to the musical hierarchy of parts, segments, and periods. Terminology of this sort, of course, invariably calls to mind Alfred Lorenz's *Geheimnis der Form bei Richard Wagner*, but Musorgsky's devices in *Boris Godunov* are far less rigid than those Lorenz attributes to Wagner. One looks in vain in *Boris* for the procrustean *Bars* and *Bogens* that Lorenz finds throughout Wagner's work. Although this is not the place to rehearse the case of Lorenz, most critics now agree that he was too inflexible in his assessments and that he pursued too zealously the correspondences that he did find. Nevertheless these objections need not prevent us from seeking, within the bounds of common sense, some significant "reciprocal relation between tonal structure and dramatic action."[37]

In *Boris Godunov*, each scene is divided into several periods corresponding to the large divisions of the text. Narrative periods and periods of dialogue usually contain many subsections and tend toward recitative-like writing. Perhaps as a result, they also often contain more frequent modulations and several tonal centers. Non-narrative periods – those involving dance (the polonaise), simple song (Varlaam's "Ballad of Kazan"), intensely emotional text (Boris's hallucination, Boris's death) – often suggest more symmetrical musical structures and remain within a single key or a few related keys.

One may understand Musorgsky's method more clearly by examining the opera's first three scenes. The first scene of the work, "Courtyard of the Novodevichy Monastery," contains five periods: the prelude and appearance of the policeman (*BorisLJ-1*, beginning – R5/14); the people's first chorus and their ensuing discussion (R6 – R14/7); the policeman's return and the people's second chorus (R15 – R23/5); Shchelkalov's narrative (R24 – R27/8); and the chorus of pilgrims (R28 – R34/10).[38] Musorgsky delineates the division by changing between solo and choral texture at the beginning of the second, fourth, and fifth periods, by recalling previously heard material at the beginning of the third, and by introducing a new key for each period: c# – f – f# – eb/Eb – Ab. Each of these keys is significant in the opera's tonal plan.

The scene begins in C# minor, the parallel minor of the opera's fundamental key Db major. C# minor, however, is heard only twice – here in the prologue, at the beginning of Boris's rise to power, and at the end of the scene in Pimen's cell, at the beginning of Grigory's rise to power. In the second and third periods of the scene (the people's choruses), Musorgsky introduces F minor and F# minor, both associated throughout the work with the people. In the fourth and fifth, he presents Eb major and minor and Ab major, keys that play a fundamental role in Boris's music and that are associated, as we shall see, with Dmitry, guilt, and Boris's desire for peace. Thus, by casting the final section of the scene in these keys, Musorgsky foreshadows these central elements of Boris's tragedy.[39]

The Coronation scene is structurally the simplest of the opera, containing just three periods arranged in the pattern A–B–A'. The first period, in C major, contains three segments comprising the introduction, Shuisky's call to the people, and the people's chorus of praise (*BorisLJ-1*, beginning – R14/5). The second period, also in three segments, is Boris's coronation monologue (R15 – R18/11). The third period (C major) is an abbreviated reprise of the chorus of the first (R19 – end). The principal key of the scene,

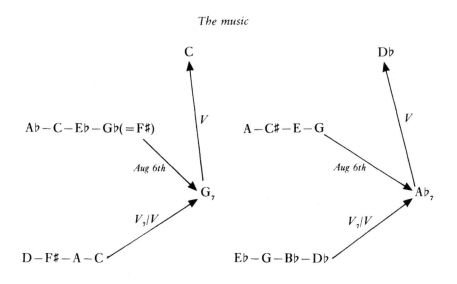

Figure 9.2

C major, plays a small part in the opera's tonal scheme. Associated with moments of public festivity, it appears for an extended time only in the choruses of the Coronation scene and in the polonaise from the scene by the fountain.

At the core of the opera's tonal plan, however, is the harmonic progression from which Musorgsky builds the introduction to this scene: two interlocking seventh chords with roots a tritone apart both of which are directed toward C major, the scene's principal key (Figure 9.2).

This introduction, when transposed to Db, the fundamental key of the opera, provides the model for the tonal depiction of Boris's struggle with Dmitry, the central conflict of the work. Two opposing ideas, Dmitry and release from Dmitry, are at war in Boris's mind throughout the opera. Musically these opposing ideas are represented by pitch-classes a tritone apart, Eb and A. The storm in his conscience leads Boris to yearn for peace; the instability between A and Eb leads to Ab. By such means Musorgsky establishes a musical and dramatic dialectic that demands resolution, but resolution for Boris comes only with death and the loss of power he obtained by murdering the child Dmitry. Thus, as we shall see, although the composer begins the progression from A/Eb through Ab to Db in all three scenes in which Boris appears, he carries it through to the end only in the Death scene. In the Coronation scene and in the *Terem* scene, the progression goes no further than Ab, the key associated with Boris's desire for peace (Figure 9.3).

245

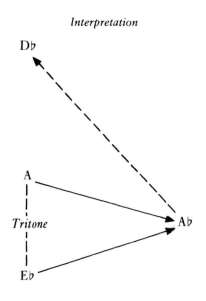

Figure 9.3

In Boris's coronation monologue, Musorgsky begins with a segment in C minor, in which Boris reveals that even at the beginning of his reign premonitions trouble his soul. In the second segment, the music progresses to Eb major with a turn toward Ab at the end, as the Tsar prays for guidance. In his moment of introspection, then, Boris's music passes through keys associated with foreboding and Dmitry to the key associated with his desire for peace. But in this scene the composer veers away from resolution, instead only suggesting it by the appearance of a Db major triad resolved plagally on Ab (Ex. 9.4). In the period's final segment, Boris breaks out of his reverie and invites everyone to his coronation feast, as the music returns without preparation to C major and the reprise of the people's chorus.

The scene in Pimen's cell is more complex than either of the first two scenes, both in its division into sections and in its key scheme. It contains five periods: Pimen's monologue (*BorisLJ-1*, beginning – R8/8); Grigory's awakening and his dialogue with Pimen (R9 – R21/7); Pimen's narrative about the legitimate tsars who reigned before Boris (R22 – R31/5); Grigory's question concerning Dmitry's age and Pimen's response (R32 – R45/10 [the shorter variant]); and conclusion (R46 – end). Perhaps because the scene is primarily narrative, each period has several segments and each segment several parts. Within each period, Musorgsky often delineates the many subdivisions by temporary digressions to closely related subregions of the

Example 9.4

period's tonic. The first period (Pimen's monologue) will serve to demonstrate how the composer treats the long narratives that characterize this
scene.

The period is in D minor. At the beginning Musorgsky introduces in the
viola an undulating sixteenth-note motive associated throughout the scene
with Pimen's writing (Ex. 9.2.3). The first segment, in three parts, consists of
a nine-measure prelude, the setting of the first three and a half lines of text,
and a slightly varied recall of the opening nine measures that cadences in the
relative major, F. This segment thus comprises a miniature A–B–A′ form. The
second segment presents the next six and a half lines of text; its first part
cadences in F, and its second prepares a return to D with a scalewise
chromatic descent in the bass from F to A. Resolution to D major marks the
beginning of the third segment. In this segment's first part, Musorgsky
introduces the motive subsequently associated with Pimen himself or with his
virtue (Ex. 9.2.4) and presents the next five lines of text. The tonal region is
the parallel D major. Turbulence in the strings at Pimen's recollection of a
distant past full of turbulent events and the subsequent plagal cadence form
the third segment's second part. The fourth segment, presenting the final two
lines of text, returns abruptly to D minor and recalls the writing figure from
the first segment. Thus the entire period forms an arch, A–BC–A′. Although
written in late 1868, when Musorgsky's adherence to *kuchkist* theories was
still strong, Pimen's monologue is surprisingly rounded, revealing a symmetry unknown in Boris's Coronation monologue, written only a few weeks
earlier. Both monologues contain several separate sections, each with its own
character and key. But since Boris's text does not return to its beginning, there
is no need for his music to return to its beginning. Pimen's text, however, does
restate its opening line as its closing line, "Just one more, the last story." This

recurrence undoubtedly motivates the rounding-off of the musical form.

In the second period – which changed subtly in revision – Grigory awakens and tells Pimen his dream. For the revision, Musorgsky adds a chorus of monks behind the scene, who project a reflective calm while Grigory expresses his agitation. By having the chorus sing while Grigory awakens from his dream, Musorgsky provides an opportunity for him to wake up, sing in agitation, and reflect on Pimen's labors without disturbing the old man. The changes give Grigory his own "space" *before* the interaction with Pimen and create an interval of "opera time" during which attention is focused away from Pimen. (They are a measure, too, of Musorgsky's fading faith in *kuchkism*: Grigory's dream in the initial version is set in a weak passage of ascending chromatic scales, with the singer's pitches drawn from the underlying harmonies, a standard cliché in *kuchkist* settings of narrative text.) At Grigory's request, Pimen blesses him – the old man's venerable serenity coalescing with that of the choir – and counsels the youth to conquer his sinful desires through prayer and fasting, but Grigory, complaining of the hermit's life, asks, "Why may I not delight in battles? Why may I not feast at the Tsar's table?" Pimen's answer – his narrative about the virtuous tsars who reigned before Boris – forms the scene's central third period.

Both the second and third periods contain many subdivisions and involve many digressions to related tonal regions. The pitch center of the second period is B, but between the opening B minor and the closing B major, one hears allusions to many transient regions, as well as one quite striking passage of triads and seventh-chords seen by Carl Dahlhaus as a compelling refutation of the charges of dilettantism often brought against Musorgsky:

In Act 1 of *Boris Godunov*, in the scene in Pimen's cell, the novice Grigory recounts a dream which starts with him climbing the stairs of a frighteningly tall tower. Musically, the narration begins (Fig. 15 [in Lamm's edition]) with a series of chords depicting the vertiginous climb with chromatic harmonies, the tonality of which could be described as "floating," in Schoenberg's expression. The progression is formed from four major chords (E–C♯–A–F♯) which are repeated sequentially a whole tone higher, except that, in the repeat, the third chord is a semitone higher again than it should be (G♭–E♭–C–A♭, where regularity demands C♭ instead of C). If we temporarily ignore the presence of that third chord, we are left with an imperfect cadence of astonishing simplicity as the basic material to be repeated: I–(V[of II])–II. To disrupt such a simple phrase with a conspicuous interpolation is certainly a conscious, considered act, not a naive one. The passage owes its expressive and symbolic effect, the realism of its depiction of Grigory's nightmare climb, to the impression of "floating tonality," and that is entirely due to the waywardness of the interpolated chord. An effect like that is not the lucky result of the "limited technical means and 'awkward writing'" of which Stravinsky accuses Musorgsky: it betrays a calculation which may be unusual, but whose steps can be traced.[40]

A♭ is the tonal center of the third period (R22 – R31/5), but Pimen's description of Tsar Ivan (R26 – R27/11) and the music preceding that description focus on E♭. Pimen's description of Tsar Feodor emphasizes F major (R28 – R29/6), and his account of the miracles seen at Feodor's death emphasizes D♭ major (R29/7 – R30/7). Of course, such excursions to related regions may be viewed as large-scale reinforcement of the prevailing tonality. Within the context of A♭, extended emphasis in turn of the pitches A♭, E♭, F and D♭ may be viewed as a large-scale simple functional progression, I–V–VI–IV. In the instance in question, the expected continuation, V–I, II–V–I, or some such, is thwarted since Pimen ends his narrative with an allusion to "the regicide" Boris while the music moves toward C (III in A♭), thence toward D. The interruption of such a basic structural progression – and its deflection toward the remote key of D – surely once again "betrays a calculation which may be unusual, but whose steps can be traced."

The central event of the scene, Grigory's decision to usurp the throne, occurs in the fourth period. The music arrives in D just as Grigory asks Pimen how old Dmitry was when murdered. At Pimen's response, "He would be your age and reigning," Musorgsky shifts abruptly into E♭, the key associated with Dmitry, introduces the motive (Ex. 9.2.5) associated throughout the opera both with the ghost of Dmitry and with the impostor Grigory and, as we have noted above, further emphasizes the moment with stage directions and a change in orchestration. At Pimen's words "I am finishing my chronicle with an account of Boris's scandalous crime," the music returns to D minor, and the remainder of the period, in which Pimen instructs Grigory to continue the chronicle of the realm and leaves to attend Matins, centers on a mixed-mode D. Just as in *Rigoletto*, a brief digression to the Neapolitan has served as the means of introducing a tonal color – in this case, E♭ – of great importance in the opera's structure.

(By eliminating Pimen's narrative about the murder of the Tsarevich, Musorgsky wrought a much more vivid introduction for the Dmitry motive. No longer foreshadowed and anticipated in the course of Pimen's narrative, it emerges with the simple force of revelation at Pimen's response to Grigory's question. The interplay between Grigory's ambition, Dmitry as Nemesis, and Pimen's role as an agent of retribution becomes more subtle and mysterious in the revision – a change that surely would have appealed to Musorgsky, as we saw in Chapter 8. And as Richard Taruskin has observed,[41] cutting the narrative also eliminates an instance in which the Dmitry motive clearly refers to the real Dmitry in the minds of characters other than Boris.)

In the final period, in C♯ minor, Grigory muses on the workings of fate. Though no one, it seems, can punish Boris for murdering the "unhappy infant," Pimen has recorded the crime for which posterity and God will judge the Tsar. As the young novice ponders his future, Musorgsky recalls the Dmitry motive in C♯ minor, thereby expressing through the music Pushkin's unspoken line, "It's settled. I'm the Tsarevich." The scene concludes with the writing motive heard above a pedal C♯.

The scene's tonal scheme is simple and carefully integrated in the tonal plan of the complete opera. Like the first scene of the prologue, the Cell scene is in C♯ minor. Tonal progression of its five periods is as follows: d–b/B–A♭–d/D–c♯, or Np–VII–V–Np–I. As noted above, the key of A♭ major dominates the scene's central third period, when Pimen is telling Grigory about Boris's predecessors who longed for repose and sought it in prayer. (Significantly, when the old monk sings of Tsar Feodor – who found peace – the music turns briefly to D♭, the key of resolution.) Equally crucial, however, is D – a tritone away from A♭. D minor accompanies Pimen's reference to Boris's crime in both the first and fourth periods, and the motive associated with Pimen and his virtue first appears in D major. Furthermore, D reappears just as Grigory assumes the guise of Dmitry. Used in this scene in conjunction with Pimen and Grigory, both agents of retribution, D becomes associated with retribution through Dmitry. The pitch-class B, represented in this scene by both B major and B minor, is associated by Allen Forte with Grigory, and of course is closely related to D.[42]

The resolution of the Cell scene to C♯ minor is logical both dramatically and musically. The idea of retribution through Dmitry leads to the beginning of Grigory's power; D is upper leading tone to C♯.[43] Thus, both claimants to the throne begin their rise to power in C♯ minor. In addition, Musorgsky's emphasis in this scene on D, in conjunction with A♭, symmetrically extends the diagram that had begun to emerge in the Coronation scene (cf. Figure 9.4 with Figure 9.3 above).

Tonality also plays a role in the Inn scene; one finds here, for example, a second instance of the representation of opposite ideas by contrasting modes. The key of A major (release from Dmitry) is heard at the beginning when Boris's police still have a chance to catch the runaway Grigory; A minor (Dmitry's victory) emerges when Grigory escapes at scene's end. Both Varlaam's songs are in keys associated with the people, the first in F♯ minor, the second in F minor (the reverse of the semitonal intensification in the first

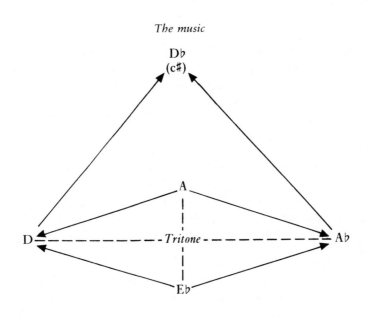

Figure 9.4

scene – as Varlaam gets drunker, his music "relaxes").

Tonality, however, is only one consideration in *Boris Godunov*. No discussion of the opera can omit some treatment of the patterns of "simple human speech" that Musorgsky composed into his music. (We discuss the convictions behind the composer's practice in Chapter 8.) Both scenes of Act I (Pimen's Cell and the Inn), adhere closely to the principles of *opéra dialogué* that were espoused in the Mighty Handful in the late 1860s. The goal of *opéra dialogué*, expressed in the composer's own words, is that "characters speak on stage as living people speak" in music that is "an artistic reproduction of human speech in all its most subtle windings."[44] Toward that end, two declamatory patterns emerge in Musorgsky's vocal writing, one found most commonly in settings of verse, the other in settings of prose. In setting a text in blank verse, like Pimen's monologue, the composer often begins phrases with an anacrusis occupying a full beat (even though such a speech pattern is not naturalistic). The musical result is not so much a naturalistic imitation of speech as a rhetorical heightening of it that complements the character of blank verse. One recent commentator finds its model in "the emotionally exalted tone Russians invariably assume when, even today and even in casual surroundings, they recite poetry."[45]

Musorgsky uses this device with restraint. In Pimen's monologue, for example, it occurs just three times. Each time, it appears in conjunction with other musical traits that help throw it into relief: a change of key and the monologue's climactic line ("Da vedayut potomki pravoslavnykh"), the restatement of Pimen's motive in the orchestra ("Minuvshee prokhodit predo mnoyu"), the repetition of the monologue's first line as its last line, with the concomitant rounding off of the musical form. It thus highlights the statement of purpose of Pimen's monologue, the moment he spends recollecting the past, and the moment he picks up his pen to continue his work.

The other declamatory pattern, as we noted in Chapter 8, is widespread in *kuchkist* settings of prose and thus in the Inn scene; it is sometimes called the "mute ending." Here a composer sets unaccented syllables occurring at the end of a word as eighth notes or triplets, with the beginning of the following beat empty. This style leads to rather choppy melodic lines, filled with rests, that strongly suggest a naturalistic manner of text delivery:

In normal, conversational Russian speech, the tonic accent is very strong and tends to fall into a pattern of fairly isochronous "beats," with the unaccented syllables arranging themselves evenly between them like gruppetti. Triplets are super-abundant in the "conversational" Inn Scene; they are almost absent in the "declaimed" Cell Scene. The two scenes sum up between them the state of the declamatory art in extremist-realist Russian music, vintage 1860s.[46]

Small wonder then that when the Inn scene was first performed, César Cui considered it "worthy of the music of *The Stone Guest*" and maintained that "the music fuses with the text to such a degree that having heard the phrases it is no longer possible to separate the text from the music."[47]

But even though the revised form of the Inn scene remains remarkably faithful to *kuchkist* ideals of declamation, it presents one subtle change worth noting, the addition of the "Song of the Drake." This animal ditty, one of several folklike genre pieces added during revision, provides not only local color, but also another interval of "opera time," during which Grigory's transformation from defiant monk to adventurer in peasant's clothing can take place in the minds of the spectators. To allow a brief interval of time to pass, like this, before bringing a character from the previous scene into a radically different setting is another device that Musorgsky easily could have taken from Verdi. In *La forza del destino*, for example, Verdi keeps Leonora offstage at the inn at Hornachuelos until after the opening chorus and the exchange between her brother and the mayor. The audience last saw Leonora fleeing with Alvaro at the end of the previous scene, after the unintentional murder of her father. She reappears at Hornachuelos only after enough time and music have passed to establish the necessary change of psychological atmosphere. The "Song of the Drake," creates precisely the same temporal

Example 9.5

space. But if the Cell scene and the Inn scene remain essentially *kuchkist* – despite certain Italianate details – the extensively revised *Terem* scene and the entirely new Polish scenes show just how far Musorgsky was prepared to retreat from *kuchkism*.

How fine *Boris* is now! It is simply magnificent. Fascinating! What variety, what contrast! How well-rounded and inspired it all is now.

ALEXANDER BORODIN

The *Terem* scene is devoted to Boris so it is no surprise to find keys associated with him playing a fundamental role. Of basic importance is the pattern revealed in the "Boris chords" of the Coronation scene: interlocking seventh chords a tritone apart directed, Janus-like, toward keys themselves a tritone apart with tonics equivalent to third and seventh of the seventh chords (see Ex. 9.5). The organization of both the first and last periods of this act centers on a transposition of this progression. Furthermore, as noted in our discussion of the Coronation scene, the relationship among the keys A, E♭, A♭, and D♭ – a relationship which lies at the heart of both Act II and the entire opera – flows directly from these selfsame chords (cf. above, Figs 9.3 and 9.1).

The six periods of Act II may be grouped in two sets of three, according to musical and dramatic symmetry:[48]

PER 1	PER 2	PER 3	PER 4	PER 5	PER 6
G	E♭	e♭	A	D/E♭	A♭
The Children	Boris with	Boris's	Boris with	Boris with	Boris's Hal-
with the Nurse	the Children	Monologue	Feodor	Shuisky	lucination
(The children's	(Boris	(Boris	(Feodor's	(Boris	(Boris
innocence.	with	alone.)	innocence.	with	alone.)
Folklike	others.)		"Song of	others.)	
songs.)			the Parrot.")		

253

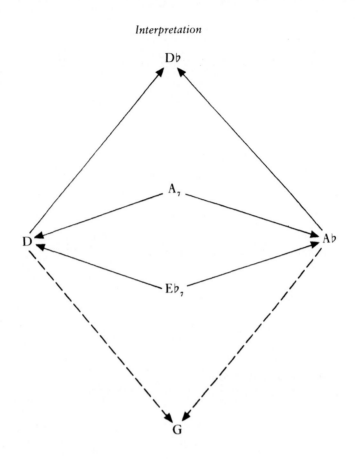

Figure 9.5

A and E♭ are the antithetical pitches of the act's tonal plan. In the first period, when the chiming clock is introduced, we hear the chords of A₇ and E♭₇, in alternation above an ostinato G–C♯. As Figure 9.5 indicates, these chords can be viewed as directed either toward D♭, the key of resolution and the fundamental key of the opera, or toward G.

At this point Musorgsky needs only to introduce the clock and to show the children's delight in it, thereby preparing for the horrible contrast to come at the end of the act. Resolution of these chords toward D♭ here would be premature, and by the end of the period Musorgsky reveals them to have been directed toward G, a pitch which Allen Forte associates with the aspirations Boris has for his family (Boris as Dynast).[49]

When Boris enters, the tonality (E♭) suggests that even though he may console his daughter and speak with his son, he is thinking about Dmitry. As he tells his son that the day may soon come when he, Feodor, will reign, the music turns to C minor, the key associated with foreboding, and we hear the motive of foreboding (Ex. 9.2.8); this motive will reappear at the beginning of Boris's farewell, when he is dying. The monologue "Dostig ya vysshey vlasti" (I have attained the highest power) reveals the fear and guilt that torment the Tsar. Musorgsky introduces in this monologue the recurring motives associated with Boris's majesty and authority and with his guilt (Ex. 9.2.9 and 9.2.10).

This is perhaps the point to pause and look more closely at this monologue and at the suggestions of Italian influence it reveals. By doing so, we may see even more clearly how far Musorgsky has traveled from a *kuchkist* preoccupation with recitative and "correct declamation," and we may perhaps reconfirm our intuition that he did not travel this path through instinct alone, but through his own ability to learn from the works of his peers.

As we have seen in Chapter 8, Musorgsky forged declamatory and conversational styles of text setting in *The Marriage* and the initial *Boris*. We saw further, in the specific example of "Dostig ya vysshey vlasti," that in his revised version Musorgsky extensively rewrote Pushkin's text, which in the initial version, good *kuchkist* that he had been, he had more faithfully preserved. From the changes that he now has made in the poet's text, one infers that his work on *The Marriage* and on the initial *Boris*, for all the practice it may have given him in setting Russian speech patterns to music, also taught him that a good play is not necessarily by itself a good libretto. Since musical setting can distort words, the extensive development of ideas is out of place. But in compensation for the loss of verbal subtlety, strong emotions can be given musical expression in opera. Thus a good libretto develops a tension between information and reflection and takes advantage of music's ability to convey what cannot be said in words. "An opera is not a play," wrote Boïto to Verdi early in the collaboration that led to *Otello*. "Our art lives by elements unknown to spoken tragedy. An ambience that has been shattered can be created once again. Eight measures are enough to resurrect a sentiment; a rhythm can revive a character; music is the most omnipotent of the arts and has a logic all its own, quicker and freer than the logic of spoken thought and more eloquent besides."[50]

Pruning away much of the "spoken thought" contained in Pushkin's text, Musorgsky creates in revision a reflective monologue of increasing psychological tension. Some two-thirds of the monologue's text is by the composer. Just the first twelve lines are taken from Pushkin, and they do not occur together but appear throughout the first three-quarters of the poet's text.[51]

Pushkin's Boris never loses his grip; reason, statecraft, and *Realpolitik* remain firmly at the forefront of his mind. By contrast, Musorgsky's hero is a pitiable creature tormented by guilt and regarding the calamities that have befallen his country as punishments for his sin. After the first third of the monologue (the part derived from Pushkin), his mind becomes so excited that he fails to complete his thoughts. The image of the child Dmitry – blood-stained, eyes ablaze, fists clenched – fills his imagination and wraps him in anguish.

Though these textual changes themselves constitute a retreat from the *kuchkist* principles embodied in the initial version, the music illustrates even more clearly than the verbal text Musorgsky's changing view of musical theater. The revised monologue is in three sections, which we may designate R, A_1, and A_2. The first section (R), beginning with the line "Dostig ya vysshey vlasti," incorporates text and music from the initial version of the monologue and is close in style to that version. Changes of meter appear in order to permit the composer to lay agogic stress on a few important accented syllables in the text; there is no extensive repetition of musical phrases within the passage, although reminiscence motives that will return in the Death scene are introduced; and the passage modulates, beginning in IV/IV of the monologue's principal key, E♭ minor, then passing through its subdominant, before cadencing on its dominant at the words "Death took off her bridegroom." The second part of the monologue (A_1), commencing with the text "Tyazhka desnitsa groznogo sudii," is in E♭ minor and exhibits a design both sectional and symmetric. If we mark the music beginning at the phrase "Tyazhka desnitsa" with the letter X (Ex. 9.6.1), the music at "I skorb'yu serdtse polno" with the letter Y (Ex. 9.6.2), and the music at the words "A tam donos" with Z (Ex. 9.6.3), then this central portion of the monologue takes the sectional form X–Y–X–Y–Z–X. A throbbing undercurrent of triplets in all but the first X section gives rhythmic stability to the passage and provides a palpable link between this section and the monologue's final part (A_2), beginning at "I dazhe son bezhit." The final section also centers on E♭, but the appearance of the highly chromatic motive associated throughout the work with Boris's guilt (Ex. 9.2.10) provides contrast and helps separate the A_1 section from the A_2 section. In sum, Musorgsky has written in this monologue a piece of music in which a character at first relates circumstances and events in a relatively free-flowing *parlando* and then expresses his emotions in a more melodious *cantilena*. The skeleton of Italian opera is visible here even if the flesh is Russian.

Setting such passages from *Boris* besides *The Marriage* shows plainly the distance Musorgsky has traveled since his apprenticeship. Though he

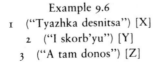

Example 9.6
1 ("Tyazhka desnitsa") [X]
2 ("I skorb'yu") [Y]
3 ("A tam donos") [Z]

continues to mimic the prosody of the text, using note values that reflect the
pace of "simple human speech," he now combines this "naturalistic"
declamation with lyricism and formal symmetry. To use his own words, from
the new conditions of "the grand stage . . . the speech acts of the characters"

Example 9.7

Example 9.8

now are "transmitted to the audience in bold relief." [52] Perhaps the measure of his success in grafting theatricality onto *kuchkism* is the bitterness of Cui's review. [53]

After the psychological stress of this monologue, Feodor's song about the parrot, in A major, provides Boris a moment's respite from his fear and guilt. Prince Shuisky, however, soon shatters the Tsar's composure. [54] The Prince interrupts Boris's sarcastic greeting to inform him that a pretender to the Russian throne has arisen in Poland and has gained the support of both the Poles and the Catholic Church. Accompanied by a motive connecting the chords of D major and Eb minor through their common enharmonic third (Ex. 9.7), Boris asks, "By what name does he dare take up arms against us?" Shuisky cunningly avoids a direct answer, but begins a long passage in which he further aggravates Boris's terror before revealing that the pretender's chosen name is Dmitry.

Boris orders Feodor from the room and instructs Shuisky to seal the border. We now hear the motive of Guilt (Ex. 9.2.10) and a variant of it (Ex. 9.8) as

Boris asks the Prince if he has ever heard of a dead child rising from the grave to challenge a consecrated tsar. Accompanied again by the music of Ex. 9.7, Boris asks Shuisky to confirm once more that Dmitry died in Uglich. This the Prince does, but Boris is still not satisfied. As we hear the motive of Boris's majesty and authority (Ex. 9.2.9) in A♭, the key associated with Boris's desire for spiritual peace, the Tsar tells Shuisky to consider well and tell the truth – for if he lies, a punishment will be devised so terrible that even Tsar Ivan would recoil in horror at the thought of it.

In F♯ major and minor (*BorisLJ-1*, R92 – R95/10), Shuisky describes how peacefully the corpse lay in state at Uglich, free from all decay. This grisly narrative is more than Boris can bear, and he collapses into his chair, dismissing Shuisky with a gesture. Each of Shuisky's revelations – the existence of a pretender, his choice of the name Dmitry, and the description of the real Dmitry's corpse – significantly involves the pitch F♯/G♭, the *odnotertsovaya svyaz'* (common-third link) between D (retribution) and e♭ (guilt). In these three increasingly terrifying revelations, Shuisky unhinges the Tsar's mind. The interview between them, perhaps an echo of the interview between King Philip and the Grand Inquisitor in *Don Carlos*, reduces Boris to desperate panic.

The act's final period, the hallucination monologue, is built upon the tritonal opposition between E♭ and A and provides another illustration of how the "Boris chords" resonate throughout the opera. The composer begins with a violent outburst of music derived from the motive of guilt, presented above a sustained pedal G♯, which soon resolves upward to A minor. As the statuettes on the chiming clock begin to move, the music settles into an ostinato on the tritone A and D♯ (E♭). Around these pitches Musorgsky builds another passage of interlocking seventh chords a tritone apart. The chords this time are B_7 and F_7, and as Fig. 9.6 shows, they are directed towards either E♭ or A, that is towards either the key associated with Dmitry or that associated with release from Dmitry.

Boris's mind teeters as though balanced on a seesaw; he may calm himself, he may slip into madness. The E_7 chord begins to appear in place of F_7, still in alternation with B_7, thereby tipping the scales momentarily toward A and self-control. But the A-sonority arising out of these progressions is unstable – A–C♯–E–G♯ – and the music becomes increasingly dissonant (Ex. 9.9).

Thus, out of the alternating interlocking sevenths emerges not A (as initially seemed likely), but E♭. Precisely when Boris mentions visions of bloody boys and begins to see Dmitry's ghost in the corner (in reality only a shadow cast by a statuette on the clock), a sustained E♭ appears (*BorisLJ-1*, R99/5 – R100/10). The recurring motives of guilt and Dmitry are heard, and

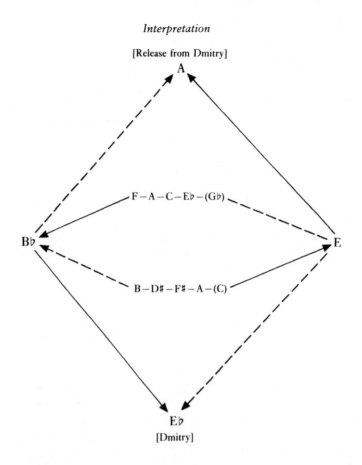

Figure 9.6

Example 9.9

12 and 13   Feodor Chaliapin as Boris, St. Petersburg, 1911

the music builds to a climax as the Tsar's hysteria mounts. Just after he cries, "It was the people's will," E♭ resolves to A♭, and the closing section begins (*BorisLJ-1*, R101 – end). We hear Ex. 9.8, a variant of the guilt motive, in sixteenth notes. Left drained and exhausted, Boris prays to God for mercy. A chromatically descending line slides toward closure on A♭ major, the sonority associated with Boris's desire for spiritual peace, and the dominant in D♭, the work's fundamental key (Ex. 9.10). In this act, however, the resolution and repose of D♭ are withheld.[55]

14 and 15   Feodor Chaliapin as Boris, St. Petersburg, 1911

With the opening of [the Polish act], we feel at once that Musorgsky is treading on alien ground.

ROSA NEWMARCH

Boris at the Bolshoi . . . I. S. [Igor Stravinsky] likes the Polish scene above all . . .

ROBERT CRAFT

As we noted in Chapter 8, many commentators have regarded the Polish act as the poorest of the opera. In Musorgsky's lifetime, critics complained that

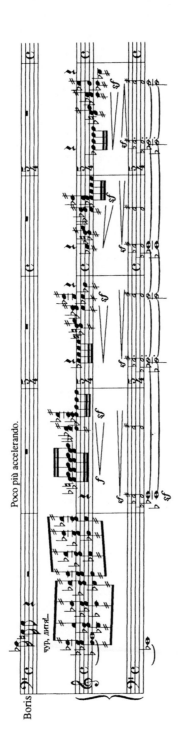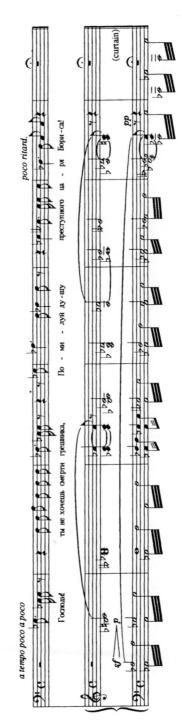

Example 9.10

Rangoni was too melodramatic and deplored the characterization of Poles by Polish dance rhythms. Serge Diaghilev believed that the omission of the scene in Marina's boudoir represented small loss; his view was defended by several Western critics shortly after the successful staging of the opera in Paris in 1908. In the early Soviet era, Boris Asafiev – who preferred Musorgsky's initial version to his revision – characterized the Polish act as "a decorative intermezzo, a digression in a direction away from the action's main line of development,"[56] and even in 1975 Joseph Kerman wrote: "Pushkin or not, the plot of the Polish act with its two scenes seems creaky in its surroundings, and the music sits strangely with the rest of the score. When it is not resolutely Polish it tends to sound rather French."[57]

One cannot dispute the pervasiveness of Polish dance rhythms in the act, though in defense of Musorgsky one might add that they probably are intended as a gesture of homage to Glinka's *Life for the Tsar*, in which Poles likewise are depicted through dances. Moreover, as we saw in Chapter 8, even though the confrontation between Marina and Rangoni in the boudoir can seem melodramatic, it is the necessary climax of the Jesuit's political manipulation of Marina. (It is neither coincidental nor insignificant that Musorgsky wrote to Stasov, at the time of the scene's composition, that the Jesuit gave him no rest for two nights in a row.[58]) What critics fail to mention, however, is that both Polish scenes are constructed just as carefully as any of the opera's Russian scenes. Both demonstrate a clear tonal plan painstakingly integrated with the plan of the entire work and subtly reflecting the organization of the text. Let us pursue, on a purely musical plane, the politics of the Polish act that we began to unravel in Chapter 8.

In the Polish act Musorgsky introduces a key he did not like – E major – to symbolize the Poles, Polish scheming, and the resulting Polish control of the pretender.[59] Marina's aria in the Boudoir scene, in which she reveals her ambition to rule through Dmitry, centers on E (mixed mode). In the Boudoir scene, Rangoni's first attempt to gain control of Marina, as well as her evasion, is in E major, and in the Fountain scene the Jesuit deceives the pretender in E. (As though to illustrate Rangoni's success, much of False Dmitry's music remains in the tonic region of E in this scene, while Rangoni's music moves into other regions of that key, notably the mediant major.) Similarly, Dmitry declares his love for Marina in E major ("Tebya, tebya odnu, Marina, ya obozhayu" [I adore you, you alone, Marina]), and their entire dialogue, preceding the love duet, is in E.

In the Boudoir scene, Musorgsky uses E minor in association with Marina and F major in association with Rangoni. The subtle interaction of these two keys and the final resolution to F reflects musically what one finds in the text:

Rangoni and Marina's conflict of will and Rangoni's ultimate victory. Though Marina's aria begins in E minor, the music falls into E major, the key of scheming, as she unfolds her plan to control the Pretender. Rangoni's first exchange with Marina, upon his entrance, establishes his key (F major), but he too turns at once to E major as he tries to gain sway over her. Her disingenuous declaration that she has no power to help him likewise is in E major. When he insists that she conquer the Pretender with her beauty, then demand of him Russia's conversion to Catholicism, she protests and orders him from her sight, but her attempt to assert her own political ambitions (reflected in the music by a pedal E) fails. As the pedal E changes to a pedal C [the dominant of F], he subjugates her with the threatening vision of Satan hovering over her – surely one of the moments in which the critic Hermann Laroche saw Meyerbeer's Bertram in this character. The Jesuit's key, F major, is heard throughout the closing measures, and an oscillating pedal E–F finally resolves to F in the last measure of the scene.[60]

Two keys, Eb major and E major, dominate the second Polish scene. Since the scene ends in Polish control of the pretender, it is not surprising that keys associated with Dmitry, Rangoni, and scheming play an important role in its structure. Musical and dramatic symmetry suggest the following grouping of the scene's six periods:[61]

PER 1	PER 2	PER 3	PER 4	PER 5	PER 6
Eb	E	C	F	E	Eb
Dmitry	*Rangoni*	*Polonaise*	*Dmitry's*	*Marina*	*Love*
alone	*manipulates*	(Lyric	*monologue*	*manipulates*	*duet*
(He reveals	*Dmitry*	interlude	(He reveals	*Dmitry*	(Lyric
his inner	(Long	incorporating	his inner	(Long	conclusion
thoughts;	recitative-	symmetric	thoughts;	recitative-	incorporating
use of Dmitry	like period	musical	use of Dmitry	like period	symmetric
motive.)	of dialogue.)	structures.)	motive.)	of dialogue.)	musical
					structures.)

The polonaise provides an interlude between the half of the scene devoted to Rangoni and Dmitry and the half devoted to Marina and Dmitry. It is in C major, a key Musorgsky seems to have used only in festive moments of the opera. Its form is an A–B–A', with each section itself comprising an a–b–a', and it also illustrates Musorgsky's predilection to modulate to regions a third away from the tonic, a trait that is visible throughout the opera. The entire middle segment is in Ab, and in all three segments there are excursions to E major: behind the festivity of the dance the scheming continues.

Dmitry begins each half of the scene with a soliloquy. In the first period, he is excited by the hope of a rendezvous with Marina. The music is in E♭, his key, and makes frequent reference to the Dmitry motive (Ex. 9.2.5). In the fourth period, frustrated by Rangoni's success in thwarting his rendezvous with Marina and jealous of her flirtations with a Polish magnate, he vows to resume his fight for Boris's crown. His resolve is expressed to the accompaniment of the Dmitry motive, presented in Rangoni's key of F and decorated with the dotted rhythm of the polonaise. One has very little hope that Dmitry will be able to maintain his posture of independence.

The second and fifth periods, both long periods of dialogue, form the core of the scene. As is the case in other lengthy narrative or dialogue periods, Musorgsky divides their text into several segments and parts, making extensive use of temporary modulations to related regions of the primary key. In the second period, Rangoni sets in motion the scheme to entrap Dmitry, aggravating the Pretender's worst fears as Shuisky had aggravated Boris's. Although the period is in E major, much of Rangoni's music is in the region of the mediant major, G♯ (enharmonically spelled A♭). Plainly, A♭ here has nothing to do with Boris's psychology but is an instance of how "related musico-dramatic events may be articulated by a fully worked-out key [in this case E major], generating its own substructure [prolonged digression to the mediant major]."[62] By contrast, Dmitry's music quickly leaves his own key, E♭, and falls into E; one wonders whether the battle is not over almost before it has begun.

The fifth period contains the heart of the scene, together with important tonal links to the rest of the opera; in it Marina carries out the scheme devised by Rangoni. To the strains of a mazurka (E major, beginning at R51/1), she tells Dmitry that she has come not to hear idle speeches of love, but to learn when he will be tsar in Moscow. The music cadences on an F♯ major triad, foreshadowing a lengthier passage in F♯ later in the scene. Dmitry is astonished at her ambition, saying that surely their love means more to her than her dreams of power and glory. Musorgsky, focusing temporarily on D major (retribution) but avoiding an unequivocal statement of it for the present, suggests through tonal color that the Pretender has forgotten his claim to Boris's throne and would rather make love than war. Accompanied again by a mazurka, Marina reminds Dmitry that if he wants only love, he will find plenty of women in Moscow, his capital city. Somewhat puzzled, he declares his passion for her in a broad melody originally composed eight years earlier, to conclude a choral prayer to the

Example 9.11

goddess Tanit in *Salammbô* (Ex. 9.11). The composer's choice of tonality for this revelation, E Major, suggests that Dmitry already is in Marina's power.

Realizing that she is in command, she spurns him brutally. Two pitch-classes are prominent in this passage, C♯ and D. The first of these, the tonic of C♯ minor, recalls that key's use in association with the beginnings of power; and, of course, her guile has rekindled his ambition. The pitch-class D, associated with retribution through Dmitry, appears most prominently as a pedal at Marina's words: "You no longer think about your throne, about your struggle with Tsar Boris." She has stated explicitly, and the music has confirmed, what before was implicit. Thoughts of love have driven retribution and the fight for the crown from his mind.

He can tolerate no more. He offers to leave for battle the next day, adding that when he has won the crown he will enjoy mocking her, for she will have lost a kingdom by having insulted him. As he once again resolves to resume the fight, this time with Marina for an audience, the Dmitry motive, still *à la*

Example 9.12

polacca, is heard in F♯ major – the region suggested earlier when she asked
"When will you be Tsar in Moscow?" The statement of the motive in F♯, of
course, recalls the parallel passage in F in the previous period. Not only do
associations with Rangoni and the Russian people overlap in ironic
juxtaposition at this moment, but the transposition up a semitone once again
suggests an intensification, this time in Dmitry's determination. We have
already noted similar effects of intensification (or relaxation) in the
Novodevichy and Inn scenes.

His anger kindled, Dmitry's music turns toward E major, as above a pedal
B♮ he tells Marina how he will relish spurning her once he is Tsar. His
determination is undermined, however, by the appearance of the unstable
sonority E–G♯–B–D♯ and the transformation of the pedal B♮ into a trill
between B♮ and A♯. After she relents, this dissonance resolves to E♭ major for
the love duet. Having spurred him into action, Marina is ready to reward him
with promises of affection (Ex. 9.12). The last word, however, is given to
Rangoni, the puppeteer who pulls the strings of both marionettes.

After Boris's death in *Boris Godunov*, the music moves to such a major key that
you can't be any more major.
ATTRIBUTED TO DMITRY SHOSTAKOVICH

The nineteenth-century romantic tragedy of the ruler Boris Godunov is
resolved in the first scene of the last act, the Death scene. Here the ideas of
retribution, guilt, escape, longing, and resolution all find their culmination. It
is no surprise, then, that the keys associated with these ideas dominate the
scene, which contains five periods – introduction and boyar's chorus, the
boyars and Shuisky, Boris's entrance, Pimen's narrative, Boris's farewell and
death.[63] The prelude (E♭ minor) and chorus of boyars (A♭ major/minor)
comprise the first period, which serves as an extended introduction to the
main part of the scene. In the second period, Shuisky tells the assembled
boyars that he has seen Boris in the throes of a fearful hallucination. At the
first mention of the Tsar, the music having shifted form A♭ to C, arrives in A
(Neapolitan of A♭), the key of escape. As Shuisky tells what he has seen,
Musorgsky shifts abruptly toward E♭. Before Boris's entrance, then, the
composer has once again established the tritonal opposition at the heart of
Boris's dilemma: the ever-present suffocating vision of Dmitry (E♭) *vs.* release
from Dmitry (A).

Boris's entrance and the appearance of the recurring motive associated
with guilt mark the beginning of the third period [e♭–(c)–d/D]. While the

boyars accuse Shuisky of lying, the Tsar lurches in, terror-stricken and begging the phantom of Dmitry to leave him in peace. The motive of guilt is heard in its characteristic tonality, E♭ minor (R25 – R26/2). As the raving Boris shouts that he is no murderer, that Dmitry lives, we hear the pitch-classes A and E♭, followed by the Dmitry motive centered on C♭(B♮), the pitch-class linked earlier with Grigory, now reminding us (in an aside) of what Boris cannot hear: Grigory lives, not Dmitry.

Shuisky speaks to Boris, and the words bring the tsar out of his hallucination. The music turns to C minor as Boris explains to his council, accompanied by the motive of foreboding, that he needs their guidance. Shuisky tells Boris that a venerable monk (Pimen) waits to speak with his sovereign and persuades Boris to admit him. In convincing the Tsar to conduct this fateful interview, Shuisky has become part of the force of retribution again, and as though to underscore this point, the music modulates from C minor to D major during Shuisky's speech (R30 – R33).

Pimen's narrative, the fourth period, is in D major/minor, associated with retribution through Dmitry. The old monk enters as the orchestra plays the motive associated both with the character Pimen and his virtue (Ex. 9.2.4). His narrative – a tale of how Dmitry, dead and sanctified, restored sight to a blind shepherd – begins in D minor. D major appears as Pimen quotes the words of the angelic Tsarevich to the shepherd. Then, in a masterful stroke of irony, Musorgsky shifts to the region of the dominant (A major, release from Dmitry) at the words, "I am Dmitry, the Tsarevich." These words prove to Boris what he has longed to know: that Dmitry really is dead. But they do not bring him peace. In his mind, profoundly vulnerable to folk superstition about the unclean dead, the corpse refuses to stay in its grave.

The Tsar topples from the throne, and with a characteristically abrupt enharmonic modulation the music returns to E♭ minor. Thus begins the fifth and final period of the scene. We hear the motive of guilt (E♭ minor) and, as Boris sends for his son, the motive associated with Feodor (C minor). Boris's farewell begins in C minor with the motive of foreboding. As he tells his son that soon he, Feodor, will begin to rule, the music turns to C major, recalling Boris's own coronation. In E♭, he warns his son against foreign intrigue and the scheming boyars, and the key suggests that he is thinking of the danger that the name Dmitry represents for his dynastic ambitions. The music moves into A♭; as we hear the theme associated with Xenia (Ex. 9.2.6), Boris instructs Feodor to protect his sister as both brother and father.

At this point the progression toward resolution has come as far as it has ever gone in the preceding scenes involving Boris. In the Coronation scene, Boris's monologue moved from C minor to E♭ major with a hint of A♭. We noted the progression in Act II from C minor to E♭ minor (second and third periods) and the overall progression of the act from A/E♭ to A♭. Here, finally, Musorgsky permits resolution to D♭. As Boris prays for God's blessing on his children, as he prays not for himself but for them, Musorgsky gives us clearest D♭ major, the key of repose and resolution, and of the loss of power.

The composer then recalls the "Boris chords" for the last time. These two alternating interlocking seventh chords a tritone apart, A₇ and E♭₇, again point toward either D♭ or G, but resolution to G (Boris as Dynast) now is out of the question. A choir of monks enters to administer the *skhima*, a rite of induction into monastic orders that all tsars commonly took at the point of death. Although their key, C# minor, recalls the opera's beginning and Boris's rise, their words ("I see the dying child") exacerbate the Tsar's deepest terror and identify the cause of his fall. Summoning all his authority and strength, he shouts that he still is Tsar (full orchestra *ff*, C major, a last echo of the Coronation scene), but death is near. We hear A♭₇ and then descending chromatic thirds in the bass under a sustained A♭. The Tsar dies, and in the final measures, we hear D♭ major, resolution and the loss of power, and a final cathartic statement of the recurring motive of Boris's majesty and authority (Ex. 9.13).

> When the leading character dies, the opera's over as far as the public is concerned.
>
> ERICH LEINSDORF

Ever since the season of 1876–77, which saw the revival of *Boris* after a year's absence from repertory, the scene in Kromy Forest has been criticized as anticlimactic because it occurs after the death of the title character. If the opera were concerned exclusively with Boris, the criticism perhaps would be justified. But as one recent commentator has observed:

Instead of a single main dramatic thread showing the consequences of Boris' drive for power, Musorgsky weaves together two such threads, the one as before showing Boris' rise and fall, the other tracing the rise of the False Dmitry to the point where, like Boris before him, he has ostensibly achieved his goal . . . In this conception a cycle is seen beginning to repeat itself; the opera closes at the peak of a second arch that intersects with and overlaps the first . . . The story is left incomplete, but the tragic ending is clear . . .[64]

The previous chapter discussed Kromy as a statement about false heroism and history; here we examine its more subtle musical profile. The Kromy Forest scene is divided into seven periods, as follows: mockery of the boyar

Example 9.13

Khrushchov, the fool and the urchins, Varlaam and Misail, anarchy, Polish Jesuits, Tsar Dmitry Ivanovich, and the fool's lament.[65] Beginning in A♭ and ending in A minor, the scene's long-term tonal arch forms a deceptive cadence in D♭, the opera's fundamental key. Such an open-ended, inconclusive cadence reflects the inconclusive ending of the drama.

The first period is in A♭ with an introductory segment in Neapolitan minor. In the key associated with Dmitry's victory (A minor), the people drag in the boyar Khrushchov, a district governor under Godunov. They sing a mock chorus of praise, cast in A♭, and prepare to avenge themselves on one of Boris's henchmen. Musorgsky's choice of A♭ for this chorus further illustrates the care with which he planned his tonal scheme. Before Boris's death, A♭ functions primarily in a family of keys related to the Tsar's psychology and symbolizes his desire for spiritual peace. In the Kromy scene, it has come to reflect, in effect, the crowd's desire to find in Boris's death and the execution of his henchman an end to *their* turmoil. Thus, despite the historical anachronism discussed in Chapter 1, Kromy Forest had to come *after* Boris's Death, for musical and psychological reasons. Small wonder that Musorgsky sensed the rightness of the shift in position when his friend Vladimir Nikolsky suggested it to him.

The people's revenge on Khrushchov is checked by the arrival of the fool and the boys. The key, A minor, is associated with Dmitry's victory; the fool, of course, is the only character in the scene who realizes the implications of that victory.

Keys associated with the people, F minor and F♯ minor, appear in the third and fourth periods. Varlaam and Misail enter, singing of the calamities that have befallen the land, and their song incites the mob to revolution. In the fifth period, two Polish Jesuits, supporters of the False Dmitry, arrive in the forest, singing their master's praise in the key associated with him, E♭ major, The crowd attempts to lynch them (F minor, R57) and is thwarted only by the approach of the pretender's army (E♭, R63).

When Dmitry arrives, he sings not in E♭, but in F, Rangoni's key. Promising "pardon and protection" to those who support him, he frees Khrushchov and invites all to follow him to the Kremlin. Dotted rhythms from the Polish act and the key, F major, suggest that though Dmitry will be crowned Tsar, the Poles will rule, and that dark times lie ahead for Russia. Perhaps to confirm that suggestion, the music shifts to E major, the key associated with Polish scheming. Dmitry frees the two Jesuits, who join the chorus of acclaim and march off with his mob toward Moscow. This section in E major also serves as the final link to the closing key of A minor (enharmonically flat submediant of D♭ major). Dmitry's victory is clear, but only the fool, left alone to sing his lament for suffering Russia, realizes that there will be no change with change. The closing page is a masterstroke of inconclusiveness (see Ex. 9.14). The fool's lament, closing in a sinuous chromatic line vaguely suggestive of the descending chromatic idea in Boris's music at the end of Act II, is followed by a short orchestral postlude, posed above a pedal A♮. Throughout the postlude, the sixth degree (F♮),

Example 9.14

upper leading tone to the dominant pitch (E♮), continues to sound in dissonance with A minor. The music winds down in a written-out ritardando, undulating gently back and forth between F♮ and E♮ in the solo bassoon, the same timbre with which the opera began. The final pitch is an eighth-note E♮, the dominant (not the tonic) in the underlying A minor. Both the overall harmonic motion in this scene (a macrolevel deceptive cadence in the opera's main key, D♭: V–♭VI) and the local events of the closing page confirm in the music's structure the drama's open-ended conclusion.

> Musorgsky was a self-taught composer, but he was also undoubtedly an intellectual one.
>
> CARL DAHLHAUS

In an essay published at the height of Serge Diaghilev's London season of 1913 – during which both *Boris Godunov* and *Khovanshchina* received their English premieres within two weeks of one another at Drury Lane – the English author Rosa Newmarch reminisced about her introduction to these works, in 1897, while studying in St. Petersburg under Vladimir Stasov's guidance. According to Newmarch, Stasov used to tell her: "Love them or hate them, but at least take the trouble to *know* every page of them. There is more vitality in Musorgsky than in any of our contemporary composers. These operas will go further afield than the rest, and you will see their day when I shall no longer be here to follow them to Germany and France, and perhaps (rather doubtfully) to England."[66]

Stasov's prophecy has been fulfilled in the twentieth century. Yet in the autumn of 1868, when Musorgsky sat down to shape the libretto for an *opéra dialogué* after Pushkin, no one could have foreseen such a result. None of the members of Musorgsky's circle had completed an opera; only Cui was getting close to doing so, with his *William Ratcliff*. Musorgsky had to his credit only two abandoned operatic projects (*Salammbô* and *The Marriage*), a handful of songs, some short orchestral works of little consequence, and one unperformed tone poem. An objective observer never would have considered him to be the leading figure of the Balakirev circle. Indeed, because of the extreme stance he had taken in *The Marriage* – surely his most exaggerated realization of mimetic, "naturalistic" text setting – he was running some risk of becoming a butt of jokes. The humorist Dmitry Minaev, writing in the satiric journal *Iskra* [The spark], characterizes Musorgsky as a "fledgling composer" and places the following speech in his mouth:

For the first, time, as an experiment, I [Musorgsky] have written an opera on the text of *The Marriage*, by Gogol, and I have succeeded in the experiment. Now I have conceived two operas: in the first I will set to music "Judicial Regulations" and in the second, the *tenth volume* of the Civil Code. The thought is really too original, but I will cope with it.[67]

Minaev's tongue-in-cheek remarks remind us that music drama is something more than text properly declaimed. By the time Musorgsky had completed the revision of *Boris*, he had outpaced those of his friends who expected nothing more from him than "correct declamation." Although it is misleading to ignore the composer's passion for the Russian language and his quest to find a musical equivalent for it, it is short-sighted and equally misleading to characterize him as a composer interested in declamation and little else. Musorgsky himself, after all, later characterized the work in which he forged his mastery of declamation – *The Marriage*, subject of Minaev's scorn – as "the best effort possible by a musician, *or more correctly a non-musician*, wishing to study and grasp the curves of human speech . . . an étude for chamber rehearsal" [emphasis added].[68] He knew that it had given him valuable experience, and he retained a measure of affection for it, as we may judge from the letter accompanying his presentation of the manuscript to Stasov.[69] But he also knew that musically *The Marriage* marked a dead end, and he retreated steadily from it in his later work. In *Boris* and later in *Khovanshchina* he combined the mimetic style of text declamation found in *The Marriage* with a clear-sighted understanding of the *musical* elements of music drama – an understanding rooted not so much in the polemics flowing from his circle as in the living works of his own great contemporaries. We do Musorgsky a great injustice to assume that his musicianship and dramatic sense remained bounded on all sides by naturalistic text setting; for, in fact, the words that he applied to Verdi describe his own growth from *The Marriage* through *Khovanshchina* equally well: "This one pushes ahead on a grand scale, this innovator doesn't feel shy . . . outdistancing everything, outdistancing everyone, even himself."

16   Modest Petrovich Musorgsky, 1876

IO

BORIS GODUNOV DURING THE
JUBILEE DECADE: THE 1980s AND
BEYOND

Chapters 8 (on the words) and 9 (on the music) undertook to trace, through an analysis of select scenes, the most important stages in Musorgsky's creative evolution as an opera composer. The 1869 *Boris* grew out of the composer's passion for "musically realized Russian speech" – and it arguably represents the highest point to which musical genius could bring orthodox *kuchkism*. The revised 1874 opera was more mainstream and cosmopolitan. It reflected its creator's increasing ability to compose dramatic spectacle on a grand scale, to command the dynamics of a mass scene, to provide onstage action with sophisticated, integrated orchestral support, and to benefit from the operatic achievements of contemporary European masters, from Wagner to Verdi. We do Musorgsky a disservice if we neglect either side of this accomplishment. As a piece of history and as an innovative exercise in melodic declamation, *Boris* is indeed rooted in the Russian language and the Russian past. But Musorgsky ultimately created, and wished to create, a European-class opera.

In this final interpretative chapter, we turn again to the native resonance of Musorgsky's masterpiece. How is the opera faring in its homeland during the final decades of the twentieth century, and what role might its famous plot come to play in the cultural and political future of Russia? Now that the Soviet Union is really over, we can begin to consider its cultural remains in some perspective. For several reasons, the Gorbachev Era (1985–91) serves as an instructive focus and summary point for evaluating the tenacious appeal of *Boris Godunov* – its themes, its composer, and its potential as a cultural document.

Throughout the 1980s, the heavily subsidized and censored production of several "restructured" disciplines (history, literature, film, ballet) were subject to painful economic accountability – usually accompanied by recrimination, soul-searching, backbiting, loss of special privilege and a deep, fully justified fear of the degrading effects of a commercial market on higher cultural values. But the spirit of *glasnost*, with all its hopes and anxieties, came late to Russian music. Unlike its sister arts, music was not immediately exhumed nor its fate under Soviet rule ritually lamented. The Union of Composers, with the apparently eternal Tikhon Khrennikov at its head, remained a relatively placid sea compared with the scandal-ridden Union of Writers or the feisty Union of Cinematographers. This benign situation began to change only toward the end of the decade.

By that time Musorgsky was well situated to become a focus for the new, more liberal and de-Sovietized approach to Russia's musical heritage. As this book has amply demonstrated, the composer was sufficiently beloved for his "folk themes," untutored genius and unhappy bohemian life under the old regime to have been pressed, during fifty years of Soviet scholarship, into pre-Marxist duty as a radical populist, a Bolshevik *avant la lettre*. Once a single ideology ceased to be mandatory, the chance to ease that carelessly applied label began to appeal to responsible scholars. Accidents of biography also helped. The 1980s was a jubilee decade for Musorgsky, with the centennial of his death celebrated in 1981 and the sesquicentennial of his birth in 1989. During that period, the Russian passion for jubilees combined with an already well-primed reforming zeal to authorize a large number of Musorgsky activities. These events included major productions of *Boris Godunov* and revivals of *Khovanshchina*; renewed efforts to fund and equip the Musorgsky museum (founded in 1978) in Naumovo, Pskov province, not far from the composer's birthplace; vocal competitions in the composer's honor and new recordings of the lesser-known songs; a flurry of commemorative essays and revisionist scholarship; and, at last, the launching of an Academy Edition of Musorgsky's works. All these activities fed the unending polemic over which version of Musorgsky's most famous work should take priority on the operatic stage.

There is a final reason why Musorgsky was something of a barometer in the unsettled cultural climate of Russia under reform. His two historical operas, *Boris Godunov* and *Khovanshchina*, both deal predominantly – one might even say excessively, to the detriment of more conventional operatic subject matter such as love – with the vexed theme of *narod i vlast'*, "the common people versus government power." Both operas are set in what the Russians call a *smuta*, a Time of Trouble marking a historical and political watershed. This historical component is crucial for understanding Musorgsky's cultural role in the century's final decade. When the fatal inadequacy of Gorbachev's reforms became manifest at the beginning of the 1990s, suggesting to some that the awful cyclicity of Russian history would again assert itself, many Russians, eager to place the turmoil in familiar context, began to refer in print to their present time as another *smuta*.

Scholars and journalists alike combed history for a key to the current disaster. As Communist ideology was publicly discredited and then jettisoned altogether, Russians began to look to earlier models of legitimacy; a cult of the tsars came into vogue. Both the *glasnost* press and *glasnost* theater began to feature the lives of Russian rulers who preceded, or were doomed to perish in, a time of trouble.

Two essays published during the summer of 1990, one year after the Musorgsky Jubilee, are especially noteworthy.[1] Both devote space to Boris Godunov. The first essay, Vyacheslav Kostikov's "Power, Living and Dead," reopens on new ground the old nineteenth-century debate over Boris's guilt for the death of Tsarevich Dmitry. Karamzin was wrong, Kostikov insists, when he blamed the collapse of Godunov's reign on some personal misdeed of the Tsar. Godunov's nemesis was not Dmitry of Uglich but Ivan the Terrible. Times of Trouble inevitably follow in the wake of tyrants – "As it was under Ivan the Terrible, so it was under Stalin," Kostikov writes darkly – and the challenge confronting the Russian people today is to break their pattern of irresponsible, sentimental explanations for political crisis. In the past only two options have presented themselves: "the temptations of anarchy or the temptations of a utopian, equalizing happiness." Both reactions, Kostikov intimates, are puerile and dangerous. A good start toward more responsible historical self-consciousness might be an objective study of that wise westernizing ruler, Boris Godunov.

In the second essay, "Emperors' Theater?," Boris Lyubimov makes a related point but transposes it to the dramatic stage. The theme of all Russian history, he claims, is *tsareubystvo, otseubystvo, detoubystvo* – killing off one's tsars, fathers, children. For this reason, he notes, the current Russian repertory is so crammed full of plays on Ivan the Terrible, Feodor Ioannovich, Boris Godunov, Peter the First, Catherine the Second, and the formerly maligned, now newly popular Paul I. All are either murderers or victims (real or alleged) of murderers. How, he asks, are we to comprehend this fascination with the violent habits of bygone tsars and, more generally, what do these new enthusiasms tell us about the traditional relation of Russia's ruled masses to her rulers? Lyubimov, too, is not optimistic. During times of trouble, he writes, Russians escape reality in two directions, each awful: they either await the Antichrist and concomitant Apocalypse or – at the other extreme – they expect a joyful utopia, a "rapid achievement of prosperity [through] economic or political experiment." What is needed, again, is some lesson from history that teaches the middle ground, that counsels neither utopia nor despair, so that the Russian people can "slowly begin the difficult climb upward." For the "horror of revolution," Lyubimov writes soberly, is precisely its tolerance of miracles and non-continuities, its suspension of any overriding moral premise, its promise of a clean start and its beguiling but deceptive vision of "changing the rules in the middle of the game."

These dark ruminations in the Soviet press speak vividly to the fate of Musorgsky's greatest opera and to his overall conflicted legacy. In a culture that has always burdened its real-life events with fictional subtexts, the popularity of "Musorgskian plots" – a fickle mob, political succession unmasked as pretendership, police arrests at a sealed border, a holy fool predicting recurrent grief and famine for Russia, true believers burning themselves in wooden churches to avoid contamination by the state – has more than musical significance. As with his great contemporary Fyodor Dostoevsky, controversy over Musorgsky has waxed with national crisis and waned in periods of hope. To take a well-known case: in 1984, the last year of the Brezhnevite stagnation, the eminent stage director Yury Lyubimov was expelled from the Taganka Theater (and from the Soviet Union) for cultural insubordination. His misdeeds included a defiant, aggressively modernized production of Pushkin's *Boris Godunov*, during which actors came down off the stage to accuse the audience of political passivity and submission to a series of shabby pretenders. At the time, it seemed as if the political potential of that 300-year-old tale was inexhaustible. But events soon proved otherwise. Several years into the Gorbachev era, in the summer of 1988, Lyubimov (again restored to favor) returned to the Taganka to mount his interrupted *Boris Godunov*. Rehearsals were uneventful and reviews mixed.[2] Critics and public had the same lukewarm response to Bondarchuk's filmed version of Pushkin's *Boris*, released in 1986. Such indifferent reception might well have been due to cultural overload and exhaustion; another factor, however, could have been a growing hope among Russia's theatergoing public that those grimly pessimistic themes in Pushkin's play and Musorgsky's two historical operas were at last giving way to something less escapist and deluded. Good news: perhaps the Boris Tale would become irrelevant to Russia of the twenty-first century.

But no. Exposure of the crimes of the Soviet period continued apace – and the more corrupt the recent past proved to be, the more the patterns of the early seventeenth century seemed to reemerge. Uneasy parallels with the present were all too easy to draw, and the Russians' intimacy with their own dark history began to bear poisonously satisfying fruit.[3] The similarities are indeed striking. The long, heroic, destructive reign of an authoritarian tyrant (Ivan the Terrible/Stalin) is followed by a succession crisis and a period of stagnation. Then, to the relief of the educated classes and the confusion of the populace, a Westernizing ruler is chosen according to a new definition of legitimacy (in each case, a variant of divine right is called into question: Boris Godunov becomes Russia's first elected Tsar after centuries of caesaro-papism; the Communist Party is forced to relinquish what it had considered its historically mandated monopoly on power after decades of unchallenged rule). Ecological and economic disasters abound. The political disintegration of the country is followed by a resurgence of national feeling and by a sense that earlier times, however awful, were more tolerable; at least they did not expose Russia as hopelessly backward to the rest of the world, and the myth of her special status among nations was sustained.

Growing disaffection with *perestroika* and nostalgic hunger for an earlier faith began to be reflected in new interpretations of Musorgsky's historical vision. Although redemptive theology plays almost no role in Musorgsky's mature work (not in Boris's repentance, the holy fool's lament, or the desperately bleak landscapes of *The Songs and Dances of Death*), during a 1989 sesquicentennial conference in Velikie Luky, Russian delegates argued for reading all of Musorgsky's work as Christian allegory.[4] This Christianiz-ation of Musorgsky, we should note, is profoundly counterintuitive: the composer was sentimental, cynical, pagan perhaps in his fascination with witchcraft and with the workings of superstition on the human psyche, but he was certainly no reverent believer. The average Soviet-bred operagoer must have been even more astonished, however, by a concomitant ideological shift: a precipitous drop in the status of the *narod*. Those cheerfully irreverent monks Varlaam and Misail – usually depicted as buffoons, and indispensable as comic relief – suddenly get a grim gloss. "After all, Musorgsky did not idealize that pair," one critic notes testily in a retrospective essay on one of the Jubilee productions, the Tarkovsky/Covent Garden *Boris*. "They are the ones who, turning up in Kromy, inspire the 'crowd of tramps' (as Musorgsky's text has it) to wild debauchery . . . Varlaam and Misail are flesh of the flesh of their people, at the head of a demonic scene. Skilfully and fervently they inflame the terrifying instincts of the herd, they fan into flame burnt-out sites of human hatred, and before disappearing they toss into the air an axe that has already tasted of someone's blood."[5]

This is revisionism of an extraordinary sort. At the 1874 premiere of *Boris*, according to Vladimir Stasov's later recollections, student radicals had turned the defiant songs of the Kromy scene into a catchword for popular resistance and a glorification of the Russian masses.[6] Not surprisingly, ever since the early Soviet period Kromy had been presented as the "proto-revolutionary" culmination of the opera, its boisterous violence exactly the sort of energy required to topple tsars, false *or* true. During the 1980s and 90s, over a century after opening night, the opera was again being interrogated in light of current political needs. But this time the spirit was quite the opposite of the idealistic populism that had cushioned the opera's reception during the 1870s. The red-tipped axe that the monk Misail brandishes throughout the Kromy scene in the Tarkovsky *Boris* is thrust violently upward just before the Pretender's entry, as the mob freezes in a gesture of defiance – a gesture uncannily reminiscent of heroic Stalinist-style statuary honoring the victorious proletariat. The centennial revivals of Musorgsky were cast not as a celebration of the people but more as a reproach, a retrospective on the people's perpetual craving for anarchy and utopia. At the center of these productions is a solitary ruler searching for faith, left alone with poor human material and a failed state.

As our survey of *Boris* criticism in Chapter 7 suggests, the ideology of these Jubilee revivals resonates powerfully in the context of the opera's history. In spirit they recall the acerbic reviews of Musorgsky's opera by the conservative critics Hermann Laroche and Nikolay Strakhov – except those reviews, we venture to add, were not quite so naive. "The mood of the entire opera is *accusatory*, [among us] a longstanding and well-known mood," Strakhov wrote in 1874. The common people are presented as "crude, drunk, oppressed, and embittered ..." Manipulating them are other characters equally egotistical and unstrung, "figures in the grip of terror, ambition, love, religious feeling . . . These aspirations have no connection among themselves, no interest for the author, and make no overall sense." Strakhov's verdict is harsh, of course, and history has proved his aesthetic judgment flawed. But his comments make marvelous counterpoint against the productions mounted one century later, in another crisis-ridden time.

With this interplay of sympathies in mind, let us look in more detail at three Jubilee productions of *Boris Godunov*.[7] The first had its beginnings in 1983, as a joint effort between Leningrad's Kirov Theater and London's Covent Garden. Its director, the filmmaker Andrey Tarkovsky, was then in exile with only three years left to live. The edition Tarkovsky used, by the British musicologist David Lloyd-Jones, is one of the more famous "supersaturated" *Borises* – that is, it stitches together the fullest versions of everything Musorgsky ever wrote for the opera. (The production was revived in 1990, played in Leningrad with a cast of English soloists, and was then brought to New York City's Metropolitan Opera House, with a Russian cast, in July 1992.) It seems no accident that Claudio Abbado first conceived the idea of inviting Tarkovsky to direct the opera after seeing the film *Andrey Rublyov*.[8] Very long but never tedious, the Kirov/Covent Garden *Boris* bears the cinematographer's signature: with a recurring white-robed specter of the murdered Tsarevich, icons staged as living *tableaux*, a heavy clerical presence (both Catholic and Orthodox) and a blind, shrouded holy fool, the production is, except for the final Kromy scene, lyrical and meditative in spirit.

In a review in *Sovetskaya kultura*, the director of the Moscow festival performance of the Kirov production, Valery Gergiev, reflected on the late Tarkovsky's interest in the Boris project. "This performance came to us when we were deeply mired in a chaos of problems and sufferings," Gergiev wrote. "Tarkovsky had no interest in the affairs of the distant past for their own sake. Painfully contemplating Russia's fate, he sought a way out – and saw it in our reawakened memory, in a troubled conscience. He sought that sense of the sacred, which should never depart from our lives, no matter what ... [In this production of *Boris* one can find] a faith capable of leading us back to a normal life."[9]

Throughout its long history, the Boris Tale has been credited with many things – but not until the 1990s could we number among its tasks "leading people toward a normal life." "Normalization" as a political aspiration took on special resonance in Russian culture of the reform years. It came to mean living one's life by internal moral criteria and in the sober spirit of small concrete deeds, not in the context of extraordinary historical claims, heroic measures, utopian fantasies, or dictated norms. To be "normal" in this way became one of the ideals of Russian citizens once the cruder ideologies governing them began to collapse – and the route to normalization, apparently, was a heightened religious consciousness, a reaffirmation of faith and an individual commitment to confronting the mistakes of the past. As one right-wing Soviet critic put the case in 1990:

The main and basic type of human personality should reject the features of the iron leader, the brilliant soldier, the willful commander and manager. It must assume the features of a gardener, a forester, a pastor. In a continuous kindly patrol he must make the rounds of his impoverished kingdom and nurture, pamper, water the drying stock and prop up what is broken. This forgotten type must be revived out of the ashes of our people. The people want him and are waiting for him.[10]

Only with some strain, of course, can such a gentle, post-Communist message be read back into the choral extravaganzas, irony-laden people's scenes, Polish coquetry, and pretenders on horseback that characterize the supersaturated *Boris*. Exclusive focus on inner spiritual torment can be found much more easily in Musorgsky's original, 1869 version of the opera. And indeed, that earlier text is the basis for two other major productions of *Boris Godunov* during the Jubilee.

Significantly, this interest in the 1869 version – which seems to recur in cycles, as our documents in Chapter 7 attest – is sustained and even nourished by the Academy Edition of Musorgsky's works. For the first time in the tangled textology of *Boris*, not only a "de-Rimskified" but also a "de-Lammified" (that is, an unconflated) set of scores will be readily available to researchers and performers.[11] Easy access to the 1869 opera will thus facilitate that portion of the Russian musical establishment eager to recast the story as a closet *Seelendrama* by excising its heroic, collective, "Italianate," too easily revolutionized components.[12] Given the perennial issue of "fidelity" that this opera raises, however, and with the lessons of our Chapters 2 and 8 in mind, it is worth remarking that the spirit of Pushkin's play is not restored to this stripped-down operatic version. Recent Soviet productions of the 1869 *Boris* reinvest in guilt and religious fervor in a way quite incompatible with the cool wit and eighteenth-century mind of Pushkin. Gone is the ribald humor, the keen sense of political necessity in conflict with personal morality; gone also is any element of spontaneous development or surprise – the very traits, in fact, that originally had made the libretto such an innovative piece of theater. The grieving conscience of the Tsar is the only thing we sense on stage, and it is an absolutely fixed value. These productions recall, in fact, the texture and tone of Pushkin's major literary inspiration, Nikolay Karamzin's *History* – without, of course, the anti-Godunov animus of Karamzin's chronicle sources.

Some details from these "original-version" productions will suggest possibilities for future tellings of the Boris Tale. The leaner of the two was mounted by the Estonia Theater from Tallinn, which had been in repertory for almost a decade.[13] Stage sets for this production were not the realistic medieval trappings we have come to expect in productions of *Boris*, but a horizontal-and-vertical abstraction of stage hangings and vaguely industrial cross-bars. Candle-bearing monks crowd into this abstract space – reminiscent of the traps of the mind – in scene after scene, eventually filling up the stage. (The production interpolates all the monks' choruses from the 1874 opera back into the original version.) Its seven scenes are separated by the tolling of bells and processions of monks. In fact, the Estonia production has ceased to be the dramatization of political struggle and has become a passion play with music – and as such it curiously recalls various late nineteenth-century attempts to re-sacralize, and thus to domesticate, Pushkin's perplexingly heroless drama by adding Christ-like features to some of its leading roles.[14] The Tallinn production has almost no trace of the noisy "people's musical drama" that *Boris* productions once so earnestly strove to realize.

Another interpretation of the 1869 *Boris*, even more radically conservative, was realized in 1989 by the Stanislavsky Theater in Moscow. This production too had no Kromy insurrection, no Polish scenes, no interpolated songs or pranks to lighten the texture. Its very austerity constituted a polemic against the conventional wisdom that Musorgsky's operatic genius had "saved" Pushkin's play by making it stageable and dramatic. As one critic remarked, Russians have had enough of these palatially kitsch "socialist-realist Bolshoy Theater" productions, which do no more than "fulfil the social-political decree for opera-style emotions obligated to reflect the power and greatness of the Fatherland."[15] Opposing itself to that task with a vengeance, the Stanislavsky production approached *Boris Godunov* in a "purely poetic and purely theatrical" way, made possible, in the words of the reviewer, by the new freedom of Russians "to read Pushkin, Karamzin and Musorgsky outside the harsh framework of an ideological *diktat.*"[16]

As a result, all the politically correct readings of the secular, materialist last century and a half fall away. The Stanislavsky production, we are told, "introduces an important religious theme, the administration of the eucharist, the search of a confused and tormented soul for peace, rest and forgiveness." Curiously, several lines belonging to the Tsarevich Feodor and Pimen are turned over to a children's chorus and resound backstage, as if these characters exist primarily as reverberations in Tsar Boris's head. The most provocative innovation is a young blond-haired boy with a candle – a specter of the murdered Tsarevich or perhaps the catharsis of Boris's crime? – who appears before the rising of the curtain to light stage candles. The Boy then becomes an actor in the drama. As the second scene opens, he is seated on the throne; when the newly-elected Tsar appears on stage amid the tolling of bells, the Boy takes up his candle and quits his seat, making an indistinct threatening gesture that causes Boris to shudder. The Boy then remains at the Tsar's side throughout the remainder of the opera.[17] What matters at every point in this production is Boris's self-absorbed preparation for the Final Judgment, wholly to the exclusion of state or society. In splendid contrast to past Soviet practice, social class does not matter at all: all are equal before God.

As is clear from the above summary – and contrary to the claims of the reviewers – the Stanislavsky Theater production does indeed reflect an ideological *diktat.* But it is far from the sort of *diktat* laid down by nineteenth-century social critics like Nikolay Chernyshevsky, sworn foe of the autocracy and inspiration for the aesthetics of *kuchkism,* or by Vladimir Stasov, singleminded propagandist for national art. True to the "binary" style regrettably characteristic of so much Russian thinking on cultural matters, an open field of nuanced, negotiable partial values is not much in evidence. What had once been forbidden now risks to become the new orthodoxy. And just as thoughtful Russian liberals are noticing with dismay that enthusiasts of the post-Communist religious renaissance are eager to reprint works by Nicolas Berdyaev and Vladimir Soloviev on the Apocalypse but not on philosophy of law or individual rights, so do thoughtful Russian theater critics lament the reductive, mechanical inversion of complex national classics. Two posters were on display in the foyer of the Stanislavsky Theater during the opera's run. One illustrated the murder of Dmitry of Uglich by Boris Godunov's minions in 1591; the other showed the Romanov heir, Tsarevich Aleksey, shot by a Bolshevik firing squad in 1918. In a wary report in *Moscow News* on two opera "revivals" – this production of *Boris Godunov* and a new staging of Glinka's *Life for the Tsar* – one reviewer concluded that "opera companies do not want to stay aloof. They want to be up to date. But the only way this aim can be achieved is through high artistic standards and professionalism: those qualities cannot be replaced by token topicality."[18]

Is "topicality" nevertheless destined to be the fate of Russian classics in Times of Trouble? Is one ideological mandate stripped away only to reveal its equally intolerant negation? One is reminded of Pushkin's irritation at those who read his drama *Boris Godunov* in the politically fraught, post-Decembrist 1820s, only to find there "allegories, hints, *allusions*," whereas his desire had been to "renounce his own style of thought and relocate himself completely in the age he was depicting."[19] A strong but fundamentally ambivalent artistic production inviting multiple hypotheses from its audience has not been realized in these *Borises*. And thus the one thing we wait for from Russian art – the possibility of it being simply art, without tendentious political lacquering pro or contra – seems as distant as ever. It is a welcome sign, one could argue, that this inadequacy has bothered many Russians as well. In 1906, the then very young Osip Mandelstam wrote a school essay entitled "Crime and Punishment in *Boris Godunov*," in which he remarked that crime was not always followed by punishment, that no work of art could conform solely to causal relations, and that art is the best arena for observing all the "narrowness, unnaturalness, falsehood and hypocrisy of a teleological point of view."[20] Now that teleological models for Russian historical experience have fallen upon hard times, we can look forward to further, more openended revisions of the current revisionist, Christianized *Boris*.

Meanwhile, the continued vulnerability of the Boris Tale to psychological and political determinism has contributed to the ancient debate over auctorial intent. According to one perceptive critic, Sergey Rumyantsev, we worry overmuch about "the author's authentic version."[21] For, he argues, any performance or edition is to a certain extent "an island in the uninterrupted stream of auctorial versions." Echoing the authenticity debates that rage in Western music circles, Rumyantsev insists that there is no way we can now return to either of the *Borises* that Musorgsky wrote. Inevitably we experience them already overladen with earlier interpretations. This tradition of reception permeates, quite properly, any new operatic production. When Valery Gergiev brought his Kirov Theater production of *Boris Godunov* to New York in 1992, he was asked, not unexpectedly, if the political and economic chaos of Russia in her reform period would help or hinder art. "There will be difficulties," he said. "But everything in Russia is now *awake*." [22]

These final comments suggest two ways to approach the rich yield of the Musorgsky Jubilee and, for that matter, two ways to approach interpretative criticism that aims – as this book does – to reconstitute the experience of an opera. The first approach is theoretical in the strong sense of that word. It aims to fit a satisfyingly closed set of postulates over a concrete cultural text. No matter how chaotically the outside world changes, it is assumed that the artwork remains a coherent island, a creative retreat where both auctorial intent and past environment are to a large extent recuperable. The success of this pole is measured by the great Russian schools of textology and scholarly commentary that have survived the most awful periods of political and cultural oppression.

Then there is a performance tradition in history. This is tradition in the sense that Rumyantsev has just invoked it: cumulative, multiply authored, messy, "awake" – and thus perpetually in hostage to the present. Any decent study of reception, of course, must take into account both poles. Nowhere is this imperative more forcefully at work than in Russian culture, for better or worse a palimpsest space literally saturated with its own history. It is, in fact, one of the reassuring paradoxes of Russian culture that a tradition so centrally concerned with apocalypse and revolution should nevertheless constitute so conscious and tenacious a continuum.

NOTES

1 Tsar Boris in history

1 For more on the Verdi–Musorgsky connection, see Chapter 9, pp. 235–39, 242, 255–56.

2 The historical material presented in this chapter is compiled from several revisionist accounts. Two accessible and reliable texts by Russian scholars available in English are: S. F. Platonov, *Boris Godunov, Tsar of Russia* [Petrograd 1921], trans. L. Rex Pyles (Gulf Breeze, Fla.: Academic International Press, 1971); and Ruslan G. Skrynnikov, *Boris Godunov* [Moscow 1978], trans. Hugh F. Graham (Gulf Breeze, Fla.: Academic International Press, 1982). Additional material from Russian sources is discussed in Caryl Emerson, *Boris Godunov: Transpositions of a Russian Theme* (Bloomington, Ind.: Indiana University Press, 1986).

3 Letter to Vladimir Stasov, 16 & 22 June 1872, in Modest Petrovich Musorgsky, *Literaturnoe nasledie*, ed. A[leksandra] A[natol'evna] Orlova and M[ikhail] S[amoylovich] Pekelis, 2 vols. (Moscow: Muzyka, 1971–72), I:132 [hereinafter: *MLN*]; in English in *The Musorgsky Reader: A Life of Modeste Petrovich Musorgsky in Letters and Documents*, ed. and trans. Jay Leyda and Sergei Bertensson (New York: W. W. Norton, 1947; reprint edn., New York: Da Capo Press, 1970), pp. 185–86 [hereinafter: *TMR*]. For the convenience of those readers who would like to place our translations in context, we shall provide both Russian and English references throughout, as follows: *MLN*, I:132/*TMR*, pp. 185–86.

4 N. M. Karamzin, *Istoriya gosudarstva Rossyskogo*, 12 vols. (St. Petersburg: Evdokimov. 1892; reprint edn., Slavistic Printings and Reprintings 189/1–12, The Hague: Mouton, 1969)., I:xvi.

5 A. S. Pushkin, *Polnoe sobranie sochineny*, 16 vols. (Moscow: Izd. Akademii Nauk SSSR, 1937–50), XIII:145.

2 Musorgsky's literary sources, Karamzin and Pushkin

1 For more detail, see Robert William Oldani, *"Boris Godunov* and the censor," *19th-Century Music* 2 (March 1979): 246–48.

2 For a thorough influence study, see J. L. Black, *Nicholas Karamzin and Russian Society in the Nineteenth Century: A Study in Russian Political and Historical*

Thought (Toronto: University of Toronto Press, 1975), esp. Ch. 4, "The history: Textbook for emperors and citizens," and Ch. 5, "The history and Russian society in the nineteenth century."

3 See the discussion by two eminent Soviet émigré musicologists, Alexandra Orlova and Maria Shneerson, "After Pushkin and Karamzin: Researching the sources for the libretto of *Boris Godunov*," in *Musorgsky: In Memoriam, 1881–1981*, ed. Malcolm Hamrick Brown, Russian Music Studies, no. 3 (Ann Arbor, Mich.: UMI Research Press, 1982), pp. 249–70, esp. pp. 249–55.

4 In the West, Richard Pipes has long appreciated Karamzin as a mature eighteenth-century political thinker; see his classic "Karamzin's conception of the monarchy," in *Essays on Karamzin: Russian Man-of-Letters, Political Thinker, Historian, 1766–1826*, ed. J. L. Black (The Hague: Mouton, 1975), pp. 105–26.

5 L. N. Luzyanina, "*Istoriya Gosudarstva Rossyskogo* N. M. Karamzina i tragediya Pushkina *Boris Godunov*," *Russkaya literatura*, no. 1 (1971), pp. 48–55.

6 The Boris Tale does not have precise boundaries within the *History*. In vol. x [1824], all four chapters are devoted to Feodor Ioannovich's reign, 1584–98 (and thus Boris's "regency"); in vol. xi [1824], chs. 1 and 2 are devoted to Godunov's reign (1598–1605), Ch. 3 to Feodor Borisovich's brief reign (1605), and Ch. 4 to the False Dmitry. The first mention of Godunov occurs much earlier, in vol. ix [1821], pp. 131–32; the final (12th) volume [1826] contains many references to the "ruins of Uglich" and other marks of Boris's legacy.

All citations of the *History* are taken from the 1892 St. Petersburg edition (first citation: Ch. 1, n. 4). Parenthetical references in the text are by roman numeral for volume and arabic numeral for page, e.g. ix, 131–32.

7 Yu. M. Lotman, *Sotvorenie Karamzina* (Moscow: Kniga, 1987), pp. 303, 313. Lotman suggests that by 1826, the time of his final illness, Karamzin had been sufficiently disillusioned by the Decembrist revolt and its cruel aftermath to have lost all hope that he could return to his role as moral adviser to the autocrat.

8 "Istoricheskiya vospominaniya i zamechaniya na puti k Troytse" [*Vestnik Evropy*, 1802], in N. M. Karamzin, *Sochineniya Karamzina*, vol. viii (Moscow: tip. Selivanskago, 1804), pp. 300–77. Quoted portions occur on pp. 359, 351–52, 365, 374.

9 Pipes, "Karamzin's conception of the monarchy," p. 107. Subsequent quote occurs on p. 121.

10 Karamzin's version of Godunov's life prevailed throughout the nineteenth century, even after more critical and positivist historiography began to be practiced. The major historians of the 1860s–90s (Kostomarov, Soloviev, Klyuchevsky) kept the presumption of guilt for the Uglich death but trimmed it of its moral significance. Sergey Platonov, the first great revisionist historian on the Time of Troubles, challenged the guilt as well. "Boris died exhausted by the grave imponderables of his reign," Platonov insists. "He did not die exhausted by a struggle with his sin-filled conscience. By the standards of his time he was guilty neither of sin or crime." Platonov, *Boris Godunov*, p. 205 [first citation: Ch. 1, n. 2].

11 For a fine discussion, see Michael Cherniavsky, *Tsar and People: Studies in*

Russian Myths (New Haven, Conn.: Yale University Press, 1961), Ch. 1; see also Alain Besançon, *Le Czarévitch immolé* (Paris: Plon, 1967), Ch. 2.

12 Ruslan Skrynnikov has traced the gradual elaboration of the Uglich events from their humble beginnings (accidental death in a courtyard) to more theatrical martyrdoms depicted in later Lives of St. Dmitry (the presence of a murder knife, a necklace, the action moved to the palace staircase, the cast of characters expanded, etc.); see his *Boris Godunov*, p. 52 [first citation: Ch. 1, n. 2]. In his description of this death, Karamzin appears to have departed from his usual practice of relying on written accounts closest in time to the historical event, drawing his material instead from a maximally distanced and "mature" hagiographic version.

13 Both Skrynnikov (*Boris Godunov*, pp. 51–65) and Platonov (*Boris Godunov*, pp. 139–52) indicate that the immediate response to Dmitry's death was rather low-key. The body was buried in Uglich, not in Moscow. The grave was forgotten or abandoned by the surviving Uglich townsfolk, who, when asked to lead the clergy to the site of the newly sainted martyr's grave in 1606, found it (after a long search) in the side of a ditch. Even Tsar Feodor, a great lover of pilgrimages, never once saw fit to visit his half-brother's grave. And the Muscovite chancellories could hardly recall the most basic information about the death when questioned on the matter in 1609. In short, evidence strongly suggests that in 1591 the whole event was simply not the scandal that it later became.

14 For a thorough treatment of the "Legend of the Returning Tsarevich," see K. V. Chistov, *Russkie narodnye sotsial'no-utopicheskie legendy* (Moscow: Nauka, 1967), Part I.

15 For more on the demonic nature of play-acting and the power of improper pretense to destroy a state, see B. A. Uspensky, "Tsar and pretender: *Samozvanchestvo* or royal imposture in Russia as a cultural-historical phenomenon," trans. David Budgen, in Yu. M. Lotman and B. A. Uspensky, *The Semiotics of Russian Culture*, ed. Ann Shukman, Michigan Slavic Contributions, no. 11 (Ann Arbor, Mich.: Michigan Slavic Contributions, 1984), pp. 259–92.

In her provocative discussion of holy foolishness and pretendership in the Age of Dostoevsky, Harriet Murav suggests that medieval Russian culture viewed the "demonic pretender" and the "holy fool" as mirror images of one another. The first was evil but pretended sanctity, the second feigned madness but was in fact blessed. In this context, it is tempting to speculate on Musorgsky's decision to use a holy fool, hard upon the False Dmitry's "triumph," to close his revised version of the opera. Read with Murav's mirror image in mind, such a juxtaposition of Holy Fool to Unholy Pretender is much richer in meaning than the St. Basil's Scene either in Pushkin (the drama, after all, deals with the issue of pretendership in a secular spirit and much more positively), or in the first version of the opera, closely modeled on Pushkin. For more on holy fools, pretenders and the importance of Karamzin for Dostoevsky's (and thus Musorgsky's) generation, see Harriet Murav, *Holy Foolishness: Dostoevsky's Novels and the Poetics of Cultural Critique* (Stanford, Calif.: Stanford University Press, 1992), Ch. 5.

16 Karamzin surprised and delighted the pre-Decembrist radicals of the early 1820s

with his volume IX and its scathingly honest indictment of Ivan IV. But we should remember that of Karamzin's three criteria for a proper monarchy – autocratic (that is, undivided) rule, legitimate dynastic succession, and enlightened rule by law – Ivan the Terrible fulfilled two of the three. In his 1811 memoir to Alexander I, Karamzin had criticized Ivan IV's reign but noted with satisfaction that Ivan's obedient subjects, alert to his legitimacy and satisfied with his undivided authority, prayed for mercy rather than plotted against his rule. No such tolerant obedience is expected (or received) from the subjects of Boris Godunov, whose misplaced ambition and elected status weakened "the moral strength of tsardom."

17 A systematic comparative analysis of Karamzin's and Pushkin's texts was undertaken only at the end of the century, by Andrey Filonov; see his *Boris Godunov A. S. Pushkina. Opyt razbora so storony istoricheskoy i esteticheskoy* (St. Petersburg: tip. Glazunova, 1899), Part I.

18 "On classical and romantic poetry" [1825], in Carl R. Proffer, ed. and trans., *The Critical Prose of Alexander Pushkin* (Bloomington, Ind.: Indiana University Press, 1969), pp. 35–38.

19 "On tragedy" [1825?], in Proffer, *Critical Prose of Pushkin*, p. 40. Pushkin discusses tragedy (what he calls the "least understood genre") at more length in a letter drafted to Nicholas Raevsky (*fils*), July (after the 19th), 1825. See A. S. Pushkin, *The Letters of Alexander Pushkin*, ed. and trans. J. Thomas Shaw (Madison, Wis.: University of Wisconsin Press, 1967), pp. 236–38.

20 The best annotated Russian text, including variants and commentary by V. O. Vinokur, is to be found in vol. VII (the only extant volume) of the 1935 edition of Pushkin's collected works, *Polnoe sobranie sochineny A. S. Pushkina* (Moscow: Izd. Akademii Nauk SSSR, 1935). A reliable, unexciting and out-of-print English version of the play exists by Philip L. Barbour: Alexander Pushkin, *Boris Godunov* (New York: Columbia University Press, 1953) [bilingual edition with notes]. At time of writing, Antony Wood is completing a new English translation of the play, appropriate for performance, to be published with essays and commentary.

21 *Letters of Pushkin*, pp. 365–67.

22 Ibid., p. 366.

23 Stephanie Sandler, *Distant Pleasures: Alexander Pushkin and the Writing of Exile* (Stanford, Calif.: Stanford University Press, 1989), p. 80.

24 V. Nepomnyashchy, *Poeziya i sud'ba: Stat'i i zametki o Pushkine* (Moscow: Sovetsky pisatel', 1983), Ch. 4 [on Boris Godunov]: "'Naimenee ponyaty zhanr'," pp. 212–50 (originally written 1974, revised 1981). The quotation is from p. 245.

25 Sandler, *Distant Pleasures*, pp. 79, 78, 88, 137. The author's second and third chapters, pp. 77–139, are devoted to Pushkin's *Boris*.

26 See K. I. Arkhangel'sky, "Problemy stseny v dramakh Pushkina (1830–1930)," in *Trudy Dal'novostochnogo pedagogicheskogo instituta* (Vladivostok), series 7, no. 1 (6) (1930): 5–16. As Arkhangelsky points out, a stage that could accommodate almost simultaneous action on various levels without the divisive effects of acts or curtains would have made possible an intense, uninterrupted flow of events, very much in Pushkin's spirit and quite unthinkable in the neoclassical

theaters of his time.

27 Vyazemsky passed on this advice in a letter to Pushkin, 6 September 1825, when by Pushkin's admission half the tragedy had been completed. Pushkin responded on 13 and 15 September 1825. See *Letters of Pushkin*, pp. 254–55.

3 Narrative and musical synopsis of the opera

1 See *The Chesterian*, new series, no. 29 (February 1923), p. 156. Robert Godet is named as the editor of this score in the firm's advertisements, though not in the score itself.

2 This score received its first performance on Friday, 6 March 1953; see Olin Downes, "Original *Boris*: Composer's ideas will be followed at the Met," *The New York Times*, 1 March 1953, sec. 2, p. 7; and Olin Downes, "*Boris Godunov* offered at Met," *The New York Times*, 7 March 1953, p. 13.

3 Richard Taruskin, "Musorgsky vs. Musorgsky: The versions of *Boris Godunov*," *19th-Century Music* 8 (1984–85): 95.

4 For example, the celebrated production at the Metropolitan Opera, unveiled on 16 December 1974, excised a large portion of the Kromy Forest scene, almost certainly in compensation for the extra length introduced by the inclusion of the St. Basil's scene and several other episodes cut by Musorgsky in revision.

5 M[odest] P[etrovich] Musorgsky, *Boris Godunov* [piano–vocal score] (St. Petersburg: V. Bessel & Co., [1874]). In 1924, Bessel published jointly with Breitkopf & Härtel a reengraving of this score, "in view of the increasing interest in this edition among foreigners." Copyright in this score was renewed in 1952, and in 1954 Bessel and Breitkopf republished it. Though not easy to find, it is still available.

6 P[etr Il'ich] Chaykovsky, *Polnoe sobranie sochineny: Literaturnye proizvedeniya i perepiska*, ed. N. A. Viktorova and others, 17 vols. (Moscow: Muzyka, 1953–81), IX:176.

7 Musorgsky to Lyudmila Shestakova, 30 July 1868, in *MLN*, I:100/*TMR*, p. 112 [first citations: Ch. 1, n. 3].

8 For a thorough discussion of Russian bell music and of how Musorgsky, in *Boris*, draws on the cultural images associated with bell ringing, see Edward V. Williams, *The Bells of Russia: History and Technology* (Princeton, N.J.: Princeton University Press, 1985), and Edward V. Williams, *The Blagovest Theme in Russian Music*, Kennan Institute for Advanced Russian Studies Occasional Papers, no. 220 (Washington, D.C.: Kennan Institute for Advanced Russian Studies, 1987), pp. 6–38.

9 Modest Mussorgsky, *Boris Godunov*, ed. David Lloyd-Jones, 2 vols. (London: Oxford University Press, 1975), I:165.

10 For details concerning the source of these texts, which involve some intriguing misidentifications, see the Appendix of Taruskin, "Musorgsky vs. Musorgsky," pp. 266–70.

11 See Chapter 4, pp. 74–75.

12 For details concerning Musorgsky's borrowings from *Salammbô*, see Gerald Abraham, "The Carthaginian element in *Boris Godunov*," *The Musical Times* 83

(1942): 9–12; revised and reissued as "The Mediterranean element in *Boris Godunov*," in *Slavonic and Romantic Music* (New York: St. Martin's Press, 1968), pp. 188–94.

13 The scene before St. Basil's Cathedral was performed at the staging of the play in 1870, and its set singled out for special praise in the reviews. Whatever reasons Musorgsky may have had for replacing this scene with the scene in Kromy Forest, censorship was not among them. For more on *Boris* and the censorship, see Chapter 6, pp. 127–33, and Oldani, "*Boris* and the censor," pp. 245–53 [first citation: Ch. 2, n. 1].

4 History of the composition, rejection, revision, and acceptance of *Boris Godunov*

1 Between 1868 and 1872, the period of *Boris*'s composition and revision, Musorgsky steadily moved away from the theoretical extremes of his circle, toward greater symmetry, greater use of periodic melody, more purely musical gestures. One sees this change not only in *Boris*, but in other works of the period as well: compare, for example, the first song of *The Nursery*, "S nyaney" (1868) with the sixth "Poekhal na palochke" (1872). Although Musorgsky's retreat from the severely "realistic" style of 1866–69 affects all his late works, including *Khovanshchina*, *Songs and Dances of Death*, even *Pictures from an Exhibition*, it has not yet received a thorough examination.

2 Taruskin, "Musorgsky *vs.* Musorgsky," p. 95 [first citation: Ch. 3, n. 3]. The "supersaturated" *Boris* may be heard in several recordings currently available on CD; see the discography for details.

3 Lloyd-Jones follows the convention of marking the first measure of the cut with the syllable *Vi–*, the last with *–de*.

4 So say Andrey Rimsky-Korsakov, Alexandra Orlova, Georgy Khubov, Emiliya Frid, Michel Calvocoressi, Rostislav Hofmann, and David Lloyd-Jones, among others. See below, n. 39.

5 See Taruskin, "Musorgsky *vs.* Musorgsky," pp. 91–118, 245–72. The author's conclusions: the initial version is "a document of a particular moment in the history of Russian opera and of its composer's creative development" (265). The revision, by contrast, "is the authentic masterpiece ... the fruit of a thorough critical reassessment born of an artistic maturity which the popular image of Musorgsky as the Oblomov of music still unjustly denies him" (265–66).

As we shall see in Chapter 10, the 1869 version of the opera came back into vogue in the Soviet Union in the 1980s, though more for political than for musical reasons.

6 See Oldani, "*Boris* and the censor," pp. 245–53 [first citation: ch. 2, n.1].

7 Musorgsky to César Cui, 3 July 1868, in *MLN*, 1:98/*TMR*, p. 109 [first citations Ch. 1, n. 3].

8 César Antonovich Cui, "Neskol'ko slov o sovremennykh opernykh formakh," *Artist*, no. 4 (1889), quoted in Richard Taruskin, *Opera and Drama in Russia As Preached and Practiced in the 1860s*, Russian Music Studies, no. 2 (Ann Arbor, Mich.: UMI Research Press, 1981), p. 348.

9 For further details, see Richard Taruskin, "Handel, Shakespeare, and Musorgsky:

The sources and limits of Russian musical realism," in *Studies in the History of Music*, vol. I: *Music and Language* (New York: Broude Brothers Limited, 1983), pp. 247–68.

10 *MLN*, 1:100/*TMR*, pp. 111–12.

11 César Cui, *La musique en Russie* (Paris: G. Fischbacher, 1880), p. 109.

12 *MLN*, 1:103/*TMR*, p. 122.

13 V[ladimir Vasil'evich] Stasov, "Modest Petrovich Musorgsky: Biografichesky ocherk," *Vestnik Evropy* 89 (May–June 1881): 520–21.

14 The Fountain scene's initial sketches, described by Stasov, probably belong to the period between January and April of 1869.

15 Musorgsky to Alexandra and Nadezhda Purgold, 13 July 1870, in *MLN*, 1:115/*TMR*, p. 147.

16 *MLN*, 1:117/*TMR*, p. 148.

17 Quoted in A[leksandra Anatol'evna] Orlova, *Trudy i dni M. P. Musorgskogo* (Moscow: Gos. Muz. Izd., 1963), p. 213 [hereinafter: *OTD*]. An English translation of this invaluable chronicle now exists: Alexandra Orlova, *Musorgsky's Days and Works: A Biography in Documents*, trans. and ed. Roy J. Guenther, Russian Music Studies, no. 4 (Ann Arbor, Mich.: UMI Research Press, 1983) [hereinafter: *MDW*]. Again for those who wish to put our translations in context, we shall provide both Russian and English references, as follows: *OTD*, p. 213/*MDW*, p. 229.

18 L[yudmila] I[vanovna] Shestakova, "Moi vechera," *Ezhegodnik imperatorskikh teatrov* 4(1893–94), second supplement: 124.

19 N[ikolay] A[ndreevich] Rimsky-Korsakov, *Letopis' moey muzykal'noy zhizni*, 8th edn. (Moscow: "Muzyka," 1980), pp. 89–90.

20 Stasov, "Musorgsky: Biografichesky ocherk," p. 523. It is curious that Stasov's account, written in 1881 and therefore the earliest of all, contains no specific indication that the committee objected to the work's "novelty" or the absence of a "female element."

21 V[ladimir] S[ergeevich] Baskin, *M. P. Musorgsky: Ocherk muzykal'noy deyatel'nosti* (Moscow: P. Jurgenson, 1886), pp. 59–60.

22 Taruskin, "Musorgsky vs. Musorgsky," p. 247.

23 Musorgsky to Arseny Golenishchev-Kutuzov, 15 August 1877, in *MLN*, 1:232/*TMR*, p. 360.

24 Taruskin, "Musorgsky vs. Musorgsky," pp. 249–50.

25 Musorgsky to Nikolay Rimsky-Korsakov, 23 July 1870, in *MLN*, 1:117/*TMR*, p. 148.

26 *OTD*, p. 216/*MDW*, p. 232.

27 Musorgsky to Vladimir Stasov, 18 April 1871, in *MLN*, 1:122/*TMR*, p. 163.

28 Musorgsky to Vladimir Stasov, 10 August 1871, in *MLN*, 1:122–23/*TMR*, p. 167.

29 A[bram Akimovich] Gozenpud, *Russky operny teatr XIX veka, 1873–1889* (Leningrad: "Muzyka," 1973), p. 74.

30 For an account of the parallels between Rimsky's *veche* scene and the Kromy Forest scene, see Richard Taruskin, "'The present in the past': Russian opera and Russian historiography, ca. 1870," in *Russian and Soviet Music: Essays for Boris Schwarz*, ed. Malcolm Hamrick Brown, Russian Music Studies, no. 11 (Ann

Arbor, Mich.: UMI Research Press, 1984), pp. 102–35.

31 *MLN*, I: 125/*TMR*, p. 171. A letter of Borodin dated 20 September 1871 catalogues the changes Musorgsky had made and includes specific reference to "a large scene where the pretender appears in Orlovsky Province, already a conqueror." Borodin also reports that Musorgsky has "radically revised a number of earlier scenes," an indication that perhaps he had already taken most of the cuts noted in Table 3.1 (pp. 63–65). See A[leksandr] P[orfir'evich] Borodin, *Pis'ma A. P. Borodina*, ed. S. A. Dyanin, 4 issues (Moscow: Gos. Muz. Izd., 1927–50), I:292.

32 Musorgsky to Alexandra Purgold, 3 January 1872, in *MLN*, I:126/*TMR*, pp. 176–77.

33 *OTD*, p. 249/*MDW*, p. 265.

34 *S.-Peterburgskie vedomosti*, 9 February 1872, quoted in *OTD*, p. 242/*MDW*, pp. 257–58.

35 *S.-Peterburgskie vedomosti*, 20 April 1872, quoted in *OTD*, pp. 248–49 /*MDW*, pp. 264–65.

36 Rimsky-Korsakov, *Letopis'*, pp. 220–21.

37 *MLN*, I: 130/*TMR*, p. 184.

38 *MLN*, I: 131/not in *TMR*.

39 See, among others, M. P. Musorgsky, *Pis'ma i dokumenty*, ed. A. N. Rimsky-Korsakov (Moscow: Gos. Muz. Izd., 1932), p. 215; *OTD*, p. 265/*MDW*, p. 283; A. A. Orlova, *Musorgsky v Peterburge* (Leningrad: Lenizdat, 1974), p. 135; Georgy Khubov, *Musorgsky* (Moscow: "Muzyka," 1969), p. 384; E[miliya Lazarevna] Frid, *Modest Petrovich Musorgsky (1839–1881)*, 4th edn. (Leningrad: "Muzyka," 1987), p. 77; Rostislav Hofmann, *Moussorgski* (Paris: Editions du Coudrier, 1952), p. 200; Mussorgsky, *Boris Godunov*, ed. Lloyd-Jones, II: 10 [first citation: Ch. 3, n. 9]. Calvocoressi states that rejection occurred in October of 1872 without specifying the source of his information; see M[ichel] D[imitri] Calvocoressi, *Modest Mussorgsky: His Life and Works* (London: Rockliff, 1956), pp. 169–70, and M. D. Calvocoressi, *Mussorgsky*, completed and rev. Gerald Abraham, The Master Musicians Series (London: J. M. Dent & Sons Ltd., 1974), p. 41. Andrey Rimsky-Korsakov (the composer's son) seems to have been the first to advance this hypothesis, in his commentary to *Pis'ma i dokumenty*.

40 The authors are indebted to Ivan Monighetti, Moscow, who provided a manuscript copy of this item from *Muzykal'ny listok*, 29 October 1872, p. 121.

41 Two reviews by César Cui provide additional evidence in support of a second rejection, but there are good reasons not to accept Cui at face value; see pp. 84–85.

42 Georgy Khubov states that the announcement was "official" but offers no evidence why it should be so regarded. See Khubov, *Musorgsky*, p. 384.

43 See Marina Sabinina, "Musorgsky i my," *Sovetskaya muzyka*, no. 3 (March 1989), p. 14. A new generation of Soviet scholars is beginning to come to grips with questions of this sort; Sabinina, for example, calls for an exposé of the monolithic friendship presumed to exist among the members of the *kuchka* and for a frank exposure of some of their unethical attitudes in the name of "nationalism." Along these lines, see also Aleksandra Orlova, "Il Potente Gruppo; La sua storia alla luce delle più recenti ricerche," in *Musorgskij: L'opera, il pensiero*, ed. Anna Maria Morazzoni (Milan: Edizioni Unicopli, [1985]), pp. 65–105; and Robert C.

Ridenour, *Nationalism, Modernism, and Personal Rivalry in 19th-Century Russian Music,* Russian Music Studies, no. 1 (Ann Arbor, Mich.: UMI Research Press, 1981).

44 According to Orlova, "no documents concerning this meeting are preserved." See Orlova, *Musorgsky v Peterburge,* p. 135.

45 B[oris L'vovich] Vol'man, *Russkie notnye izdaniya XIX-nachala XX veka* (Leningrad: "Muzyka," 1970), p. 115; Chaykovsky, *Polnoe sobranie sochineny: Literaturnye proizvedeniya i perepiska,* v:330–34 [First citation: Ch. 3, n. 6].

46 Quoted in *OTD,* p. 253/*MDW,* p. 269. According to a private communication from Alexandra Orlova, there no longer can be any question concerning the date of this letter; it belongs definitely to 1872 since elsewhere in it Bessel refers to Rimsky's impending marriage and honeymoon. The wedding occurred on 30 June 1872, and the couple's European honeymoon lasted through the second half of August.

47 *MLN,* 1:133/*TMR,* p. 188.

48 Stasov, "Musorgsky: Biografichesky ocherk," pp. 523ff.; Shestakova, "Moi vechera," pp. 124ff.; Rimsky-Korsakov, *Letopis',* pp. 89ff.

49 V. V. Stasov, "Pamyati Musorgskogo" [1886], in *Izbrannye sochineniya,* 3 vols., ed. E. D. Stasova and others (Moscow: "Iskusstvo," 1952), III:31–43.

50 [Yuliya Fedorovna Platonova], "Novye materialy dlya biografii M. P. Musorgskogo: Pis'mo Yu. Platonovoy k V. V. Stasovu po povodu pervoy postanovki *Borisa,*" *Russkaya muzykal'naya gazeta,* no. 12 (December 1895), cols. 779–83.

51 Musorgsky, *Pis'ma i dokumenty,* p. 285; *OTD,* pp. 291–92/*MDW,* p. 313.

52 One may cite, for example, the fact that Gedeonov returned from Paris on 22 October, not in mid-August.

53 Stasov, *Izbrannye sochineniya,* III:42.

54 Yu. F. Platonova, "Iz *Avtobiografii,*" in *M. P. Musorgsky v vospominaniyakh sovremennikov,* ed. E. M. Gordeeva (Moscow: "Muzyka," 1989), p. 121.

55 Ibid., p. 122. *Khovanshchina* was rejected for performance shortly after its completion by Rimsky-Korsakov, following Musorgsky's death.

56 Platonova was let go in 1876, thirteen years after her debut. She could not have had too many seasons in which to imagine herself in *Khovanshchina.*

57 None of Musorgsky's letters supports the soprano's assertions; nor does the inscription that he placed in her copy of the published piano–vocal score of *Boris* refer to her having single-handedly brought the opera to the stage. See *OTD,* p. 400/*MDW,* p. 425.

58 *S.-Peterburgskie vedomosti,* 6 February 1874, quoted in *OTD,* p. 355/*MDW,* p. 378.

59 [César Antonovich Cui,] "Muzykal'nye zametki: *Ermak* opera Santisa, odobrennaya vodevil'nym komitetom," *S.-Peterburgskie vedomosti,* 6 December 1873, p. 1.

60 Ibid.

61 C. A. Cui, *Izbrannye pis'ma,* ed. I. L. Gusin (Leningrad: Gos. Muz. Izd., 1955), pp. 74–75.

62 M. Musorgsky, *Boris Godunov* [libretto] (St. Petersburg: V. Bessel & Co., [1873]).

63 The critic for *Peterburgskaya gazeta* wrote: "The success of the latter two scenes

was great, but the success of the first was enormous . . . Such a success was all the more remarkable in that all preceding works by our composers (*Ratcliff, The Power of the Fiend, The Stone Guest, The Maid of Pskov*), as is well known, had at their first performances if not fiascos, then at least something a long way from enthusiasm." Quoted in *OTD*, p. 278/*MDW*, p. 298.

64 *Golos* (St. Petersburg), 9 February 1873, p. 3, col. 6.

65 Quoted in *OTD*, p. 290/*MDW*, p. 309.

66 *Golos* (St. Petersburg), 17 January 1872, p. 5, col. 3; *Golos*, 22 September 1874, p. 5, col. 6.

67 *Golos*, 26 February 1882, p. 5, col. 2.

68 See Rimsky-Korsakov, *Letopis'*, p. 103.

69 V. V. Stasov, *Pis'ma k rodnym*, 4 parts (Moscow: Gos. Muz. Izd., 1953–54), II:102. According to the agreement between Musorgsky and Bessel, the composer received 600 rubles for *Boris*, 300 in the course of the opera's first season on the stage, the remaining 300 in its second; see Musorgsky, *Pis'ma i dokumenty*, p. 524.

70 As things turned out, the Maryinsky presented only two evenings of spoken theater and one final performance of *Lohengrin* in the post-Lenten season of 1873 – inauspicious surroundings for the unveiling of a major new work. See *Golos* (St. Petersburg), 9 April – 15 May 1873.

71 A[leksandr] I[vanovich] Vol'f, *Khronika Peterburgskikh teatrov s kontsa 1855 do nachala 1881 goda* (St. Petersburg: R. Golike, 1884), p. 126.

72 A. A. Orlova and V[ladimir] N[ikolaevich] Rimsky-Korsakov, *Stranitsy zhizni N. A. Rimskogo-Korsakova: Letopis' zhizni i tvorchestva*, 4 issues (Leningrad: "Muzyka," 1969–73), II:73. See also Rimsky-Korsakov, *Letopis'*, pp. 102–103.

73 *MLN*, I:146/*TMR*, p. 207.

74 *MLN*, I:170/*TMR*, p. 251.

75 Borodin, *Pis'ma*, II:63.

76 Cui, *Izbrannye pis'ma*, pp. 74–75 and p. 546, fn. 2 to letter 43.

77 Orlova and Rimsky-Korsakov, *Stranitsy*, II:68.

78 *Golos* (St. Petersburg), 12 April 1874, p. 5, col. 1.

79 Quoted in Musorgsky, *Pis'ma i dokumenty*, pp. 172–73.

80 Tat'yana Mikhailovna Rodina, "Gedeonov, Stepan Aleksandrovich," *Teatral'naya entsiklopediya*, 5 vols. (Moscow: "Sovetskaya entsiklopediya," 1961–67), I:1132.

81 L. M. Kutateladze, ed., *E. F. Napravnik: Avtobiograficheskie, tvorcheskie materialy, dokumenty, pis'ma*, (Leningrad: Gos. Muz. Izd., 1959), p. 40.

82 See Vol'f, *Khronika teatrov s 1855 do 1881*, pp. 142–43.

83 Oldani, "*Boris* and the censor," pp. 245–53; Taruskin, "Musorgsky *vs.* Musorgsky," pp. 245–72.

5   A tale of two productions – St. Petersburg (1874–1882), Paris (1908)

1 See, for example, Rosa Newmarch, *The Russian Opera* (London: Herbert Jenkins Ltd., 1914), pp. 237–40; Mary Ellis Peltz and Robert Lawrence, *The Metropolitan Opera Guide*, The Modern Library (New York: Random House, 1942), pp.

338–48: and Milton Cross, *Complete Stories of the Great Operas* (Garden City, N.Y.: Doubleday and Co., 1947), pp. 89–98.

2 Quoted in B[oris] P[avlovich] Gorodetsky, *Tragediya A. S. Pushkina "Boris Godunov"* (Leningrad: "Prosveshchenie," 1969), pp. 70–71. Pushkin finally was allowed to publish the play in 1831.

3 See Chapter 6 for selected censorship documents.

4 Quoted in N[ikolay] V[asil'evich] Drizen, *Dramaticheskaya tsenzura dvukh epokh, 1825–1881* (Petrograd: "Prometey," 1917), p. 222.

5 This arrangement is confirmed in an album of lithographs of the sets, published immediately after the performance; see A[dol'f] I[osifovich] Sharleman', *"Boris Godunov": Risunky dekoratsy k tragedii A. S. Pushkina* (St. Petersburg: Izd. M. A. Shishkova, 1870).

6 Quoted in N[ina] F[edorovna] Filippova, *Narodnaya drama A. S. Pushkina "Boris Godunov"* (Moscow: "Kniga," 1972), pp. 105–6. Transforming the Patriarch into an Old Boyar, of course, was simply the stratagem required to get the character past the censor.

7 Vol'f, *Khronika teatrov s 1855 do 1881*, p. 44 [first citation: Ch. 4, n. 71].

8 Quoted in *OTD*, p. 329/*MDW*, p. 354 [first citation: Ch. 4, n. 17].

9 See Oldani, "*Boris* and the censor," pp. 251–53 [first citation: Ch. 2, n. 1].

10 Two types of cuts are shown in Musorgsky's holograph, distinguished by verbal instructions either to copy or not to copy the passage crossed out. Passages marked "Do not write" were cut by Musorgsky himself, out of artistic conviction, and do not appear in the published piano–vocal score of 1874. By contrast, passages marked "Write" were cut by Nápravník (probably with Musorgsky's consent) as a performance expedient; all these passages are fully restored in the published piano–vocal score. The directions to "write" or "not write" probably were inserted to enable copyists employed by Musorgsky's publisher to prepare rental materials that would coincide with the published score. For further details, see Robert W. Oldani, "Editions of *Boris Godunov*," in *Musorgsky: In Memoriam, 1881–1981*, ed. Malcolm Hamrick Brown, Russian Music Studies, no. 3 (Ann Arbor, Mich.: UMI Research Press, 1982), pp. 179–213.

11 A[rseny] A[rkad'evich] Golenishchev-Kutuzov, "Vospominaniya o M. P. Musorgskom," in *Muzykal'noe nasledstvo*, issue I, ed. M. V. Ivanov-Boretsky (Moscow: Muzgiz, 1935), p. 19. All the passages mentioned by Golenishchev-Kutuzov were in fact cut at the performance.

12 [German Avgustovich] Larosh, "Novaya russkaya opera," *Golos* (St. Petersburg), 29 January 1874, p. 3.

13 *Muzykal'ny listok*, no. 16 (10 February 1874), quoted in Gozenpud, *Russky operny teatr 1873–1889*, p. 87 [first citation: Ch. 4, n. 29].

14 Unpublished diary of I[l'ya Fedorovich] Tyumenev, quoted in Gozenpud, *Russky operny teatr 1873–1889*, p. 88.

15 N[ikolay Ivanovich] Kompaneysky, "K novym beregam: M. P. Musorgsky (1839–1881)," *Russkaya muzykal'naya gazeta*, no. 17 (1906), col. 432.

16 All six sets are illustrated in Robert William Oldani, "Musorgsky's *Boris* on the stage of the Maryinsky Theater," *The Opera Quarterly* 4 (Summer 1986): 82–84.

We are indebted to the editor of *The Opera Quarterly* for permission to incorporate this article into the present discussion.

17 Quoted in Gozenpud, *Russky operny teatr 1873–1889*, pp. 84–85.

18 Ibid., p. 83. This stage detail of the parrot in its cage – which, as Karamzin notes, the historical Tsar Boris had received as a gift from the Austrian ambassador – almost surely led Musorgsky to add the "Song of the Parrot" when he began to revise his opera in 1871, soon after the play's production.

19 *S.-Peterburgskie vedomosti*, 6 February 1874, quoted in *OTD*, p. 334/MDW, p. 359.

20 *Birzhevye vedomosti*, 2 February 1874, quoted in *OTD*, p. 352/MDW, p. 376.

21 N. Strakhov, "*Boris Godunov* na stsene," in *Zametki o Pushkine i drugikh poetakh*, 2nd ed. (Kiev: tip. Chokolova, 1897; reprint edn., Russian Reprint Series no. 43, The Hague: Europe Printing, 1967), p. 80.

22 In fairness to Baskin, he notes too that "in designing Boris's role, the composer has shown himself to be a philosopher-musician, expressing with rare accuracy the character's psychological make-up," and he concludes, "*Boris*'s composer . . . is not limited to [comedy], since much in art is accessible to his multifaceted talent." See *OTD*, pp. 338–40/*MDW*, pp. 364–65.

23 *Birzhevye vedomosti*, 2 February 1874, excerpted in *OTD*, pp. 348–52/*MDW*, pp. 373–76.

24 *Birzhevye vedomosti*, 29 January 1874, quoted in *OTD*, p. 336/*MDW*, p. 362.

25 Larosh, "Novaya russkaya opera," p. 3. Longer excerpts from several of the most significant reviews appear in Chapter 7, "The opera through the years: selected texts in criticism."

26 *Muzykal'ny listok*, no. 15 (3 February 1874), quoted in A. A. Khokhlovkina, "Pervye kritiki *Borisa Godunova*," in *Musorgsky: "Boris Godunov" – Stat'i i issledovaniya* (Moscow: Gos. Muz. Izd., 1930), p. 142.

27 *Muzykal'ny listok*, no. 16 (10 February 1874), quoted in *OTD*, p. 362/*MDW*, p. 385.

28 *S.-Peterburgskie vedomosti*, 6 February 1874, quoted in *OTD*, p. 360/*MDW*, p. 383.

29 *S.-Peterburgskie vedomosti*, 6 February 1874, quoted in *OTD*, p. 357/*MDW*, p. 380.

30 *S.-Peterburgskie vedomosti*, 6 February 1874, quoted in *OTD*, p. 357–58/ *MDW*, p. 380–81.

31 *S.-Peterburgskie vedomosti*, 6 February 1874, quoted in *OTD*, p. 359/*MDW*, p. 381.

32 *S.-Peterburgskie vedomosti*, 6 February 1874, quoted partly from *OTD*, p. 360/ *MDW*, pp. 382–83, and partly from Khubov, *Musorgsky*, p. 400 [first citation: Ch. 4, n. 39].

33 Musorgsky to Vladimir Stasov, 6 February 1874, in *MLN*, 1:175–76/*TMR*, pp. 266–67. Despite the anger shown in this letter, Musorgsky apparently held no grudge against Cui. On 4 May 1875, an examination committee on which he served voted unanimously to accept Cui's opera *Angelo* for production by the Imperial Theaters. Musorgsky's opinion: "the opera is rich in musical beauties."

See *MLN*, 1:190/not in *TMR*.

34 Lyudmila Ivanovna Shestakova, "Moi vechera," quoted in *OTD*, p. 360/*MDW*, p. 383.

35 Quoted in *OTD*, p. 354/*MDW*, p. 378.

36 Quoted in Gozenpud, *Russky operny teatr 1873–1889*, p. 83.

37 Erich Leinsdorf used the same argument to justify the sequence St. Basil scene, Kromy Forest scene, Death scene at the Metropolitan Opera's production of 1960–61. See J[ohn] W. F[reeman], "Boris and Dmitri," *Opera News* 25 (7 January 1961): 15.

38 *Golos* (St. Petersburg), 3 February 1879, quoted in *OTD*, p. 526/*MDW*, pp. 558–59.

39 *S.-Peterburgskie vedomosti*, 20 January 1879, quoted in *OTD*, p. 524–25/*MDW*, p. 557.

40 *Voskresny listok muzyki i ob"yavleny*, 21 January 1879, quoted in *OTD*, p. 525/*MDW*, pp. 557–58.

41 Quoted in *OTD*, p. 629/*MDW*, p. 664. Sarah Bernhardt was in St. Petersburg at the time of the revival, and at least one of the capital's newspapers – the German-language daily – took no notice at all of this native opera, devoting its theatrical columns instead to the doings of the French actress. See *St. Petersburger Zeitung*, 11–18 December 1881.

42 P. Stolpyansky, "Letopis' SPb. imperatorskikh teatrov: Sezon 1882–1883 godov," *Ezhegodnik imperatorskikh teatrov*, issue 2 (1913), supplement, pp. LII-LIII.

43 *Golos* (St. Petersburg), 13 October 1882, p. 3.

44 N. Rimsky-Korsakov, *Polnoe sobranie sochineny: Literaturnye proizvedeniya i perepiska*, 8 vols. [to date] (Moscow: Gos. Muz. Izd., 1955–), v:509.

45 Rimsky-Korsakov, *Letopis' moey muzykal'noy zhizni*, p. 94 [first citation: Ch. 4, n. 19].

46 Ibid., pp. 185–86.

47 Ibid., p. 186.

48 M. P. Musorgsky, *Boris Godunov* [piano–vocal score], ed. and orch. by N. A. Rimsky-Korsakov (St. Petersburg: V. Bessel & Co., 1896), unpaginated preface.

49 Rimsky-Korsakov, *Letopis' moey muzykal'noy zhizni*, p. 265.

50 César Cui, "Teatr i muzyka. Moskovskaya chastnaya russkaya opera. *Boris Godunov* Musorgskogo," *Novosti i birzhevaya gazeta*, 9 March 1899 p. 3.

51 Yu[ly] D[mitrievich] Engel', "*Boris Godunov* M. P. Musorgskogo," *Russkie vedomosti* (Moscow), 10 December 1898, p. 3.

52 Ibid.

53 Rimsky-Korsakov, *Letopis' moey muzykal'noy zhizni*, p. 294.

54 Alexandre Benois, *Reminiscences of the Russian Ballet*, trans. by Mary Britnieva (London: Putnam, 1941), p. 166.

55 Richard Buckle, *Diaghilev* (New York: Atheneum, 1979), p. 27; Serge Lifar, *Serge Diaghilev: His Life, His Work, His Legend* (New York: G. P. Putnam's Sons, [1940]). p. 36.

56 A[bram Akimovich] Gozenpud, *Russky operny teatr mezhdu dvukh revolyutsy, 1905–1917* (Leningrad: "Muzyka," 1975), p. 197.

57 See, for example, Buckle, *Diaghilev*, pp. 91–101. New organization and fresh perspectives are brought to this material in Lynn Garafola, *Diaghilev's Ballets Russes* (New York: Oxford University Press, 1989).

58 M[ichel] D[imitri] Calvocoressi, *Musicians Gallery: Music and Ballet in Paris and London; Recollections of M. D. Calvocoressi* (London: Faber and Faber Limited, [1933]), p. 169. Calvocoressi, perhaps best known for his three books on Musorgsky, was thirty years old and already enthusiastic about the composer when he was invited to help Diaghilev in France. He became deeply involved in the production of *Boris Godunov* and ultimately received the Tsarist Order of St. Anne in recognition of his services to Russian music.

59 I. S. Zil'bershteyn and V. A. Samkov, eds., *Sergey Dyagilev i russkoe iskusstvo: Stat'i, otkrytye pis'ma, interv'yu. Perepiska. Sovremenniki o Dyagileve*, 2 vols. (Moscow: "Izobrazitel'noe iskusstvo," 1982), II: 102–03.

60 Gozenpud, *Teatr mezhdu revolyutsy*, p. 205.

61 Quoted in Arnold Haskell, *Diaghileff: His Artistic and Private Life*, 2nd edn. (London: Victor Gollancz Ltd., 1955), p. 179.

62 For a synopsis of Diaghilev's version, see Théâtre National de l'Opéra, *"Boris Godounow": Opéra en 3 actes et 7 tableaux de Modest Moussorgsky* (Paris: Théâtre National de l'Opéra, 1908), pp. 41–46. Calvocoressi maintains that it was he who convinced Diaghilev to restore the episode of the Tsarevich's geography lesson and who prevented the omission of the Kromy Forest scene. See *Musicians Gallery*, pp. 181–84.

63 *Musicians Gallery*, pp. 182–83.

64 Alexandre Benois, *Memoirs*, trans. by Moura Budberg, 2 vols. (London: Chatto & Windus, 1960–64), II: 251.

65 *Chaliapin: An Autobiography As Told to Maxim Gorky*, ed. and trans. Nina Froud and James Hanley (New York: Stein and Day, [1967]), p. 165.

66 Théâtre National de l'Opéra, *"Boris Godounow,"* title page. Calvocoressi gives an entertaining account of the problems and intrigues, real and imaginary, which Diaghilev and his troupe encountered in bringing the opera to the stage; see *Musicians Gallery*, pp. 184–94.

67 Prince Peter Lieven, *The Birth of Ballets-Russes*, trans. by L. Zarine (London: George Allen & Unwin Ltd., 1936), p. 51.

68 Rosa Newmarch, "Russian opera in Paris: Moussorgsky's *Boris Godounov*," *The Monthly Musical Record* 38 (July 1908): 147.

69 M., "Les concerts russes de l'opéra," *La revue musicale: Publication bimensuelle* 7 (1 June 1907): 281.

70 "Le baromètre musical: I. Opéra; Recettes détaillées du 16 mai au 15 juin 1908," *La revue musicale: Publication bimensuelle* 8 (1 July 1908): 397. Of the eighteen performances of other works given in the period between 16 May and 15 June, only one, a performance of Massenet's *Thaïs*, generated receipts in excess of 20,000 francs.

71 Haskell, *Diaghileff*, pp. 182–83. Insight into Diaghilev's audience is provided by Lynn Garafola's examination of the booking lists for *Boris*. These documents, in her words, "reveal that his public was not primarily an aristocratic one, despite

the Proustian-sounding titles reported in the society columns of *Figaro*. Rather, Diaghilev's audience was an amalgam of financiers, bankers, and diplomats, members of the city's foreign and Franco-Jewish communities, and personalities from the worlds of fashion, music, entertainment, and the press." See Garafola, *Diaghilev's Ballets Russes*, p. 279.

72 *La Liberté* (Paris), quoted in M. D. Calvocoressi, "Early criticisms of Moussorgsky in Western Europe," *Musical Opinion* 52 (1929): 643.

73 Newmarch, "Russian opera in Paris," p. 149: "Compared with his fellow-countrymen, Musorgsky has never been considered a master of brilliant orchestration. But in *Boris Godunov* all subtle and prodigious effects are entrusted to the human voice, individual, or massed closely together – frequently in unison. The orchestra plays a comparatively restrained and discreet part in complete contradiction to the superb and complicated commentary of Wagner and Strauss. Yet it does its work effectively, and is often quite as moving as the colossal expenditure of sound to which we are growing too accustomed. For instance, in the scene in which Boris is inwardly torn by the fiends of madness and despair, an accompaniment for strings, pianissimo, reproducs the psychological atmosphere with a subtle horror and poignancy that no loud brass or percussion effects could possibly have evoked."

74 M. D. Calvocoressi, *Moussorgsky*, Les Maîtres de la Musique (Paris: Felix Alcan, 1908), p. 202, fn. 1: "In 1896 a new edition of *Boris Godunov* appeared, revised and adapted by Mr. Rimsky-Korsakov. Certain of the alterations which one notes there have a purely practical goal, which is to facilitate performance; others are motivated only by the desire to attenuate the unusual aspect of the work, to make it less disconcerting to the public."

75 Eugene E. Simpson, *Travels in Russia, 1910 and 1912* (Taylorville, Ill.: By the Author, 1916), pp. 47–48.

76 Calvocoressi, *Musicians Gallery*, p. 178.

77 Only 200 copies of Pavel Lamm's edition were printed; the edition was never put on sale. Parts were never easily obtainable, even after E. F. Kalmus reprinted the full score in the 1960s. Indeed, the publication in 1975 of David Lloyd-Jones's edition, for which score and parts are readily available, already has generated far many more performances of *Boris* without Rimsky than did all the critical polemics of the previous seven decades combined.

78 A copyright declaration in the first edition of the libretto of *Boris*, published in 1873, warns that scores and parts must be obtained from the publisher. See M. Musorgsky, *Boris Godunov* [libretto] (St. Petersburg: V. Bessel & Co., [1873]), title page.

79 [V. Bessel & Co.], *Katalog izdany muzykal'noy torgovli Vasily Bessel' i Ko.* (St. Petersburg: [V. Bessel & Co.], 1898), section 3, p. 1.

80 [V. Bessel & Co.], *Extrait du catalogue général W. Bessel & Cie., Editeurs: M. Moussorgsky* (Paris: Dépot des Éditions "Musique Russe," n.d.), p. 5.

81 Quoted in *OTD*, p. 393/*MDW*, p. 416.

82 One probably should not assume, as some writers have done, that Diaghilev had easy access to the complete full score of Musorgsky's version (and thus could have

produced it had he chosen to do so) merely because he reproduces in facsimile six pages of Musorgsky's holograph full score in his program book. All six pages are taken from the scene in Pimen's cell, the manuscript of which was in Rimsky-Korsakov's possession.

83 Calvocoressi, *Musicians Gallery*, p. 178.
84 Serge Diaghilev, "Memoirs," quoted in Buckle, *Diaghilev*, p. 104.
85 *Rech'*, no. 267 (1910), quoted in Gozenpud, *Teatr mezhdu revolyutsy*, p. 207.
86 Serge Diaghilev, "Memoirs," quoted in Buckle, *Diaghilev*, p. 105.
87 M. D. Calvocoressi, "The genuine score of *Boris*," *Christian Science Monitor*, 9 March 1929, p. 6, col. 4.
88 Zil'bershteyn and Samkov, *Dyagilev i russkoe iskusstvo*, II:104.
89 Diaghilev, "Memoirs," quoted in Buckle, *Diaghilev*, p. 111.

6 Boris and the censor: documents

1 *Svod zakonov Rossyskoy imperii, izdaniya 1857 goda*, 15 vols. (St. Petersburg: Printing House of the Second Section of His Majesty's Private Chancellery, 1857), vol. XIV, *Ustav o preduprezhdenii i presechenii prestupleny*, article 188.
2 *Polnoe sobranie zakonov Rossyskoy imperii, s 1649 goda*, 45 vols. ([St. Petersburg:] Printing House of the Second Section of His Majesty's Private Chancellery, 1830), XIII:392.
3 Quoted in Gorodetsky, *Tragediya A. S. Pushkina "Boris Godunov"*, pp. 68–71 [first citation: Ch. 5, n. 2].
4 Ibid.
5 Quoted in V. M. Abramkin, "Pushkin v dramaticheskoy tsenzure (1828–1917)," in *Literaturny arkhiv*, vol. I, ed. O. V. Tsekhnovitser, S. D. Balukhaty, and N. K. Piksanov (Moscow: Izd. Akademii Nauk SSSR, 1938), p. 231.
6 Quoted in N[ikolay] V[asil'evich] Drizen, *Dramaticheskaya tsenzura dvukh epokh, 1825–1881* ([Petrograd:] "Prometey," 1917), pp. 19–20.
7 Quoted in Abramkin, "Pushkin v dramaticheskoy tsenzure," p. 233.
8 Quoted in Abramkin, "Pushkin v dramaticheskoy tsenzure," p. 234.
9 *Antrakt*, no. 11 (1866), quoted in M[ikhail Borisovich] Zagorsky, *Pushkin i teatr* (Moscow: "Iskusstvo," 1940), p. 285.
10 Quoted in Drizen, *Dramaticheskaya tsenzura dvukh epokh*, p. 222.
11 Quoted in OTD, p. 243–44/MDW, p. 260 [first citations: Ch. 4, n. 17].
12 Quoted in OTD, pp. 246–47/MDW, pp. 262–63.
13 *Polnoe sobranie zakonov Rossyskoy imperii: Sobranie vtoroe*, 55 vols. (St. Petersburg: Printing House of the Second Section of His Majesty's Private Chancellery, 1830–84), vol XL, article 41988, section I, paragraph A-2. See also article 41990, section III, paragraph 15.
14 M[odest Petrovich] Musorgsky, *Boris Godunov* [libretto] (St. Petersburg: V. V. Bessel & Co., [1873]). A listing in the store catalogs of V. Bazanov's bookstore confirms that the libretto was indeed offered for sale.
15 See *Svod zakonov Rossyskoy imperii, izdaniya 1857 goda*, 15 vols. (St. Petersburg: Printing House of the Second Section of His Majesty's Private Chancellery, 1857),

vol. XIV, *Ustav tsenzurny*, articles 65, 169.

16 For a more thorough discussion of these and other censorship matters, see Oldani, "*Boris* and the censor," pp. 245–53 [first citation: Ch. 2, n. 1].

7 The opera through the years: Selected texts in criticism

1 Excerpt from: Vladimir Vasil'evich Stasov, "Modest Petrovich Musorgsky: Biografichesky ocherk," *Vestnik Evropy* 89 (May–June 1881): 285–316, 506–45; reprinted in V. V. Stasov, *Izbrannye sochineniya*, ed. E. D. Stasova et al., 3 vols. (Moscow: Iskusstvo, 1952), II:161–213. Other documents and reviews, covering this period of the premiere and rediscovery in Rimsky's edition, are quoted extensively in Chapters 4 and 5.

2 Excerpt from: César Cui, "Tri kartiny iz zabrakovannoy vodevil'nym komitetom opery Musorgskogo 'Boris Godunov.' Nechto o budushchem russkoy opery," *S-Peterburgskie vedomosti*, 9 February 1873, pp. 1–2; reprinted in C. A. Cui, *Izbrannye stat'i*, compiled with introduction and notes by I. L. Gusin (Leningrad: Gos. Muz. Izd., 1952), pp. 225–35. A shorter, different excerpt from this review can be found in *OTD*, pp. 278–79/*MDW*, pp. 299–300 [first citations: Ch. 4, n. 17].

3 Excerpt from: César Cui, "M. P. Musorgsky (Kritichesky etyud)," *Golos* (St. Petersburg), 8 April 1881, reprinted in Cui, *Izbrannye stat'i*, pp. 286–96. Cf. *OTD*, pp. 625–26/*MDW*, pp. 659–60.

4 Excerpt from: G. A. Larosh, "Muzykal'nye ocherki," *Golos* (St. Petersburg), 14 February 1873, pp. 1–2. Cf. *OTD*, pp. 282–86/*MDW*, pp. 302–05.

5 Excerpt from: G. A. Larosh, "Myslyashchy realist v russkoy opere," *Golos* (St. Petersburg), 13 February 1874, pp. 1–3. Cf. *OTD*, p. 365–69/*MDW*, pp. 388–91.

6 Excerpt from: G. A. Larosh, "Muzykal'nye ocherki," *Golos* (St. Petersburg), 15 November 1876, pp. 1–3. Cf. *OTD*, p. 483/*MDW*, p. 512.

7 All excerpts here are translated from the full texts gathered in N. Strakhov, "*Boris Godunov* na stsene," in *Zametki o Pushkine i drugikh poetakh*, 2nd edn. (Kiev: tip. Chokolova, 1897; reprint edn., Russian Reprint Series 43, The Hague: Europe Printing, 1967), pp. 79–104. Greatly abbreviated versions of the three letters can be found in *OTD*/*MDW*: no. 1, pp. 372–73/394–95; no. 2, pp. 379–80/400–01; no. 3, pp. 385–87/407–08.

8 Excerpt from: A. A. Golenishchev-Kutuzov, "Vospominaniya o M. P. Musorgskom," in *Muzykal'noe nasledstvo*, issue 1, ed. M. Ivanov-Boretsky (Moscow: MuzGiz, 1935), pp. 13–49. Though written in 1888, Golenishchev-Kutuzov's memoirs were discovered only in 1932 and first published in 1935.

9 Nikolay Rimsky-Korsakov, Editor's preface to *Boris Godunov*, by Modest Musorgsky (St. Petersburg: V. Bessel & Co., 1896), unpaginated.

10 Nikolay Rimsky-Korsakov, Editor's preface to *Boris Godunov*, by Modest Musorgsky (St. Petersburg: V. Bessel & Co., 1908), unpaginated.

11 Excerpt from: Fedor Shalyapin [Feodor Chaliapin], *Stranitsy iz moey zhizni. Maska i dusha* (Moscow: Knizhnaya palata, 1990), pp. 316–18.

12 Excerpt from: Claude Debussy, "*La chambre d'enfants*: Poème et musique de M.

Notes to pages 157–70

Moussorgsky," *La revue blanche* 24 (January–April 1901): 623–24; reprinted in *Monsieur Croche Antidilettante* (Paris: Dorbon Aîné/Nouvelle Revue Française, 1921). A full-length biography in documents of Marie Olénine d'Alheim has recently been written by Alexander Tumanov of the University of Alberta–Edmonton (*K dal'nym beregam. Zhizn' i tvorchestvo M. A. Oleninoy-d'Al'geim*, 1992), which contains invaluable information on the early reception of Musorgsky in France.

13 Excerpt from: Arthur Pougin, *A Short History of Russian Music*, trans. Lawrence Haward (London: Chatto & Windus, 1915), pp. 232–47 passim. Pougin's book was first published in 1897 under the title *Essai historique sur la musique en Russie*; we have introduced several adjustments in Haward's translation, which appeared in the wake of Diaghilev's successful "Russian seasons" of opera and ballet at Drury Lane prior to World War I.

14 Excerpt from: Jean Marnold, "M. Rimsky-Korsakoff et *Boris Godounoff*," *Mercure de France*, modern series, 75 (September–October 1908): 332–37; reprinted in Jean Marnold, *Musique d'autrefois e d'aujourd'hui* (Paris: Dorbon-Aîné, n.d.), pp. 270–81.

15 Excerpt from: A. V. Lunacharsky, "*Boris Godunov* Musorgskogo," first published as a fifteen-page brochure (Moscow, 1920), republished in the journal *Kul'tura i zhizn'* (Moscow, 1921), translated from A. V. Lunacharsky, *V mire muzyki* (Moscow: Sovetsky Kompozitor, 1971), pp. 57–63.

16 Excerpt from: Igor Glebov [Boris Vladimirovich Asaf'ev], "Pochemu nado ispol'nyat' *Borisa Godunova* Musorgskogo v podlinnom vide?" in *K vosstanov-leniyu "Borisa Godunova" Musorgskogo* (Moscow: Gos. Izd. Muz. Sek., 1928), pp. 12–27; reprinted in B. V. Asaf'ev, *Izbrannye trudy*, 5 vols. (Moscow: Izd. AN SSR, 1952–57), III:68–77.

17 Excerpt from: Igor Glebov [Boris Vladimirovich Asaf'ev], "Operny orkestr Musorgskogo," in *K vosstanovleniyu "Borisa Godunova" Musorgskogo*, pp. 28–38; reprinted in Asaf'ev, *Izbrannye trudy*, III:32–37.

18 Excerpt from: "*Boris Godunov* kak muzykal'ny spektakl' iz Pushkina (zametki)," in Asaf'ev, *Izbrannye trudy*, III:100–159.

19 A. K. Glazunov, "O novoy postanovke opery *Boris Godunov* Musorgskogo," *Krasnaya gazeta*, 28 February 1928, reprinted in A. K. Glazunov, *Pis'ma, stat'i, vospominaniya: Izbrannoe* (Moscow: Gos. Muz. Izd., 1958), pp. 471–74.

20 Excerpt from: *Izvestiya*, 1 May 1941, quoted in D. Shostakovich, *O vremeni i o sebe (1926–1975)*, ed. G. Pribegina (Moscow: Sovetsky Kompozitor, 1980), pp. 87–88.

Commenting on the production of Lamm's score at Sadler's Wells in 1935, a staff critic for *The Musical Times* also noted Asafiev's interpretation of Musorgsky's orchestration, and replied: "The coronation scene was ineffective. Musorgsky intended to make it a half-hearted jubilation on the part of the crowd and therefore wrote music that was half-hearted in construction. A wrong principle, to represent an awkward affair by awkwardly-made music." See W. McN[aught], "*Boris Godounov* at Sadler's Wells," *The Musical Times* 76 (November 1935): 1029.

306

21 Excerpt from: M[ichel]-D[imitri] Calvocoressi, "New chapters in the history of *Boris Godunov*," *The Musical Times* 68 (1927); 512–13.
22 Excerpt from: M. D. Calvocoressi, "*Boris Godunov* as Moussorgsky wrote it," *The Musical Times* 69 (1928): 318–20, 408–12, 506–08. The musical analysis in this article – including the passage quoted concerning the *Terem* scene – reappears verbatim in M. D. Calvocoressi, *Mussorgsky*, compl. Gerald Abraham, The Master Musicians (London: J. M. Dent and Sons, 1946; revised edn., London: J. M. Dent & Sons, 1974).
23 Excerpt from: Willy Schmid, "*Boris Godounov* again," *The Chesterian*, new series, 9 (July–August 1928): 245–51.
24 Excerpt from: Carl Dahlhaus, *Realism in Nineteenth-Century Music*, trans. Mary Whittall (Cambridge: Cambridge University Press, 1985), pp. 77–78.
25 Excerpt from: Sergey Slonimsky, "Tragediya razobshchennosti lyudey," *Sovetskaya muzyka*, no. 3 (March 1989), pp. 20–30.

8 The *Boris* libretto as a formal, literary, and historical problem

1 There have been some preliminary moves toward a poetics of the libretto. See two essays by Ulrich Weisstein, "The libretto as literature," *Books Abroad: An International Literary Quarterly* (Winter 1961): 16–22, and "Librettology: The fine art of coping with a Chinese twin," *Komparatistische Hefte*, Heft 5/6 (1982) (Universität Bayreuth): 23–42. See also Gary Schmidgall, *Literature as Opera* (New York: Oxford University Press, 1977); Herbert Lindenberger, *Opera: The Extravagant Art* (Ithaca, N.Y.: Cornell University Press, 1984), Chs. 1–4. An excellent book that omits Slavic repertory because of its author's honestly admitted "ignorance of Czech and Russian" is Patrick J. Smith, *The Tenth Muse: A Historical Study of the Opera Libretto* (New York: Schirmer, 1970). On the nineteenth-century French (and to a lesser extent, Russian) tradition of librettowriting, see Hugh MacDonald, "The prose libretto," *Cambridge Opera Journal* 1 (July 1989): 155–66.
2 Taruskin, "Handel, Shakespeare, and Musorgsky," pp. 247–68 [first citation: Ch. 4, n. 9]. Boris Asafiev makes this same "mimetic" point in his 1928 defense of a de-Rimskified *Boris*; see Chapter 7, pp. 163–65.
3 For general background, see Charles A. Moser, *Esthetics as Nightmare: Russian Literary Theory, 1855–1870* (Princeton, N.J.: Princeton University Press, 1989); for the specific application to musical art of Chernyshevsky's 1855 manifesto "The Aesthetic Relations of Art to Reality," see Richard Taruskin, "Realism as preached and practiced: The Russian *opéra dialogué*," *The Musical Quarterly* 56 (July 1970): 431–54.
4 The quotation is from Musorgsky's autobiographical sketch for Hugo Riemann's *Musik-Lexikon* (June 1880). This document is printed in full in *MLN*, 1:270/ *TMR*, p. 420 [first citations: Ch. 1, n. 3].
5 Musorgsky to Vladimir Nikolsky, 28 June 1870, in *MLN*, 1:114/*TMR*, p. 145.
6 Musorgsky to Vladimir Nikolsky, 15 August 1868, in *MLN*, 1:103/*TMR*, p. 122.
7 See I. Ya. Belenkova, "Printsipy dialoga v *Borise Godunove* Musorgskogo i ikh

razvitie v sovetskoy opere," in *M. P. Musorgsky i muzyka XX veka*, ed. G. L. Golovinsky (Moscow: Muzyka, 1990), pp. 110–36, esp. 112–27.

8 Carl Dahlhaus, "What is a musical drama?" *Cambridge Opera Journal* 1 (July 1989): 96.

9 See V. A. Vasina-Grossman, "Muzyka i proza: k izucheniyu naslediya Musorgskogo," in *Tipologiya russkogo realizma vtoroy poloviny XIX veka*, ed. G. Yu. Sternin (Moscow: Nauka, 1979), pp. 14–16.

10 For an exemplary discussion of "double hypocrisy" in the opening scenes of the 1869 *Boris*, see E. Levashev, "Drama naroda i drama sovesti v opere *Boris Godunov*," *Sovetskaya muzyka* 5 (1983): 32–45, esp. 34. Levashev is reviewing the Estonian Tallinn Theater revival of the original version (for more on this production, see Chapter 10).

11 Dmitry Pisarev, "Pushkin i Belinsky," *Russkoe slovo*, April–June 1865, quoted in Moser, *Esthetics as Nightmare*, p. 55. In a recent discussion by the Soviet musicologist Boris Kats, Musorgsky's principled stand against "unconditional beauty" in art is positioned between Dostoevsky ("Beauty will save the world") and the utilitarian Pisarev: "If one accepts the distinction current at that time [the 1860s] between 'aesthetes' and 'nihilists,' then Musorgsky was too nihilistic for the aesthetes and too aesthetic for the nihilists." B. A. Kats, "Tri zametki k probleme: Musorgsky i kul'tura ego vremeni," in *Muzyka. Kultura. Chelovek* (Sverdlovsk: Izd. Ural'skogo universiteta, 1988), pp. 110–23, esp. 120.

12 Taruskin, "Musorgsky vs. Musorgsky," p. 102 [first citation: Ch. 3, n. 3].

13 See the discussion of this creative relationship in Taruskin, "Russian opera and Russian historiography," pp. 77–146, esp. 124–36 [first citation: Ch. 4, n. 30].

14 The general prospectus of the Full Academy Edition, with some early results of research on *Boris*, is discussed by V. I. Antipov et al., "Polnoe akademicheskoe: Itogi predvaritel'nogo etapa raboty," *Sovetskaya muzyka*, no. 3 (March 1989), pp. 65–77. Quoted material occurs on p. 70.

15 See, for example, June Turner, "Musorgsky," *Music Review* 47 (1986–87): 153–75. Working without Russian and with little attention to Musorgsky's peculiar letter-writing style or to the conventions of Russian male-to-male discourse, Turner sees homosexuality and mother-fixation as surface manifestations of a more basic psychosis: male sado-masochism. For a more cautious and responsible speculation, see Richard Taruskin's Introduction to his *Musorgsky: Eight Essays and an Epilogue* (Princeton, N.J.: Princeton University Press, 1993).

16 For an excellent analysis of these newly loosened gender roles, see Irina Paperno, *Chernyshevsky and the Age of Realism: A Study in the Semiotics of Behavior* (Stanford, Calif.: Stanford University Press, 1988), Ch. 2. See also Kats, "Tri zametki," pp. 110–15, for the suggestion that Musorgsky was waging a polemic against "romanticism" in all its forms: love scenarios, stereotypical musical expression, banal idealization.

17 This and all subsequent quotations from the libretto of *Boris Godunov* are taken from the text published in *MLN*, II:57–112 [hereinafter in the text: *BGLibr 74*]. For the lines cited above, see p. 60.

The opera's literary text is preserved in a multitude of variants both with and without music, including a full author's manuscript libretto in a separate notebook and an incomplete libretto (prologue and first two acts) written by Musorgsky and interleafed in a volume of Pushkin's works containing the play. The text appearing in *BGLibr 74* is conflationist but clarifies in footnotes which lines came from which source.

18 See Taruskin, "Musorgsky *vs.* Musorgsky," pp. 256–58, and Taruskin, "Russian opera and Russian historiography," pp. 127–28.

19 Taruskin, "Musorgsky *vs.* Musorgsky," p. 261.

20 Ibid., p. 248–51.

21 *BGLibr 74*, p. 72.

22 See the discussion in A. S. Ogolevets, *Vokal'naya dramaturgiya Musorgskogo* (Moscow: Muzyka, 1966), p. 174.

23 For a good sampling of these subtle adjustments, see R[uzana Karpovna]. Shirinyan, "Pushkin i Musorgsky," *Sovetskaya muzyka*, no. 9 (September 1969), p. 88.

24 These four basic modes are described in Ogolevets, *Vokal'naya dramaturgiya Musorgskogo*, pp. 8–10.

25 For our reading we draw on Emerson, *Boris Godunov*, pp. 113–17 [first citation: Ch. 1, n. 2], and Robert W. Oldani, "Sealing Pushkin to his place," in *Musicological Essays from the Middle Ages to the 20th Century: A Seventieth Birthday Tribute to Gwynn McPeek from His Friends and Colleagues*, ed. C. Comberiati and M. Steel (New York: Gordon and Breach, 1988), pp. 201–12. Our individual statements have been extensively revised in this conflation.

26 The translation of this first monologue is revised from Emerson, *Boris Godunov*, pp. 113 – 14, which in turn is indebted to Paul Schmidt's version in *Meyerhold at Work*, ed. Paul Schmidt (Austin, Tex.: University of Texas Press, 1980), pp. 89–91.

27 But we should mention one detail of the 1869 setting (which is largely Pushkin's text, with some cuts): Musorgsky adds to the list of Boris's rumored victims (Irina, Tsar Feodor) "that unfortunate child, the young tsarevich." By specifically entering the death of Dmitry of Uglich into the libretto on the same plane of rumor as the other slander circulating at court, Musorgsky, in his first version, equivocates even more than Pushkin on the question of actual historical guilt.

28 Musorgsky to Vladimir Stasov, 10 August 1871, in *MLN*, 1:122–23/*TMR*, p. 167.

29 See Linda J. Ivanits, *Russian Folk Belief* (Armonk, N.Y.: M. E. Sharpe, 1989), Ch. 3 ("The Devil"), esp. p. 39.

30 Felix J. Oinas, "The devil in Russian folklore," in *Essays on Russian Folklore and Mythology* (Columbus, Ohio: Slavica, 1984), p. 98.

31 Pushkin to N. N. Raevsky, in *Letters of Pushkin*, p. 365 [first citation: Ch. 2. n. 19].

32 See Otets Pierling, *Dimitry Samozvanets*, trans. from the French into Russian by V. P. Potemkin (Moscow: Sfinks, 1912), pp. 59–113, esp. 59.

33 James H. Billington, *The Icon and the Axe: An Interpretive History of Russian Culture*, Vintage Books (New York: Random House, 1966), p. 122.

34 "Musorgsky *vs.* Musorgsky," pp. 256–61, and "Russian opera and Russian historiography," pp. 124–35.

35 Richard Taruskin documents the most probable source of events depicted in the

Kromy scene: *The Time of Troubles of the Russian State* (1866) by the populist historian Nikolay Kostomarov. See "Russian opera and Russian historiography," pp. 132–35.

36 Arnold Whittall, *Romantic Music: A Concise History from Schubert to Sibelius* (London: Thames & Hudson, 1987), p. 134.

9 The music

1 Willy Schmid, "*Boris Godunov* again," *The Chesterian*, new series 9 (July–August 1928): 251.

2 Examination of the composer's published letters reveals no resentment of the criticisms leveled at his opera; see *MLN*, 1: 120–33/*TMR*, pp. 159–88 passim [first citations: Ch. 1, n. 3].

3 Musorgsky to Vladimir Stasov, 31 March 1872, in *MLN*, 1: 129/*TMR*, p. 182. In 1872, Stepan Gedeonov, Director of the Imperial Theaters, commissioned the opera-ballet *Mlada* from Musorgsky, Rimsky-Korsakov, Borodin, Cui, and the staff ballet composer Ludwig Minkus; the project collapsed before it was finished, but Musorgsky managed to recycle much of the music he had written for it into other works.

4 Musorgsky to Mily Balakirev, 24 September 1867, in *MLN*, 1:94–95/*TMR*, pp. 99–100.

5 Roland John Wiley, "The tribulations of nationalist composers: A speculation concerning borrowed music in *Khovanshchina*," in *Musorgsky: In Memoriam, 1881–1981*, ed. Malcolm Hamrick Brown, Russian Music Studies, no. 3 (Ann Arbor, Mich.: UMI Research Press, 1982), p. 167.

6 There are at least two versions of each of the following: *Intermezzo in B Minor*, the songs "Where Art Thou, Little Star?" "The Joyous Hour," "King Saul," "Night," "Kalistratushka," "Gopak," "The Seminarist," "Gathering Mushrooms," "The Classicist," "The Orphan," "Eremushka's Lullaby," "A Child's Song," "Lullaby" (from *Songs and Dances of Death*), the chorus *Destruction of Sennacherib*, the operatic fragment *The Marriage*, *St. John's Night on Bald Mountain* (1867) and its revision for the abortive *Mlada* (1872) and later *Fair at Sorochintsy* (1880), and of course *Boris*.

7 Musorgsky to Vladimir Stasov, 13 August 1876, in *MLN*, 1:223/*TMR*, p. 343.

8 Pavel Lamm, "Vosstanovlenie podlinnogo teksta *Borisa Godunova*," in *Musorgsky: "Boris Godunov" – Stat'i i issledovaniya* (Moscow: Gos. Muz. Izd., 1930), pp. 15–16.

9 M. D. Calvocoressi, "The strange case of Mussorgsky," *Christian Science Monitor*, 14 February 1925, p. 12.

10 B. H. Haggin, "Music," *The Nation* 167 (25 December 1948): 732. Polemic was still with us in the mid-1980s: "That any producer could think, ever again, of giving Rimsky's whorish bedizening, a pervasive trivialization, when the composer's stark, stunning, utterly masterful original exists [. . .] boggles the mind." Roger Dettmer, "Cassettes considered," *Fanfare* 8 (July–August 1985): 40.

11 A recent exception is Allen Forte, "Musorgsky as modernist: The phantasmic

episode in *Boris Godunov*," *Music Analysis* 9 (March 1990): 3–46.

12 See, for example, Calvocoressi, *Mussorgsky Life and Works*, pp. 234–301 [first citation: Ch. 4, n. 39].

13 Wiley, "Tribulations," p. 169.

14 Taruskin, "Musorgsky *vs.* Musorgsky," pp. 263–64 [first citation: Ch. 3, n. 3].

15 Quoted in *TMR*, p. 130. It is impossible to clarify in a footnote the complex issues of aesthetic philosophy, personal antagonism, rivalry, and vested interest that lurk behind Stasov's dismissal of Wagner; see Ridenour, *Nationalism, Modernism, and Personal Rivalry*; Taruskin, *Opera and Drama* [first citation: Ch. 4, n. 8]; and Wiley, "Tribulations," pp. 173–76.

16 Musorgsky to Nikolay Rimsky-Korsakov, before 4 October 1867, in *MLN*, 1:95/*TMR*, p. 101.

17 Kompaneysky, "K novym beregam," col. 439 [first citation: Ch. 5, n. 15].

18 César Cui, "Operny sezon v Peterburge: Pervoe i vtoroe predstavlenie *Ruslana i Lyudmily*," *S.-Peterburgskie vedomosti*, 16 September 1864, reprinted in *Musykal'no-kriticheskie stat'i* (Petrograd: "Prosveshchenie," 1918), p. 111.

19 Musorgsky to Lyudmila Shestakova, 19 December 1879, in *MLN*, 1:258/*TMR*, pp. 397–98.

20 David Brown, *Mikhail Glinka: A Biographical and Critical Study* (London: Oxford University Press, 1974), p. 218; Richard Taruskin, "Serov and Musorgsky," in *Slavonic and Western Music: Essays for Gerald Abraham*, ed. Malcolm Hamrick Brown and Roland John Wiley, Russian Music Studies, no. 12 (Ann Arbor, Mich.: UMI Research Press, 1985), pp. 144–45.

21 Musorgsky to Vladimir Stasov, 18 October 1872, in *MLN*, 1:141/*TMR*, p. 199.

22 Musorgsky to Vladimir Stasov, 23 July 1873, in *MLN*, 1:156/*TMR*, p. 227.

23 Consider, for example, a parallel between Musorgsky's tone poem and the "Dream of a Witches' Sabbath" from the *Symphonie Fantastique*. Quite apart from the obvious points of similarity in the subject matter, both Musorgsky and Berlioz state their initial sections twice, the second time a semitone higher, and both emphasize the tritone melodically.

24 V[asily] V[asil'evich] Yastrebtsev, *Nikolay Andreevich Rimsky-Korsakov: Vospominaniya*, ed. A. V. Ossovsky, 2 vols. (Leningrad: Gos. Muz. Izd., 1959–60), II:460.

25 Donald Jay Grout, *A Short History of Opera*, 2nd edn. (New York: Columbia University Press, [1965]), pp. 366–67. The quotation is Grout's description of Verdi's practice.

26 Taruskin, "Musorgsky *vs.* Musorgsky," p. 254: "A mezza notte, ai giardin della Regina" and "Polnoch', v sadu, u fontana."

27 Julian Budden, *The Operas of Verdi*, vol. III: *From Don Carlos to Falstaff* (New York: Oxford University Press, 1981), p. 120.

28 *MLN*, 1:207/*TMR*, p. 319.

29 Musorgsky to Nikolay Rimsky-Korsakov, 15 July 1867, in *MLN*, 1:91/*TMR*, p. 95.

30 Musorgsky to Nikolay Rimsky-Korsakov, before 4 October 1867, in *MLN*, 1:95–96/*TMR*, p. 101; see the epigram at the head of this section.

31 Musorgsky to Nikolay Rimsky-Korsakov, 15 August 1868, in *MLN*, I:106/*TMR*, p. 120.

32 Yastrebtsev, *Vospominaniya*, I:173. Rimsky's version of the scene begins and ends in E♭ major, just as Musorgsky's does.

33 David Lawton, "On the 'Bacio' theme in *Otello*," *19th-Century Music* I (March 1978): 214–15.

34 Guy Marco, "Viewpoint: On key relations in opera," *19th-Century Music* 3 (July 1979): 86–87. As Jonathan D. Kramer has remarked, in another context, relationships of this sort "are not consciously perceived: they are all the more powerful because they are subliminal, reaching us through our intuition and emotion." *Listen to the Music* (New York: Schirmer Books, 1988), p. 48.

35 Roger Parker and Matthew Brown, "Motivic and tonal interaction in Verdi's *Un Ballo in Maschera*," *Journal of the American Musicological Society* 36 (Summer 1983): 263.

36 Wiley, "Tribulations," pp. 165–66. For more on the structural use of tonality in *Rigoletto*, see David Lawton, "Tonal structure and dramatic action in *Rigoletto*," *Verdi: Bollettino dell'istituto di studi Verdiani* 3 (1982): 1559–81.

37 Lawton, "Tonal structure in *Rigoletto*," p. 1560.

38 Unless otherwise noted, all references to *Boris Godunov* in this chapter are to vol. I of the full orchestral score edited by David Lloyd-Jones (London: Oxford University Press, 1975), which we have abbreviated with the siglum *BorisLJ-I*. Although vol. I of this edition contains just the nine scenes of the revision – scenes unique to the initial version appear in the appendices of vol. II – Lloyd-Jones nonetheless presents each of the nine in its maximally supersaturated form, reinserting into the main text all the sections cut by the composer during the course of revision. Even though we are convinced that the vocal score of 1874 represents Musorgsky's final thoughts concerning the structure of his opera, episode by episode, we have chosen to base our discussion on Lloyd-Jones's edition since it is the most easily obtained. To extract Musorgsky's final conception from it – to bring it into line with the vocal score of 1874 – the reader must *always take* the cuts marked *Vi–de* by Lloyd-Jones.

The figure preceding the virgule indicates rehearsal number; the number following – if one appears – indicates the subsequent measure number. Thus the figure R28 refers to rehearsal number 28, and R34/10 refers to the tenth measure of rehearsal 34. We explain this system at some length since published editions of *Boris* vary widely in format and content. Not all editions contain rehearsal numbers, and there is no standardization among those that do. Furthermore, editorial restorations of material cut by Musorgsky make a clear consecutive enumeration of the measures of the opera impossible. For example, m. 749 of Act II in Bessel's first edition is different from m. 749 of Act II in Pavel Lamm's edition, and neither corresponds to m. 749 of Act II in Lloyd-Jones's edition. For further discussion, see Oldani, "Editions of *Boris Godunov*," pp. 179–213 [first citation: Ch. 5, n. 10].

39 In the opera's initial version (1869), Musorgsky ended this first scene with an additional *tableau* in which the people discuss what the pilgrims have said, the

policeman returns to give them further orders, and they indifferently accept these new orders. Dramatically the section seems redundant, making no points that have not been made earlier in the scene. Musically it is well-crafted: Musorgsky brings back the opening theme of the prelude and returns to C♯ minor, thereby rounding off the scene both thematically and tonally. But it seems to us that it is precisely this careful closing of the form that ultimately makes this initial ending unsatisfactory. Too much has happened to warrant closing the circle at this point. Finishing the scene open-endedly on the dominant, as the pilgrims enter the monastery, does not alter the listener's realization that Boris will be Tsar, and by avoiding resolution so early in the opera, Musgorsky leaves a clear path toward further development.

40 Dahlhaus, *Realism in Nineteenth-Century Music*, p. 77 [first citation: Ch. 7, n. 24].

41 Taruskin, "Musorgsky *vs*. Musorgsky," p. 262.

42 Forte, "Musorgsky as modernist," p. 6.

43 The crucial dramatic events of *Rigoletto* likewise hinge on a tonal relationship of Neapolitan to tonic.

44 Musorgsky to Lyudmila Shestakova, 30 July 1868, in *MLN*, I: 100/*TMR*, p. 112.

45 Taruskin, "Musorgsky *vs*. Musorgsky," pp. 100–01.

46 Ibid., p. 102.

47 César Cui, "Muzykal'nye zametki: Tri kartiny iz zabrakovannoy vodevil'nym komitetom opery g. Musorgskogo *Boris Godunov*," *S.-Peterburgskie vedomosti*, 9 February 1873, p. 1.

48 Per. 1, *BorisLJ-1*, beginning – R35; Per. 2, R35/2 – R42/9; Per. 3, R43 – R53/6; Per. 4, R54 – R67/10; Per. 5, R69/3 – R95/10; Per. 6, R96 – end. Take all cuts marked *Vi–de*.

49 Forte, "Musorgsky as modernist," p. 6.

50 *Carteggio Verdi-Boïto*, ed. Mario Medici and Marcello Conati with the collaboration of Marisa Casati, 2 vols. (Parma: Istituto di Studi Verdiani, 1978), I: 5.

51 Musorgsky's practice of freely combining passages of Pushkin with his own text is further illustrated in the text of the revision's hallucination scene, part of which is paraphrased from the last twelve lines of Pushkin's "Dostig ya vysshey vlasti," part of which is taken from an entirely different scene in the play, and part of which is by the composer himself. See Chapter 8 for further details.

52 Musorgsky to Arseny Golenishchev-Kutuzov, 15 August 1877, in *MLN*, I:232/ *TMR*, p. 360.

53 We have adapted this discussion of "Dostig ya vysshey vlasti," with the addition of new material, from Oldani, "Sealing Pushkin to his place," pp. 201–12 [first citation: Ch. 8, n. 25].

54 In a passage appearing just before Shuisky's entrance in the libretto of 1873, but cut from the piano–vocal score of 1874, Musorgsky indicates that Boris does not trust Shuisky and regards him as an antagonist. The passage provides a motive for Shuisky's clever manipulation of the Tsar's terror, but it also tends to reduce the scene between Shuisky and Boris merely to a struggle for power. By eliminating these few lines of characterization from the score, Musorgsky permits one to view Shuisky not merely as a powerful noble who wants to be tsar himself, but as yet

another instrument of retribution. The change is perhaps fortuitous, but as we are about to see, much of Shuisky's music revolves around the pitch-class D, associated with retribution through Dmitry.

55 For a detailed theoretical exegesis of this scene, see Forte, "Musorgsky as modernist," pp. 21–41.

56 Asaf'ev, *K vosstanovleniyu*, p. 68 [first citation: ch. 7, n. 16].

57 Joseph Kerman, "The puzzle of *Boris*," *Opera News* 39 (25 January 1975): 11.

58 Musorgsky to Vladimir Stasov, 18 April 1871, in *MLN*, 1:122/*TMR*, p. 163.

59 In a letter to Balakirev, dated 31 March 1862, Musorgsky states: "I don't like E major," See *MLN*, 1:61/*TMR*, p. 42.

60 Compare the ending of the Kromy Forest scene.

61 Per. 1, *BorisLJ-1*, beginning – R6/2; Per. 2, R6/3 – R24/6; Per. 3, R25 – R38/7; Per 4, R39 – R49/7; Per. 5, R49/8 – R71/6; Per. 6, R72 – end.

62 Parker and Brown, "Motivic and Tonal Interaction," pp. 263.

63 Per. 1, *BorisLJ-1*, beginning – R11/7; Per. 2, R12 – R24/8; Per. 3, R25 – R34/5; Per. 4, R35 – R46/7; Per 5, R47 – end. Take all cuts marked *Vi–de*.

64 Edward R. Reilly, *The Music of Mussorgsky: A Guide to the Editions* (New York: The Musical Newsletter, [1980]), p. 8.

65 Per. 1, *BorisLJ-1*, beginning – R19/9; Per. 2, R20 – R24/9; Per. 3, R25 – R28/8; Per. 4, R29 – R51/5; Per. 5, R52 – R62/6; Per. 6, R63 – R72/8; Per. 7, R73 – end.

66 Rosa Newmarch, "Moussorgsky's Operas," *The Musical Times* 54 (July 1913): 433.

67 M. B. [Dmitry Dmitrievich Minaev], "V nogu, rebyata, raz, dva! (Zastol'nye besedy otstavnogo mayora Mikhaila Burbonova)," *Iskra*, no. 19 (9 May 1871), col. 584.

68 Musorgsky to Arseny Golenishchev-Kutuzov, 15 August 1877, in *MLN*, 1:232/*TMR*, p. 360.

69 Musorgsky to Vladimir Stasov, 2 January 1873, in *MLN*, 1:144/*TMR*, p. 203.

10 *Boris Godunov* during the jubilee decade: the 1980s and beyond

1 Vyacheslav Kostikov, "Vlast' mertvaya i vlast' zhivaya: zametki pri chtenii otechestvennoy istorii," *Sovetskaya kul'tura*, 11 August 1990, p. 4: and Boris Lyubimov, "Imperatorsky teatr?" *Literaturnaya gazeta*, 13 June 1990. For these references we are indebted to the text of Robert C. Tucker's Presidential Address to the AAASS, "What time is it in Russia's history?" (Washington, D.C., 19 October 1990).

2 For an eyewitness account of the scandalous first run, see Paul Debreczeny, "*Boris Godunov* at the Taganka: A Note on a Non-Performance," *Slavic and East European Journal* 28 (1984): 99–101; for an exemplary review of the "revival" four years later, see A. Amelin, "Dva puti," *Sovetskaya kul'tura*, 17 September 1988, p. 8.

3 For a concrete and extensive parallel between Boris Godunov and Mikhail Gorbachev, see Oleg Moroz, "Zhivaya vlast' dlya cherni nenavistna?" *Literaturnaya gazeta*, 1 May 1991, p. 3. The title ("Is living power hateful to the mob?")

transforms a line from Pushkin's *Boris* into a fateful question. Both of these rulers had taken great risks and rendered great services to the people, Moroz writes, and neither had been rewarded. "The hardest thing to understand about Pushkin's Godunov is why the people don't love him. It seems as if he does everything for the people's good ... History moves in circles, and the same situation obtains with our current president ... Without a doubt, Gorbachev is the greatest Russian political figure of the twentieth century. We should fall down at his feet. But instead a hundred thousand voices cry from the public squares: 'Gorbachev, resign! Gorbachev, resign! Gorbachev, resign!'" The rapidity with which Gorbachev – neither reliable Communist nor repentant liberal – subsequently faded from his country's view does indeed recall the complete eclipse of the brief, provisional "Godunov dynasty" in the seventeenth century.

4 See D. Logbas, "God Musorgskogo prodolzhaetsya: v kontekste XX veka," *Sovetskaya muzyka*, no. 11 (November 1989), pp. 89–91.

5 Marina Kornakova, "Tarkovsky prodolzhaetsya," *Muzykal'naya zhizn'*, January 1991, pp. 3–5, esp. p. 4. According to Musorgsky's stage directions in the Kromy scene, Varlaam and Misail enter only after the introductory musical episodes are complete, presumably as part of Dmitry's advance guard; in this production, however, the two renegade monks are present from the beginning, maneuvering the crowd into various line-dances and coordinating the torture of the boyar and the Jesuits. Throughout, Misail brandishes a red-tipped axe. But this resistance is not presented as a positive, intelligent, or conscious force, which seems to be Kornakova's point.

6 "With its fresh and still unspoiled feeling, youth understood that a great artistic force had created and entrusted to our people a new, marvelous, national work, and youth rejoiced, and was glad, and celebrated. Twenty [sic] performances were given to a full theater; more than once a crowd of young people sang 'The Coronation of the Boyar by the People' and other choruses [from the Kromy scene] throughout the night in the streets ..." Stasov, "Musorgsky: Biografichesky ocherk," pp. 529–30 [first citation: Ch. 4, n. 13].

7 For a survey of Jubilee *Boris* productions, see Genrikh Isakhanov, "Liki festival'nykh *Borisov*," *Sovetskaya muzyka*, no. 12 (December 1990), pp. 39–46.

8 See the 1988 tribute to Tarkovsky by Abbado in the Kirov Opera/Royal Opera House guide to the Leningrad premiere, April 1990, p. 8.

9 "Segodnya – *Boris* Tarkovskogo," *Sovetskaya kul'tura*, 27 October 1990, p. 1.

10 Aleksandr Prokhanov, "Tragediya tsentralizma," *Literaturnaya Rossiya*, no. 1 (5 January 1990), pp. 4–5; cited here from a translation in *National Affairs*, 26 January 1990, p. 97.

11 See V. I. Antipov et al., "Polnoe akademicheskoe," *Sovetskaya muzyka*, no. 3 (March 1989), p. 66. The thirty-two-volume project will proceed along two tracks: vols. I-XVII will contain all of Musorgsky's own surviving scores with commentary; vols. XVIII-XXXII, arrangements and completions by the hands of other masters (Rimsky-Korsakov, Shostakovich, Stravinsky, Ravel). In the words of the editors, the order of publication will not be chronological but according to "cultural value": the earliest volumes will be on the historical operas, followed by

the comic operas and finally the songs, piano works and incidental orchestral pieces.

12 See the case made for the 1869 version by the well-known Soviet bass and interpreter of Boris, Evgeny Nesterenko: "Operedivshy vremya," *Sovetskaya muzyka,* no. 3 (March 1989), pp. 40–42.

13 See Isakhanov, "Liki festival'nykh *Borisov,*" pp. 43–45.

14 Boris's daughter the Tsarevna Xenia, victimized and then incarcerated by the Pretender, was especially favored for such Christianizing treatment. The historical Xenia ended her life as a nun, and in art she became the spiritual center of martyr plays that portrayed her as a complex symbol of bride, nun, Virgin Mary, and the Savior himself. See the discussion of Alexander Fedotov's 1868 play "The Godunovs" (premiered in Moscow in 1884) in Caryl Emerson, "Pretenders to history: Four plays for undoing Pushkin's *Boris Godunov,*" *Slavic Review* 44 (Summer 1985): 257–79.

15 Sergey Korobkov, "Venchanie na tsarstvo," *Muzykal'naya zhizn'* 14 (1990): 9.

16 Ibid.

17 Aleksey Kandinsky, "Tsena podlinnika," *Sovetskaya muzyka,* no. 8 (August 1990), p. 47. Kandinsky, sympathetic to the old school, does not approve of these interpolations and considers them an unwarranted liberty. Both Pushkin's drama and Musorgsky's opera, he claims, strive for balance between psychological and historical factors, and the Stanislavsky Theater production destroys that balance by reducing the whole to a "bad dream." Kandinsky notes that this *Boris* takes place not on a stage but in the madhouse of the Tsar's mind, and he regrets that "one cannot see the Tsar's suite, the Tsar's bodyguard, and, most importantly, the people."

18 Nora Grigoryieva, "Two Operatic Premieres in Moscow," *Moscow News,* no. 4, 1990.

19 A. S. Pushkin, "Pis'mo k izdatel'yu *Moskovskogo vestnika,*" in *Polnoe sobranie sochineny,* 16 vols. (Moscow: Izd. Akademii Nauk SSSR, 1937–50), XI:68.

20 "Prestuplenie i nakazanie v 'Borise Godunove,'" *Sokhrani moyu rech': Mandel'shtamovskii sbornik* (Moscow: Obnovlenie, 1991), pp. 5–9, esp. p. 6.

21 Sergei Rumyantsev, "Podlinnost' istiny: Eshche raz o *Borise Godunove,*" *Sovetskaya muzyka,* no. 8 (August 1990), pp. 49–52.

22 "Intrepid" [An Interview with Valery Gergiev by Stephanie von Buchau], *Opera News* (June 1992), 16.

DISCOGRAPHY
A GUIDE TO RECORDINGS OF *BORIS GODUNOV*

In 1992, 118 years after the premiere of *Boris Godunov* at the Maryinsky Theater in St. Petersburg, there is still no recording of Musorgsky's masterpiece that presents the opera in the final form he gave it, as documented in the published piano–vocal score of 1874. The reasons for this are not hard to find and will be thrice familiar to the reader who has come this far in this book: two composer's versions, extraneous versions by Rimsky-Korsakov and a host of others, and critical editions, when they appear, that blend and mix the composer's distinct conceptions, all in the name of "authenticity." It is certainly ironic that of all the recordings listed below, the one closest to Musorgsky's final conception – episode for episode, provided the listener play the Death scene before the Kromy Forest scene – is no. 6, a straightforward, uncut, unaltered, unamplified performance of Rimsky-Korsakov's final redaction – with no added St. Basil scene, no bits and snatches reinserted from the initial version, no attempt made to have the best of both Musorgsky's worlds with the necessary concomitant of devising new cuts to scale the resulting behemoth down to reasonable size.

In such circumstances it can hardly be surprising that the first-time buyer of *Boris Godunov* often is bewildered by the sheer complexity of who wrote what when and frequently is uncertain whether a particular recording offers Musorgsky, Musorgsky/Rimsky-Korsakov, Musorgsky/Shostakovich, or Musorgsky/Somebody Else. The purpose of the present discography, then, is to provide a short guide to recordings of the opera and to what the consumer can expect of various offerings. We have discussed recordings currently available, in 1992, in either the United States or the United Kingdom. Because of high documentary or artistic value, however, we also have included several European recordings never released in the United States and several out-of-print recordings (identified by the letters OP preceding the manufacturer's name and catalog number). Seeking only to provide guidance to the contemporary record buyer and to those curious about the sound of the many redactions, we have made no attempt to produce a comprehensive discography. We hope, accordingly, that readers will forgive the exclusion of some of their favorites.

Boris Godunov. An Opera in Four Acts with Prologue. Complete

MUSORGSKY'S ORCHESTRATION

1 Alexander Vedernikov, Vladislav Piavko, Irina Arkhipova, and others. USSR TV and Radio Large Chorus, "Spring" Studio Children's Chorus, USSR TV and Radio Large Orchestra. Vladimir Fedoseyev, cond.

The revision, but with every scene in its longest possible form. Thus, the recording does not contain the St. Basil scene, but it does restore all the material from the initial version that Musorgsky, in revision, cut from the five scenes common to both versions.

CD: Philips 412 281-2PH3 (3 CDs).
LP: Philips 412 281-1 (4 discs: OP).

2 Aage Haugland, Stig Fogh Andersen, and others. DR Radio Choir, DR Radio Symphony Orchestra. Dimitri Kitaenko, cond.

Following Boris Christoff's lead (see nos. 6 and 7), Aage Haugland sings the three bass roles – Boris, Pimen, and Varlaam. Billing itself as a "concert version based on the 1868/69 version," this performance in fact mixes the composer's two versions without representing either one adequately. Only six scenes are performed, an incomplete text no matter what the version. Although the two scenes of the Prologue appear exactly as in the 1869 score, the Cell scene is given according to the revision (omitting Pimen's narrative about the tsarevich's murder and including both the first two choruses of monks offstage and the revised form of Grigory's dream). The *Terem* scene likewise is given according to the revision, but with cuts. The version of the Death scene heard here falls between two stools, following some of the cuts Musorgsky took in revision while ignoring others. The St. Basil scene, very much part of the 1869 score, is omitted entirely. (The two Polish scenes and the Kromy Forest scene, of course, do not appear in the "1868/69 version," and so they play no part here.) It is ironic that this set, which tries to sell itself as the *initial* version, is in fact the only recording from which one can hear the *revised* Cell scene exactly as Musorgsky left it, without the narrative about Dmitry's murder stitched back in!

CD: Kontrapunkt 32036/37 (2 CDs).

3 Ruggero Raimondi, Vyacheslav Polozov, Galina Vishnevskaya, and others. The Chevy Chase Elementary School Chorus, The Choral Arts Society of Washington, The Oratorio Society of Washington, National Symphony Orchestra. Mstislav Rostropovich, cond.

The "supersaturated" *Boris*, with everything in the longest possible form. Stitches the St. Basil scene back in (before the Death scene), as well as all the material from the initial version that Musorgsky, in revision, cut from the five scenes common to both versions. Even a short twelve-bar passage which Musorgsky scratched out of the revised *Terem* scene is performed here – despite David Lloyd-Jones's having included it in the OUP edition with great hesitation, a note of caution, and an explicit warning that the passage was not contained in the Oxford parts. Somewhat unusually, the episode of the fool with the boys is heard in both the St. Basil and the Kromy Forest scene. The only significant omission in this recording is the initial version of the *Terem* scene – which, of course, cannot be combined in a single narrative line with the revision of the same scene.

    CD: Erato 2292-45418-2 zb (3 CDs).

4 Martti Talvela, Nicolai Gedda, Bozena Kinasz, and others. Polish Radio Chorus of Kraków, Boys Chorus from the Kraków Philharmonic Chorus, Polish Radio National Symphony Orchestra. Jerzy Semkow, cond.

    This is the earliest complete recording of the opera to be made using the composer's score. It presents the "supersaturated" *Boris*, offering the same musical text as no. 3, with one exception. The episode of the fool with the boys, having been heard once in the St. Basil scene, is here cut from the Kromy Forest scene – the usual practice in most performances that include both these scenes. Apart from this, the only significant omission, as in no. 3, is the initial version of the *Terem* scene.

    CD: Not currently available.

    LP: Angel sx-3844 (q) (4 discs: OP).

5 Nicolai Ghiaurov, Michail Svetlev, Stefka Mineva, and others. Sofia National Opera Chorus, Sofia Festival Orchestra. Emil Tchakarov, cond.

    The "supersaturated" *Boris* once again, essentially the same as no. 3. Stitches the St. Basil scene back in (before the Death scene, but with a disclaimer that it need not be played), as well as all the material from the initial version that Musorgsky, in revision, cut from the five scenes common to both versions. The episode of the fool with the boys is heard in both the St. Basil and the Kromy Forest scene, but the twelve bars of the revised *Terem* scene questioned by David Lloyd-Jones are omitted.

    CD: Sony Classical s3k 45763 (3 CDs).

None of the recordings of the complete opera based on Musorgsky's orchestration includes the initial version of the *Terem* scene (for which, see no. 14 below).

RIMSKY-KORSAKOV'S ORCHESTRATION

6 Boris Christoff, Dmitr Uzunov, Evelyn Lear, and others. Chorus of the National Opera of Sofia, Paris Conservatoire Orchestra. André Cluytens, cond.

    The second recording of Boris Christoff, who sings all three bass roles (Boris, Pimen, Varlaam). Uses the Rimsky-Korsakov score of 1908. Though obviously incorporating Rimsky's many changes in orchestration, pitch, melodic line, and so forth, this recording nevertheless comes closer than any other to Musorgsky's final conception in terms of plot, incident, and scene sequence – provided, of course, that the listener play Side 8 (the Death scene) before Side 7 (the Kromy Forest scene).

CD: Angel CDCC-47993 (3 CDs: OP).

LP: Angel S-3633 D/L (4 discs: OP).

7 Boris Christoff, Nicolai Gedda, Eugenia Zareska, and others. Choeurs Russes de Paris, Orchestre National de la Radiodiffusion Française. Issay Dobrowen, cond.

The first recording of Boris Christoff, who sings all three bass roles (Boris, Pimen, Varlaam). The young Nicalai Gedda, as Grigory/Dmitry, remains unsurpassed in this role. Though following the shorter versions of the Cell scene and the Fountain scene from 1896, this performance adheres to Rimsky's score of 1908 in the other scenes.

CD: Not currently available.

LP: Capitol GDR-7164 (4 discs: OP); reissued, Seraphim ID-6101 (4 discs: OP); reissued, EMI Pathé Marconi 1141613 (4 discs: OP).

8 Evgeny Nesterenko, Vladimir Atlantov, Elena Obraztsova, and others. Chorus and orchestra of the Bolshoi Theater (Moscow). Mark Ermler, cond.

The full Rimsky-Korsakov score of 1908, but with the addition of the St. Basil's scene in Ippolitov-Ivanov's orchestration (see below, no. 9). The episode of the fool with the boys, having been heard once in the St. Basil scene, is cut from the Kromy Forest scene – the usual practice in most performances that include both these scenes. The order of the last three scenes here is unusual: St. Basil's, Kromy Forest, and Boris's Death. All the other conflationary performances discussed in this discography follow the order found in Pavel Lamm's edition: St. Basil's, Boris's Death, and Kromy Forest.

CD: Chant du Monde LDC 278 853/55 (3 CDs).

LP: Melodiya (Russia) A10 00137 008 (4 discs).

9 Mark Reizen, Georgy Nelepp, M. Maksakova, and others. Chorus and Orchestra of the Bolshoi Theater (Moscow). Nikolai Golovanov, cond.

This recording, documenting the Bolshoy Theater production of 1948, presents a stable late-Soviet state of a conflation first produced in Moscow in 1927; that production combined Rimsky-Korsakov's orchestration of Musorgsky's revision with a newly-commissioned orchestration by Mikhail Ippolitov-Ivanov (in the style of Rimsky) of the then-newly-discovered "additional people's scene" in front of St. Basil's Cathedral. The following year, 1928, saw the production in Leningrad of "Musorgsky's original" – in reality a conflation of the composer's two versions. (This Leningrad production is discussed in Chapter 7 above; see pp. 162–68.) Interest in the composer's own scoring waned in the Soviet Union during the 1930s and 40s, and in 1948, when the Bolshoy mounted a sumptuous new production of *Boris Godunov*, the score chosen was Rimsky's, augmented by Ippolitov-Ivanov's St. Basil scene. To compensate for the extra length of this additional scene, the production reverted to Rimsky's shorter 1896 score in the Cell scene and the Fountain scene. The *Terem* scene was presented in a version that restored a few of Rimsky's cuts from 1896 (e.g., Feodor's geography lesson, the chiming clock) but allowed others to stand (e.g., the uproar among the nurses offstage and Feodor's song of the parrot). The episode of the fool with the boys, having been heard once in the St. Basil scene, is cut from the Kromy Forest scene – the usual practice in most performances that include both these scenes. This version of the opera –shortened Cell, *Terem*, and Fountain scenes, additional St. Basil scene, shortened Kromy Forest scene – became the standard text at Moscow's Bolshoy Theater in the 1950s, 60s, and 70s and is preserved in several recordings of Soviet provenance.

> CD: Not currently available.
> LP: Melodiya M10-37403-10 (4 discs: OP); reissued, Educational Media Associates RR-440 (3 discs: OP).

10 Nicolai Ghiaurov, Ludovic Spiess, Galina Vishnevskaya, and others. Vienna Boys Choir, Sofia Radio Chorus, Vienna State Opera Chorus, Vienna Philharmonic Orchestra. Herbert von Karajan, cond.

The full Rimsky-Korsakov score of 1908, but with the addition of the St. Basil scene in Ippolitov-Ivanov's orchestration. The episode of the fool with the boys, having been heard once in the St. Basil scene, is again cut from the Kromy Forest scene.

> CD: London 411 862-2 (3 CDs).
> LP: London OSA-1439 (4 discs: OP).

11 George London, Vladimir Ivanovsky, Irina Arkhipova and others. Chorus and Orchestra of the State Academic Bolshoi Theater USSR. Alexander Melik-Pashaev, cond.

Preserving George London's interpretation of the title role, this recording has musical text identical to no. 9.

> CD: Not currently available.
> LP: Columbia M4S-696 (4 discs: OP).

12 Ivan Petrov, Vladimir Ivanovsky, Irina Arkhipova and others. Chorus and Orchestra of the State Academic Bolshoi Theater USSR. Alexander Melik-Pashaev, cond.

An all-Russian cast performing the same musical text heard in no. 9.

> CD: Not currently available.
> LP: Melodiya (Russia) 33D-010953-60 (4 discs: OP); reissued, Musical Heritage Society MHS 4007/10 (4 discs: OP); reissued, Ariola/Eurodisc 78701XIR (4 discs: OP).

13 Nikola Ghiuzelev, Dimiter Damyanov, Alexandrina Milcheva, and others. Chorus and Orchestra of the National Opera of Sofia. Assen Naidenov, cond.

The full Rimsky-Korsakov score of 1908, but with the addition of the St. Basil scene in Ippolitov-Ivanov's orchestration. The episode of the fool with the boys, having been heard once in the St. Basil scene, is cut from the Kromy Forest scene. Cf. nos. 8 & 10.

> CD: Fidelio 1824/5/6 (3 CDs).
> LP: Harmonia Mundi (France) HMU-4-144 (4 discs: OP).

No complete commercial recording has yet been made using Shostakovich's, Rathaus's, or Melngailis's orchestrations. See the "Excerpts" section, below.

Boris Godunov. An Opera in Four Acts with Prologue. Excerpts

MUSORGSKY'S ORCHESTRATION

14 Vaclovas Daunoras, Sergei Larin, Antonijas Kesada. Lithuanian TV and Radio Chorus. Lithuanian National Philharmonia SO. Juozas Domarkas, cond.

The most noteworthy feature of this recording is the inclusion of the *Terem* scene according to the 1869 score. But the decision to substitute the 1874 version of Boris's monologue "Dostig ya vysshei vlasti," though symptomatic of the modern urge to conflate, is hard to justify.

CD: Not currently available.

LP: Medodiya (Russia) A10 00603-007.

15 Gottlob Frick, Martti Talvela, Rudolf Schock, and others. Chorus and Orchestra of the German Opera Berlin. Lovro von Matacic, cond. (sung in German).

Talvela, well-known subsequently as Boris, sings Pimen here. The disc includes the Coronation scene, the *Terem* scene from Boris's entrance through "Dostig ya vysshei vlasti," the Death scene from Pimen's entrance through the end, and the Kromy Forest scene from Dmitry's entrance through the end.

CD: Not currently available.

LP: Eurodise (Germany) 72765KR (1 disc: OP).

RATHAUS'S ORCHESTRATION

16 Giorgio Tozzi, Albert da Costa, Nell Rankin, and others. The Metropolitan Opera Orchestra and Chorus. Dimitri Mitropoulos, cond. (sung in English).

About half the opera: Coronation scene, Cell scene, revised *Terem* scene (cut), Boudoir scene (from Rangoni's entrance), Fountain scene (from just after the polonaise), St. Basil scene, Death scene. Since Rathaus based his work on Pavel Lamm's edition, his score reinserts material from the initial version that Musorgsky cut, in revision, from the scenes common to both versions.

CD: Not currently available.

LP: RCA Victor LM-6063 (2 discs: OP).

SHOSTAKOVICH'S ORCHESTRATION

17 Boris Shtokolov, Vladimir Ulyanbov, and others. Orchestra of the Leningrad Kirov Theater. Sergei Eltsin, cond.

Terem scene only, in the 1869 version, but with one conflationist lapse! The performers follow Shostakovich's recommendation (given in a note in the score) to shift to the 1874 version for Shuisky's narrative about Dmitry's corpse. Thus, both extant recordings of the 1869 *Terem* scene (nos. 14 and 17) incorporate music from the 1874 score.

CD: Not currently available.

LP: Melodiya (Russia) 33S-281-82 1 10" disc: OP); reissued, Melodiya/ Columbia (US) M 34569 (1 disc: OP).

18 Theo Adam, Peter Schreier, Siegfried Vogel, and others. Kinderchor des Philharmonischen Chores Dresden, Rundfunkchor Leipzig, Staatskapelle Dresden. Herbert Kegel, cond. (sung in German).

A good way to sample Shostakovich's orchestration. The disc contains the Coronation scene, "Dostig ya vysshei vlasti," Boris's hallucination monologue, the polonaise, the love duet, an excerpt from the St. Basil scene, Pimen's narrative (Death scene), and Boris's farewell and death.

CD: Not currently available.

LP: Telefunken (UK) SAT-22526 (1 disc: OP).

OF HISTORICAL INTEREST
(ALL IN RIMSKY-KORSAKOV'S ORCHESTRATION)

19 Feodor Chiliapin, various supporting performers and conductors.

CD: Angel CDH-61009; Nimbus NI 7823/4.

LP: Angel "Great Recordings of the Century" COLH-100 (1 disc: OP); reissued, Seraphim S-60211 (1 disc: OP).

20 Igor Kipnis and others, Victor Symphony Orchestra and Chorus, Nicolai Berezovsky, cond.

CD: RCA Gold Seal (Victor Vocal Series) 60522-2-RC.

LP: RCA Victrola VIC-1396 (1 disc: OP). The LP contains a four-minute excerpt from the Novodevichy scene, in which Kipnis is not heard, omitted from the CD.

21 Nicola Rossi-Lemeni and others. San Francisco Opera Chorus, San Francisco Symphony Orchestra. Leopold Stokowski, cond.

A miscellany of basso and choral scenes, linked generally by transitions of Stokowski's devising. Even though Stokowski gave the first performance using Pavel Lamm's edition outside Russia (Philadelphia Orchestra, 1929–30), here he reverts to Rimsky-Korsakov's score, albeit with occasional reference to a Musorgskian gesture. The opening melody, for example, is heard in Musorgsky's soli bassoons rather than in Rimsky's bassoon plus English horn.

CD: Not currently available.

LP: RCA Victor LM-1764 (1 disc: OP); reissued, Dell'Arte Records DA-9002 (1 disc: OP).

22 Dmitry Smirnov and M. S. Davydova. Unnamed ensemble and conductor.

The love duet only (beginning from "Stoy, Marina"), in a three-record set entitled *Outstanding Russian Singers of the Past*. Smirnov sang the role of Grigory/Dmitry at Diaghilev's production in Paris in 1908.

CD: Not currently available.

LP: Melodiya (Russia) 33 D 014921-26 (OP).

SELECT BIBLIOGRAPHY

Music

Musorgsky, Modest Petrovich. *Boris Godunov* [holograph full score]. St. Petersburg, C.I.S. Central Music Library of the Kirov Theater, MS 3695.

Boris Godunov [first edition, libretto]. St. Petersburg: V. Bessel & Co., [1873].

Boris Godunov [first edition, piano–vocal score]. St. Petersburg: V. Bessel & Co., [1874].

Boris Godunov [piano–vocal score]. Edited and orchestrated by N[ikolay] A[ndreevich] Rimsky-Korsakov. Transcribed for voice and piano by N. A. Rimsky-Korsakov. St. Petersburg: V. Bessel & Co., 1896.

Boris Godunov [piano–vocal score]. Edited and orchestrated by N[ikolay] A[ndreevich] Rimsky-Korsakov. French translation by M[ichel] Delines and L[ouis] Laloy. St. Petersburg: V. Bessel & Co., 1908.

Boris Godunov [full orchestral score]. Edited by David Lloyd-Jones. 2 vols. London: Oxford University Press, 1975.

Boris Godunov [full orchestral score]. Redaction of N. A. Rimsky-Korsakov with the addition of the St. Basil scene in the orchestration of M. M. Ippolitov-Ivanov. Edited by I[rina Nikolaevna] Iordan and G[eorgy Vasil'evich] Kirkor. Moscow: Gos. Muz. Izd., 1959; reprint edn., New York: Dover, 1987.

Boris Godunov [full orchestral score]. Edited by P. A. Lamm. Orchestrated by Dmitry Dmitrievich Shostakovich. 2 vols. Moscow: Sovetsky Kompozitor, 1963; reprint edn., with new preface by R. W. Oldani, Miami: Kalmus, 1990.

Polnoe sobranie sochineny. Edited by Pavel Aleksandrovich Lamm. 8 vols. Moscow: Gos. Muz. Izd., 1928–34; reprint edn., 23 vols., New York: Kalmus, n.d.

Polnoe akademicheskoe sobranie sochineny M. P Musorgskogo v tridtsati dvukh tomakh. Moscow: "Muzyka," 1989– [projected].

Letters and documents

Musorgsky, Modest Petrovich. *Literaturnoe nasledie: Pis'ma, Biograficheskie materialy i dokumenty, Literaturnye proizvedeniya.* Edited by A. A. Orlova and M. S. Pekelis. 2 vols. Moscow: Muzyka, 1971–72.

The Musorgsky Reader: A Life of Modeste Petrovich Musorgsky in Letters and

Select bibliography

Documents. Edited and translated by Jay Leyda and Sergei Bertensson. New York: W. W. Norton, 1947; reprint edn., New York: Da Capo Press, 1970.

Pis'ma. Moscow: "Muzyka," 1981; 2nd edn., 1984.

Pis'ma i dokumenty. Edited by A. N. Rimsky-Korsakov. Moscow: Gos. Muz. Izd., 1932.

Pis'ma k A. A. Golenishchevu-Kutuzovu. Edited by Yu. V. Keldysh. Commentary by P. Aravin. Moscow: Gos. Muz. Izd., 1939.

Selected readings

Abraham, Gerald. "The Carthaginian element in *Boris Godunov.*" *The Musical Times* 83 (January 1942): 9–12. Revised and reissued as "The Mediterranean element in *Boris Godunov.*" In *Slavonic and Romantic Music*, pp. 188–94. New York: St. Martin's Press, [1968].

"Musorgsky, Modest Petrovich." *The New Grove Dictionary of Music and Musicians.* Edited by Stanley Sadie. London: Macmillan, 1980. Vol. 12, pp. 865–874.

"Mussorgsky's *Boris* and Pushkin's." *Music and Letters* 26 (January 1945): 31–38. Reprinted in *Slavonic and Romantic Music*, pp. 178–87. New York: St. Martin's Press, [1968].

Alheim, Marie Olénine d'. *Le legs de Moussorgski.* Paris: Eugène Rey, 1908.

Alheim, Pierre d'. *Moussorgski.* Paris: Société du Mercure de France, 1896.

Asaf'ev, Boris Vladimirovich [Igor Glebov]. "Die ästhetischen Anschauungen Mussorgskijs." Translated by Jacques Handschin. *Die Musik* 21 (May 1929): 561–75.

Boris Godounov restauré." *La revue musicale*, no. 6 (1 April 1928), pp. 274–76.

Izbrannye trudy. 5 vols. Moscow: Izd. AN SSSR, 1952–57.

K vosstanovleniyu "Borisa Godunova" Musorgskogo. Moscow: Gos. Izd. Muz. Sek., 1928.

Baskin, V[ladimir] S[ergeevich]. *M. P. Musorgsky: Ocherk muzykal'noy deyatel'nosti.* Moscow: P. Jurgenson, 1886.

Baughan, E. A. "Moussorgsky's operas." *The Fortnightly Review* 94 (July–December 1913): 539–45.

Belenkova, I. Ya. "Printsipy dialoga v *Borise Godunove* Musorgskogo i ikh razvitie v sovetskoy opere." In *M. P. Musorgsky i muzyka XX veka*, pp. 110–36. Edited by G. L. Golovinsky. Moscow: Muzyka, 1990.

Bellaigue, Camille. "Un grand musicien réaliste: Moussorgski." *Revue des deux mondes*, ser. 5, 2 (March–April 1901): 858–89.

Belyaev, Viktor Mikhaylovich [Victor Belaiev]. "The battle over *Boris.*" *Christian Science Monitor*, 21 April 1928, p. 7, cols. 1–3.

"*Boris Godunov*; Lenigr. Gosud. Academ. Teatr Opery i Baleta." *Zhizn' iskusstva*, no. 9 (28 February 1928), pp. 8–10.

Musorgsky's "Boris Godunov" and Its New Version. Translated by S. W. Pring.

London: Oxford University Press, 1928.

Belyaev, Viktor Mikhaylovich, and others. *Musorgsky. "Boris Godunov". Stat'i i issledovaniya.* Moscow: Gos. Izd. Muz. Sek., 1930.

Billington, James H. *The Icon and the Axe: An Interpretive History of Russian Culture.* Vintage Books. New York: Random House, 1966.

Buckle, Richard. *Diaghilev.* New York: Atheneum, 1979.

Calvocoressi, M[ichel] D[imitri]. "*Boris Godounov.*" *Mercure Musical* 4 (1908): 61–78.

"*Boris Godunov* as Moussorgsky wrote it." *The Musical Times* 69 (1928): 318–20, 408–12, 506–508.

"*Boris Godunov*: Genuine and otherwise." *The Musical Times* 65 (February 1924): 117–19.

"Early criticisms of Moussorgsky in Western Europe." *Musical Opinion* 52 (1929): 642–43, 736–38.

"The genuine score of *Boris.*" *Christian Science Monitor,* 9 March 1929, p. 6, cols. 3–4.

"The genuine scoring of *Boris Godunof.*" *The Monthly Musical Record* 58 (1928): 328–31, 359–61.

"Glazunov contra *Boris Godunov.*" *The Musical Times* 69 (1928): 514.

Modest Mussorgsky: His Life and Works. London: Rockliff, 1956; Fair Lawn, N.J.: Essential Books, 1956.

Moussorgsky. Les maîtres de la musique. Paris: Félix Alcan, 1908. Revised and enlarged edition, 1911. Translated by A. Eaglefield Hull as *Musorgsky: The Russian Musical Nationalist.* London: Kegan, Paul, Trench, Trubner & Co. 1919.

Musicians Gallery: Music and Ballet in Paris and London; Recollections of M. D. Calvocoressi. London: Faber and Faber, [1933].

Mussorgsky. [Completed by Gerald Abraham.] The Master Musician Series. London: J. M. Dent & Sons Ltd., 1946; rev. edn., by G. Abraham, London: J. M. Dent & Sons Ltd., 1974.

"New chapters in the history of *Boris Godunov.*" *The Musical Times* 68 (1927): 512–13.

"The opening motive in *Boris Godunov.*" *The Musical Times* 69 (January 1928): 19–20.

"La révélation de *Boris Godounov.*" *La revue musicale,* no. 6 (1 April 1928), pp. 202–15.

"A Russian critic on Mussorgsky's orchestration." *Dominant* 1 (May 1928): 24–26.

"The strange case of Moussorgsky." *Christian Science Monitor,* 14 February 1925, p. 12, cols. 1–2.

"Il vero e completo *Boris Godunof.*" *Rassegna musicale* 1 (1928): 217–25.

Cherniavsky, Michael. *Tsar and People: Studies in Russian Myths.* New Haven, Conn.: Yale University Press, 1961.

Csampai, Attila, and Holland, Dietmar, eds. *Modest Mussorgskij "Boris Godunow":*

Texte, Materialien, Kommentare. Hamburg: Rowohlt, 1982.

Cui, César Antonovich. *Izbrannye pis'ma.* Compiled with introduction and notes by I. L. Gusin. Leningrad: Gos. Muz. Izd., 1955.

Izbrannye stat'i. Compiled with introduction and notes by I. L. Gusin. Leningrad: Gos. Muz. Izd., 1952.

La musique en Russie. Paris: G. Fischbacher, 1880.

"Teatr i muzyka. Moskovskaya chastnaya russkaya opera. *Boris Godunov* Musorgskogo," *Novosti i birzhevaya gazeta,* 9 March 1899, p. 3.

Debussy, Claude. "*La chambre d'enfants*: Poème et musique de M. Moussorgsky." *La revue blanche* 24 (January–April 1901): 623–24; reprinted in *Monsieur Croche antidilettante.* Paris: Dorbon Aîné/Nouvelle Revue Française, 1921.

Emerson, Caryl. *Boris Godunov: Transpositions of a Russian Theme.* Bloomington, Ind.: Indiana University Press, 1986.

"Musorgsky's libretti on historical themes: From the two *Borises* to *Khovanshchina.*" In *Reading Opera,* pp. 235–67. Edited by Arthur Groos and Roger Parker. Princeton, N.J.: Princeton University Press, 1988.

"Pretenders to history: Four plays for undoing Pushkin's *Boris Godunov.*" *Slavic Review* 44 (Summer 1985): 257–79.

English National Opera; The Royal Opera Covent Garden. *"Boris Godunov": Modest Mussorgsky.* Edited by Nicholas John. Opera Guide Series, English National Opera and The Royal Opera Covent Garden, no. 11. London: John Calder, 1982.

Fel'dman, O. M. *Sud'ba dramaturgii Pushkina.* Moscow: "Iskusstvo," 1975.

Forte, Allen. "Musorgsky as modernist: The phantasmic episode in *Boris Godunov.*" *Music Analysis* 9 (March 1990): 3–46.

Frid, E[miliya Lazarevna]. *M. P. Musorgsky: Problemy tvorchestva.* Leningrad: "Muzyka," 1981.

Modest Petrovich Musorgsky (1839–1881). 4th edn. Leningrad: "Muzyka," 1987.

Fulle, Gerlinde. *Modest Mussorgskijs "Boris Godunow": Geschichte und Werk, Fassungen und Theaterpraxis.* Wiesbaden: Breitkopf & Härtel, 1974.

Garafola, Lynn. *Diaghilev's Ballets Russes.* New York: Oxford University Press, 1989.

Gavazzeni, Gianandrea. *Musorgskij e la musica russa dell'800.* Florence: G. C. Sansoni, 1943.

Glazunov, Aleksandr Konstantinovich. "O novoy postanovke opery *Boris Godunov* Musorgskogo." *Krasnaya gazeta,* 28 February 1928; reprinted in *Pis'ma, stat'i, vospominaniya: Izbrannoe.* Moscow: Gos. Muz. Izd., 1958.

Godet, Robert. "Les deux Boris." *La revue musicale,* no. 6 (1 April 1922), pp. 1–17.

En marge de "Boris Godounof": Notes sur les documents iconographiques de l'édition Chester. Paris: F. Alcan, 1926.

"The true and false Boris." *The Chesterian,* new series, no. 23 (May 1922), pp. 193–99.

Golenishchev-Kutuzov, Arseny Arkad'evich. "Vospominaniya o M. P. Musorgskom." In *Muzykal'noe nasledstvo,* issue 1, pp. 13–49. Edited by M. Ivanov-

Boretsky. Moscow: OGiz/MuzGiz, 1935.

Gordeeva, E. M., ed. *M. P. Musorgsky v vospominaniyakh sovremennikov*. Moscow: "Muzyka," 1989.

Gorodetsky, B[oris] P[avlovich] *Tragediya A. S. Pushkina "Boris Godunov"*. Leningrad: "Prosveshchenie," 1969.

Gozenpud, A[bram Akimovich]. *Russky operny teatr XIX veka, 1873–1889*. Leningrad: "Muzyka," 1973.

Russky operny teatr mezhdu dvukh revolyutsy, 1905–1917. Leningrad: "Muzyka," 1975.

Haskell, Arnold. *Diaghileff: His Artistic and Private Life*. 2nd edn. London: Victor Gollancz Ltd., 1955.

Hofmann, Rostislav. *Moussorgski*. Paris: Editions du Coudrier, 1952.

La vie de Moussorgski. Paris: Editions du Sud, [1964].

Hoops, Richard Allen. "V. V. Stasov, Selected articles on Musorgsky: A critical annotated translation with introduction." Ph.D. dissertation, The Florida State University, 1977.

Ivanits, Linda J. *Russian Folk Belief*. Armonk, N.Y.: M. E. Sharpe, 1989.

Kabalevskaya, O. "Vokal'naya interpretatsiya partii Borisa Godunova Shaliapinym." In *Voprosy teorii i estetiki muzyki*, issue 11, pp. 201–22. Edited by L. N. Raaben. Leningrad: "Muzyka," 1972.

Karamzin, N. M. *Istoriya gosudarstva Rossyskogo*. 12 vols. St. Petersburg: Evdokimov, 1892; reprint edn., Slavistic Printings and Reprintings 189/1–12, The Hague: Mouton, 1969.

Karatygin, V[iacheslav Gavrilovich]. *I. Musorgsky. II. Shalyapin*. Petersburg [sic]: Izd. Biblioteki Gosud. Akad. Teatra, Opery, Baleta, 1922.

Keldysh, Yury [Vsevolodovich], and Yakovlev, Vas[ily Vasil'evich], eds. *M. P. Musorgsky: K pyatidesyatiletiyu so dnya smerti, 1881–1931; Stat'i i materialy*. Moscow: Gos. Muz. Izd., 1932.

Khubov, Georgy [Nikitich]. *Musorgsky*. Moscow: "Muzyka," 1969.

Larosh, German Avgustovich [Hermann Laroche]. "Muzykal'nye ocherki," *Golos* (St. Petersburg), 14 February 1873, pp. 1–2.

"Muzykal'nye ocherki," *Golos* (St. Petersburg), 15 November 1876, pp. 1–3.

"Myslyashchy realist v russkoy opere," *Golos* (St. Petersburg), 13 February 1874, pp. 1–3.

"Novaya russkaya opera," *Golos* (St. Petersburg), 29 January 1874, p. 3.

Le Roux, Maurice. *Moussorgski. "Boris Godounov"*. Collection les grands opéras. Paris: Editions Aubier-Montaigne, 1980.

Levashev, E[vgeny], comp. and gen. ed. *Nasledie M. P. Musorgskogo: Sbornik materialov k vypusku Polnogo akademicheskogo sobraniya sochineny M. P. Musorgskogo v tridtsati dvukh tomakh*. Moscow: "Muzyka," 1989.

Lloyd-Jones, David. "*Boris Godunov*: analisi critica dell'orchestrazione originale." In *Musorgskij: l'opera, il pensiero*, pp. 175–84. Edited by A. M. Morazzoni. Milan: Edizioni Unicopli, 1985.

Lunacharsky, Anatoly Vasil'evich. *V mire muzyki*. Moscow: Sovetsky Kompozitor, 1971.

MacDonald, Hugh. "The prose libretto." *Cambridge Opera Journal* 1 (July 1989): 155–66.

McN[aught], W. "*Boris Godounov* at Sadler's Wells." *The Musical Times* 76 (November 1935): 1029.

Marco, Guy. "Viewpoint: On key relations in opera." *19th-Century Music* 3 (July 1979): 83–88.

Marnold, Jean. "M. Rimsky-Korsakoff et *Boris Godounoff*," *Mercure de France*, modern series, 75 (September–October 1908): 332–37; reprinted in *Musique d'autrefois e d'aujourd'hui*. Paris: Dorbon-Aîné, n.d.

Mila, Massimo. "Classicità del *Boris*." In *Musorgskij: l'opera, il pensiero*, pp. 165–74. Edited by A. M. Morazzoni. Milan: Edizioni Unicopli, 1985.

Muzykal'ny sovremennik, nos. 5–6 (1917).

Newmarch, Rosa. *The Russian Opera*. London: Herbert Jenkins Ltd., 1914.

"Russian opera in Paris: Moussorgsky's *Boris Godounov*." *The Monthly Musical Record* 38 (July 1908): 147–49.

Ogolevets, A[leksey Stepanovich]. *Vokal'naya dramaturgiya Musorgskogo*. Moscow: Muzyka, 1966.

Oldani, Robert William. "*Boris Godunov* and the censor." *19th-Century Music* 2 (March 1979): 245–53.

"Editions of *Boris Godunov*." In *Musorgsky: In Memoriam, 1881–1981*, pp. 179–213. Edited by Malcolm Hamrick Brown. Russian Music Studies, no. 3. Ann Arbor, Mich.: UMI Research Press, 1982.

"Musorgskij e la critica del suo tempo." In *Musorgskij: l'opera, il pensiero*, pp. 131–49. Edited by A. M. Morazzoni. Milan: Edizioni Unicopli, 1985.

"Mussorgsky's *Boris* on the stage of the Maryinsky Theater: A chronicle of the first production." *The Opera Quarterly* 4 (Summer 1986): 75–92.

"Sealing Pushkin to his place." In *Musicological Essays from the Middle Ages to the 20th Century: A Seventieth Birthday Tribute to Gwynn McPeek from His Friends and Colleagues*, pp. 201–12. Edited by C. Comberiati and M. Steel. New York: Gordon and Breach, 1988.

Orlov, Georgy [Pavlovich]. *Letopis' zhizni i tvorchestva M. P. Musorgskogo*. Moscow: Gos. Muz. Izd., 1940.

Orlova, A[leksandra Anatol'evna]. *Musorgsky v Peterburge*. Leningrad: Lenizdat, 1974.

"Il Potente Gruppo; La sua storia alla luce delle più recenti ricerche." In *Musorgskij: L'opera, il pensiero*, pp. 65–105. Edited by Anna Maria Morazzoni. Milan: Edizioni Unicopli, [1985].

Trudy i dni M. P. Musorgskogo: Letopis' zhizni i tvorchestva. Moscow: Gos. Muz. Izd., 1963. Translated and edited by Roy J. Guenther as *Musorgsky's Days and Works: A Biography in Documents*. Russian Music Studies, no. 4. Ann Arbor, Mich.: UMI Research Press, 1983.

Orlova, Aleksandra Anatol'evna, ed. *Musorgsky Remembered*. Translated by Véronique Zaytzeff and Frederick Morrison. Bloomington, Ind.: Indiana University Press, 1991.

Orlova, Aleksandra Anatol'evna, and Rimsky–Korsakov, V[ladimir] N[ikolaevich]. *Stranitsy zhizni N. A. Rimskogo-Korsakova: Letopis' zhizni i tvorchestva*. 4 issues. Leningrad: "Muzyka," 1969–73.

Orlova, Alexandra, and Shneerson, Maria. "After Pushkin and Karamzin: Researching the sources for the libretto of *Boris Godunov*." In *Musorgsky: In Memoriam, 1881–1981*, pp. 249–70. Edited by Malcolm Hamrick Brown. Russian Music Studies, no. 3. Ann Arbor, Mich.: UMI Research Press, 1982.

Pipes, Richard. *Essays on Karamzin: Russian Man-of-Letters, Political Thinker, Historian, 1766–1826*. Edited by J. L. Black. The Hague: Mouton, 1975.

Platonov, S. F. *Boris Godunov, Tsar of Russia*. Translated by L. Rex Pyles. Gulf Breeze, Fla.: Academic International Press, 1971.

Pougin, Arthur. *Essai historique sur la musique en Russie*. Paris: Fischbacher, 1897; 2nd edn., 1904. Translated by Lawrence Haward as *A Short History of Russian Music*. London: Chatto & Windus, 1915.

Pushkin, Alexander Sergeevich. *Boris Godunov*. Translated by Philip L. Barbour. New York: Columbia University Press, 1953.

The Critical Prose of Alexander Pushkin. Edited and translated by Carl R. Proffer. Bloomington, Ind.: Indiana University Press, 1969.

The Letters of Alexander Pushkin. Edited and translated by J. Thomas Shaw. Madison, Wis.: University of Wisconsin Press, 1967.

Polnoe sobranie sochineny. 16 vols. Moscow: Izd. Akademii Nauk SSSR, 1937–50.

Rassadin, Stanislav Borisovich. *Dramaturg Pushkin*. Moscow: "Iskusstvo," 1977.

Ravel, Maurice. "*Boris Godounoff*." *Commœdia illustré*, 5 June 1913, unpaginated.

Reilly, Edward R. *The Music of Mussorgsky: A Guide to the Editions*. New York: The Musical Newsletter, [1980].

Ridenour, Robert C. *Nationalism, Modernism, and Personal Rivalry in 19th-Century Russian Music*. Russian Music Studies, no. 1. Ann Arbor, Mich.: UMI Research Press, 1981.

Riesemann, Oskar von. *Modest Petrowitsch Mussorgski*. Monographien zur russischen Musik, Bd. 2. Munich: Drei Masken Verlag, 1926. Translated [English] by Paul England as *Moussorgsky*. New York: Alfred A. Knopf, 1929; reprint edn., New York: Dover, 1971.

Rimsky-Korsakov, N[ikolay] A[ndreevich]. *Letopis' moey muzykal'noy zhizni*. 8th edn. Moscow: "Muzyka," 1980.

Sandler, Stephanie. *Distant Pleasures: Alexander Pushkin and the Writing of Exile*. Stanford, Calif.: Stanford University Press, 1989.

Schandert, Manfred. *Das Problem der originalen Instrumentation des Boris Godunow von M. P. Mussorgski*. Schriftenreihe zur Musik, vol. XV. Hamburg: Karl Dieter Wagner, 1979.

Schmid, Willy. "*Boris Godounov* again." *The Chesterian*, new series, 9 (July–August 1928): 245–51.

Schmidgall, Gary. *Literature as Opera*. New York: Oxford University Press, 1977.

Shalyapin, Fedor [Feodor Chaliapin]. *Chaliapin: An Autobiography As Told to Maxim Gorky*. Edited and translated by Nina Froud and James Hanley. New York: Stein and Day, [1967].

Stranitsy iz moey zhizni. Maska i dusha. Moscow: Knizhnaya palata, 1990.

Shirinyan, R[uzana Karpovna]. *Evolyutsiya opernogo tvorchestva Musorgskogo*. Moscow: "Muzyka," 1973.

M. P. Musorgsky. [Al'bom]. Series: Chelovek, Sobytiya, Vremya. Moscow: "Muzyka," 1987.

Shostakovich, Dmitry Dmitrievich. *O vremeni i o sebe (1926–1975)*. Edited by G. Pribegina. Moscow: Sovetsky Kompozitor, 1980. Translated by Angus and Neilian Roxburgh as *Dmitry Shostakovich: About Himself and His Times*. Moscow: Progress Publishers, 1981.

Sincero, Dino. "*Boris Godounow* al Teatro alla Scala di Milano." *Rivista musicale italiana* 16 (1909): 385–94.

Skrynnikov, Ruslan G. *Boris Godunov*. Translated by Hugh F. Graham. Gulf Breeze, Fla.: Academic International Press, 1982.

Sovetskaya muzyka, no. 4 (April 1939); no. 3 (March 1989).

Stasov, Vladimir Vasil'evich. *Izbrannye sochineniya*. Edited by E. D. Stasova and others. 3 vols. Moscow: "Iskusstvo," 1952.

"Modest Petrovich Musorgsky: Biograficheskyi ocherk." *Vestnik Evropy* 89 (May–June 1881): 285–316, 506–45.

Selected Articles on Musorgsky. See Hoops, Richard Allen.

Selected Essays on Music. Translated by Florence Jonas. New York: Frederick A. Praeger, 1968.

Strakhov, Nikolay Nikolaevich. "*Boris Godunov* na stsene." In *Zametki o Pushkine i drugikh poetakh*, pp. 79–104, 2nd edn. Kiev: tip. Chokolova, 1897; reprint edn., Russian Reprint Series 43, The Hague: Europe Printing, 1967.

Taruskin, Richard. "Handel, Shakespeare, and Musorgsky: The sources and limits of Russian musical realism." In *Studies in the History of Music*, vol. 1: *Music and Language*, pp. 247–68. New York: Broude Brothers Limited, 1983.

Musorgsky: Eight Essays and an Epilogue. Princeton, N.J.: Princeton University Press, 1992. [Includes reprints of the articles cited in our text according to their initial places of publication: "Handel, Shakespeare, and Musorgsky: The sources and limits of Russian musical realism"; "Musorgsky *vs.* Musorgsky: The versions of *Boris Godunov*"; "'The present in the past': Russian opera and Russian historiography, ca. 1870"; and "Serov and Musorgsky".]

"Musorgsky *vs.* Musorgsky: The versions of *Boris Godunov*." *19th-Century Music* 8 (1984–85): 91–118, 245–72.

Opera and Drama in Russia As Preached and Practiced in the 1860s. Russian Music Studies, no. 2. Ann Arbor, Mich.: UMI Research Press, 1981.

"'The present in the past': Russian opera and Russian historiography, ca. 1870." In *Russian and Soviet Music: Essays for Boris Schwarz*, pp. 102–35. Edited by Malcolm Hamrick Brown. Russian Music Studies, no. 11. Ann Arbor, Mich.:

UMI Research Press, 1984.

"Serov and Musorgsky." In *Slavonic and Western Music: Essays for Gerald Abraham*, pp. 139–61. Edited by Malcolm Hamrick Brown and Roland John Wiley. Russian Music Studies, no. 12. Ann Arbor, Mich.: UMI Research Press, 1985.

Théâtre National de l'Opéra. *"Boris Godounow": Opéra en 3 actes et 7 tableaux de Modeste Moussorgsky*. Paris: Théâtre National de l'Opéra, 1908.

Tibaldi Chiesa, Mary. *Mussorgsky*. Milan: S. A. Fratelli Treves Editori, [1935].

Troyat, Henri. *Pouchkine*. Paris: Editions Albin Michel, 1946. Translated as *Pushkin* by Nancy Amphoux. Garden City, N.Y.: Doubleday & Co., 1970.

Vol'f, A[leksandr] I[vanovich]. *Khronika Peterburgskikh teatrov s kontsa 1855 do nachala 1881 goda*. St. Petersburg: R. Golike, 1884.

Wiley, Roland John. "The tribulations of nationalist composers: A speculation concerning borrowed music in *Khovanshchina*." In *Musorgsky: In Memoriam, 1881–1981*, pp. 163–77. Edited by Malcolm Hamrick Brown. Russian Music Studies, no. 3. Ann Arbor, Mich.: UMI Research Press, 1982.

Williams, Edward V. *The Bells of Russia: History and Technology*. Princeton, N.J.: Princeton University Press, [1985].

The Blagovest Theme in Russian Music. Kennan Institute for Advanced Russian Studies Occasional Papers, no. 220. Washington, D.C.: Kennan Institute for Advanced Russian Studies, 1987.

Wolfurt, Kurt von. *Mussorgskij*. Stuttgart: Deutsche Verlagsanstalt, 1927.

"Das Problem Mussorgskij/Rimskij-Korssakoff: Ein Vergleich zwischen dem Original-Klavierauszug von Mussorgskijs *Boris Godunoff* und Rimskij-Korssakoffs Bearbeitung." *Die Musik* 17 (April 1925): 481–91.

Worbs, Hans Christoph. *Modest P. Mussorgsky in Selbstzeugnissen und Bilddokumenten*. Hamburg: Rowohlt, 1976.

Yastrebtsev, V[asily] V[asil'evich]. *Nikolay Andreevich Rimsky-Korsakov: Vospominaniya*. Edited by A. V. Ossovsky. 2 vols. Leningrad: Gos. Muz. Izd., 1959–60.

Zaporozhets, N[ataliya Vladimirovna]. *Opery Musorgskogo "Boris Godunov" i "Khovanshchina"*. Moscow: Muzyka, 1966.

Zil'bershteyn, I. S., and Samkov, V. A., eds. *Sergey Dyagilev i russkoe iskusstvo: Stat'i, otkrytye pis'ma, interv'yu. Perepiska. Sovremenniki o Dyagileve*. 2 vols. Moscow: "Izobrazitel'noe iskusstvo," 1982.

INDEX

Notes

(1) Page numbers in *italics* refer to illustrations.
(2) Opera characters, scenes, etc. are indexed as "Boris Godunov," "Dmitry," etc.

Abbado, Claudio, 283
Alexander I, Tsar, 11, 13, *16*
Alexander II, Tsar, 79, 130, 132
Alexander III, Tsar, 107
Alheim, Marie Olénine d', 157
Alheim, Pierre d', 157, 158
Asafiev, Boris Vladimirovich (Igor
    Glebov), 162–67, 169, 173–74, 264

Balakirev, Mili Alexeivich, 49, 62, 79,
    226, 239
Baskin, Vladimir, 75, 101
Beecham, Sir Joseph, 67
Beethoven, Ludwig van, 41, 175, 235
Benckendorff, Alexander, 128–29
Benois, Alexandre, 92, 108, 114, 117
Berdyaev, Nicholas, 287
Berlioz, Hector, 135, 139, 157, 230–31,
    234–35
    Symphonie Fantastique, 230, 235
Bessel, Vassily, & Co. (publisher), 14,
    68, 79–82, 85–86, 88, 95, 109, 113,
    120–21
Betz, Eduard, 74
Bilibin, Ivan, 92, 108
Billington, James, 219
Blumenfeld, Felix, 108

Bocharov, Mikhail, 85, 98, 100
Boïto, Arrigo, 255
Bolotnikov, 9
Bondarchuk, Sergey, 281
Boris, St., 18
Boris Godunov, Tsar, 4–10, 209,
    219–20
    in Karamzin's history, 15–18, 20–23
Boris Godunov (Musorgsky)
    and censorship, 92, 127–33
    composition, rejection, revision and
        acceptance of, 67–90
    criticism of, 134–79
    and Karamzin's history, 12–23
    Kirov/Covent Garden production,
        283–85
    libretto, 11, 183–224
    music, 225–76
    Musorgsky's revisions of, 36–37,
        59–69, 78, 79, 105, 164, 166, 169,
        171–73, 190, 225–27
    narrative and synopsis, 35–66
    Paris production (1908), 107–24
    and Pushkin's play, 23–34, 38–39,
        43, 46, 79, 134, 140, 148–49,
        161–62, 184, 189–220 *passim*, 192,
        250, 255–56

333